S0-BYS-490

**Asheville-Buncombe
Technical Community College
Learning Resources Center
340 Victoria Road
Asheville, NC 28801**

ADOBE® WEB PACK: PHOTOSHOP® 7.0, LIVEMOTION™ 2.0, AND GOLIVE™ 6.0

Discarded

Date SEP 1 3 2024

By Beskeen/Foley/Reding

04 - 0835

COURSE
PUBLISHING

Adobe® Web Pack: Photoshop® 7.0, LiveMotion™ 2.0, and GoLive™ 6.0
by Beskeen/Foley/Reding

Managing Editor:
Nicole Jones Pinard

Senior Product Manager:
Rebecca Berardy

Associate Product Manager:
Christina Kling Garrett

Editorial Assistant:
Elizabeth Harris

Production Editors:
Aimee Poirier and Melissa Panagos

Developmental Editors:
Jeanne Herring and Holly Lancaster

Composition House:
GEX Publishing Services

QA Manuscript Reviewers:
Shawn Day, Matt DeGraff, Serge
Palladino, Max Prior, Jeff Schwartz,
Ashlee Welz

Text Designer:
Ann Small

Illustrator:
Philip Brooker

Cover Design:
Philip Brooker

COPYRIGHT © 2003 Course
Publishing, a division of Course
Technology. Thomson Learning™ is a
trademark used herein under license.

Printed in the United States of
America

1 2 3 4 5 6 7 8 9 BU 06 05 04 03 02

For more information, contact Course
Technology, 25 Thomson Place,
Boston, Massachusetts, 02210.

Or find us on the World Wide Web
at: www.premierpressbooks.com

ALL RIGHTS RESERVED. No part
of this work covered by the copyright
hereon may be reproduced or used in
any form or by any means—graphic,
electronic, or mechanical, including
photocopying, recording, taping, Web
distribution, or information storage

and retrieval systems—without the
written permission of the publisher.

For permission to use material from
this text or product, contact us by

Tel (800) 730-2214
Fax(800) 730-2215

www.thomsonrights.com

Trademarks
Some of the product names and company names used in this book have
been used for identification purposes
only and may be trademarks or registered trademarks of their respective
manufacturers and sellers.

Credit
Some of the images used in this book
are the property of GettyImages'™
royalty-free CD-ROM collections,

including: Travel Souvenirs (PhotoDisc);
Working Bodies (PhotoDisc); Tools of
the Trade (Artville); Just Flowers 2
(PhotoDisc); Educational Elements
(Artville); Symbols & Icons (Artville);
Portraits of Diversity (PhotoDisc);
Sports and Recreation (PhotoDisc).

Adobe® Photoshop®, Adobe®
LiveMotion™, and Adobe® GoLive® are
trademarks or registered trademarks of
Adobe Systems Incorporated.

Disclaimer
Course Publishing reserves the right
to revise this publication and make
changes from time to time in its content without notice.

ISBN 1-59200-052-5

Acknowledgements

We would like to spend a moment and thank a few people who helped us turn a bunch of thoughts and ideas into a finished body of work. A special thanks to Jeanne Herring and Holly Lancaster, whose input transformed the sections and to Rebecca Berardy, Aimee Poirier, and Nicole Jones Pinard at Course Technology for their support on the project. We would also like to thank all of the QA testers: Harris Bierhoff, Shawn Day, Matt DeGraff, Max Prior, Jeffrey Schwartz, and Ashlee Welz who followed behind us and worked out technical issues and other inconsistencies. We especially appreciated the insightful reviewer feedback from: Jeff Kushner, James Madison University; Piyush Patel, Northern Oklahoma College; and Rick Sheridan, California State University. —The Authors

David W. Beskeen The LiveMotion portion of this book completes the creative circle, along with Adobe Photoshop and Adobe GoLive, for designing a powerful, interactive Web site. A big thanks to Karen, Jordan, Jen, and Justin for "living without me" for a short time while I wrote.

Christine Foley I hope that this book inspires designers in making the Web a more beautiful space. The clients that allowed me to use and modify their sites for the projects in this book may not realize the full value of their contribution, saving hours and hours of project development. Special thanks to Jayme Canaday of Grow Up Gardening, John Martinson of ChinaMist, Leon Silver of BenjaminKay Galleries, Karleen Kelso and Jan Elizabeth of CPCPrint, Lou Skorish of Uncle Louie's, and Evelyn Foley, Mom, of Eucalyptus Extraordinaire. Thank you, too, to the people that let me use images of their exemplary sites, including Linda Enger, Don Giannatti and the people at CityofOrlando.net: Michael McCarthy, Dena Wild, Alex Law, Marcia Clark, Scott Brockmeier, Natalie Spencer, and Rob Spindler. Lastly, thank you to my personal support team: to all my friends and clients for not giving up on me, to Dad and Mom for your continued belief, and to Bridget Miller for raising yourself!

Elizabeth Eisner Reding This project was quite enjoyable because Photoshop is so much fun to use and so integral to enhancing the Web. My sincere thanks goes to everyone who worked on this project—David, Jeanne, Holly, and Christine. Without our families we are lost, I would like to thank my husband, Michael, for his input on all matters large and small, and to my mother, Mary Eisner, for her support and enthusiasm.

Asheville-Buncombe
Technical Community College
Learning Resources Center
340 Victoria Road
Asheville, NC 28801

ACKNOWLEDGEMENTS

Introduction

Welcome to *Adobe® Web Pack: Photoshop® 7.0, LiveMotion™ 2.0, and GoLive™ 6.0*. This book offers creative projects, concise instructions, and complete coverage of basic to intermediate Photoshop, LiveMotion and GoLive skills, helping you to create dynamic Web sites!

This book is organized into 17 sections. In these sections, you will learn many skills including how to enhance Photoshop images and then optimize the files for the Web; create objects, rollovers, and animations in LiveMotion; and then create and publish a GoLive Web site with images, text, links, tables, actions, and forms. The integration section in this book will teach you the powerful capabilities of bringing all three of these applications together!

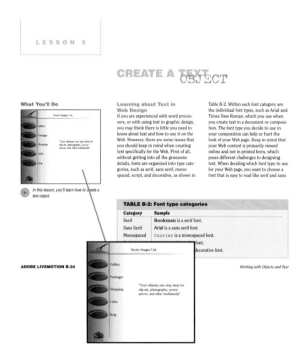

What You'll Do

A What You'll Do figure begins every lesson. This figure gives you an at-a-glance look at the skills covered in the section and shows you the completed data file of the lesson. Before you start the lesson, you will know—both on a technical and artistic level—what you will be creating.

Comprehensive Conceptual Lessons

Before jumping into instructions, in-depth conceptual information tells you "why" skills are applied. This book provides the "how" and "why" through the use of professional examples. Also included in the text are helpful tips and sidebars to help you work more efficiently and creatively.

Step-by-Step Instructions

This book combines in-depth conceptual information with concise steps to help you learn the skills of each of the applications. Each set of steps guides you through a lesson where you will apply tasks to a dynamic and professional data file. Step references to large colorful images and quick step summaries round out the lessons.

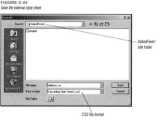

Create an external style sheet

1. Click File on the menu bar, point to Export, then click Internal Style Sheet.

    TIP The CSS Editor must be open, with the CSS Definitions tab in front, in order for the Export command to be active.

2. In the Save As dialog box, type the filename **biditems.css**, then save the CSS file in the IslandFever! site folder, as shown in Figure C-24.

    The external style sheet, biditems.css, opens in a new window, as shown in Figure C-25.

    TIP The Save As dialog box will default to the last folder you saved to—be sure you are saving to the IslandFever! site folder! (The .html files are not displayed in the window because the style sheet file type is .css.)

3. Close biditems.css and services.html.

    The services.html CSS Editor closes with services.html.

You exported services.html's internal style sheet to an external style sheet named biditems.css.

FIGURE C-24
Save the external style sheet

IslandFever! site folder

CSS file format

FIGURE C-25
External style sheet

ADOBE GOLIVE C-28

Formatting and Stylizing Text

China Mist Gourmet Iced Tea Company is very pleased with the visual appearance of the page you designed for them listing their teas—it is fresh and flavorful. They have asked you to add the names of the teas to the page, keeping with the same fresh style for the text used on the page. They have provided some introductory text about their teas you can copy into the page, but the tea names will need to be typed in manually.

1. Navigate to the drive and folder containing your project files, copy the contents of the SiteC-4 folder to the China Mist project folder you created in Section B, then open China Mist.site.

2. Open teas.html, then add the tea names in text boxes next to each of the flavor icons, as shown in Figure C-40, tagging each tea name as an Address element. (*Hint:* Although you can experiment with combining tea names in a single text box, differences in line height handling by different browsers makes individual text boxes a more consistent method of aligning text to images.)

3. Add the text from teaintro.txt in a text box just under the navigation buttons. Tag this text as a Paragraph element, then create and define styles for the paragraph and address elements in an internal style sheet so that the page is visually appealing. Feel free to use Figure C-40 as a guideline.

FIGURE C-40
Completed Project 2

Formatting and Stylizing Text

ADOBE GOLIVE C-43

Projects

At the end of each section, you will find hands-on projects that require you to apply the skills you've learned in the section to create Web sites, rollovers, animations, and enhance graphics.

Photoshop

SECTION A   GETTING STARTED WITH ADOBE PHOTOSHOP 7.0

SECTION E · PLACING TYPE IN AN IMAGE

BONUS SECTION A · CREATING WEB DOCUMENTS

LiveMotion

SECTION A   GETTING STARTED WITH ADOBE LIVEMOTION 2.0

SECTION C WORKING WITH IMPORTED IMAGES AND OBJECT LAYERS

SECTION D WORKING WITH COLOR, EFFECTS, AND ROLLOVERS

GoLive

SECTION B   ADDING AND MODIFYING IMAGES

SECTION C   FORMATTING AND STYLIZING TEXT

SECTION D   CREATING NAVIGATION LINKS

Intended Audience

This book is for you if, you want to learn how to use Adobe Photoshop 7.0, LiveMotion 2.0, and GoLive 6.0. The book is designed to provide basic and in-depth instruction to help you explore the nuances of these exciting programs.

Platforms

This book is written for both the Windows and Macintosh platforms. Both versions of each software program are generally the same. The images in this book are all from Windows and may vary in some ways on the Mac. When there are differences between the instructions for the two platforms, instructions written specifically for the Windows version end with the notation (Win) and instructions for the Macintosh version end with the notation (Mac).

Fonts

Data and solution files contain a variety of fonts, and there is no guarantee that any of these fonts will be available on your computer. In cases where less common fonts are used in files, these fonts are identified. Every effort has been made to use commonly available fonts in the lessons. If any of the fonts in use are not available on your computer, please make a substitution.

Icons, Buttons, and Pointers

Symbols for icons, buttons, and pointers are shown each time they are used.

Additional Information for the Adobe Photoshop 7.0 Units

Measurements in Photoshop

When measurements are shown, needed, or discussed, they are given in pixels. Use the following instructions to change the units of measurement to pixels.

1. Click Edit on the menu bar, point to Preferences, then click Units and Rulers.
2. Click the Rulers list arrow, then click Pixels.
3. Click OK.

You can display rulers by clicking View on the menu bar, then clicking Rulers, or by pressing [Ctrl][R] (Win) or [command][R] (Mac). You can hide visible rulers by clicking View on the menu bar, then clicking Rulers, or by pressing [Ctrl][R] (Win) or [command][R] (Mac). A checkmark to the right of the Rulers command indicates that the Rulers are displayed.

Skills Reference in Photoshop Sections

As a bonus, a Power User Shortcuts table is included at the end of every Photoshop section. This table contains the most expedient method of completing tasks covered in the section. It is meant for the more experienced user, or for the user who wants to become more experienced. Tools are

shown, not named. In the tables, menu commands are abbreviated using the following format: Edit ➤ Preferences ➤ Units and Rulers. This command translates as follows: Click Edit on the menu bar, point to Preferences, then click Units and Rulers.

Additionial Information for the GoLive 6.0 Sections

Internet Connection

The GoLive portion of this book is best used with an Internet connection and FTP access to a Web server for uploading files. However, lessons that involve a connection are followed by an alternate set of steps for readers without a connection.

Working With Data Files

To complete many of the sections in this book, you will need to use data files found on the accompanying CD-ROM. Use the **Data Files List** at the back of the book to organize your files to a zip drive, network folder, hard drive, or other storage device.

Create a subfolder for each section in the location where you are storing your files, and name it according to the section title (e.g., GoLive Section A).

For each section you work with, copy the data files listed in the **Data Files Supplied** column of the Data Files List into that section's folder.

Store the files you modify or create in each section in the section folder.

SECTION A

GETTING STARTED WITH ADOBE PHOTOSHOP 7.0

1. Start Adobe Photoshop 7.0.

2. Learn how to open and save a document.

3. Examine the Photoshop window.

4. Use the Layers and History palettes.

5. Learn about Photoshop by using Help.

6. View and print a document.

7. Close a document and exit Photoshop.

Using PhotoShop

Adobe Photoshop is an image-editing program that lets you create and modify digital images. A **digital image** is a picture in electronic form. Using Photoshop, you can create original artwork, manipulate color images, and retouch photographs. In addition to being a robust application popular with graphics professionals, it is practical for anyone who wants to enhance existing artwork or create new masterpieces. For example, you can repair and restore damaged areas within an image, combine images, and create graphics and special effects for the Web.

Understanding Platform Interfaces

Photoshop is available in both Windows and Macintosh platforms. Regardless of which type of computer you use, the features and commands are very similar. Some of the Windows and Macintosh keyboard commands differ in name, but they have equivalent functions. For example, the [Ctrl] and [Alt] keys are used in Windows, and the [command] and [option] keys are used on Macintosh computers. There is a dramatic visual difference between the two platforms from the moment the program is started. These differences are due to the user-interface found in each type of computer.

Understanding Sources

Photoshop allows you to work with images from a variety of sources. You can create your own original artwork in Photoshop, use images downloaded from the Web, or use images that have been scanned or created using a digital camera. Whether you create Photoshop images to print in high resolution or optimize them for multimedia presentations, Web-based functions, or animation projects, Photoshop is a powerful tool for communicating your ideas visually.

Tools You'll Use

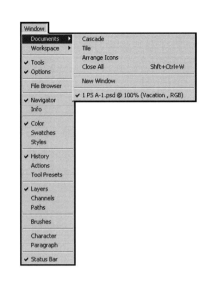

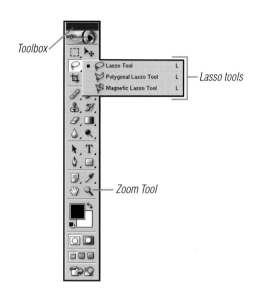

Toolbox

Lasso tools

Zoom Tool

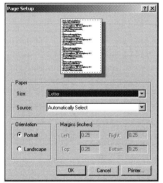

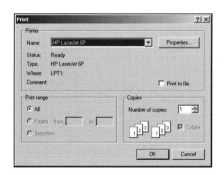

Tool options bar

Palette well

START ADOBE PHOTOSHOP 7.0

What You'll Do

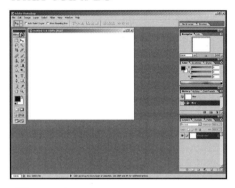

 In this lesson, you'll start Photoshop for Windows or Macintosh (depending on the platform you are using), then create a file.

Defining Image-Editing Software

Photoshop is an image-editing program. An **image-editing** program allows you to manipulate graphic images so that they can be reproduced by professional printers using full-color processes. Using a toolbar, windows, various tools, menus, and a variety of techniques, you can modify a Photoshop image by rotating it, resizing it, changing its colors, or adding text to it. You can also use Photoshop to create and open different kinds of file formats, which enables you to create your own images, import them from a digital camera or scanner, or use files (in other formats) purchased from outside sources. Table A-1 lists the file formats that Photoshop can open and create.

Understanding Images

Every image is made up of dots, which are called **pixels**, and each pixel represents a color or shade. Pixels within an image can be added, deleted, or modified.

QUICKTIP

Photoshop files can become quite large. After a file is complete, it can be **flattened**, an irreversible process that combines all layers and reduces the file size.

Using Photoshop Features

Photoshop includes many tools that you can use to manipulate images and text. Within an image, you can add new items and modify existing elements, change colors, and draw shapes. For example, using the Lasso Tool, you can outline a section of an image and drag the section onto another area of the image. You can also isolate a foreground or background image. You can extract all or part of a complex image from nearly any background and use it elsewhere.

QUICKTIP

You can create a logo in Photoshop. A **logo** is a distinctive image that you can create by combining symbols, shapes, colors, and text. Logos give graphic identity to organizations, such as corporations, universities, and retail stores.

You can also create and format text, called type, in Photoshop. You can apply a variety of special effects to type; for example, you can change the appearance of text and the distance between characters. You can also edit type after it has been created and formatted.

QUICKTIP

Photoshop records each change you make to a document in the History palette. You can undo or redo a recorded action as necessary. Photoshop records actions for the current session only; it discards actions when the program closes.

Adobe ImageReady 7.0, a Web production software program included with Photoshop, allows you to optimize, preview, and animate images. Because ImageReady is fully integrated with Photoshop, you can jump seamlessly between the two programs.

You can also quickly turn any graphics image into a GIF animation. Photoshop and ImageReady let you compress file size (while optimizing image quality) to ensure that your files download quickly from a Web page. Using optimization features, you can view multiple versions of an image and select the one that best suits your needs.

Starting Photoshop and Creating a File

The way that you start Photoshop depends on the computer platform you are using. However, when you start Photoshop in either platform, the computer displays a splash screen, a window that displays information about the software, and then the Photoshop window opens.

After you start Photoshop, you can create a file from scratch. You use the New dialog box to create a file. You can also use the New dialog box to set the size of the image you're about to create by typing dimensions in the Width and Height text boxes.

TABLE A-1: Graphic File Formats Supported in Photoshop

file format	filename extension	file format	filename extension
Photoshop	.PSD	Filmstrip	.VLM
Bitmap	.BMP	Kodak PhotoCD	.PCD
PC Paintbrush	.PCX	Pixar	.PXR
Graphics Interchange Format	.GIF	Scitex CT	.SCT
Photoshop PostScript	.EPS	Photoshop PDF	.PDF
Tagged Image Format	.TIF or .TIFF	Targa	.TGA or .VDA
JPEG Picture Format	.JPG, .JPE, or .JPEG	PICT file	.PCT, .PIC, or .PICT
CorelDraw	.CDR	Raw	.RAW

Start Photoshop (Windows)

1. Click the Start button on the taskbar. 🏁Start

2. Point to Programs, then click Adobe Photoshop 7.0, as shown in Figure A-1.

   TIP The Adobe Photoshop 7.0 program might be found in the Adobe folder, which is in the Program Files folder on the hard drive.

3. Click File on the menu bar, then click New.

4. Double-click the number in the Width text box, type **500**, click the Width list arrow, then click pixels, if necessary.

5. Double-click the number in the Height text box, type **400**, click the Height list arrow, then click pixels, if necessary.

6. Click OK.

You started Photoshop for Windows, then created a file with custom dimensions.

FIGURE A-1
Starting Photoshop 7.0 (Windows)

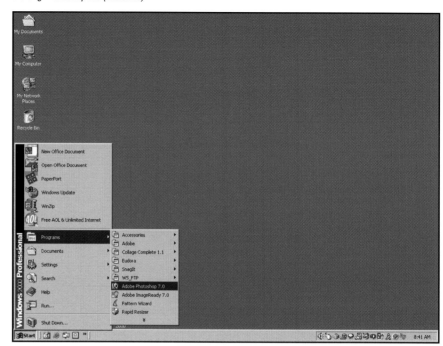

Understanding hardware requirements (Windows)

Adobe Photoshop 7.0 has the following minimum system requirements:

- Processor: Intel Pentium class III or 4
- Operating System: Microsoft® Windows® 98, Windows 98 Second Edition, Windows Millennium Edition, Windows NT with Service Pack 6a, Windows 2000 with Service Pack 2, or Windows XP
- Memory: 128 MB of RAM (192 MB recommended)
- Storage space: 280 MB of available hard-disk space
- Monitor: 800x600 color monitor with 16-bit color or greater video card

Starting Photoshop 7.0 (Macintosh)

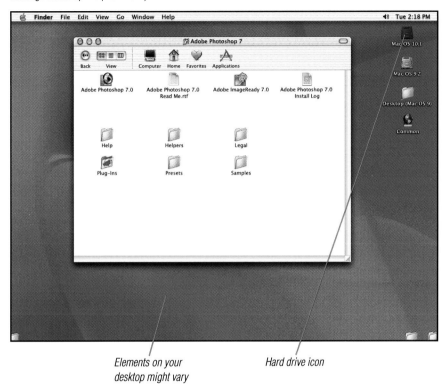

Elements on your
desktop might vary

Hard drive icon

Start Photoshop (Macintosh)

1. Double-click the hard drive icon, then double-click the Adobe Photoshop 7.0 folder.

2. Double-click the Adobe Photoshop 7.0 program icon. Compare your screen to Figure A-2.

3. Click File on the menu bar, then click New.

4. Double-click the number in the Width text box, type **500**, click the Width list arrow, then click pixels, if necessary.

5. Double-click the number in the Height text box, type **400**, click the Height list arrow, then click pixels, if necessary.

6. Click OK.

You started Photoshop for the Macintosh, then created a file with custom dimensions.

Understanding hardware requirements (Macintosh)

Adobe Photoshop 7.0 has the following minimum system requirements:

- Processor: PowerPC® processor (G3, G4, or G4 dual)
- Operating System: Mac OS software version 9.1, 9.2, or Mac OS X version 10.1.3
- Memory: 128 MB of RAM (192 MB recommended)
- Storage space: 320 MB of available hard-disk space
- Monitor: 800x600 color monitor with 16-bit color or greater video card

LEARN HOW TO OPEN AND SAVE A DOCUMENT

What You'll Do

 In this lesson, you'll locate and open files using the File menu and the File Browser, then save a file with a new name.

Opening and Saving Files

Photoshop provides several options for opening and saving a file. Often, the project you're working on determines the techniques you use for opening and saving files. For example, you might want to preserve the original version of a file while you modify a copy. You can open a file, then immediately save it with a different filename, as well as open and save files in many different file formats. For example, you can open a Photoshop file that has been saved as a bitmap (.bmp) file, then save it as a JPEG (.jpg) file to use on a Web page.

Customizing How You Open Files

You can customize how you open your files by setting preferences. **Preferences** are options you can set that are based on your

Using the File Info dialog box

You can use the File Info dialog box to identify a file, add a caption or other text, or add a copyright notice. The Caption section allows you to enter printable text, as shown in Figure A-4. For example, to add your name to a document, click File on the menu bar, click File Info, then click in the Caption text box. (You can move from field to field by pressing [Tab] or by clicking in individual text boxes.) Type your name, course number, or other identifying information in the Caption text box. You can enter additional information in the other text boxes, then save all the File Info data as a separate file that has an .XMP extension. To select the caption for printing, click File on the menu bar, click Print with Preview. Verify that the Show More Options check box is selected, then select the Caption check box. To print the filename, select the Labels check box. You can also print crop marks and registration marks. If you choose, you can even add a background color or border to your image. After you select the items you want to print, click Print.

work habits. For example, you can use the Open Recent command on the File menu to instantly locate and open the files that you recently worked on, or you can allow others to preview your files as thumbnails. Figure A-3 shows the Preferences dialog box options for handling your files.

Browsing Through Files

You can easily find the file you're looking for by using the File Browser feature. You can open the File Browser by clicking the File Browser tab in the **palette well** (which is an area that is located near the top-right corner of the screen where you can assemble windows used to modify documents). You can also open the File Browser from the File menu. When you open the File Browser, a hierarchical tree for your computer's hard drive is displayed. You can use this tree to find the file you are searching for. When you locate a file, you can click its thumbnail to see information about its size, format, and creation and modification dates. You can open a file using the File Browser by double-clicking its thumbnail. If the File Browser is docked in the palette well, you can close it by pressing [Esc].

Using Save As Versus Save

Sometimes it's more efficient to create a new image by modifying an existing one, especially if it contains elements and special effects that you want to use again. The Save As command on the File menu creates a copy of the file, prompts you to give the duplicate file a new name, and then displays the new filename in the document's title bar. You use the Save As command to name an unnamed document or to save an existing document with a new name. For example, throughout this book, you will be instructed to open your project files and use the Save As command. Saving your project files with new names keeps them intact in case you have to start the lesson over again or you want to repeat an exercise. When you use the Save command, you save the changes you made to the open document.

FIGURE A-3
Preferences dialog box

Select option for thumbnail preview

Enter number of files to appear in Open Recent list

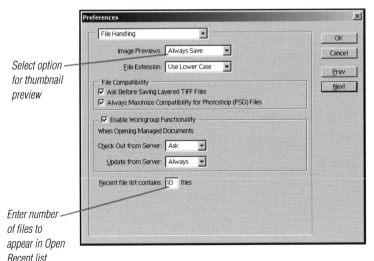

FIGURE A-4
File Info dialog box

Type information that you want to be printed

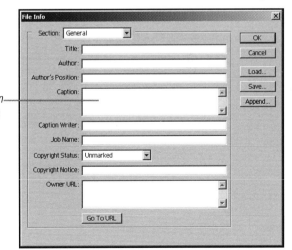

Open a file using the File menu

1. Click File on the menu bar, then click Open.

2. Click the Look in list arrow (Win) or the From list arrow (Mac), as shown in Figure A-5, navigate to the location where your Section A project files are stored, then click Open.

3. Click PS A-1.psd, then click Open.

   TIP If you receive a message stating that some text layers need to be updated before they can be used for vector-based output, click Update (Mac).

You used the Open command on the File menu to locate and open a file.

Open a file using the File Browser

1. Click the File Browser tab in the palette well. [File Browser]

   TIP If the File Browser is not visible in the palette well, set your monitor resolution to greater than 800 × 600 pixels and click File on the menu bar, then click Browse. You can add the File Browser to the palette well by clicking the list arrow in the upper-right corner, then by clicking Dock to Palette Well.

2. Navigate through the hierarchical tree to the location where your Section A project files are stored. Compare your File Browser palette to Figure A-6.

(continued)

FIGURE A-5
Open dialog box for Windows and Macintosh

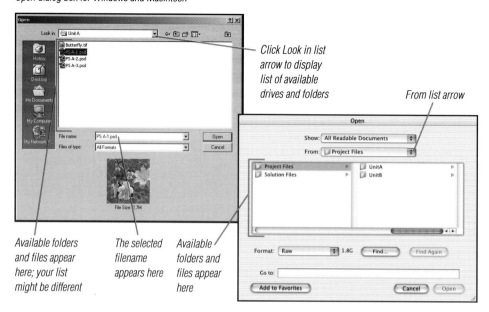

Click Look in list arrow to display list of available drives and folders

From list arrow

Available folders and files appear here; your list might be different

The selected filename appears here

Available folders and files appear here

FIGURE A-6
Docked File Browser palette

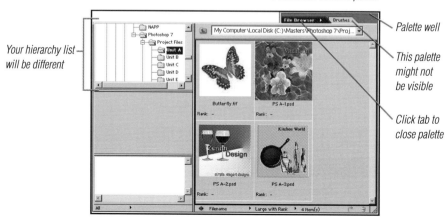

Your hierarchy list will be different

Palette well

This palette might not be visible

Click tab to close palette

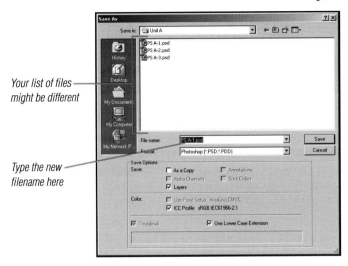

Your list of files —
might be different

Type the new —
filename here

Duplicate file with
new name

Lesson 2   Learn How to Open and Save a Document

3. Double-click Butterfly.tif.

> TIP If you receive a message stating that
> some text layers need to be updated before
> they can be used for vector-based output,
> click Update (Mac).

The File Browser palette automatically closed
when the Butterfly file opened.

You used the File Browser to locate and open a file.

Use the Save As command

1. Click the PS A-1.psd window to activate it.

2. Click File on the menu bar, click Save As,
   then compare your Save As dialog box to
   Figure A-7.

3. If the drive containing your project files is
   not displayed, click the Save in list arrow
   (Win) or the Where list arrow (Mac), then
   navigate to the location where your Section
   A data files are stored.

4. Select the current filename in the File name
   text box, if necessary; type **Vacation**, then
   click Save. Compare your image to Figure A-8.

*You used the Save As command on the File menu
to save the file with a new name.*

EXAMINE THE PHOTOSHOP WINDOW

What You'll Do

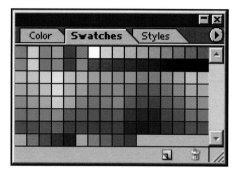

 In this lesson, you'll select a tool on the toolbox, use a shortcut key to cycle through the hidden tools, select and add a tool to the Tool Preset picker, use the Window menu to show and hide palettes in the workspace, and then create a customized workspace.

Learning About the Workspace

The **workspace** is the area within the program window that includes the entire window, from the command menus at the top of your screen to the status bar (Win) at the bottom. Desktop items are visible in this area (Mac). The workspace is shown in Figure A-9.

The **title bar** displays the program name (Adobe Photoshop) and the filename of the open document (for a new document, **Untitled-1**, because the file has not been named). The title bar also contains a Close button, and Minimize, Maximize, and Restore buttons (Win).

The **menu bar** contains menus from which you can choose Photoshop commands. You can choose a menu command by clicking it or by pressing [Alt] plus the underlined letter in the menu name (Win). Some commands display shortcut keys on the right side of the menu. Shortcut keys provide an alternative way to activate menu commands. Some commands might appear dimmed, which means they are not currently available. An ellipsis after a command indicates additional choices.

Finding Tools Everywhere

The **toolbox** contains tools associated with frequently used Photoshop commands.

Overcoming information overload

One of the most common experiences shared by first-time Photoshop users is information overload. There are just too many places and things to look at! When you feel your brain overheating, take a moment and step back. Remind yourself that the document window is the central area where you can see a composite of your work. All the tools and palettes are there to help you, not to add to the confusion.

The face of a tool contains a graphical representation of its function; for example, the Zoom Tool shows a magnifying glass. You can place the pointer over each tool to display a ScreenTip, which tells you the name or function of that tool. Some tools have additional hidden tools, indicated by a small black triangle in the lower-right corner of the tool.

The **tool options bar**, located directly under the menu bar, displays the current settings for each tool. For example, when you click the Type Tool, the default font and font size appear on the tool options bar, which can be changed if desired. You can move the tool options bar anywhere in the workspace for easier access. The tool options bar also contains the Tool Preset picker. This is the leftmost tool on the tool options bar and displays the active tool. You can click the list arrow on this tool to select another tool without having to use the toolbox. The tool options bar also contains the palette well, an area where you can assemble palettes for quick access.

QUICKTIP

The palette well is only available when your monitor resolution is greater than 800 pixels × 600 pixels.

Palettes are small windows used to verify settings and modify documents. By default, palettes appear in stacked groups at the right side of the window. You can display a palette by simply clicking the palette's name tab, which makes it the active palette. Palettes can be separated and moved

FIGURE A-9
Workspace

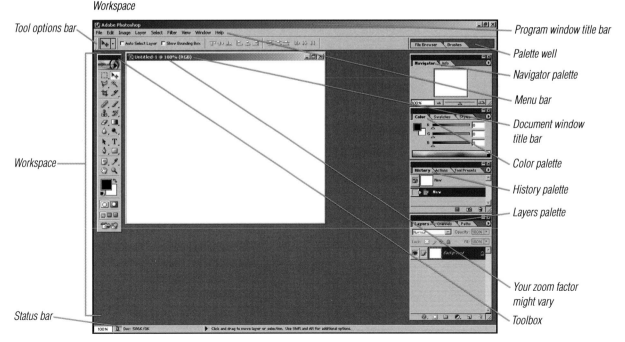

Tool options bar

Workspace

Status bar

Program window title bar
Palette well
Navigator palette
Menu bar
Document window title bar
Color palette
History palette
Layers palette
Your zoom factor might vary
Toolbox

anywhere in the workspace by dragging their name tabs to new locations. Each palette contains a menu that you can view by clicking the list arrow in its upper-right corner.

QUICKTIP
You can reset palettes to their default locations at any time by clicking Window on the menu bar, pointing to Workspace, then clicking Reset Palette Locations.

The **status bar** is located at the bottom of the program window (Win) or the document window (Mac). It displays information, such as the file size of the active window and a description of the active tool. You can display other information on the status bar, such as the current tool, by clicking the black triangle to view a pull-down menu with more options.

Rulers can help you precisely measure and position an object in the workspace. The rulers do not appear the first time you use Photoshop, but you can display them by clicking Rulers on the View menu.

Using Tool Shortcut Keys

Each tool has a corresponding shortcut key. For example, the shortcut key for the Type Tool is T. After you know a tool's shortcut key, you can select the tool on the toolbox by pressing its shortcut key. To select and cycle through a tool's hidden tools, you press and hold [Shift] then press the tool's shortcut key until the desired tool appears. See the Power User Shortcuts table at the end of each section for a description of tool shortcut keys.

Customizing Your Environment

Photoshop makes it easy for you to position elements you work with just where you want them. If you move elements around to make your environment more convenient, you can always return your workspace to its original appearance by resetting the default palette locations. You can create a customized workspace by clicking Window on the menu bar, pointing to Workspace, then clicking Save Workspace. A named workspace appears in the Window menu under Workspace. So, if you want to open a named workspace, click Window on the menu bar, point to Workspace, then click the workspace you want to use.

FIGURE A-10

Hidden tools

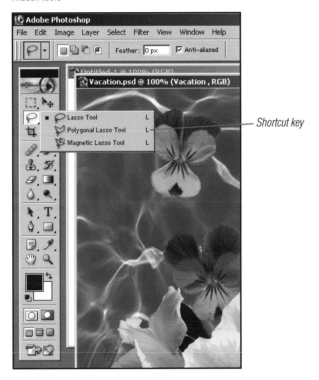

Shortcut key

Select a tool

1. Click the Lasso Tool on the toolbox, then press and hold the mouse button until a list of hidden tools appears, as shown in Figure A-10.

2. Click the Polygonal Lasso Tool, then note the shortcut key, L, next to the tool name.

3. Press and hold [Shift], press [L] three times to cycle through the list of tools, then release [Shift].

   TIP You can return the tools to their default setting by clicking the Click to open the Tool Preset picker list arrow on the tool options bar, clicking the list arrow, then clicking Reset All Tools.

You selected the Lasso Tool on the toolbox and used its shortcut key to cycle through the Lasso tools.

Select a tool from the Tool Preset picker

1. Click the Click to open the Tool Preset picker list arrow on the tool options bar. See Figure A-11.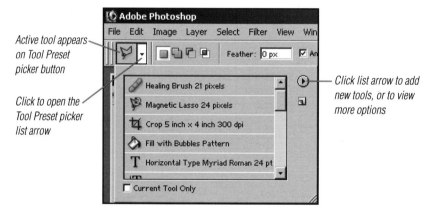

   A button gets its name from its ScreenTip (descriptive text that appears when you place the pointer over the button).

2. Deselect the Current Tool Only check box, if necessary.

3. Double-click the Magnetic Lasso 24 pixels tool.

You selected the Magnetic Lasso Tool using the Tool Preset picker.

FIGURE A-11
Using the Tool Preset picker

Active tool appears on Tool Preset picker button

Click to open the Tool Preset picker list arrow

Click list arrow to add new tools, or to view more options

Healing Brush 21 pixels
Magnetic Lasso 24 pixels
Crop 5 inch x 4 inch 300 dpi
Fill with Bubbles Pattern
Horizontal Type Myriad Roman 24 pt

Current Tool Only

1. Click the Move Tool on the toolbox. ⊞

2. Click the Click to open the Tool Preset picker list arrow on the tool options bar. ⊞⊡

3. Click the list arrow on the Tool Preset picker. ⊙

4. Click New Tool Preset, then click OK to accept the default name (Move Tool #1). Compare your list to Figure A-12.

   TIP   You can display the currently selected tool alone by selecting the Current Tool Only check box.

You added the Move Tool to the Tool Preset picker.

FIGURE A-12
Move Tool added to Tool Preset picker

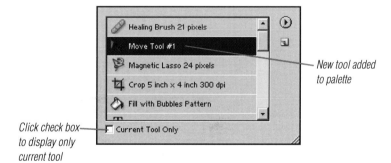

New tool added to palette

Click check box to display only current tool

Show and hide palettes

1. Click Window on the menu bar, then verify that Color has a check mark next to it.

2. Click the Swatches tab next to the Color tab to make the Swatches palette active, as shown in Figure A-13.

3. Click Window on the menu bar, then click Swatches to deselect it.

   TIP   You can hide all open palettes by pressing [Shift], then [Tab], then show them by pressing [Shift], then [Tab] again. To hide all open palettes, the tool options bar, and the toolbox, press [Tab], then show them by pressing [Tab] again.

4. Click Window on the menu bar, then click Swatches to redisplay the Swatches palette.

You used the Window menu to show and hide the Swatches palette.

FIGURE A-13
Active Swatches palette

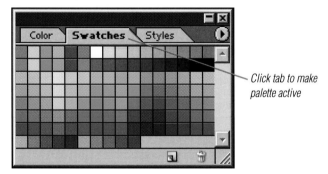

Click tab to make
palette active

Create a customized workspace

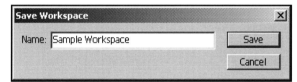

1. Click and drag the toolbox title bar so it appears to the right of the document.
2. Click Window on the menu bar, point to Workspace, then click Save Workspace.
3. Type **Sample Workspace** in the Name text box, as shown in Figure A-14.
4. Click Save.
5. Click Window on the menu bar, then point to Workspace.

   The name of the new workspace appears on the Window menu.
6. Click Reset Palette Locations.

You created a customized workspace, then reset the palette locations.

FIGURE A-14
Save Workspace dialog box

USE THE LAYERS AND HISTORY PALETTES

What You'll Do

 In this lesson, you'll hide and display a layer, move a layer on the Layers palette, and then undo the move by deleting the Layer Order state on the History palette.

Learning About Layers

A **layer** is a section within an image that can be manipulated independently. Layers allow you to control individual elements within a document and create great dramatic effects and variations of the same document. Each Photoshop document can consist of one layer, many individual layers, or groups of layers.

You can think of layers in a Photoshop image as individual sheets of clear plastic that are in a stack. It's possible for your document to quickly accumulate dozens of layers. Layers enable you to easily manipulate individual characteristics within an image. The **Layers palette** displays all the layers in an open document. You can use the Layers palette to create, copy, delete, display, hide, merge, lock, or reposition layers.

QUICKTIP

In Photoshop, using and understanding layers is the key to success.

Setting preferences

The Preferences dialog box contains several topics, each with its own settings: General, File Handling, Display and Cursors, Transparency and Gamut, Sections and Rulers, Guides, Grids and Slices, Plug-ins and Scratch Disks, and Memory and Image Cache. To open the Preferences dialog box, click Edit on the menu bar, point to Preferences, then click a topic that represents the settings you want to change. If you move palettes around the workspace, or make other changes to them, you can choose to retain those changes the next time you start the program. To always start a new session with default palettes, click General on the Preferences menu, deselect the Save Palette Locations check box, then click OK. Each time you start Photoshop, the palettes will be reset to their default locations and values.

Understanding the Layers Palette

The order in which the layers appear in the Layers palette matches the order in which they appear in the document; the topmost layer in the Layers palette is the topmost layer in the image. You can make a layer active by clicking its name in the Layers palette. When a layer is active, it is highlighted in the Layers palette, a paintbrush icon appears next to the thumbnail, indicating that you can edit the layer, and the name of the layer appears in parentheses in the document title bar. Only one layer can be active at a time. Figure A-15 shows a document with its Layers palette. Did you notice that this image contains 5 layers? Each layer can be moved or modified individually within the palette to give a different effect to the overall document. If you look at the Layers palette, you'll see that the Finger Painting layer is dark, indicating that it is currently active.

QUICKTIP

Get in the habit of shifting your eye from the document to the Layers palette. Knowing which layer is active will save you time and help you troubleshoot an image.

Displaying and Hiding Layers

You can use the Layers palette to control which layers are visible in a document. You can show or hide a layer by clicking the Indicates layer visibility button next to the layer thumbnail. When a layer is hidden, you are not able to merge it with another, select it, or print it. Hiding some layers can make it easier to focus on particular areas of an image.

Using the History Palette

Photoshop records each task you complete in a document in the **History palette.** This record of events, called states, makes it easy to see what changes occurred and the tools or commands that you used to make the modifications. The History palette, also shown in Figure A-15, displays up to 20 states and automatically updates the list to display the most recently performed tasks. The list contains the name of the tool or command used to change the image. You can delete a state in the History palette by selecting it and dragging it to the Delete current state button. Deleting a state is equivalent to using the Undo command. You can also use the History palette to create a new document from any state.

QUICKTIP

When you delete a History state, you undo all the events that occurred after that state.

FIGURE A-15
Layers and History palettes

History states

Click a layer name to make the layer active

Hide and display a layer

1. Click the Azaleas layer on the Layers palette.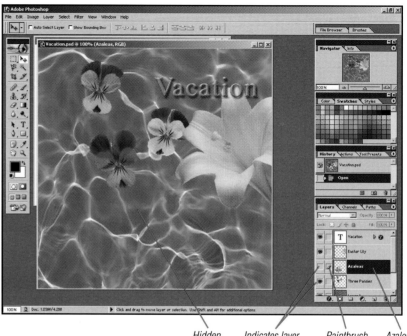

   > TIP Depending on the size of the window, you might only be able to see the initial characters of the layer name.

2. Click the Indicates layer visibility button on the Azaleas layer to hide the image, as shown in Figure A-16.

   > TIP By default, transparent areas of an image have a checkerboard display on the Layers palette.

3. Click the Indicates layer visibility button on the Azaleas layer to reveal the image.

You made the Azaleas layer active on the Layers palette, then clicked the Indicates layer visibility button to hide and display a layer.

FIGURE A-16
Azaleas layer hidden

Hidden Azaleas layer

Indicates layer visibility buttons

Paintbrush icon

Azaleas layer

Considering ethical implications

Because Photoshop enables you to make so many incredible changes to images, you should consider the ethical ramifications and implications of altering images. Is it proper or appropriate to alter an image just because you have the technical expertise to do so? Are there any legal responsibilities or liabilities involved in making these alterations? Because the topic of **intellectual property** (an image or idea that is owned and retained by legal control) has become more pronounced with the increased availability of information and content, you should make sure you have the legal right to alter an image, especially if you plan on displaying or distributing the image to others. Know who retains the rights to an image, and if necessary, make sure you have written permission for its use, alteration, and/or distribution. Not taking these precautions could be costly.

Layer moved in Layers palette

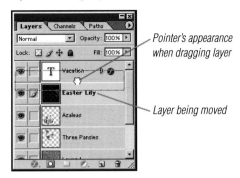

Pointer's appearance
when dragging layer

Layer being moved

FIGURE A-18
Result of moved layer

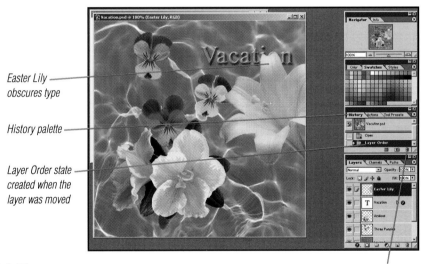

Easter Lily
obscures type

History palette

Layer Order state
created when the
layer was moved

Delete current
state button

FIGURE A-19
Deleting a History state

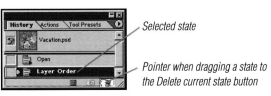

Selected state

Pointer when dragging a state to
the Delete current state button

Lesson 4   Use the Layers and History Palettes

Move a layer on the Layers palette and delete a state on the History palette

1. Click the Easter Lily layer on the Layers palette, then drag it to the top position in the palette, as shown in Figure A-17. 🖑

   The object in the Easter Lily layer obscures part of the type. See Figure A-18.

2. Click Layer Order on the History palette, then drag it to the Delete current state button on the History palette, as shown in Figure A-19. 🗑

   TIP Each time you close and reopen a document, the History palette is cleared.

   The text is no longer obscured.

3. Click File on the menu bar, then click Save.

You moved the Easter Lily layer to the top of the Layers palette, then returned it to its original position by dragging the Layer Order state to the Delete current state button on the History palette.

LEARN ABOUT PHOTOSHOP BY USING HELP

What You'll Do

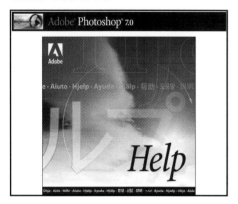

In this lesson, you'll open Help, then view and find information from the following Help links: Contents, Index, Site Map, and Search.

Understanding the Power of Help

Photoshop features an extensive Help system that you can use to access definitions, explanations, and useful tips. Help information is displayed in a browser window, so you must have Web browser software installed on your computer to view the information; however, you do not need an Internet connection to use Photoshop Help.

Using Help Topics

The Help window has five links that you can use to retrieve information about Photoshop commands and features: Using Help, Contents, Index, Site Map, and Search, as shown in Figure A-20. The

Using Help link displays information about the Help system. The Contents link allows you to browse topics by category; the Index link provides the letters of the alphabet, which you can click to view keywords and topics alphabetically. Each entry in the Index section is followed by a number, which represents the number of articles about the particular subject. The Site Map link displays a variety of links that take you directly to specific topics. The Search link allows you to enter keywords as your search criteria. When you choose a topic using any of the five methods, information about that topic appears in the right pane of the browser window.

FIGURE A-20
Links in the Help window

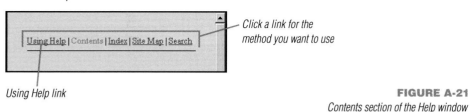

Click a link for the
method you want to use

Using Help link

FIGURE A-21
Contents section of the Help window

Using the Layers palette

The Layers palette lists all layers, layer sets, and layer effects in an image. You can accomplish many tasks--such as creating, hiding, displaying, copying, and deleting layers--using the buttons in the Layers palette. You can access additional commands and options in the Layers palette menu and the Layers menu.

Photoshop Layers palette: **A.** Layers palette menu **B.** Layer set **C.** Layer **D.** Layer thumbnail **E.** Layer effect

Displaying the Layers palette

Choose Window > Layers.

Click Contents topic   Subtopic

Find information in Contents

1. Click Help on the menu bar, then click Photoshop Help.

   | TIP You can also open the Help window by pressing [F1] (Win) or [command] [?] (Mac).

2. If it's not already selected, click the Contents link, scroll down the left pane, then click the Using Layers link.

3. Click the Using the Layers palette link in the right pane. See Figure A-21.

You used the Photoshop Help command on the Help menu to open the Help window and viewed a topic in Contents.

Understanding the Help links

Many Help topics contain links at the bottom of the right pane that indicate the hierarchy of the current entry in Help and link to related topics. If you want to see a list of related topics, click the link to go up a level. Browsing the hierarchy of Help topics can help you understand Photoshop functionality. To ensure that the Help window is displayed properly, use Netscape 4.75 and later or Internet Explorer 5.0.

Find information in the Index

1. Open Help, if necessary, then click the Index link in the Help window.

2. Click the L link, scroll down the left pane to layers, then click the 1 link next to about. Compare your Help window to Figure A-22.

You clicked an alphabetical listing and viewed an entry in the Index.

Find information in the Site Map

1. Open Help, if necessary, then click the Site Map link in the Help window.

2. Scroll down the left pane, then click the If you are new to Photoshop link. Compare your Help window to Figure A-23.

You clicked a link in the site map to find information on Photoshop.

FIGURE A-22
Topics in the Index window

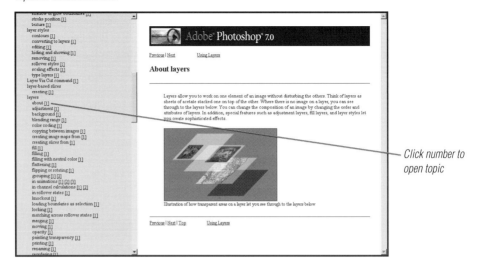

Click number to open topic

FIGURE A-23
Topics in the Site Map window

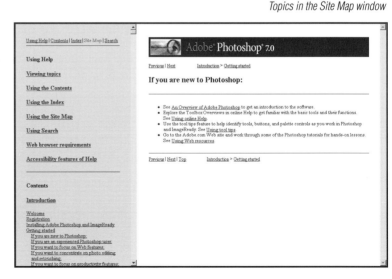

1. Open Help, if necessary, then click the Search link in the Help window.

2. Type **print quality**, then click Search.

   > TIP You can search for multiple words by inserting a space; do not use punctuation in the text box.

3. Scroll down the left pane, if necessary, click the About printing link, then compare your Help screen to Figure A-24.

4. Click File on the menu bar, then click Close (Win) or Quit (Mac) when you are finished reading the topic.

You entered a search term, viewed search results, and exited the Help window.

FIGURE A-24

Search topic in Help

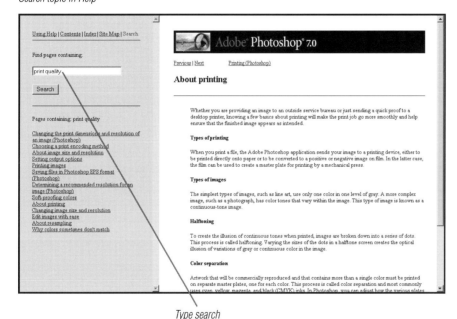

Type search
term here

VIEW AND PRINT A DOCUMENT

What You'll Do

 In this lesson, you'll use the Zoom Tool on the toolbox to increase and decrease your views of the image. You'll also change the page orientation settings in the Page Setup dialog box, and print the document.

Getting a Closer Look

When you edit an image in Photoshop, it is important that you have a good view of the area that you are focusing on. Photoshop has a variety of methods that allow you to enlarge or reduce your current view. You can use the Zoom Tool by clicking the image to zoom in on (magnify the view) or zoom out of (reduce the view) areas of your document. Zooming in or out enlarges or reduces your *view*, not the actual image. The maximum zoom factor is 1600%. The current zoom percentage appears in the document's title bar, in the Navigator palette, and on the status bar. When the Zoom Tool is selected, the tool options bar provides additional choices for changing your view as shown in Figure A-25. For example, the Resize Windows To Fit check box automatically resizes the window whenever you magnify or reduce the view. You can also change the zoom percentage using the Navigator palette and the status bar by typing a new value in the zoom text box.

Printing Your Document

In many cases, a professional print shop might be the best option for printing a Photoshop document to get the highest quality. You can, however, print a Photoshop document using a standard black-and-white or color printer. Regardless of the number of layers in an image, your printed image will be a composite of all visible layers. Of course, the quality of your printer and paper will affect the appearance of your output. The Page Setup dialog box displays options for printing, such as paper orientation. **Orientation** is the direction in which an image appears on the page. In **portrait orientation**, a document is printed with the short edges of the paper at the top and bottom. In **landscape orientation**, a document is printed with the long edges of the paper at the top and bottom.

Viewing a Document in Multiple Views

You can use the New Window command on the Window ➢ Documents menu to open multiple views of the same document. You can change the zoom percentage in each view so you can spotlight the areas you want to modify, and then modify the specific area of the image in each view. Because you are working on the same document in multiple views, not in multiple versions, Photoshop automatically applies the changes you make in one view to all views. Although you can close the views you no longer need at any time, Photoshop will not save any changes until you save the document.

FIGURE A-25
Zoom Tool choices on the tool options bar

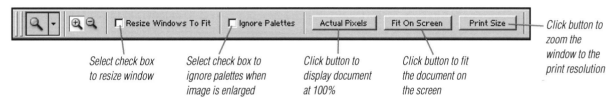

Select check box to resize window

Select check box to ignore palettes when image is enlarged

Click button to display document at 100%

Click button to fit the document on the screen

Click button to zoom the window to the print resolution

Using a scanner and a digital camera

If you have a scanner, you can use print images, such as those taken from photographs, magazines, or line drawings, in Photoshop. Make sure you remember that images taken from magazines are owned by others, and that you need permission to distribute them. Scanners are relatively inexpensive and easy to use. They come in many types, including flatbed or single-sheet feed. After you scan an image and save it as an electronic file, you can open and use it in Photoshop. You can also use a digital camera to create your own images. Although it operates much like a film camera, a digital camera captures images on some form of electronic medium, such as a floppy disk or SmartMedia card. After you upload the images from your camera to your computer, you can use the images in Photoshop.

So how can you use that scanned image or digital picture in Photoshop? Well, you can open the image (which usually has a .JPG extension or another file format) by clicking File on the menu bar, then by clicking Open. (Since All Formats is the default file type, you should be able to see all available image files.) After the Open dialog box opens, locate the folder containing your scanned or digital images, click the file you want to open, then click Open. A scanned or digital image will contain all its imagery in a single layer. You can add layers to the image, but you can only save these new layers if you save the image as a Photoshop document (with the extension .PSD).

Use the Zoom Tool

1. Click the Zoom Tool on the toolbox.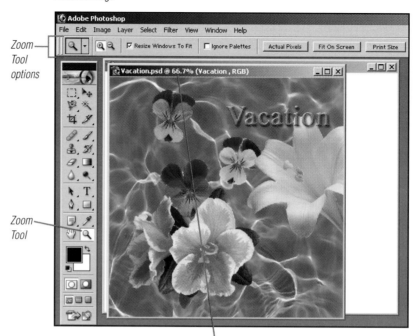

2. Select the Resize Windows To Fit check box on the tool options bar. ☐ Resize Windows To Fit

3. Position the pointer over the center of the image, then click the image. ⊕

   | TIP Position the pointer over the part of the image you want to keep in view.

4. Press [Alt] (Win) or [option] (Mac), then click the center of the image twice. ⊖

5. Release [Alt] (Win) or [option] (Mac), then compare your image to Figure A-26.

   The zoom factor for the document is 66.7%.

You selected the Zoom Tool on the toolbox and used it to zoom in to and out of the image.

FIGURE A-26
Reduced image

Zoom Tool options

Zoom Tool

Zoom percentage changed

Using the Navigator palette

You can change the magnification factor of an image using the Navigator palette or the Zoom Tool on the toolbox. By double-clicking the Zoom box on the Navigator palette, you can enter a new magnification factor, then press [Enter] (Win) or [return] (Mac). The magnification factor—shown as a percentage—is displayed in the lower-left corner of the Navigator palette. The red border in the palette, called the Proxy Preview Area, defines the area of the image that is magnified. You can drag the Proxy Preview Area inside the Navigator palette to view other areas of the image at the current magnification factor.

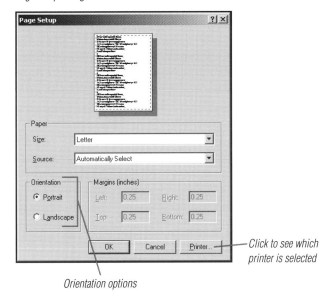

*Click to see which
printer is selected*

Orientation options

*Name of
selected printer*

Number of copies

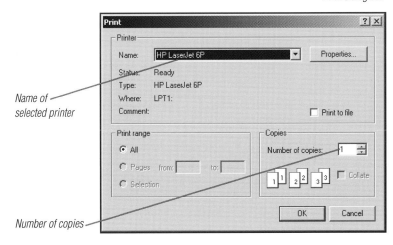

Modify print settings

1. Click File on the menu bar, then click Page Setup to open the Page Setup dialog box, as shown in Figure A-27.

   TIP If you have not selected a printer using the Chooser, a warning box might appear (Mac).

   Page setup and print settings vary slightly in Macintosh.

2. Click the Landscape option button, then click OK.

   TIP Choose either Landscape option (Mac).

3. Click File on the menu bar, click Print, then click Proceed.

4. Make sure that the All option button is selected in the Print range section, and that 1 appears in the Number of copies text box (Win), or the From option button is selected in the Copies & Pages section (Mac), then click OK (Win) or Print (Mac), as shown in Figure A-28.

You used the Page Setup command on the File menu to open the Page Setup dialog box, changed the page orientation, then printed the document.

CLOSE A DOCUMENT AND EXIT PHOTOSHOP

What You'll Do

 In this lesson, you'll use the Close and Exit (Win) or Quit (Mac) commands to close documents and exit Photoshop.

Concluding Your Work Session

At the end of your work session, you might have opened several documents; you now need to decide which ones you want to save.

QUICKTIP

If you share a computer with other people, it's a good idea to reset Photoshop's preferences back to their default settings. You can do so when you start Photoshop by pressing and holding [Shift][Alt][Ctrl] (Win) or [Shift][option][command] (Mac).

Closing Versus Exiting

When you are finished working on a document, you need to save and close it. You can close one document at a time, or close all open documents at the same time by exiting the program. Closing a file leaves Photoshop open, which allows you to open or create another file. Exiting Photoshop closes the file, closes Photoshop, and returns you to the desktop, where you can choose to open another program or shut down the computer. Photoshop will prompt you to save any changes before it closes the files. If you do not modify a new or existing document, Photoshop will close it automatically when you exit.

QUICKTIP

To close all open documents, click Window on the menu bar, point to Documents, then click Close All.

Using Adobe online

Periodically, when you start Photoshop, an Update dialog box might appear, prompting you to search for updates or new information on the Adobe Web site. If you click Yes, Photoshop will automatically notify you that a download is available; however, you do not have to select it. You can also obtain information about Photoshop from the Adobe Photoshop Web site (www.adobe.products/photoshop/main.html), where you can link to downloads, tips, training, galleries, examples, and other support topics.

FIGURE A-29
Closing a document using the File menu

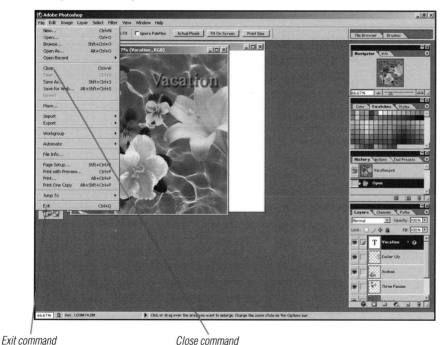

Exit command   Close command

1. Click File on the menu bar, then compare your screen to Figure A-29.

2. Click Close.

   > TIP   You can close an open file (without closing Photoshop) by clicking the Close button in the document window. Photoshop will prompt you to save any unsaved changes before closing the document.

3. If asked to save your work, click Yes (Win) or Save (Mac).

4. Click File on the menu bar, then click Exit (Win) or click Photoshop on the menu bar, then click Quit (Mac).

   > TIP   To exit Photoshop and close an open file, click the Close button in the program window. Photoshop will prompt you to save any unsaved changes before closing.

5. If asked to save your work, click No.

You closed the current document and exited the program by using the Close and Exit (Win) or Quit (Mac) commands.

As a new Photoshop user, you are comforted knowing that Photoshop's Help system provides definitions, explanations, procedures, and other helpful information. It also includes examples and demonstrations to show how Photoshop features work. You use the Help system to learn about managing the color in your images.

1. Open the Photoshop Help window.
2. Click the Producing Consistent Color (Photoshop) link in the Contents pane.
3. Click the Why colors sometimes don't match link.
4. After you read this topic, use the Previous link to return to the previous screen.
5. Click the About color management link.
6. Print out the About color management topic, then compare your results to the sample shown in Figure A-30.

FIGURE A-30
Completed Project 1

Kitchen World, your local specialty cooking shop, has just added herb-infused oils to its product line. They have hired you to draft a flyer that features their new products. You use Photoshop to create a flyer.

1. Open PS A-3.psd, then save it as **Kitchen World**.
2. Make the Measuring Spoons layer visible.
3. Drag the Oils layer behind the Skillet layer.
4. Drag the Measuring Spoons layer in front of the Skillet layer.
5. Save the document, then compare your document to the sample shown in Figure A-31.

FIGURE A-31
Completed Project 2

SECTION B

WORKING WITH LAYERS

1. Examine and convert layers.

2. Add and delete layers.

3. Add a selection from one document to another.

4. Organize layers with layer sets and colors.

SECTION B
WORKING WITH LAYERS

Layers Are Everything

You can use Photoshop to create sophisticated images because you can create multiple layers. Each object created in Photoshop exists on its own individual layer, making it easy to control the position and quality of each layer in the stack. Depending on your computer's resources, you can have a maximum of 8000 layers in each Photoshop document with each layer containing as much or as little detail as necessary. Adding layers to an image increases its file size, so after your document is finished, you can dramatically reduce its file size by combining all the layers.

> **QUICK**TIP
>
> The transparent areas in a layer do not increase file size.

Understanding the Importance of Layers

Layers make it possible to manipulate the tiniest detail within your document, which gives you tremendous flexibility when you make changes. By placing images, effects, styles, and type on separate layers, you can modify them individually *without* affecting other layers. The advantage to using multiple layers is that you can isolate effects and images on one layer without affecting the others. The disadvantage of using multiple layers is that your file size might become very large.

Using Layers to Modify a Document

You can add, delete, and move layers in your document. You can also drag a portion of an image, called a **selection**, from one Photoshop document to another. When you do this, a new layer is automatically created. Copying layers from one document to another makes it easy to transfer a complicated effect, a simple image, or a piece of type. You can also hide and display each layer, or change its opacity. **Opacity** is the ability to see through a layer so that layers beneath it are visible. You can continuously change your document's overall appearance by changing the order of your layers, until you achieve just the look you want.

Tools You'll Use

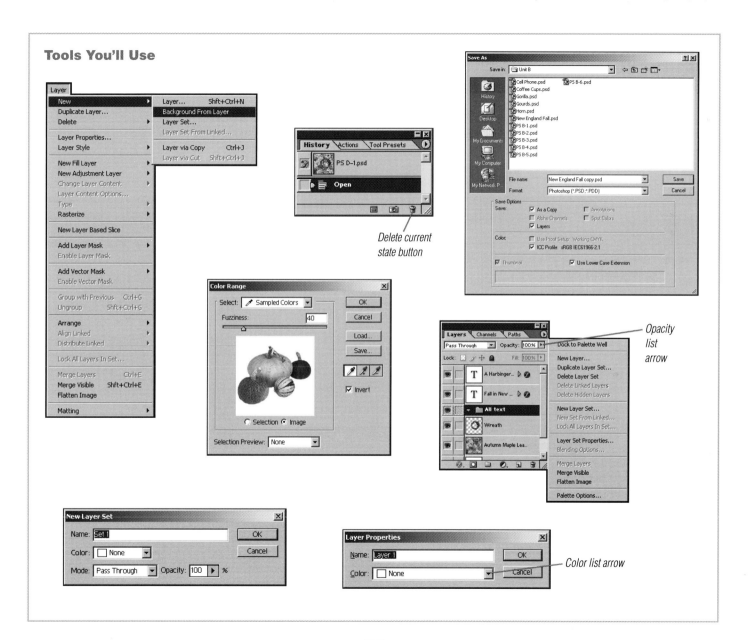

Delete current state button

Opacity list arrow

Color list arrow

EXAMINE AND CONVERT LAYERS

What You'll Do

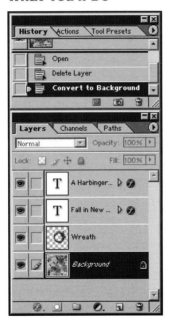

 In this lesson, you'll use the Layers palette to delete a Background layer and the Layer menu to create a Background layer from an image layer.

Learning About the Layers Palette

The **Layers palette** lists all the layer names within a Photoshop file and enables you to manipulate one or more layers at a time. By default, this palette is located in the lower-right corner of the screen, but it can be moved to a new location by dragging the palette's tab. In some cases, the entire name of the layer might not appear in the palette. If a layer name is too long, an ellipsis appears, indicating that part of the name is hidden from view. You can view a layer's entire name, by holding the pointer over the name until the full name appears. The **layer thumbnail** appears to the left of the layer name and contains a miniature picture of the layer's content, as shown in Figure B-1. To the left of the layer thumbnail, you can add color, which allows you to easily identify layers. The Layers palette also contains common buttons, such as the Delete layer button and the Create new layer button.

QUICKTIP

You can hide or resize Layers palette thumbnails to improve your computer's performance. To remove or change the size of layer thumbnails, click the Layers palette list arrow, then click Palette Options to open the Layers Palette option dialog box. Click the option button next to the desired thumbnail size, or click the None option button to remove thumbnails, then click OK. A paintbrush icon appears in place of a thumbnail.

Recognizing Layer Types

The Layers palette includes several types of layers: Background, type, and image (non-type). The Background layer—whose name appears in italics—is always at the bottom of the stack. Type layers—layers that contain text—contain the type layer icon in the layer thumbnail, and image layers display a thumbnail of their contents, as shown in Figure B-1. In addition to dragging selections from one Photoshop document to another, you can also drag objects created in other applications, such as Adobe Illustrator, InDesign, or Macromedia Flash, onto a Photoshop document, which creates a layer containing objects created in another program.

QUICKTIP

It is not necessary for a Photoshop document to have a Background layer.

Organizing Layers

One of the benefits of using layers is that you can create different design effects by rearranging their order. Figure B-2 contains the same layers as Figure B-1, but they are arranged differently. Did you notice that the wreath is partially obscured by the gourds and the title text? This reorganization was created by dragging the Wreath layer below the Gourds layer on the Layers palette.

QUICKTIP

Did you notice the lines in the figures? These are moveable guides that you can use to help you place objects.

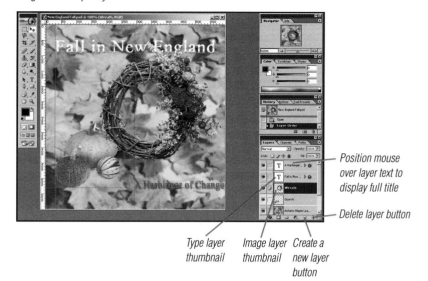

Position mouse over layer text to display full title

Delete layer button

Type layer thumbnail   Image layer thumbnail   Create a new layer button

New layer order

Wreath obscured

Converting Layers

When you open an image created with a digital camera, you'll notice that the entire image appears in the Background layer. The Background layer of any document is the initial layer and is always located at the bottom of the stack. You cannot change its position in the stack, nor can you change its opacity or lighten or darken its colors. You can convert a Background layer into an image layer (nontype layer), and you can convert an image layer into a Background layer. You need to modify the image layer *before* converting it to a Background layer. You might want to convert a Background layer into an image layer so that you can use the full range of editing tools on the layer content. You might want to convert an image layer into a Background layer after you have made all your changes and want it to be the bottommost layer in the stack.

QUICKTIP

When converting an image layer to a Background layer, you must delete the existing Background layer. You can delete a Background layer by clicking it on the Layers palette, then dragging it to the Delete layer button on the Layers palette.

FIGURE B-3
Preferences dialog box

Rulers list arrow

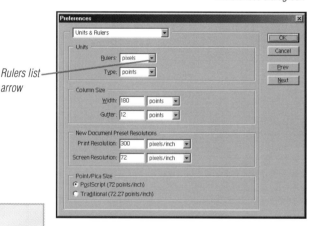

Using rulers and changing units of measurement

You can display horizontal and vertical rulers to help you better position elements. To display or hide rulers, you click View on the menu bar, then click Rulers. (A check mark to the right of the Rulers command indicates that the Rulers are displayed.) In addition to displaying or hiding rulers, you can also choose from various units of measurement. Your choices include pixels, inches, centimeters, micrometers, points, picas, and percentages. Pixels, for example, display more tick marks and can make it easier to make tiny adjustments. You can change the units of measurement by clicking Edit [Win] or Photoshop [Mac] on the menu bar, pointing to Preferences, then clicking Units & Rulers [Win]. In the Preferences dialog box, as shown in Figure B-3, click the Rulers list arrow, click the units you want to use, then click OK.

FIGURE B-4

Warning box

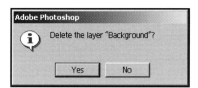

FIGURE B-5

Background layer deleted

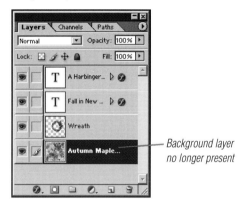

Background layer
no longer present

FIGURE B-6

New Background layer added to Layers palette

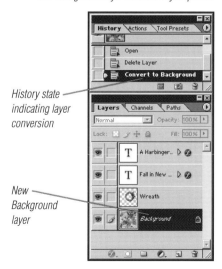

History state
indicating layer
conversion

New
Background
layer

Convert an image layer into a Background layer

1. Open PS B-1.psd, then save it as **New England Fall**.

   TIP   If you receive a message stating that some of the text layers need to be updated before they can be used for vector-based output, click Update (Mac).

2. Click View on the menu bar, click Rulers if your rulers are not visible, then verify that your rulers are displayed in pixels.

   TIP   If you are unsure which units of measurement are used, click Edit (Win) or Photoshop (Mac) on the menu bar, point to Preferences, then click Units & Rulers (Win). Click the Rulers list arrow, click Pixels, then click OK.

3. On the Layers palette, scroll down, click the Background layer, then click the Delete layer button.

4. Click Yes in the warning box, as shown in Figure B-4, then compare your Layers palette to Figure B-5.

5. Click Layer on the menu bar, point to New, then click Background From Layer.

   The Autumn Maple Leaves layer has been converted into the Background layer. Did you notice that in addition to the image layer being converted to the Background layer that a state now appears in the History palette that says Convert to Background? See Figure B-6.

6. Save your work.

You displayed the rulers, deleted the Background layer, then converted an image layer into the Background layer.

ADD AND DELETE LAYERS

What You'll Do

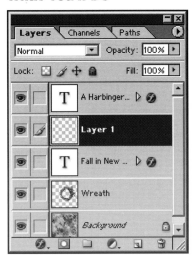

 In this lesson, you'll create a new layer using the New command on the Layer menu, delete a layer, and create a layer using buttons on the Layers palette.

Adding Layers to a Document

Because it's so important to make use of multiple layers, Photoshop makes it easy to add and delete layers. You can create layers in three ways:

- Use the New command on the Layer menu.
- Use the New Layer command on the Layers palette menu.
- Click the Create a new layer button on the Layers palette.

Objects on new layers have a default opacity setting of 100%, which means that objects on lower layers are not visible. Each layer has the Normal (default) blending mode applied to it. (A **blending mode** is a feature that affects a layer's underlying pixels, and is used to lighten or darken colors.)

Merging layers

You can combine multiple image layers into a single layer using the merging process. Merging layers is useful when you want to make specific edits permanent. In order for layers to be merged, they must be visible and next to each other on the Layers palette. You can merge all visible layers within an image, or just the ones you select. Type layers cannot be merged until they are **rasterized** (turned into a bitmapped image layer), or converted into uneditable text. To merge two layers, make sure that they are next to each other and that the Indicates layer visibility button is visible on each layer, then click the layer in the higher position on the Layers palette. Click Layer on the menu bar, then click Merge Layers. The active layer and the layer immediately beneath it will be combined into a single layer. To merge all visible layers, click the Layers palette list arrow, then click Merge Visible. Most layer commands that are available on the Layers menu, such as Merge Layers, are also available using the Layers palette list arrow.

Naming a Layer

Photoshop automatically assigns a sequential number to each new layer name, but you can rename a layer at any time. After all, calling a layer "Layer 12" is fine, but you might want to use a more descriptive name so it is easier to distinguish one layer from another. If you use the New command on the Layers menu, you can name the layer when you create it. You can rename a layer at any time by using any of these methods:

- Click the Layers palette list arrow, click Layer Properties, type the name in the Name text box, then click OK.
- Double-click the name on the Layers palette, type the new name, then press [Enter] (Win) or [return] (Mac).

Deleting Layers From a Document

You might want to delete an unused or unnecessary layer. You can use four methods to delete a layer:

- Click the name on the Layers palette, click the Layers palette list arrow, then click Delete Layer as shown in Figure B-7.
- Click the name on the Layers palette, click the Delete layer button on the Layers palette, then click Yes in the warning box.
- Drag the layer name on the Layers palette to the Delete layer button on the Layers palette.

- Click the name on the Layers palette, press and hold [Alt] (Win) or [option] (Mac), then click the Delete layer button on the Layers palette.

You should be certain that you no longer need a layer before you delete it. If you delete a layer by accident, you can restore it during the current editing session by deleting the Delete Layer state on the History palette.

> **QUICKTIP**
> Photoshop always numbers layers sequentially, no matter how many layers you add or delete.

FIGURE B-7
Layers palette menu

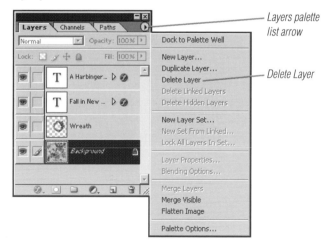

Layers palette list arrow

Delete Layer

Add a layer using the Layer menu

1. Click the Fall in New England layer on the Layers palette.

   A new layer will be added above the active layer.

2. Click Layer on the menu bar, point to New, then click Layer to open the New Layer dialog box, as shown in Figure B-8.

   > TIP By default, Photoshop names new layers consecutively, starting with Layer 1. You can change the layer name in the New Layer dialog box before it appears on the Layers palette.

3. Click OK.

   The New Layer dialog box closes and the new layer appears above the Fall in New England layer on the Layers palette. The New Layer state is added to the History palette. See Figure B-9.

   You created a new layer above the Fall in New England layer, using the New command on the Layer menu.

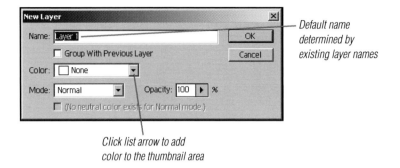

Default name determined by existing layer names

Click list arrow to add color to the thumbnail area

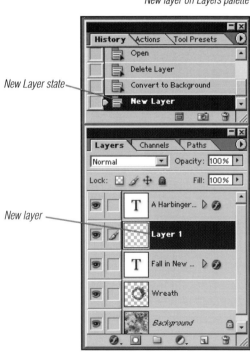

New Layer state

New layer

Delete a layer

1. Position the pointer over Layer 1 in the Layers palette. 🖑

2. Drag Layer 1 to the Delete layer button on the Layers palette. 🗑

   TIP You can also delete the layer by dragging the New Layer state in the History palette to the Delete current state button.

You used the Delete layer button on the Layers palette to delete a layer.

Add a layer using the Layers palette

1. Click the Fall in New England layer on the Layers palette.

2. Click the Create a new layer button on the Layers palette, then compare your Layers palette to Figure B-10. 🔲

   TIP You can rename a layer by clicking the Layers palette list arrow, clicking Layer Properties, typing a new name in the Name text box, then clicking OK.

3. Save your work.

You used the Create a new layer button on the Layers palette to add a new layer.

FIGURE B-10
New layer with default settings

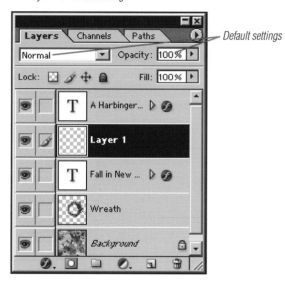

Default settings

ADD A SELECTION FROM ONE
DOCUMENT TO ANOTHER

What You'll Do

In this lesson, you'll use the Invert check box in the Color Range dialog box to make a selection, drag the selection to another document, and remove the fringe from a selection.

Understanding Selections

Often the Photoshop document you want to create involves using an image or part of an image from another file. To use an image or part of an image, you must first select it. Photoshop refers to this as "making a selection." A selection is an area of an image surrounded by a **marquee**, a dashed line that surrounds the area you want to edit or move to another document, as shown in Figure B-11. You can drag a marquee around a selection using four marquee tools: Rectangular Marquee, Elliptical Marquee, Single Row Marquee, and Single Column Marquee. Table B-1 displays the four marquee tools and other selection tools. You can set options for

each tool on the tool options bar when the tool you want to use is active.

Understanding the Extract and Color Range Commands

In addition to using selection tools, Photoshop provides other methods for incorporating imagery from other documents. The **Extract command**, located on the Filter menu, separates an image from a background or surrounding imagery. You can use the **Color Range** command, located on the Select menu, to select a particular color contained in an existing image. Depending on the area you want, you can use the Color Range dialog box to extract a portion of an image. For

Cropping an image

You might find an image that you really like, except that it contains a particular portion that you don't need. You can exclude, or **crop**, certain parts of an image by using the Crop Tool on the toolbox. Cropping hides areas of an image from view *without* losing resolution quality. To crop an image, click the Crop Tool on the toolbox, drag the pointer around the area you *want to keep*, then press [Enter] (Win) or [return] (Mac).

example, you can select the Invert check box to choose one color and then select the portion of the image that is every color *except* that one. After you select all the imagery you want from another document, you can drag it into your open document.

Making a Selection and Moving a Selection

You can use a variety of methods and tools to make a selection, which can be used as a specific part of a layer or the entire layer.

You use selections to isolate an area you want to alter. For example, you can use the Magnetic Lasso Tool to select complex shapes by clicking the starting point, tracing an approximate outline, then clicking the ending point. Later, you can use the Crop Tool to trim areas from a selection. When you use the Move Tool to drag a selection to the destination document, Photoshop places the selection in a new layer above the previously active layer.

Defringing Layer Contents

Sometimes when you make a selection, then move it into another document, the newly selected image can contain unwanted pixels that give the appearance of a fringe, or halo. You can remove this effect using a Matting command called Defringe. This command is available in the Layers menu and allows you to replace fringe pixels with the colors of other nearby pixels. You can determine a width for replacement pixels between 1 and 200. It's magic!

FIGURE B-11
Marquee selections

Area selected using the Rectangular Marquee Tool

Specific element selected using the Magnetic Lasso Tool

TABLE B-1: Selection Tools

tool	tool name	tool	tool name
	Rectangular Marquee Tool		Lasso Tool
	Elliptical Marquee Tool		Polygonal Lasso Tool
	Single Row Marquee Tool		Magnetic Lasso Tool
	Single Column Marquee Tool		Eraser Tool
	Crop Tool		Background Eraser Tool
	Magic Wand Tool		Magic Eraser Tool

Make a color range selection

1. Open Gourds.psd, click the title bar, then drag it to an empty portion of the workspace so that you can see both documents.

2. Click Select on the menu bar, then click Color Range.

   TIP If the background color is solid, you can select the Invert check box to pick only the pixels in the image area.

3. Click the Image option button, then type **0** in the Fuzziness text box (or drag the slider all the way to the left until you see 0).

   TIP When more than one document is open, each has its own set of rulers.

4. Position the pointer in the white background of the image in the Color Range dialog box, and click the background. 🖋

5. Select the Invert check box. Compare your dialog box to Figure B-12.

6. Click OK, then compare your Gourds.psd document to Figure B-13.

You opened a document and used the Color Range dialog box to select the image pixels by selecting the image's inverted colors.

FIGURE B-12
Color Range dialog box

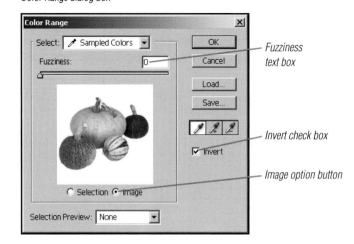

Fuzziness text box

Invert check box

Image option button

FIGURE B-13
Marquee surrounding selection

Marquee surrounds everything that is the inverse of the white background

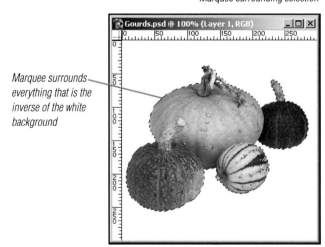

Working with Layers

FIGURE B-14
Gourds image dragged to New England Fall document

White fringe
surrounds image

FIGURE B-15
Gourds layer defringed

Gourds image
in document

Gourds moved to active
layer in document

Move a selection to another document

1. Click the Move Tool on the toolbox.
2. Position the pointer anywhere over the selection in the Gourds document.
3. Drag the selection to the New England Fall document, then release the mouse button.

   The gourds image moves to the New England Fall document appearing on Layer 1.
4. If necessary, drag the gourds to the precise location shown in Figure B-14.

You dragged a selection from one document to another.

Defringe the selection

1. Click Layer on the menu bar, point to Matting, then click Defringe.
2. Type **2** in the Width text box, then click OK.
3. Save your work.
4. Close Gourds.psd, then compare your open document to Figure B-15.

You removed the fringe from a selection.

ORGANIZE LAYERS WITH LAYER SETS AND COLORS

What You'll Do

In this lesson, you'll use the Layers palette menu to create, name, and color a layer set, and then add layers to it. You'll add finishing touches to the document, save it as a copy, then flatten it.

Understanding Layer Sets

A layer set is a Photoshop feature that allows you to organize your layers on the Layers palette. In the same way that a folder on your hard drive can contain individual computer files, a layer set contains individual layers. For example, you can create a layer set that contains all the type layers in your document. To create a layer set, you click the Layers palette list arrow, then click New Layer Set. As with layers, it is helpful to choose a descriptive name for a layer set.

Organizing Layer Sets

After you create a layer set, you simply drag layers on the Layers palette directly on top of the layer set. You can remove layers from a layer set by dragging them out of the layer set to a new location on the Layers palette or by deleting them. Some changes made to a layer set, such as blending mode or opacity changes, affect every layer in the layer set. You can choose to expand or collapse layer sets, depending on the amount of information you need to see. Expanding a layer set

Duplicating a layer

When you add a new layer by clicking the Create a new layer button on the Layers palette, the new layer contains default settings. However, you might want to create a new layer that has the same settings as an existing layer. You can do so by duplicating an existing layer to create a copy of that layer and its settings. Duplicating a layer is also a good way to preserve your modifications, because you can modify the duplicate layer and not worry about losing your original work. To create a duplicate layer, select the layer you want to copy, click the Layers palette list arrow, click Duplicate Layer, then click OK. The new layer will appear above the original.

shows all of the layers in the layer set, and collapsing a layer set hides all of the layers in a layer set. You can expand or collapse a layer set by clicking the triangle to the left of the layer set icon. Figure B-16 shows one expanded layer set and one collapsed layer set.

Adding Color to a Layer

If your document has relatively few layers, it's easy to locate the layers. However, if your document contains several layers, you might need some help in organizing them. You can organize layers by color-coding them, which makes it easy to find the group you want, regardless of its location on the Layers palette. For example, you can put all type layers in red or put the layers associated with a particular portion of an image in blue. To color a layer, click the Layers palette list arrow, click Layer Properties, click the Color list arrow, click a color, then click OK. To color the Background layer, you must first convert it to a regular layer.

QUICKTIP

You can also color-code a layer set without losing the color-coding you applied to individual layers.

Flattening an Image

After you make all the necessary modifications to your document, you can greatly reduce the file size by flattening the image. **Flattening** merges all visible layers into a single Background layer and discards all hidden layers. Make sure that all layers that you want to display are visible before you flatten the document. Because flattening removes a document's individual layers, it's a good idea to make a copy of the original document *before* it is flattened. The status bar displays the document's current size and the size it will be when flattened. If you work on a Macintosh, you'll find this information in the lower-left corner of the document window.

FIGURE B-16
Layer sets

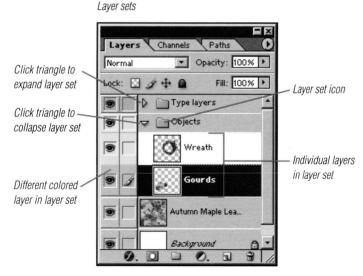

Click triangle to expand layer set

Click triangle to collapse layer set

Different colored layer in layer set

Layer set icon

Individual layers in layer set

Create a layer set

1. Verify that Layer 1 is active, click the Layers palette list arrow, then click New Layer Set.

   The New Layer Set dialog box opens, as shown in Figure B-17.

   > TIP Photoshop automatically places a new layer set above the active layer.

2. Type **All Type** in the Name text box.

3. Click the Color list arrow, click Red, then click OK.

   The New Layer Set dialog box closes. Compare your Layers palette to Figure B-18.

You used the Layers palette menu to create a layer set, then named and applied a color to it.

Move layers to the layer set

1. Click the Fall in New England type layer on the Layers palette, then drag it to the All Type layer set.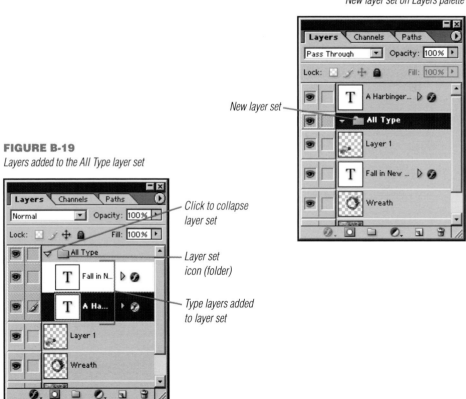

2. Click the A Harbinger of Change type layer, drag it to the All Type layer set, then compare your Layers palette to Figure B-19.

3. Click the triangle to the left of the layer set icon (folder) to collapse the layer set.

4. Click the Wreath layer.

5. Click Layer on the menu bar, point to Matting, then click Defringe.

6. Type 2 in the Width text box, then click OK.

You moved two layers into a layer set, then defringed a layer.

FIGURE B-17
New Layer Set dialog box

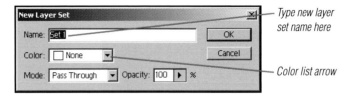

Type new layer set name here

Color list arrow

FIGURE B-18
New layer set on Layers palette

New layer set

FIGURE B-19
Layers added to the All Type layer set

Click to collapse layer set

Layer set icon (folder)

Type layers added to layer set

FIGURE B-20
Finished document

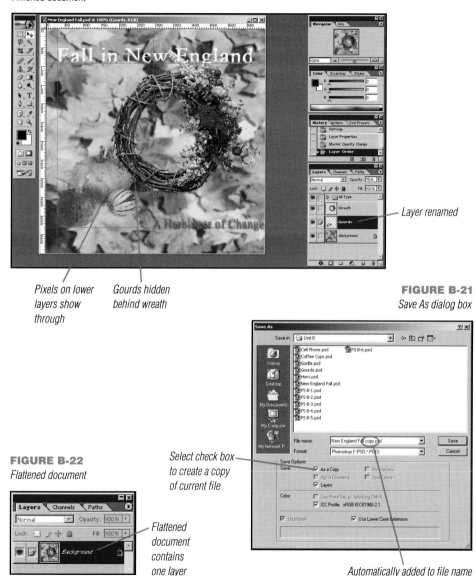

Layer renamed

Pixels on lower layers show through

Gourds hidden behind wreath

FIGURE B-21
Save As dialog box

FIGURE B-22
Flattened document

Select check box to create a copy of current file

Flattened document contains one layer

Automatically added to file name

Rename a layer and adjust opacity

1. Double-click Layer 1, type **Gourds**, then press [Enter] (Win) or [return} (Mac).

2. Double-click the Opacity text box on the Layers palette, type **75**, then press [Enter] (Win) or [return] (Mac).

3. Drag the Gourds layer on top of the Wreath layer, then compare your image to Figure B-20.

4. Save your work.

You renamed the new layer, adjusted opacity, and rearranged layers.

Flatten an image

1. Click File on the menu bar, then click Save As.

2. Select the As a Copy check box, then compare your dialog box to Figure B-21.

3. Click Save.

   Photoshop saves and closes a copy of the document containing all the layers and effects.

4. Click Layer on the menu bar, then click Flatten Image. Compare your Layers palette to Figure B-22.

5. Save your work.

You saved the document as a copy, and then flattened the document.

A credit union is developing a hotline for members to use to help abate credit card fraud as soon as it occurs. They're going to distribute 10,000 refrigerator magnets over the next three weeks. As part of their effort to build community awareness of the project, they've sponsored a contest for the magnet design. You decide to enter the contest.

1. Open PS B-3.psd, then save it as **Fraud Magnet**.
2. Open Cell Phone.psd, use the Color Range dialog box or any selection tool on the toolbox to select the image, then drag it to the Fraud Magnet document.
3. Rename the newly created layer **Cell Phone**, if necessary, then apply a color to the layer on the Layers palette.
4. Convert the Background layer to an image layer, then rename it **Banner**.
5. Change the opacity of the Banner layer to any setting you like.
6. Defringe the Cell Phone layer using the pixel width of your choice.
7. Save your work, then compare your document to Figure B-23.

FIGURE B-23
Completed Project 1

One of the gorillas in your local zoo is pregnant. The zoo hires you to create a promotional billboard commemorating this event for the upcoming season. The Board of Directors decides that the billboard should be humorous.

1. Open PS B-4.psd, then save it as **Zoo Billboard**.
2. Open Gorilla.psd, use the Color Range dialog box or any selection tool on the toolbox to create a marquee around the gorilla, then drag the selection to the Zoo Billboard document.
3. Name the new layer **Great Ape**.
4. Change the opacity of the Great Ape layer to 88%.
5. Save your work, then compare your document to Figure B-24.

FIGURE B-24
Completed Project 2

SECTION

MAKING C

SELECTIONS

1. Make a selection using shapes.

2. Modify a marquee.

3. Select using color and modify a selection.

4. Add a vignette effect to a selection.

SECTION C
MAKING SELECTIONS

Combining Images

Most Photoshop documents are created using a technique called **compositing**— combining images from different sources. These sources include other Photoshop documents, royalty-free images, pictures taken from digital cameras, and scanned artwork. How you get that extraneous imagery into your Photoshop documents is an art unto itself. You can include additional images by using tools on the toolbox and menu commands.

Understanding Selection Tools

You can use two basic methods to make selections: using a tool or using color. You can use three freeform tools to create your own unique selections, four fixed area tools to create circular or rectangular selections, and a wand tool to make selections using colors. In addition, you can use menu commands to increase or decrease selections that you made with these tools, or you can make selections based on color.

Understanding Which Selection Tool to Use

With so many tools available, how do you know which one to use? After you know the different selection options, you'll learn how to look at images and evaluate selection opportunities. With experience, you'll learn how to identify edges that can be used to isolate imagery, and how to spot colors that can be used to isolate a specific object.

Combining Imagery

After you decide on an object that you want to place in a Photoshop document, you can add the object by cutting, copying, and pasting, dragging and dropping objects using the Move Tool, and using the **Clipboard**, the temporary storage area provided by your operating system.

Tools You'll Use

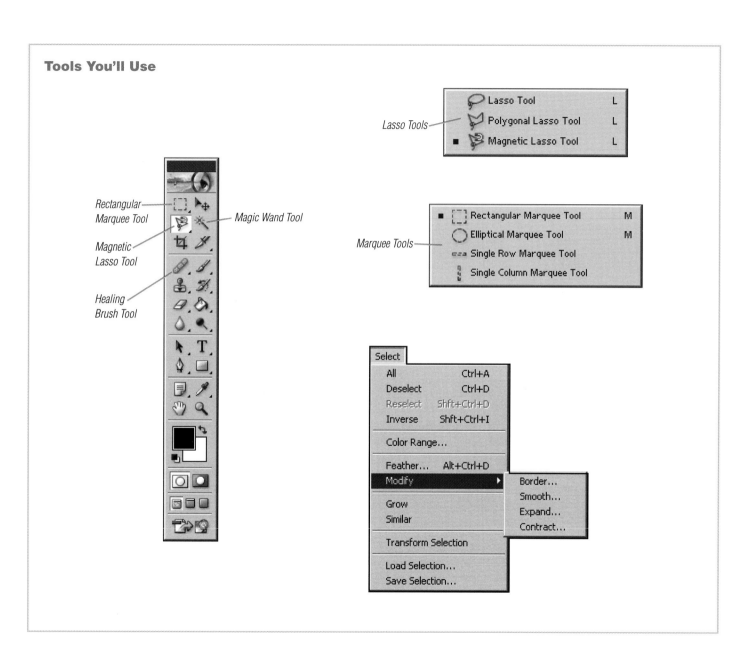

Lasso Tools
- Lasso Tool — L
- Polygonal Lasso Tool — L
- ■ Magnetic Lasso Tool — L

Rectangular Marquee Tool

Magic Wand Tool

Magnetic Lasso Tool

Healing Brush Tool

Marquee Tools
- ■ Rectangular Marquee Tool — M
- Elliptical Marquee Tool — M
- Single Row Marquee Tool
- Single Column Marquee Tool

Select
All	Ctrl+A
Deselect	Ctrl+D
Reselect	Shft+Ctrl+D
Inverse	Shft+Ctrl+I
Color Range...	
Feather...	Alt+Ctrl+D
Modify ▶	
Grow	
Similar	
Transform Selection	
Load Selection...	
Save Selection...	

Modify submenu:
- Border...
- Smooth...
- Expand...
- Contract...

MAKE A SELECTION USING SHAPES

What You'll Do

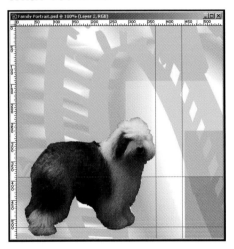

 In this lesson, you'll make selections using a marquee tool and a lasso tool, position a selection with the Move Tool, deselect a selection, and drag a complex selection into another document.

Selecting by Shape

The Photoshop selection tools make it easy to select objects that are rectangular or elliptical in nature. Wouldn't it be a lovely world if every image we wanted fell into one of those categories? Well, unfortunately, they don't. While some objects are round or square, most are unusual in shape. Making selections can sometimes be a painstaking process because many objects don't have clearly defined edges. To select an object by shape, you need to click the appropriate tool on the toolbox, then drag the pointer around the object. The selected area is defined by a **marquee**, or series of dotted lines, as shown in Figure C-1.

Creating a Selection

Drawing a rectangular marquee is easier than drawing an elliptical marquee, but with practice, you'll be able to create both marquees easily. Table C-1 lists the tools you can use to make selections using

shapes. Figure C-2 shows a marquee surrounding an irregular shape.

> **QUICKTIP**
>
> A marquee is sometimes referred to as *marching ants* because the dots within the marquee appear to be moving.

Using Fastening Points

Each time you click one of the marquee tools, a fastening point is added to the image. A **fastening point** is an anchor within the marquee. When the marquee pointer reaches the initial fastening point (after making its way around the image), a very small circle appears on the pointer, indicating that you have reached the starting point. Clicking the pointer when this circle appears closes the marquee. Some fastening points, such as those in a circular marquee, are not visible, while others, such as those created by the Polygonal or Magnetic Lasso Tools, are visible.

Selecting, Deselecting, and Reselecting

After a selection is made, you can move, copy, transform, or make adjustments to it. A selection stays selected until you unselect, or **deselect**, it. You can deselect a selection by clicking Select on the menu bar, then clicking Deselect. You can also reselect a deselected object by clicking Select on the menu bar, then clicking Reselect.

QUICKTIP

You can select an entire image by clicking Select on the menu bar, then clicking All.

FIGURE C-1
Elliptical Marquee Tool used to create marquee

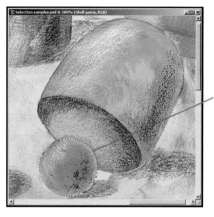

Elliptical marquee surrounding object

FIGURE C-2
Marquee surrounding irregular shape

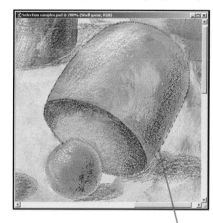

Marquee surrounding irregular shape

TABLE C-1: Selection Tools by Shape

tool	button	effect
Rectangular Marquee Tool		Creates a rectangular selection. Press [Shift] while dragging to create a square.
Elliptical Marquee Tool		Creates an elliptical selection. Press [Shift] while dragging to create a circle.
Single Row Marquee Tool		Creates a 1-pixel-wide row selection.
Single Column Marquee Tool		Creates a 1-pixel-wide column selection.
Lasso Tool		Creates a freehand selection.
Polygonal Lasso Tool		Creates straight line selections. Press [Alt] (Win) or [option] (Mac) to create freehand segments.
Magnetic Lasso Tool		Creates selections that snap to an edge of an object. Press [Alt] (Win) or [option] (Mac) to alternate between freehand and straight line segments.

Placing a Selection

You can place a selection into a Photoshop document in many ways. You can copy or cut a selection, then paste it to a different location in the same document or to a different document. You can also use the Move Tool to drag a selection to a new location.

Using Guides

Guides are non-printable horizontal and vertical lines that you can add to a document to help you position a selection. You can create an unlimited number of horizontal and vertical guides. You can create a guide by positioning the pointer on either ruler, then clicking and dragging the guide into position. You can delete a guide by selecting the Move Tool on the toolbox, positioning the pointer over the guide, then clicking and dragging it back to its ruler. If the Snap feature is enabled, as you drag an object toward a guide, the object will be pulled toward the guide. To turn on the Snap feature, click View on the menu bar, then click Snap. A check mark appears to the left of the command if the feature is enabled.

QUICKTIP

You can temporarily change *any selected tool* into the Move Tool by pressing and holding [Ctrl] (Win) or [command] (Mac). When you're finished dragging the selection, release [Ctrl] (Win) or [command] (Mac), and the functionality of the originally selected tool returns.

FIGURE C-3

Rectangular Marquee Tool selection

TABLE C-2: Working with a Selection

if you want to	then do this
Move a selection (within a document, or between documents) by positioning ➤✛ over the selection, then dragging the marquee and its contents	Move Tool ➤✛
Copy a selection to the Clipboard	Activate document containing the selection, click Edit ➤ Copy
Cut a selection to the Clipboard	Activate document containing the selection, click Edit ➤ Cut
Paste a selection from the Clipboard	Activate document where you want the selection, click Edit ➤ Paste
Delete a selection	Make selection, then press [Delete] (Win) or [delete] (Mac)

1. Start Photoshop, open PS C-1.psd, then save it as **Family Portrait**.

2. Click View on the menu bar, then click Rulers to select it, if necessary.

   TIP You can quickly change the unit of measurement by right-clicking a ruler and selecting the desired measurement.

3. Change the current unit of measurement to pixels, if necessary.

4. Open Sheepdog.tif, then display the rulers, if necessary.

5. Click the Rectangular Marquee Tool on the toolbox. 🔲

6. Make sure the value in the Feather text box on the tool options bar is 0 px.

   Feathering determines the amount of blur between the selection and the pixels surrounding it.

7. Drag the pointer from 90 H/20 V to 450 H/340 V. See Figure C-3. ✛

   The first measurement refers to the horizontal ruler (H); the second measurement refers to the vertical ruler (V).

8. Click the Move Tool, then drag the selection to the Family Portrait document.

   The selection now appears in the Family Portrait document on a new layer (Layer 1).

   TIP Table C-2 describes methods you can use to move selections in a document.

Using the Rectangular Marquee Tool, you created a selection in an image, then you dragged the object into another document.

Position a selection with the Move Tool

1. Verify that the Move Tool is selected on the toolbox.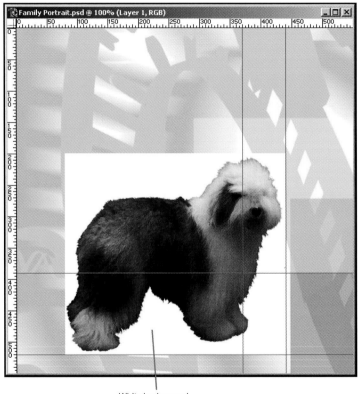

2. If you do not see guides, click View on the menu bar, point to Show, then click Guides.

3. Drag the object so that the bottom-right corner snaps to the ruler guides at 440 H/520 V. Compare your image to Figure C-4.

   Did you feel the snap to effect as you positioned the selection within the guides? This feature makes is easy to properly position objects within a document.

   You used the Move Toola to reposition the selection in an existing document.

FIGURE C-4

Rectangular selection in document

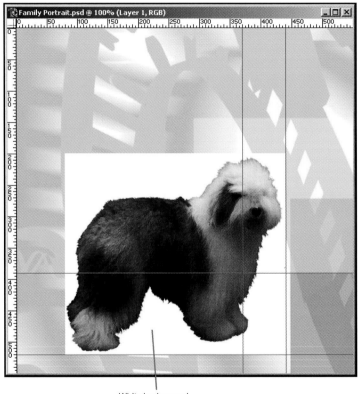

White background
included in selection

FIGURE C-5

Deselect command

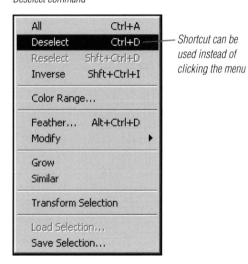

All	Ctrl+A
Deselect	Ctrl+D
Reselect	Shft+Ctrl+D
Inverse	Shft+Ctrl+I
Color Range...	
Feather...	Alt+Ctrl+D
Modify	▶
Grow	
Similar	
Transform Selection	
Load Selection...	
Save Selection...	

Shortcut can be used instead of clicking the menu

1. Click the Indicates layer visibility button on Layer 1 on the Layers palette. 👁️
   Layer 1 is now hidden.
2. Click Window on the menu bar, point to Documents, then click Sheepdog.tif.
3. Click Select on the menu bar, then click Deselect, as shown in Figure C-5.

You hid the active layer, then eliminated the marquee from the source document using the Deselect command on the Select menu.

Create a selection with the Magnetic Lasso Tool

1. Click the Magnetic Lasso Tool on the toolbox.

2. Change the settings on the tool options bar so that they are the same as those shown in Figure C-6. Table C-3 describes Magnetic Lasso Tool settings.

3. Click the Magnetic Lasso Tool pointer once anywhere on the edge of the dog, to create your first fastening point.

4. Drag the pointer slowly around the dog until the dog is almost entirely selected, as shown in Figure C-7, then click directly over the initial fastening point.

   Don't worry about all the nooks and crannies surrounding the dog: the Magnetic Lasso Tool will take care of them for you. You will see a small circle next to the pointer when it is directly over the initial fastening point, indicating that you are closing the selection. The individual segments turn into a marquee. In Figure C-7, the selection was started at approximately 320 H/85 V.

   > TIP You can insert additional fastening points by clicking the pointer while dragging. For example, click the mouse button at a location where you want to change the selection shape.

You created a selection with the Magnetic Lasso Tool.

FIGURE C-6
Options for the Magnetic Lasso Tool

FIGURE C-7
Creating a selection with the Magnetic Lasso Tool

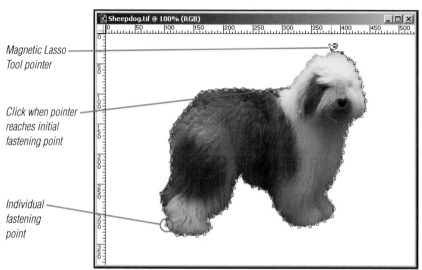

Magnetic Lasso Tool pointer

Click when pointer reaches initial fastening point

Individual fastening point

Mastering the art of selections

You might feel like a total goof when you first start making selections. Making selections is a skill, and like most skills, it takes a lot of practice to become proficient. In addition to practice, make sure that you're comfortable in your work area, that your hands are steady, and that your mouse is working well. A non-optical mouse that is dirty will make selecting an onerous task, so make sure your mouse is well cared for and is functioning correctly.

FIGURE C-8

Selection moved into document

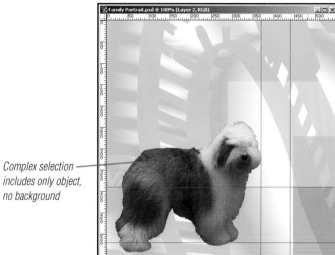

Complex selection includes only object, no background

TABLE C-3: Magnetic Lasso Tool settings

setting	description
Feather	Determines the amount of blur between the selection and the pixels surrounding it. This setting is measured in pixels and can be a value between 0 and 250.
Anti-aliased	Determines the smoothness of the selection by softening the color transition between edge and background pixels.
Width	Determines the width within by detecting an edge from the pointer. This setting is measured in pixels and can have a value from 1 to 40.
Edge Contrast	Determines the tool's sensitivity. This setting can be a value between 1% and 100%: high values detect high-contrast edges.
Frequency	Determines the rate at which fastening points are applied. This setting can be a value between 0 and 100: high values insert more fastening points.

Move a complex selection to an existing document

1. Click the Move Tool on the toolbox.

   TIP   You can also click the Click to open the Tool Preset picker list arrow on the tool options bar, then double-click the Move Tool.

2. Drag the selection to the Family Portrait document.

   The selection appears on a new layer (Layer 2).

3. Drag the object so that the right edge of the dog's cheek snaps to the guide at 370 H and the bottom of the dog's front paw snaps to the guide at 520 V.

4. Drag Layer 1 to the Delete layer button on the Layers palette.

5. Save your work, then compare your image to Figure C-8.

6. Click Window on the menu bar, point to Documents, then click Sheepdog.tif.

7. Close the Sheepdog.tif document without saving your changes.

You dragged a complex selection into an existing Photoshop document. You positioned the object using ruler guides and deleted an unnecessary layer.

MODIFY A MARQUEE

What You'll Do

 In this lesson, you'll move and enlarge a marquee, drag a selection into a Photoshop document, then position a selection using ruler guides.

Changing the Size of a Marquee

Not all objects are easy to select. Sometimes, when you make a selection, you might need to change the size of the marquee.

The tool options bar contains selection buttons that help you add to and subtract from a marquee, or intersect with a selection. The marquee in Figure C-9 was modified into the one shown in Figure C-10 by clicking the Add to selection button. After the Add to selection button is active, you can draw an additional marquee (directly adjacent to the selection), and it will be added to the current marquee.

One method you can use to increase the size of a marquee is the Grow command. After you make a selection, you can increase the marquee size by clicking Select on the menu bar, then by clicking Grow. The Grow command selects pixels adjacent to the marquee.

QUICKTIP

Sometimes all that is needed to enlarge a marquee is to create a small selection then use the Grow command on the Select menu.

Modifying a Marquee

While a selection is active, you can modify the marquee by expanding or contracting it, smoothing out its edges, or enlarging it to add a border around the selection. These four commands: Border, Smooth, Expand, and Contract are submenus of the Modify command, which is found on the Select menu. For example, you might want to enlarge your selection. Using the Expand command, you can increase the size of the selection, as shown in Figure C-11.

Moving a Marquee

After you create a marquee, you can move the marquee to another location in the same document or to another document entirely. To do this, position the pointer in the center of the selection, then drag the marquee to the new location.

QUICKTIP

You can always hide and display layers as necessary to facilitate making a selection.

FIGURE C-9
New selection

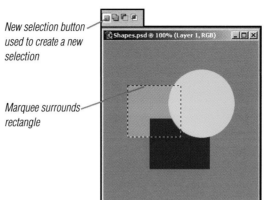

New selection button used to create a new selection

Marquee surrounds rectangle

FIGURE C-10
Selection with additions

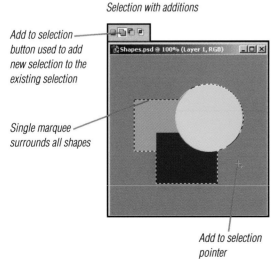

Add to selection button used to add new selection to the existing selection

Single marquee surrounds all shapes

Add to selection pointer

FIGURE C-11
Expanded marquee

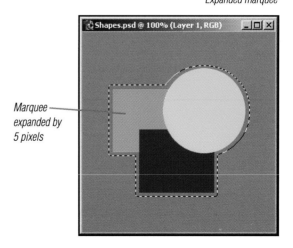

Marquee expanded by 5 pixels

Move a marquee

1. Open Butterfly.tif.

2. Click the Elliptical Marquee Tool on the toolbox.

3. Click the New selection button on the tool options bar, if necessary.

4. Drag the pointer from 50 H/50 V to 80 H/70 V. Compare your document to Figure C-12. ✛

5. Position the pointer in the center of the selection.

6. Drag the pointer to 140 H/70 V, as shown in Figure C-13. ▶

   TIP You can also nudge a selection using the arrow keys. Each time you press an arrow key, the selection moves one pixel in the direction of the key.

You created a marquee, then dragged the marquee to reposition it.

FIGURE C-12
Marquee in document

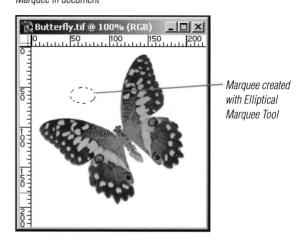

Marquee created
with Elliptical
Marquee Tool

FIGURE C-13
Moved marquee

New marquee
location

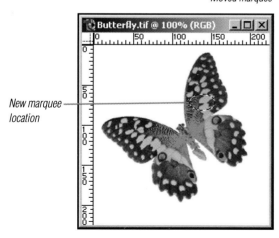

FIGURE C-14
Expand Selection dialog box

FIGURE C-15
Expanded marquee

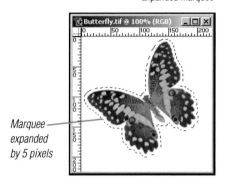

Marquee expanded by 5 pixels

FIGURE C-16
Expanded selection moved to the Family Portrait document

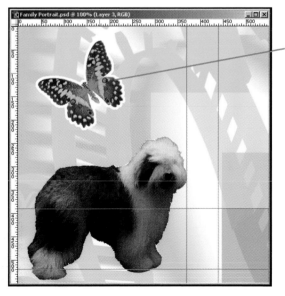

Border formed by expanding the marquee

Enlarge a marquee

1. Click Select on the menu bar, then click Grow.

2. Click Select on the menu bar, then click Similar.

3. Click Select on the menu bar, point to Modify, then click Expand.

4. Type **5** in the Expand By text box of the Expand Selection dialog box, as shown in Figure C-14.

5. Click OK, then compare your selection to Figure C-15.

6. Click the Move Tool on the toolbox.

7. Position the pointer over the selection, then drag the selection to the Family Portrait document.

8. Drag the butterfly so that the top-left wing is at 30 H/100 V.

9. Save your work, then compare your image to Figure C-16.

10. Make Butterfly.tif active.

11. Close Butterfly.tif without saving your changes.

You enlarged a selection marquee by using the Grow, Similar, and Expand commands, then you dragged the selection into an open document.

SELECT USING COLOR AND MODIFY A SELECTION

What You'll Do

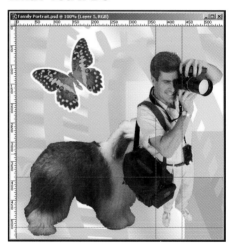

In this lesson, you'll make selections using both the Color Range command and the Magic Wand Tool. You'll also flip a selection, then fix an image using the Healing Brush Tool.

Selecting with Color

Selections based on color can be easy to make, especially when the background of an image is different from the image itself. High contrast between colors is an ideal condition for making selections based on color. You can make selections using color with the Color Range command on the Select menu, or you can use the Magic Wand Tool on the toolbox.

Using the Magic Wand Tool

When you select the Magic Wand Tool, the following options are available on the tool options bar:

- The four selection buttons.
- The Tolerance setting, which allows you to specify whether similar pixels will be selected. This setting has a value from 0 to 255, and the lower the value, the closer in color the selected pixels will be.
- The Anti-aliased check box, which softens the selection's appearance.
- The Contiguous check box, which lets you select pixels that are next to one another.
- The Use All Layers check box, which lets you select pixels from all layers.

Knowing which selection tool to use

The hardest part of making a selection might be determining which selection tool to use. How are you supposed to know if you should use a marquee tool or a lasso tool? The first question you need to ask yourself is, "What do I want to select?" Becoming proficient in making selections means that you need to assess the qualities of the object you want to select, and then decide which method to use. Ask yourself: Does the object have a definable shape? Does it have an identifiable edge? Are there common colors that can be used to create a selection?

See Figure C-17 to view the tool options bar when the Magic Wand Tool is selected.

Using the Color Range Command

You can use the Color Range command to make the same selections as with the Magic Wand Tool. When you use the Color Range command, the Color Range dialog box opens. This dialog box lets you use the pointer to identify which colors you want to use to make a selection. You can also select the Invert check box to *exclude* the chosen color from the selection. The **fuzziness** setting is similar to tolerance, in that the lower the value, the closer in color pixels must be to be selected.

QUICKTIP

The Color Range command does not give you the option of excluding contiguous pixels as does the Magic Wand Tool.

Transforming a Selection

After you place a selection in a Photoshop document, you can change its size and other qualities by clicking Edit on the menu bar, pointing to Transform, then clicking any of the commands on the submenu. After you select certain commands, small squares called **handles** surround the selection. To complete the command, you drag a handle until the image has the look you want, then press [Enter] (Win) or [return] (Mac). You can also use the Transfer submenu to flip a selection horizontally or vertically.

Using the Healing Brush Tool

If you place a selection then notice that the image has a few imperfections, you can fix the image. You can fix many imperfections (such as dirt, scratches, bulging veins on skin, or wrinkles on a face) using the Healing Brush Tool on the toolbox. This tool lets you sample an area that you want to duplicate, then paint over the imperfections. What is the result? The less-than-desirable pixels seem to disappear into the surrounding image. In addition to matching the sampled pixels, the Healing Brush Tool also matches the texture, lighting, and shading of the sample. This is why the painted pixels blend so effortlessly into the existing image.

QUICKTIP

A sample is taken by pressing and holding [Alt] (Win) or [option] (Mac) while dragging the pointer over the area you want to duplicate.

FIGURE C-17
Options for the Magic Wand Tool

Select using color range

1. Open Photographer.tif.
2. Click Select on the menu bar, then click Color Range.
3. Click the Image option button, if necessary.
4. Select the Invert check box.
5. Click anywhere in the white area surrounding the sample image.
6. Verify that your settings match those shown in Figure C-18, then click OK.

   The Color Range dialog box closes and the man in the image is selected.
7. Click the Move Tool on the toolbox.
8. Drag the selection into Family Portrait.psd, then position the selection as shown in Figure C-19.

You made a selection within an image using the Color Range command on the Select menu, and dragged the selection to an existing document.

FIGURE C-18
Completed Color Range dialog box

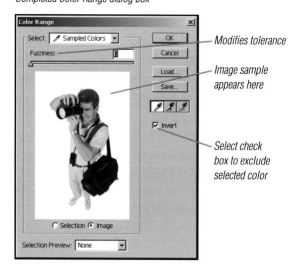

— *Modifies tolerance*

— *Image sample appears here*

— *Select check box to exclude selected color*

FIGURE C-19
Selection in document

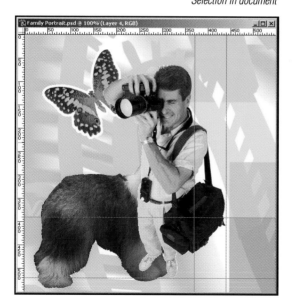

FIGURE C-20
Magic Wand Tool settings

FIGURE C-21
Selected area

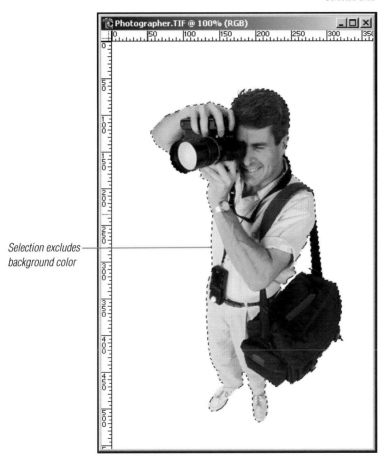

Selection excludes
background color

Select using the Magic Wand Tool

1. Click the Indicates layer visibility button on Layer 4 of the Layers palette to hide it.

2. Make Photographer.tif active.

3. Click Select on the menu bar, then click Deselect.

4. Click the Magic Wand Tool on the toolbox.

5. Change the settings on the tool options bar to match those in Figure C-20.

6. Click anywhere in the white area of the image (such as 50 H/50 V).

7. Click Select on the menu bar, then click Inverse. Compare your selection to Figure C-21.

8. Click the Move Tool on the toolbox, then drag the selection into Family Portrait.psd.

You made a selection using the Magic Wand Tool, then dragged it into an existing document.

Lesson 3 Select Using Color and Modify a Selection

Flip a selection

1. Click Edit on the menu bar, point to Transform, then click Flip Horizontal.

2. Drag Layer 4 to the Delete layer button on the Layers palette, because it is no longer necessary.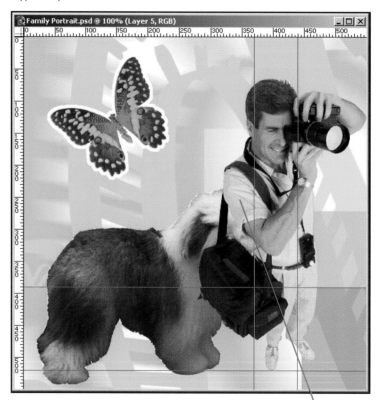

3. Click Layer on the menu bar, point to Matting, then click Defringe.

4. Type **2** in the Width text box.

5. Click OK.

6. Drag the flipped selection so it is positioned as shown in Figure C-22.

7. Make Photographer.tif the active document, then close Photographer.tif without saving your changes.

You flipped and repositioned a selection.

FIGURE C-22
Flipped and positioned selection

Flipped selection defringed

FIGURE C-23
Healing Brush Tool options

FIGURE C-24
Healed area

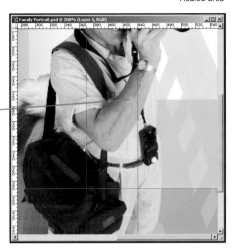

Veins removed
from image

FIGURE C-25
Image with fixed imperfections

1. Click the Zoom Tool on the toolbox.
2. Click the image at 400 H/300 V.
3. Click the Healing Brush Tool on the toolbox. Change the setting on your tool options bar to match those shown in Figure C-23.

   > TIP   If you need to change the Brush settings, you can click the Click to open the Brush picker list arrow, then drag the sliders so the settings are 10 px diameter, 100% hardness, 25% spacing, 0° angle, 100% roundness, and pen pressure size.

4. Press and hold [Alt] (Win) or [option] (Mac), click the image at 400 H/300 V, then release [Alt] (Win) or [option] (Mac).

   You sampled an area so that you can use the Healing Brush Tool to paint a damaged area with the sample.

5. Click and drag the pointer over the photographer's vein (from approximately 435 H/250 V to 430 H/270 V).

6. Click and drag the pointer over the vein (from approximately 430 H/270 V to 410 H/285 V). Compare the repaired area to Figure C-24.

7. Click the Zoom Tool on the toolbox.

8. Press and hold [Alt] (Win) or [alt] (Mac), click the center of the image, then release [Alt] (Win) or [alt] (Mac).

9. Save your work, then compare your image to Figure C-25.

You used the Healing Brush Tool to fix imperfections in an image.

ADD A VIGNETTE EFFECT TO A SELECTION

What You'll Do

In this lesson, you'll create a vignette effect, using a layer mask and feathering.

Understanding Vignettes

Traditionally, a **vignette** is a picture or portrait whose border fades into the surrounding color at its edges. You can use a vignette effect to give an image an old-world appearance. You can also use a vignette effect to tone down an overwhelming background. You can create a vignette effect in Photoshop by creating a mask with a blurred edge. A **mask** lets you protect or modify a particular area and is created using a marquee.

Creating a Vignette

A **vignette effect** uses feathering to fade a marquee shape. The **feather** setting blurs the area between the selection and the surrounding pixels, which creates a distinctive fade at the edge of the selection. You can create a vignette effect by using a marquee or lasso tool to create a marquee in an image layer. After the selection is created, you can modify the feather setting (a 10- or 20-pixel setting creates a nice fade) to increase the blur effect on the outside edge of the selection. Click Layer on the menu bar, point to Add Layer Mask, then click Reveal Selection; the mask forms a frame resulting in a vignette.

FIGURE C-26
Marquee in document

FIGURE C-28
Vignette effect in document

Vignette effect
fades border

FIGURE C-27
Layers palette

Feathered mask creates
vignette effect

1. Click the Backdrop layer on the Layers palette.
2. Click the Elliptical Marquee Tool on the toolbox.
3. Change the Feather setting on the tool options bar to 20.
4. Create a selection from 0 H/0 V to 550 H/550 V, as shown in Figure C-26.
5. Click Layer on the menu bar, point to Add Layer Mask, then click Reveal Selection.

   The vignette effect is added to the layer.
6. Click Layer 5 on the Layers palette, then drag it beneath Layer 2 to move the dog in front of the photographer. Compare your Layers palette to Figure C-27.
7. Click Layer 2, click Layer on the menu bar, point to Matting, then click Defringe.
8. Type **2** in the Width text box, then click OK.
9. Click View on the menu bar, then click Rulers to hide them.
10. Save your work, then compare your document to Figure C-28.

You created a vignette effect by adding a feathered layer mask. You also rearranged layers and defringed a selection.

Lesson 4   Add a Vignette Effect to a Selection

The FBI has hired you to create a new image for its personal investigation division. You have created the background artwork, but need to find other images to complete the assignment. Your employers want to stay with the theme of surveillance, and request that you use legal sources of artwork.

1. Open PS C-3.psd, then save it as **FBI**. (*Hint*: Click Update to close the warning box regarding missing fonts, if necessary.)
2. Open Plug.tif, then use the Magnetic Lasso Tool to select the plug and the wire.
3. Position the selection within FBI. (*Hint*: You can scale a selection, using the Transform command on the Edit menu, if you want it to be larger or smaller.)
4. Close Plug.tif without saving any changes.
5. Open Satellite.tif, then use the Color Range dialog box or the Magnetic Lasso Tool to isolate the antennae and satellites within the image. (*Hint*: You might have to use a combination of several methods to isolate the image.)
6. Position the selection within FBI.
7. Close Satellite.tif without saving any changes.
8. Open Headphones.tif, then use any selection method to select the Headphones.
9. Position the selection within FBI.
10. Close Headphones.tif without saving any changes.
11. Display the Type layer, then move the type to the top of the document.

FIGURE C-29
Completed Project 1

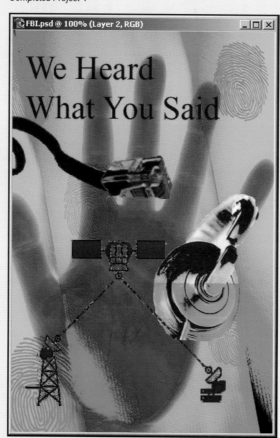

12. Defringe any layers, as necessary.
13. Save your work, then compare your document to the sample in Figure C-29.

The Boston Athletic Association, which sponsors the Boston Marathon, is holding a contest for artwork to announce the upcoming marathon. Submissions can be created on paper or computer-generated. You feel you have a good chance at winning this contest, using Photoshop as your tool.

1. Open PS C-4.psd, then save it as **Marathon Contest**.
2. Locate at least two pieces of appropriate artwork—either on your hard disk, in a royalty-free collection, or from scanned images—that you can use in this document.
3. Use any appropriate methods to select imagery from the artwork.
4. After the selections have been made, copy each selection into Marathon Contest.
5. Arrange the imagery in a professional design that is sure to win the contest.
6. Deselect the selections in the files you are no longer using, and close them without saving the changes.
7. Add a vignette effect to the Backdrop layer.
8. Display the type layers.
9. Defringe any layers, as necessary.
10. Save your work, then compare your document to the sample in Figure C-30.

FIGURE C-30
Completed Project 2

INCORPORATING COLOR TECHNIQUES

1. Work with color to transform a document.

2. Use the Color Picker and the Swatches palette.

3. Place a border around an image.

4. Blend colors using the Gradient Tool.

5. Add color to a grayscale image.

6. Use filters, opacity, and blending modes.

SECTION D
INCORPORATING COLOR TECHNIQUES

Using Color

Color can make or break an image. Sometimes colors can draw us into an image; other times they can repel us. We all know what colors we like, but when it comes to creating an image, it is helpful to have some knowledge of color theory and be familiar with color terminology.

Understanding how Photoshop measures, displays, and prints color can be valuable when you create new images or modify existing images. Some colors you choose might be difficult for a professional printer to reproduce or might look muddy when printed. As you become more experienced using colors, you will learn which colors can be reproduced well and which ones cannot.

Understanding Color Modes and Color Models

Photoshop displays and prints images using specific color modes. A **mode** is the amount of color data that can be stored in a given file format, based on an established model. A **model** determines how pigments combine to produce resulting colors. This is the way your computer or printer associates a name or numbers with colors. Photoshop uses standard color models as the basis for its color modes.

Displaying and Printing Images

An image shown on your monitor, such as an icon on your desktop, is a **bitmap**, a geometric arrangement of different color dots on a rectangular grid. Each dot, called a **pixel**, represents a color or shade. Bitmapped images are *resolution-dependent* and can lose detail—often demonstrated by a jagged appearance—when highly magnified. When printed, images with high resolutions tend to show more detail and subtler color transitions than low-resolution images.

Tools You'll Use

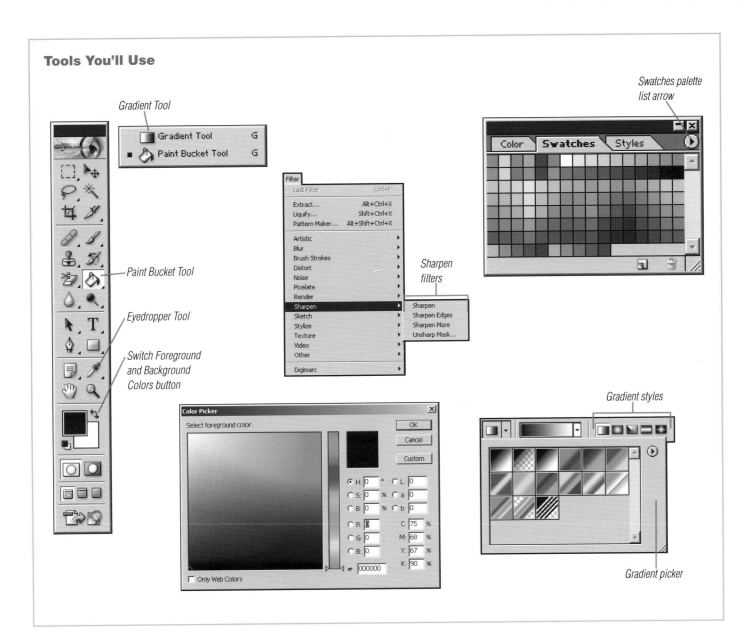

Gradient Tool

Paint Bucket Tool

Eyedropper Tool

Switch Foreground and Background Colors button

Sharpen filters

Swatches palette list arrow

Gradient styles

Gradient picker

WORK WITH COLOR TO TRANSFORM A DOCUMENT

What You'll Do

 In this lesson, you'll use the Color palette, the Paint Bucket Tool, and the Eyedropper Tool to add a new color to the background.

Learning About Color Models

Photoshop reproduces colors using models of color modes. The range of displayed colors, or **gamut**, for each model, is shown in Figure D-1. The shape of each color gamut indicates the range of colors it can display. If a color is out of gamut, it is beyond the color space that your monitor can display or that your printer can print. You select the color mode from the Mode command on the Image menu.

QUICKTIP

A color mode is used to determine which color model will be used to display and print an image.

Understanding the psychology of color

Have you ever wondered why some colors make you react a certain way? You might have noticed that some colors affect you differently than others. Color is such an important part of our lives, and in Photoshop, it's key. Specific colors are used in print and Web pages to evoke the following responses:

- Blue tends to instill a feeling of safety and stability and is commonly used by financial services.
- Certain shades of green can generate a soft, calming feeling, while others suggest youthfulness and growth.
- Red commands attention and can be used as a call to action; it can also distract a reader's attention from other content.
- White evokes the feeling of purity and innocence, looks cool and fresh, and is often used to suggest luxury.
- Black conveys feelings of power and strength, but can suggest darkness and negativity.

L*a*b Model

The L*a*b model is based on one luminance (lightness) component and two chromatic components (from green to red, and from blue to yellow). Using the L*a*b model has distinct advantages: you have the largest number of colors available to you and the greatest precision with which to create them. You can also create all the colors contained by other color models, which are limited in their respective color ranges. The L*a*b model is device-independent—the colors will not vary, regardless of the hardware. Use this model when working with photo CD images so that you can independently edit the luminance and color values.

HSB Model

Based on the human perception of color, the HSB (Hue, Saturation, Brightness) model has three fundamental characteristics: hue, saturation, and brightness. The color reflected from or transmitted through an object is called **hue**. Expressed as a degree (between 0° and 360°), each hue is identified by a color name (such as red or green). **Saturation** (or *chroma*) is the strength or purity of the color, representing the amount of gray in proportion to hue. Saturation is measured as a percentage from 0% (gray) to 100% (fully saturated). **Brightness** is the measurement of relative lightness or darkness of a color and is measured as a percentage from 0% (black) to 100% (white). Although you can use the HSB model to define a color on the Color palette or in the Color Picker dialog box, Photoshop does not offer HSB mode as a choice for creating or editing images.

RGB Mode

Photoshop uses color modes to determine how to display and print an image. Each mode is based on established models used in color reproduction. Most colors in the visible spectrum can be represented by mixing various proportions and intensities of red, green, and blue (RGB) colored light. RGB colors are additive colors. **Additive colors** are used for lighting, video, and computer monitors; color is created by light passing through red, green, and blue phosphors. When the values of red, green, and blue are zero, the result is black; when the values are all 255, the result is white. Photoshop assigns each component of the RGB mode an intensity value. Your colors can vary from monitor to monitor even if you are using the exact RGB values on different computers.

FIGURE D-1
Photoshop color gamuts

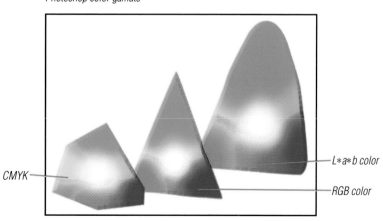

CMYK

L*a*b color

RGB color

QUICKTIP

Colors vary because color monitors use the RGB mode, which uses red, green, and blue phosphors to create a pixel. Variables such as the manufacturing technique used to apply phosphors to the glass, and the capabilities of your video adapter affect how your monitor displays color.

CMYK Mode

The light-absorbing quality of ink printed on paper is the basis of the CMYK (Cyan, Magenta, Yellow, Black) mode. Unlike the RGB mode—in which components are *combined* to create new colors—the CMYK mode is based on colors being partially *absorbed* as the ink hits the paper and being partially *reflected* back to your eyes. CMYK colors are **subtractive colors**—the *absence* of cyan, magenta, yellow, and black creates white. Subtractive (CMYK) and additive (RGB) colors are complementary colors; a pair from one model creates a color in the other. When combined, cyan, magenta, and yellow absorb all color and produce black. The CMYK mode—in which the lightest colors are assigned the highest percentages of ink colors—is used in four-color process printing. Converting an RGB image into a CMYK image produces a **color separation** (the commercial printing process

of separating colors for use with different inks). Note, however, that because your monitor uses RGB mode, you will not see the exact colors until you print the image, and even then the colors can vary depending on the printer and offset press.

Understanding the Bitmap and Grayscale Modes

In addition to the RGB and CMYK modes, Photoshop provides two specialized color modes: bitmap and grayscale. The **bitmap mode** uses black or white color values to represent image pixels, and is a good choice for images with subtle color gradations, such as photographs or painted images. The **grayscale mode** uses up to 256 shades of gray, assigning a brightness value from 0 (black) to 255 (white) to each pixel. Displayed colors can vary from monitor to monitor even if you use identical color settings on different computers.

Using Foreground and Background Colors

In Photoshop, the **foreground color** is black by default and is used to paint, fill, and apply a border to a selection. The **background color** is white by default and is used

to make **gradient fills** (gradual blends of multiple colors) and fill in areas of an image that have been erased. You can change the foreground and background colors using the Color palette, the Swatches palette, the Color Picker, or the Eyedropper Tool. You can restore the default colors by clicking the Default Foreground and Background Colors button on the toolbox, shown in Figure D-2. You can apply a color to the background of a layer using the Paint Bucket Tool. When you click an image with the Paint Bucket Tool, the current foreground color on the toolbox fills the background of the active layer.

FIGURE D-2
Foreground and background color buttons

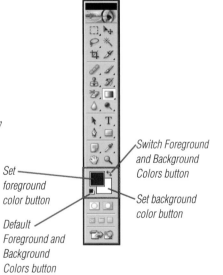

Switch Foreground and Background Colors button

Set foreground color button

Set background color button

Default Foreground and Background Colors button

FIGURE D-3

Document with rulers displayed

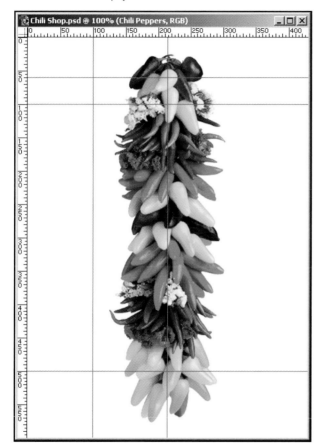

1. Start Photoshop, open PS D-1.psd, then save it as **Chili Shop**.

2. Click the Default Foreground and Background Colors button on the toolbox. ■₋

3. Display the rulers in pixels if necessary, then compare your screen to Figure D-3.

   TIP You can right-click (Win) or [control] click (Mac) one of the rulers to choose Pixels, Inches, Centimeters, Millimeters, Points, Picas, or Percent as a unit of measurement, instead of using the Rulers and Units Preferences dialog box.

You set the default foreground and background colors and displayed rulers in pixels.

Change the background color using the Color palette

1. Click the Background layer on the Layers palette.

2. Click the Color palette tab. Color

3. Drag each color slider on the Color palette to the right until you reach the values shown in Figure D-4.

   The active color changes to the new color. Did you notice that this document is using the RGB mode?

   TIP   You can also double-click each component's text box on the Color palette and type the color values.

4. Click the Paint Bucket Tool on the toolbox.

   TIP   If the Paint Bucket Tool is not visible on the toolbox, click the Gradient Tool on the toolbox, press and hold the mouse button until the list of hidden tools appears, then click the Paint Bucket Tool.

5. Click the image.

6. Drag the Paint Bucket state on the History palette onto the Delete current state button.

   TIP   You can also undo the last action by clicking Edit on the menu bar, then clicking Undo Paint Bucket.

You set new values in the Color palette, used the Paint Bucket Tool to change the background to that color, then undid the change.

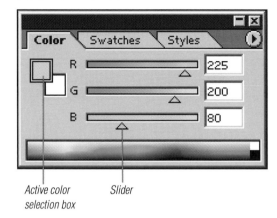

Active color   Slider
selection box

Using ruler coordinates

Photoshop rulers run along the top and left-hand sides of the document window. Each point on an image has a horizontal and vertical location. These two numbers, called x and y coordinates, appear in the Info palette (which is located behind the Navigator palette). The x coordinate refers to the horizontal location, and the y coordinate refers to the vertical location. You can use the guides to identify coordinates of a location, such as a color you want to sample. If you have difficulty seeing the ruler markings, you can increase the size of the image; the greater the zoom factor, the more detailed the measurement hashes.

FIGURE D-5

New foreground color applied to Background layer

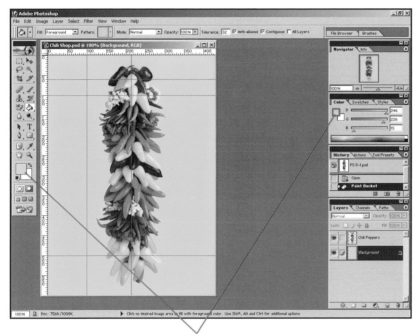

New foreground color

1. Click the Background layer on the Layers palette to make it active.

2. Click the Eyedropper Tool on the toolbox.

3. Click the image at 215 H/60 V, using the blue guides to help ensure accuracy.

   The Set foreground color button displays the color that you clicked (or sampled).

4. Click the Paint Bucket Tool on the toolbox.

5. Click the image, then compare your document to Figure D-5.

   TIP Your color values on the Color palette might vary from the sample.

6. Save your work.

You used the Eyedropper Tool to sample a color as the foreground color, then used the Paint Bucket Tool to change the background color to the color you sampled.

USE THE COLOR PICKER AND THE SWATCHES PALETTE

What You'll Do

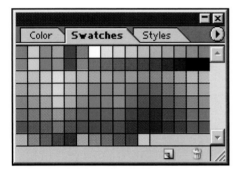

In this lesson, you'll use the Color Picker and the Swatches palette to select new colors, then you'll add a new color to the background and the swatches palette.

Making Selections from the Color Picker

Depending on the color model you are using, you can select colors using the **Color Picker**, a feature that lets you choose a color from a color spectrum or lets you numerically define a custom color. You can change colors in the Color Picker dialog box by using the following methods:

- Drag the sliders along the vertical color bar.
- Click inside the vertical color bar.

- Click inside the Color field.
- Enter a value in any of the text boxes.

A circular marker indicates the active color. The color slider displays the range of color levels available for the active color component. The adjustments you make by dragging or clicking on a new color are reflected in the text boxes; when you choose a new color, the previous color appears beneath it.

Using the Swatches Palette

You can also change colors using the Swatches palette. The **Swatches palette** is a visual display of colors you can choose from. You can add your own colors to the palette by sampling a color from an image, and you can also delete colors. When you add a swatch to the Swatches palette, Photoshop assigns a default name that has a sequential number, or you can name the swatch whatever you like. Photoshop places new swatches in the first available space at the end of the palette. You can view swatch names by clicking the Swatches palette list arrow, then clicking Small List. You can restore the default Swatches palette by clicking the Swatches palette list arrow, clicking Reset Swatches, then clicking OK. Figure D-6 shows a color in the Color Picker dialog box and on the Swatches palette.

FIGURE D-6

Color Picker dialog box and Swatches palette

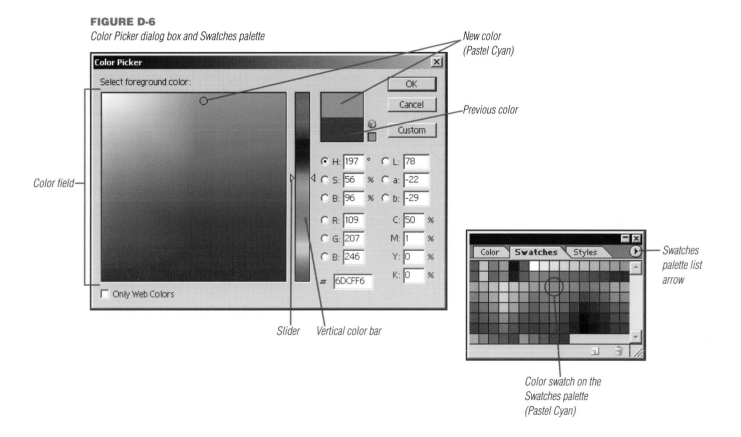

Select a color from the Color Picker

1. Click the Set foreground color button on the toolbox, then verify that the Hue (H) option button is selected in the Color Picker dialog box.

2. Click the R (Red) option button.

3. Click the bottom-right corner of the Color field (fuchsia), as shown in Figure D-7.

   TIP If the out-of-gamut indicator appears next to the color, then this color exceeds the printable range.

4. Click OK.

You opened the Color Picker dialog box, selected a different color palette, and then selected a new color.

Select a color from the Swatches palette

1. Click the Swatches palette tab.

   Swatches

2. Click the second swatch from the left in the first row, as shown in Figure D-8.

   Did you notice that the foreground color (on the toolbox) changed to a lighter, brighter yellow?

3. Click the Paint Bucket Tool on the toolbox.

4. Click the image, then compare your screen to Figure D-9.

You opened the Swatches palette, selected a color, and then used the Paint Bucket Tool to change the background to that color.

FIGURE D-7
Color Picker dialog box

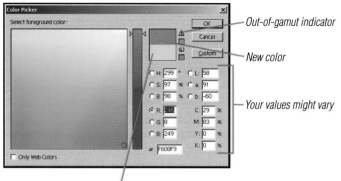

Out-of-gamut indicator

New color

Your values might vary

Previous color

FIGURE D-8
Swatches palette

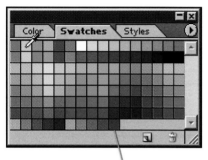

Your swatches on the last row might vary

FIGURE D-9
New foreground color applied to Background layer

FIGURE D-10

Swatch added to Swatches palette

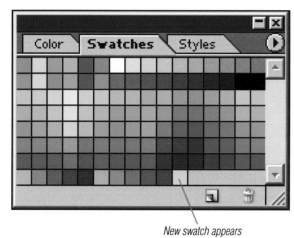

New swatch appears
in last row

1. Click the Eyedropper Tool on the toolbox.

2. Click one of the light yellow peppers.

3. Click an empty position in the last row of the Swatches palette.

4. Click OK to accept the default swatch name in the Color Swatch Name dialog box.

   TIP To delete a color from the Swatches palette, press [Alt] (Win) or [command] (Mac), position the pointer over a swatch, then click the swatch.

5. Save your work, then compare the new swatch in your Swatches palette to Figure D-10.

You used the Eyedropper Tool to sample a color, and then added the color to the Swatches palette.

PLACE A BORDER AROUND AN IMAGE

What You'll Do

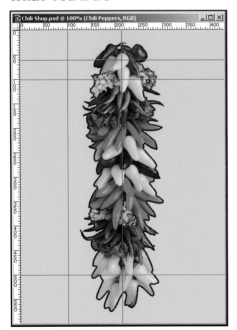

In this lesson, you'll add a border to an image.

Emphasizing an Image

You can emphasize an image by placing a border along its edges. This process is called **stroking the edges**. The default color of the border is the current foreground color on the toolbox. You can change the width, color, location, and blending mode of a border using the Stroke dialog box. The default stroke width is the setting last applied; you can apply a width from 1 to 16 pixels. The location option buttons determine where the border will be placed. If you want to change the location of the stroke, you must first delete the previously applied stroke, or Photoshop will apply the new border over the existing one.

Locking Transparent Pixels

As you modify layers, you can lock some properties to protect their contents. The ability to lock—or protect—elements within a layer is controlled from within the Layers palette, as shown in Figure D-11. It's a good idea to lock transparent pixels when you add borders so that stray marks

will not be included in the stroke. You can lock the following layer properties:
- Transparency: Limits editing capabilities to areas in a layer that are opaque.
- Image: Makes it impossible to modify layer pixels using painting tools.
- Position: Prevents pixels within a layer from being moved.

QUICKTIP

You can only lock transparency or image pixels in a layer containing an image, not type.

FIGURE D-11
Layers palette locking options

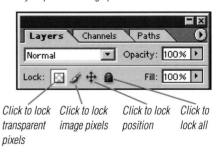

Click to lock transparent pixels   Click to lock image pixels   Click to lock position   Click to lock all

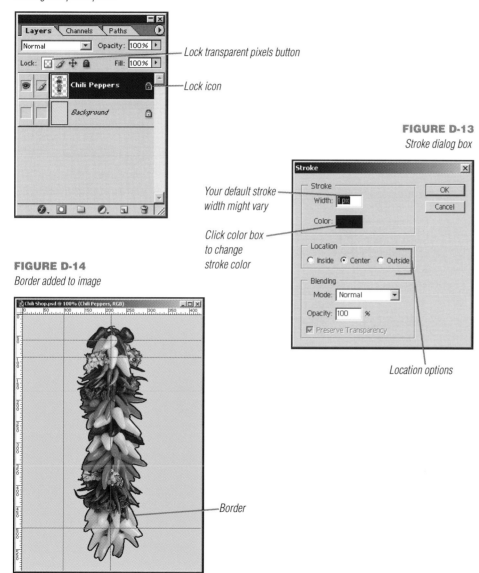

FIGURE D-12

Locking transparent pixels

Lock transparent pixels button

Lock icon

FIGURE D-13

Stroke dialog box

Your default stroke width might vary

Click color box to change stroke color

FIGURE D-14

Border added to image

Location options

Border

Create a border

1. Click the Indicates layer visibility button on the Background layer on the Layers palette.

   TIP You can click the Indicates layer visibility button to hide distracting layers.

2. Click the Default Foreground and Background Colors button on the toolbox to change the Foreground Color button to black.

   The foreground color will become the default border color.

3. Click the Chili Peppers layer on the Layers palette.

4. Click the Lock transparent pixels button on the Layers palette. See Figure D-12.

   The border will only be applied to the pixels on the edge of the chili peppers.

5. Click Edit on the menu bar, then click Stroke to open the Stroke dialog box. See Figure D-13.

6. Type **3** in the Width text box, click the Inside option button, then click OK.

   TIP Determining the correct border location can be confusing. Try different settings until you achieve the look you want.

7. Click the Indicates layer visibility button on the Background layer on the Layers palette.

8. Save your work, then compare your image to Figure D-14.

You hid a layer, changed the foreground color to black, locked transparent pixels, then used the Stroke dialog box to apply a border to the image.

BLEND COLORS USING THE GRADIENT TOOL

What You'll Do

In this lesson, you'll create a gradient fill from a sampled color and a swatch, then apply it to the background.

Understanding Gradients

A **gradient fill**, or simply **gradient**, is a blend of colors used to fill a selection of a layer or an entire layer. A gradient's appearance is determined by its beginning and ending points, and its length, direction, and angle. Gradients allow you to create dramatic effects, using existing color combinations or your own colors. The Gradient picker, as shown in Figure D-15, offers multicolor gradient fills and a few that use the current foreground or background colors on the toolbox.

FIGURE D-15
Gradient picker

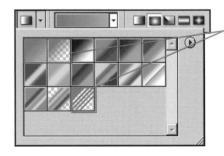

Gradient fills that use current foreground or background colors

Incorporating Color Techniques

Using the Gradient Tool

You use the Gradient Tool to create gradients in Photoshop. When you choose the Gradient Tool, five gradient styles become available on the tool options bar. The five gradient styles—Linear, Radial, Angle, Reflected, and Diamond—are shown in Figure D-16. In each example, the gradient was drawn from 50 H/50 V to 100 H/100 V.

Customizing Gradients

Using the **gradient presets**—predesigned gradient fills that are displayed in the Gradient picker—is a great way to learn how to use gradients. But as you become more familiar with Photoshop, you might want to venture into the world of the unknown and create your own gradient designs. You can create your own designs by modifying an existing gradient using the Gradient Editor. You can open the Gradient Editor, shown in Figure D-17, by clicking the selected gradient pattern that appears on the tool options bar. After it's open, you can use it to make the following modifications:

- Create a new gradient from an existing gradient.
- Modify an existing gradient.
- Add intermediate colors to a gradient.
- Create a blend between more than two colors.
- Adjust the opacity values.
- Determine the placement of the midpoint.

FIGURE D-16
Sample gradients

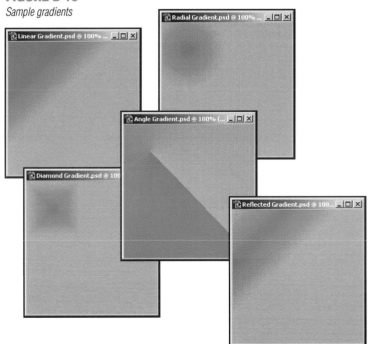

FIGURE D-17
Gradient Editor dialog box

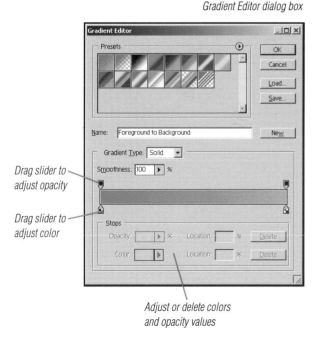

Drag slider to adjust opacity

Drag slider to adjust color

Adjust or delete colors and opacity values

Create a gradient from a sample color

1. Verify that the Eyedropper Tool is selected.

2. Click the image at 245 H/450 V.

   | TIP To accurately select the coordinates, adjust the zoom factor as necessary.

3. Click the Switch Foreground and Background Colors button on the toolbox.

4. Click Swatch 1 on the Swatches palette (the new swatch you previously added to the Swatches palette).

5. Click the Indicates layer visibility button on the Chili Peppers layer.

6. Click the Background layer on the Layers palette to make it active, as shown in Figure D-18.

7. Click the Paint Bucket Tool on the toolbox, then press and hold the mouse button until the list of hidden tools appears.

8. Click the Gradient Tool, then click the Linear Gradient button on the tool options bar, if necessary.

9. Click the Click to open Gradient picker list arrow on the tool options bar, then click Foreground to Background (the first gradient fill in the first row), as shown in Figure D-19.

You sampled a color on the image to set the background color, changed the foreground color using an existing swatch, selected the Gradient Tool, and then chose a gradient fill and style.

FIGURE D-18
Chili Peppers layer hidden

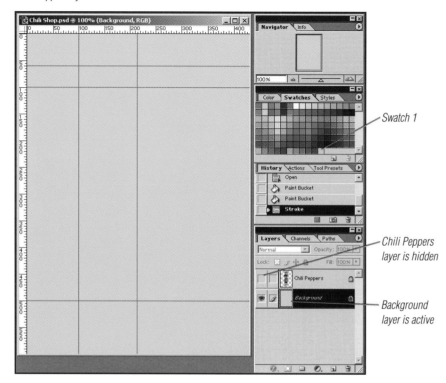

Swatch 1

Chili Peppers layer is hidden

Background layer is active

FIGURE D-19
Gradient picker

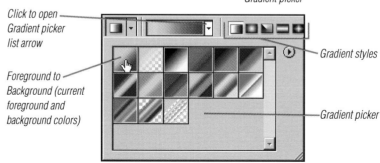

Click to open Gradient picker list arrow

Foreground to Background (current foreground and background colors)

Gradient styles

Gradient picker

FIGURE D-20
Gradient fill applied to Background layer

1. Click the Click to open Gradient picker list arrow to close the Gradient picker.

   TIP You can also close the Gradient picker by pressing [Esc](Win) or [esc](Mac).

2. Drag the pointer from 100 H/60 V to 215 H/500 V in the document window.

3. Click the Indicates layer visibility button on the Chili Peppers layer.

   The chili peppers layer appears against the new background, as shown in Figure D-20.

   TIP It is a good idea to save your work early and often in the creation process, especially before making significant changes or printing.

4. Save your work.

You applied the gradient fill to the background.

ADD COLOR TO A GRAYSCALE IMAGE

What You'll Do

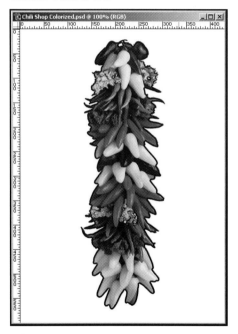

 In this lesson, you'll convert an image to grayscale, change the color mode, then colorize a grayscale image using the Hue/Saturation dialog box.

Colorizing Options

Grayscale images can contain up to 256 shades of gray, assigning a brightness value from 0 (black) to 255 (white) to each pixel. Since the earliest days of photography, people have been tinting grayscale images with color to create a certain mood or emphasize an image in a way that brightly colored photographs could not. To capture this effect in Photoshop, you convert an image to the Grayscale mode, then choose the color mode you want to work in before you continue. When you apply a color to a grayscale image, each pixel becomes a shade of that particular color instead of gray.

Converting Grayscale and Color Modes

When you convert a color image to grayscale, the light and dark values—called the **luminosity**—remain, while the color information is deleted. When you change from grayscale to a color mode, the foreground and background colors on the toolbox change from black and white to the previously selected colors.

Colorizing a Grayscale Image

In order for a grayscale image to be colorized, you must change the color mode to one that accommodates color. After you change the color mode, and then adjust settings in the Hue/Saturation dialog box, Photoshop will determine the colorization range based on the hue of the currently selected foreground color. If you want a different colorization range, you need to change the foreground color.

FIGURE D-21

Gradient Map dialog box

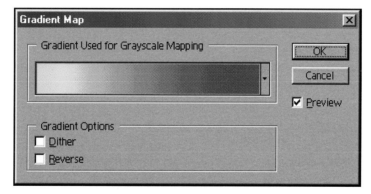

Applying a gradient effect

You can also use the Gradient Map to apply a colored gradient effect to a grayscale image. The Gradient Map uses gradient fills (the same ones displayed in the Gradient picker) to colorize the image, which can produce some stunning effects. You use the Gradient Map dialog box, shown in Figure D-21, to apply a gradient effect to a grayscale image. You can access the Gradient Map dialog box using the Adjustments command on the Image menu.

Change the color mode

1. Open PS D-2.psd, then save it as **Chili Shop Colorized**.

2. Click Image on the menu bar, point to Mode, then click Grayscale.

3. Click Flatten to close the warning box.

   The color mode of the document is changed to grayscale, and the image is flattened so there is only a single layer. All the color information in the image has been discarded.

4. Click Image on the menu bar, point to Mode, then click RGB Color.

   The color mode is changed back to RGB color, although there is still no color in the image.

5. Click Image on the menu bar, point to Adjustments, then click Hue/Saturation to open the Hue/Saturation dialog box, as shown in Figure D-22.

6. Select the Colorize check box in the Hue/Saturation dialog box.

You converted the image to Grayscale, then you changed the color mode to RGB color.

FIGURE D-22
Hue/Saturation dialog box

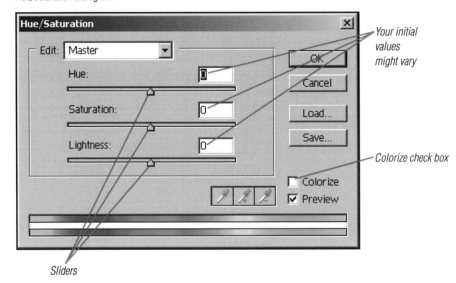

Your initial values might vary

Colorize check box

Sliders

FIGURE D-23

Colorized image

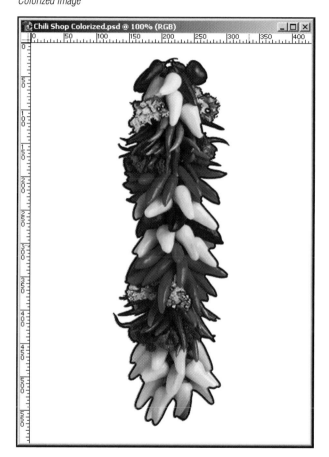

Colorize a grayscale image

1. Drag the Hue slider until the text box displays 240.

   TIP You can also type values in the text boxes in the Hue/Saturation dialog box. Negative numbers must be preceded by a minus symbol or a hyphen. Positive numbers can be preceded by a plus sign (+), but it is optional.

2. Drag the Saturation slider until the text box displays 45.

3. Drag the Lightness slider until the text box displays +10.

4. Click OK.

5. Save your work, then compare your document to Figure D-23.

You colorized a grayscale image by adjusting settings in the Hue/Saturation dialog box.

USE FILTERS, OPACITY AND BLENDING MODES

What You'll Do

 In this lesson, you'll adjust the brightness and contrast, apply a Sharpen filter, and adjust the opacity of the lines applied by the filter. You'll also adjust the color balance of the Chili Shop document.

Manipulating an Image

As you work in Photoshop, you might realize that some images have fundamental problems that need correcting, while others just need to be further enhanced. For example, you might need to adjust an image's contrast and sharpness, or you might want to colorize an otherwise dull image. You can use a variety of techniques to change the way an image looks. For example, you can use the Adjustments command on the Image menu to modify hue and saturation, as well as brightness and contrast.

Understanding Filters

Filters are Photoshop commands that can significantly alter an image's appearance. Experimenting with Photoshop's filters is a fun way to add a different effect to your image. For example, the Watercolor filter gives the illusion that your image was

Fixing blurry scanned images

An unfortunate result of scanning a picture is that the image can become blurry. You can fix this, however, using the Unsharp Mask filter. This filter both sharpens and smoothes the image by increasing the contrast along element edges. Here's how it works: the smoothing effect removes stray marks, and the sharpening effect emphasizes contrasting neighboring pixels. Most scanners come with their own Unsharp Masks built into the TWAIN driver, but using Photoshop, you have access to a more powerful version of this filter. You can use Photoshop's Unsharp Mask to control the sharpening process by adjusting key settings. In most cases, your scanner's Unsharp Mask might not give you this flexibility. Regardless of the technical aspects, the result is a sharper image. You can apply the Unsharp Mark by clicking Filter on the menu bar, pointing to Sharpen, then click Unsharp Mask.

painted using traditional watercolors. Sharpen filters can appear to add definition to the entire image, or just the edges. Compare the different Sharpen filters applied in Figure D-24. The **Sharpen More filter** increases the contrast of adjacent pixels and can focus a blurry image. Be careful not to overuse sharpening tools (or any filter), because you can create high-contrast lines or add graininess in color or brightness.

Choosing Blending Modes

A **blending mode** controls how pixels are either made darker or lighter based on underlying colors. Photoshop provides a variety of blending modes, listed in Table D-1, to combine the color of the pixels in the current layer with those in layer(s) beneath it. You can see a list of blending modes by clicking the Add a layer style button on the Layers palette.

Understanding Blending Mode Components

You should consider the following underlying colors when planning a blending mode: **base color**, which is the original color of the image; **blend color**, which is the color you apply with a paint or edit tool; and **resulting color**, which is the color that is created as a result of applying the blend color.

Softening Filter Effects

Opacity can soften the line that the filter creates, but it doesn't affect the opacity of the entire layer. After a filter has been applied, you can modify the opacity and apply a blending mode using the Layers palette or the Fade dialog box. You can open the Fade dialog box by clicking Edit on the menu bar, then clicking the Fade command.

QUICKTIP

The Fade command appears only after a filter has been applied. When available, the command name includes the name of the applied filter.

Balancing Colors

As you adjust settings, such as hue and saturation, you might create imbalances in your document. You can adjust colors to correct or improve a document's appearance. For example, you can decrease a color by increasing the amount of its opposite color. You use the Color Balance dialog box to balance the color in an image.

FIGURE D-24
Sharpen filters

Original image

Sharpen filter applied

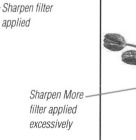

Sharpen More filter applied excessively

TABLE D-1: Blending Modes

blending mode	description
Dissolve, Behind, and Clear modes	Dissolve mode creates a grainy, mottled appearance. The Behind mode paints on the transparent part of the layer—the lower the opacity, the grainier the image. The Clear mode paints individual pixels. All modes are available only when the Lock transparent pixels check box is *not* selected.
Multiply and Screen modes	Multiply mode creates semitransparent shadow effects. This mode assesses the information in each channel, then multiplies the value of the base color by the blend color. The resulting color is always *darker* than the base color. The Screen mode multiplies the value of the inverse of the blend and base colors. After it is applied, the resulting color is always *lighter* than the base color.
Overlay mode	Dark and light values (luminosity) are preserved, dark base colors are multiplied (darkened), and light areas are screened (lightened).
Soft Light and Hard Light modes	Soft Light lightens a light base color and darkens a dark base color. The Hard Light blending mode creates a similar effect, but provides greater contrast between the base and layer colors.
Color Dodge and Color Burn modes	Color Dodge mode brightens the base color to reflect the blend color. The Color Burn mode darkens the base color to reflect the blend color.
Darken and Lighten modes	Darken mode selects a new resulting color based on whichever color is darker—the base color or the blend color. The Lighten mode selects a new resulting color based on the lighter of the two colors.
Difference and Exclusion modes	The Difference mode subtracts the value of the blend color from the value of the base color, or vice versa, depending on which color has the greater brightness value. The Exclusion mode creates an effect similar to that of the Difference mode, but with less contrast between the blend and base colors.
Color and Luminosity modes	The Color mode creates a resulting color with the luminance of the base color, and the hue and saturation of the blend color. The Luminosity mode creates a resulting color with the hue and saturation of the base color, and the luminance of the blend color.
Hue and Saturation modes	The Hue mode creates a resulting color with the luminance of the base color and the hue of the blend color. The Saturation mode creates a resulting color with the luminance of the base color and the saturation of the blend color.

1. Click Image on the menu bar, point to Adjustments, then click Brightness/Contrast to open the Brightness/Contrast dialog box.

2. Drag the Brightness slider until +15 appears in the Brightness text box.

3. Drag the Contrast slider until +25 appears in the Contrast text box. Compare your screen to Figure D-25.

4. Click OK.

You adjusted settings in the Brightness/Contrast dialog box.

FIGURE D-25

Brightness/Contrast dialog box

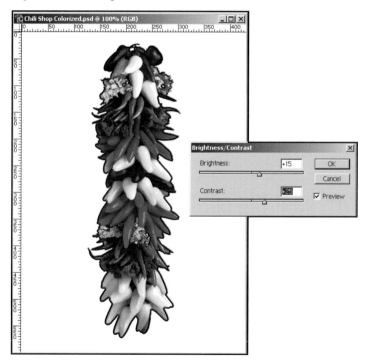

Work with a filter, blending mode, and an opacity setting

1. Click Filter on the menu bar, point to Sharpen, then click Sharpen More.

   The border and other features of the image are intensified.

2. Click Edit on the menu bar, then click Fade Sharpen More to open the Fade dialog box, as shown in Figure D-26.

3. Drag the Opacity slider until 55 appears in the Opacity text box.

   The opacity setting softened the lines applied by the Sharpen More filter.

4. Click the Mode list arrow, then click Dissolve to blend the surrounding pixels.

5. Click OK.

6. Save your work, then compare your document to Figure D-27.

You applied the Sharpen More filter, then adjusted the opacity and changed the color mode in the Fade dialog box.

FIGURE D-28
Color Balance dialog box

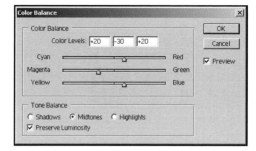

1. Click Window on the menu bar, point to Documents, then click Chili Shop.psd (Win) or Chili Shop (Mac).

   The original (color) document becomes active.

2. Click Image on the menu bar, point to Adjustments, then click Color Balance.

3. Drag the Cyan-Red slider until +20 appears in the first text box.

4. Drag the Magenta-Green slider until –30 appears in the middle text box.

5. Drag the Yellow-Blue slider until +20 appears in the last text box, as shown in Figure D-28.

   Subtle changes were made in the color balance in the image.

6. Click OK.

7. Save your work, then compare your document to Figure D-29.

You switched to the Chili Shop document, and then adjusted settings in the Color Balance dialog box.

FIGURE D-29
Finished project

You are finally able to leave your current job and pursue your lifelong dream of opening a furniture repair and restoration business. While you're waiting for the laser stripper and refinisher to arrive, you start work on a sign design.

1. Open PS D-5.psd, then save it as **Restoration**.
2. Move the objects to any location.
3. Take a sample of the blue pliers (in the tool belt), then switch the foreground and background colors.
4. Take a sample of the red tape measure (in the tool belt).
5. Use any Gradient Tool to create an interesting effect on the Background layer.
6. Save the document, then compare your document to the sample shown in Figure D-30.

FIGURE D-30
Completed Project 1

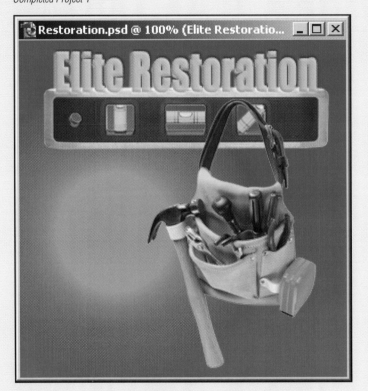

You're painting the swing set at the Artful Dodgers Preschool, when you notice a staff member struggling to create a flyer for the school. Although the basic flyer is complete, it doesn't convey the high energy of the school. You offer to help, and soon find yourself in charge of creating an exciting background for the image.

1. Open PS D-6.psd, then save it as **Preschool**.
2. Select a foreground color and apply it to the Background layer.
3. Add a new layer (Layer 3), then select a background color and apply a gradient you have not used before to the layer. (*Hint*: Immediately undo a gradient that you don't want.)
4. Add the foreground and background colors to the Swatches palette.
5. Apply a Sharpen filter to Layer 2 and adjust the opacity of the filter.
6. Save your work.
7. Compare your document to the sample shown in Figure D-31.

FIGURE D-31
Completed Project 2

SECTION 5

PLACING TYPE IN AN IMAGE

1. Learn about type and how it is created.

2. Change spacing and adjust baseline shift.

3. Use the Drop Shadow style.

4. Apply anti-aliasing to type.

5. Modify type with the Bevel and Emboss style.

6. Apply special effects to type using filters.

SECTION E

PLACING TYPE IN AN IMAGE

Learning About Type

Text can play an important role when used along with images, such as in magazine and newspaper advertisements. In Photoshop, text is referred to as type. You can use type to express the ideas displayed in a document's imagery or to deliver an additional message. You can manipulate type in many ways to convey or reinforce the meaning behind an image. As in other programs, type has its own unique characteristics in Photoshop. For example, you can change its appearance by using different typefaces and colors.

Understanding the Purpose of Type

Type is typically used along with imagery to deliver a message quickly and with flare. Because type is used sparingly (typically there's not a lot of room for it), its appearance is very important; color and imagery are often used to *complement* or *reinforce* the message within the text. Type should be short in length, but direct and to the point. It should be large enough for easy reading, but should not overwhelm or distract from the central image. For example, a vibrant and daring advertisement should contain just enough type to interest the reader, without demanding too much reading.

Getting the Most Out of Type

Type expresses ideas, but the appearance of the type can drive the point home. After you decide on the content you want to use and create the type, you can experiment with its appearance by changing its **font** (characters with a similar appearance), size, and color. You can also apply special effects that make it stand out, or appear to pop off the page.

Tools You'll Use

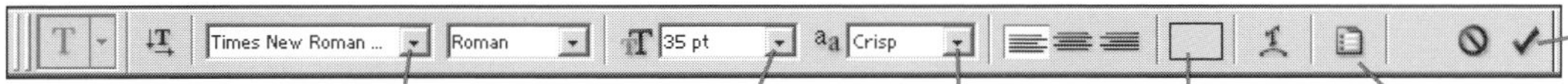

Times New Roman ...
Roman
35 pt
Crisp
Commit any current edits button
Set the font family list arrow
Set the font size list arrow
Set the anti-aliasing method list arrow
Set the text color button
Show the Character & Paragraph palettes button

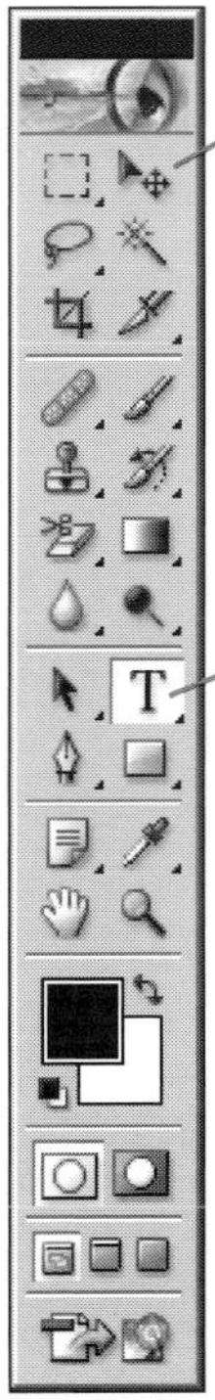

Move Tool
Horizontal Type Tool

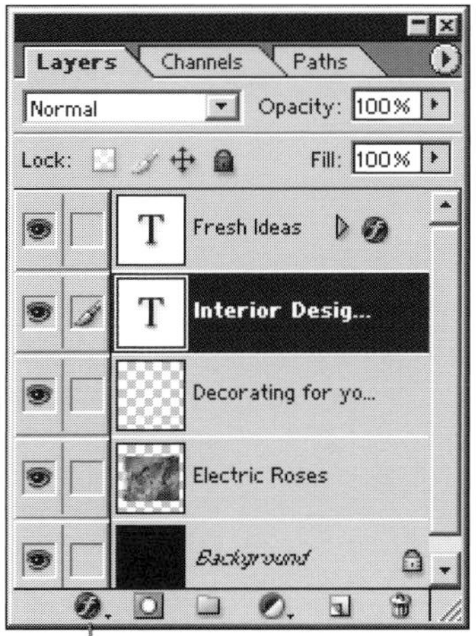

Layers
Channels
Paths
Normal
Opacity: 100%
Lock:
Fill: 100%
Fresh Ideas
Interior Desig...
Decorating for yo...
Electric Roses
Background
Add a layer style button

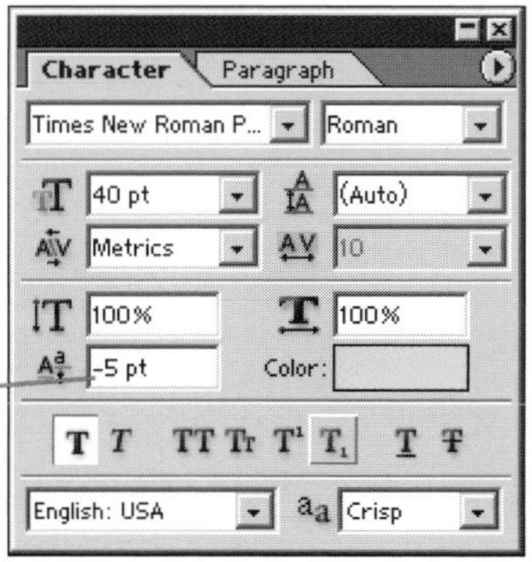

Character
Paragraph
Times New Roman P...
Roman
40 pt
(Auto)
Metrics
10
100%
100%
-5 pt
Color:
English: USA
Crisp
Set the baseline text box

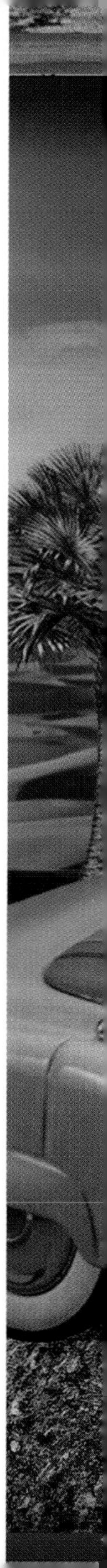

LEARN ABOUT TYPE AND HOW IT IS CREATED

What You'll Do

In this lesson, you'll create a type layer, then change the alignment, font family, size, and color of the type.

Introducing Type Types

Outline type is mathematically defined, which means that it can be scaled to any size without losing its sharp, smooth edges. Some programs, such as Adobe Illustrator, create outline type. **Bitmap type** is composed of pixels, and, like images, can develop jagged edges when enlarged. The type you create in Photoshop is initially outline type, but it is converted into bitmap type when you apply special filters. Using the type tools and the tool options bar, you can create horizontal or vertical type and modify its font size and alignment. You use the Color Picker dialog box to change type color. When you create type in Photoshop, it is automatically placed on a new type layer on the Layers palette.

QUICKTIP

Keeping type on separate layers makes it much easier to modify and change positions within the document.

Getting to Know Font Families

Each **font family** represents a complete set of characters, letters, and symbols for a particular typeface. Font families are generally divided into three categories: serif, sans serif, and symbol. Characters in **serif fonts** have a tail, or stroke, at the end of some characters. These tails make it easier for the eye to recognize words. For this reason, serif fonts are generally used in text passages. **Sans serif fonts** do not have tails and are commonly used in headlines. **Symbol fonts** are used to display unique characters (such as $, ÷, or ™). Table E-1 lists commonly used serif and sans serif fonts. After you select the Horizontal Type Tool, you can change font families using the tool options bar.

Measuring Type Size

The size of each character within a font is measured in **points**. **PostScript**, a programming language that optimizes printed text and graphics, was introduced by Adobe in 1985. In PostScript measurement, 1 inch is equivalent to 72 points or 6 picas. Therefore, 1 pica is equivalent to 12 points. In traditional measurement, 1 inch is equivalent to 72.27 points. The default Photoshop type size is 12 points. In Photoshop, you have the option of using PostScript or traditional character measurement.

Acquiring Fonts

Your computer probably has many fonts installed on it, but no matter how many fonts you have, you probably can use more. Fonts can be purchased from private companies, individual designers, computer stores, catalog companies, or from the Internet. Using your browser and your favorite search engine, you can locate Web sites that let you purchase or download fonts. Many Web sites offer specialty fonts, such as the Web site shown in Figure E-1. Other Web sites offer these fonts free of charge or for a nominal fee.

TABLE E-1: Commonly Used Serif and Sans Serif Fonts

serif fonts	sample	sans serif fonts	sample
Lucida Handwriting	Adobe Photoshop	Arial	Adobe Photoshop
Rockwell	Adobe Photoshop	Bauhaus	Adobe Photoshop
Times New Roman	Adobe Photoshop	Century Gothic	Adobe Photoshop

Create and modify type

1. Start Photoshop, open PS E-1.psd, then save the file as **Fresh Ideas**.

2. If necessary, display the rulers in pixels.

   TIP   You can quickly display the rulers by pressing [Ctrl][R] (Win) or [command][R] (Mac).

3. Click the Default Foreground and Background Colors button.

4. Click the Horizontal Type Tool on the toolbox. T.

5. Click the Set the font family list arrow on the tool options bar, click Times New Roman (or a similar substitute), if necessary, then verify that Roman appears in the text box next to the Set the font family list arrow.

6. Click the Left align text button on the tool options bar, if necessary.

7. Click the Set the font size list arrow on the tool options bar, then click 60 pt, if necessary.

8. Click the document at 240 H/250 V, then type **Fresh Ideas**, as shown in Figure E-2. [T]

   TIP   Type should be short enough to be read in a glance. Thinking during the reading process means there's too much type.

You created a type layer by using the Horizontal Type Tool on the toolbox, then modified the font family, alignment, and font size.

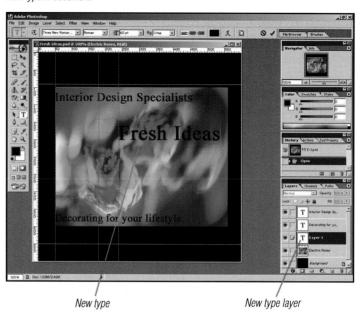

New type   New type layer

Using the active layer palette background (Macintosh)

Icons used in Macintosh to identify type layers are similar to those found in Windows. In Macintosh, the active layer has the same Type and Layer style buttons. The active layer's background color is the same color as the Highlight Color chosen in the Appearance control panel menu item. (In Windows, the active layer's background color is navy blue.)

FIGURE E-3
Type with new color

Type with new color —

Using the Swatches palette to change type color
You can also use the Swatches palette to change type color. Select the type, then click a color on the Swatches palette. The new color that you click will appear in the Set foreground color button on the toolbox and will be applied to type that is currently selected.

1. Press [Ctrl][A] (Win) or [command][A] (Mac) to select all the text.
2. Click the Set the font family list arrow, scroll up, then click Arial.
3. Click the Set the text color button on the tool options bar. ■
4. Click the image at 60 H/370 V. 〔I〕

   TIP   Drag the Color Picker dialog box out of the way if it blocks your view of the image.

   As you position the pointer over the image, the pointer automatically becomes an Eyedropper pointer. The new color is now the active color in the Color Picker dialog box.
5. Click OK in the Color Picker dialog box.
6. Click the Commit any current edits button on the tool options bar. ✔

   Clicking the Commit any current edits button accepts your changes and makes them permanent in the document.
7. Click the Move Tool on the toolbox. ⊞
8. Drag the Fresh Ideas type to 240 H/90 V, as shown in Figure E-3.
9. Save your work.

You changed the font family, modified the color of the font by using the Eyedropper pointer and an existing document color. You also moved the type within the document.

CHANGE SPACING AND ADJUST BASELINE SHIFT

What You'll Do

 In this lesson, you'll adjust the spacing between characters and change the baseline of type.

Spacing Between Lines and Type Characters

Competition for readers on the visual landscape is fierce. To get and maintain an edge over other designers, Photoshop provides tools that make finite adjustments to your type, thereby making your type more distinctive. These adjustments might not be very dramatic, but they can influence readers in subtle ways. For example, type that is too small and difficult to read might make the reader angry (at the very least), and he or she might not even look at the document (at the very worst). You can make finite adjustments, called **type spacing**, to the space between characters and between lines of type. Adjusting type spacing affects the ease with which words are read.

Understanding Character and Line Spacing

Fonts in desktop publishing and word processing programs use proportional spacing, whereas typewriters use monotype spacing. In **monotype spacing**, each character occupies the same amount of space. This means that characters such as "o" and "w" take up the same area as "i" and "l". In **proportional spacing**, each character can take up a different amount of space, depending on its width. **Kerning** controls the amount of space between characters and can affect several characters, a word, or an entire paragraph. **Tracking** inserts a *uniform* amount of space between selected characters. Figure E-4 shows an example of type before and after it has been kerned.

The second line of text takes up less room and has less space between its characters, making it easier to read. You can also change the amount of space between lines of type, or **leading**, to add or decrease the distance between lines of text.

Using the Character Palette

The **Character palette**, shown in Figure E-5, helps you manually or automatically control type properties such as kerning, tracking, and leading. You open the Character palette from the tool options bar.

Adjusting the Baseline Shift

Type rests on an invisible line called a **baseline**. Using the Character palette, you can adjust the **baseline shift**, the vertical distance that type moves from its baseline.

You can add interest to type by changing the baseline shift.

QUICKTIP

Clicking the Set the text color button on either the tool options bar or the Character palette opens the Color Picker dialog box.

FIGURE E-4
Kerned characters

FIGURE E-5
Character palette

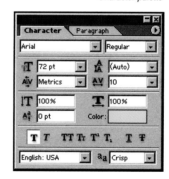

Kern characters

1. Click the Fresh Ideas type layer on the Layers palette, if necessary.

2. Click the Horizontal Type Tool on the toolbox. T.

3. Click the Toggle the Character and Paragraph palettes button on the tool options bar.

   TIP You can close the Character palette by clicking the Close button in the upper-right corner of its title bar or by clicking the Toggle the Character and Paragraph palettes button.

4. Click between "I" and "d" in the word "Ideas."

   TIP You can drag the Character palette out of the way if it blocks your view.

5. Click the Set the kerning between two characters list arrow on the Character palette, then click –25. Metrics

   The spacing between the two characters decreases.

6. Click between "r" and "e" in the word "Fresh."

7. Click the Set the kerning between two characters list arrow, then click –10, as shown in Figure E-6. Metrics

8. Click the Commit any current edits button on the tool options bar. ✔

You modified the kerning between characters by using the Character palette.

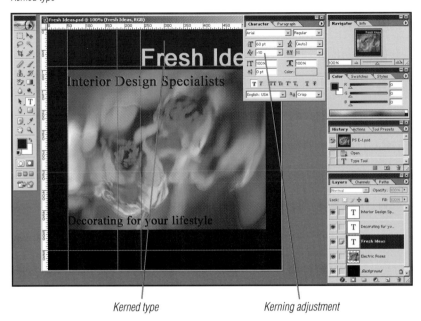

Kerned type   Kerning adjustment

Correcting spelling errors

Are you concerned that your gorgeous image will be ruined by misspelled words? Photoshop understands your pain and has included a spelling checker to make sure you are never plagued by incorrect spellings. If you want, the spelling checker will check the type on the current layer, or all the layers in the document. First, make sure the correct dictionary for your language is selected. English: USA is the default, but you can choose another language by clicking the Set the language on selected characters for hyphenation and spelling list arrow at the bottom of the Character palette. To check spelling, click Edit on the menu bar, then click Check Spelling. The spelling checker will automatically stop at each word not already appearing in the dictionary. One or more suggestions might be offered, which you can either accept or reject.

FIGURE E-7
Color Picker dialog box

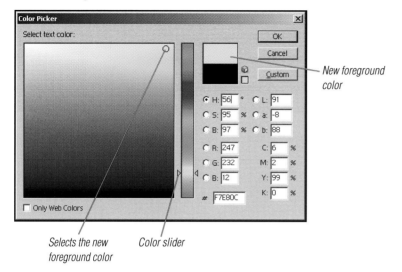

Selects the new
foreground color

Color slider

New foreground
color

FIGURE E-8
Type with baseline shifted

1. Double-click the layer thumbnail on the Interior Design Specialists type layer.

2. Click the Set the text color button on the tool options bar. ▬

3. If necessary, click the H (Hue) option button in the Color Picker dialog box, click yellow in the color slider, click in the upper-right corner of the color field, as shown in Figure E-7, then click OK. ◯

4. Select the capital "I" in "Interior," double-click 35 in the Set the font size text box on the Character palette, type 40, double-click 0 in the Set the baseline shift text box on the Character palette, then type **–5**.

5. Select "D" in "Design," double-click 35 in the Set the font size text box, type **40**, double-click 0 in the Set the baseline shift text box, then type **–5**.

6. Select "S" in "Specialists," double-click 35 in the Set the font size text box, type **40**, double-click 0 in the Set the baseline shift text box, then type **–5**.

7. Click the Commit any current edits button on the tool options bar. ✔

8. Click the Toggle the Character and Paragraph palettes button on the tool options bar. ▤

9. Click the Move Tool on the toolbox, then drag the Interior Design Specialists type to 50 H/550 V, as shown in Figure E-8.

10. Save your work.

You changed the type color, then adjusted the baseline of the first character in each word.

USE THE DROP SHADOW STYLE

What You'll Do

 In this lesson, you'll apply the drop shadow style to a type layer, then modify drop shadow settings.

Adding Effects to Type

Layer styles (effects which can be applied to a type or image layer) can greatly enhance the appearance of type and improve its effectiveness. A type layer is indicated by the appearance of the T icon in the layer's thumbnail box. When a layer style is applied to any layer, the Indicates layer effects icon (*f*) appears in that layer when it is active. The Layers palette is a great source of information. You can see which effects have been applied to a layer by clicking the arrow to the left of the Indicates layer effects icon on the Layers palette if the layer is active or inactive. Figure E-9 shows a layer that has two type layer styles applied to it. Layer styles are linked to the contents of a layer, which means that if a type layer is moved or modified, the layer's style will still be applied to the type.

QUICKTIP

Type layer icons used in the Macintosh version of Photoshop are similar to those found in the Windows version of Photoshop.

Using the Drop Shadow

One method of placing emphasis on type is to add a drop shadow to it. A **drop shadow** creates an illusion that another colored layer of identical text is behind the selected type. The drop shadow default color is black, but can be changed to another color using the Color Picker dialog box, or any of the other methods for changing color.

Applying a Style

You can apply a style, such as a drop shadow, to the active layer, by clicking Layer on the menu bar, pointing to Layer Style, then clicking a style. (The settings in the Layer Style dialog box are "sticky," meaning that they display the settings that you last used.) An alternative method to using the menu bar is to select the layer that you want to apply the style to, click the Add a layer style button on the Layers palette, then click a style. Regardless of which method you use, the Layer Style dialog box opens. You use this dialog box to add all kinds of effects to type. Depending on which style you've chosen, the Layer Style dialog box displays options appropriate to that style.

QUICK**TIP**

You can apply styles to objects as well as type.

Controlling a Drop Shadow

You can control many aspects of a drop shadow's appearance, including its angle, its distance behind the type, and the amount of blur it contains. The **angle** determines where the shadow falls relative to the text, and the **distance** determines how far the shadow falls from the text. The **spread** determines the width of the shadow

text, and the **size** determines the clarity of the shadow. Figure E-10 contains two samples of drop shadow effects. The first line of type uses the default background color (black), has an angle of 160 degrees, distance of 10 pixels, a spread of 0%, and a size of 5 pixels. The second line of type uses a blue background color, has an angle of 120 degrees, distance of 20 pixels, a spread of 10%, and a size of 5 pixels. As you modify the drop shadow, the preview window displays the changes.

FIGURE E-9

Effects in an inactive type layer

FIGURE E-10

Sample drop shadows

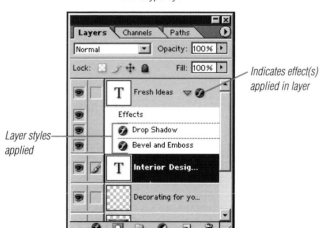

Layer styles applied

Indicates effect(s) applied in layer

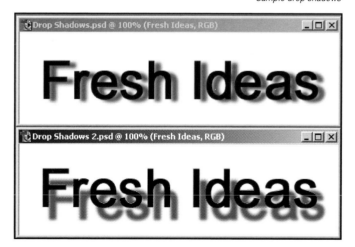

Add a drop shadow

1. Double-click the layer thumbnail on the Decorating for your lifestyle type layer.

2. Click the Set the text color button on the tool options bar. ▉

3. Click the "F" in "Fresh." ⌶

4. Click OK in the Color Picker dialog box.

5. Click the Commit any current edits button on the tool options bar. ✔

6. Click the Add a layer style button on the Layers palette. ⊘.

7. Click Drop Shadow.

   The default drop shadow settings are applied to the type as shown in Figure E-11. Table E-2 explains drop shadow settings.

   TIP You can also open the Layer Style dialog box by double-clicking a layer on the Layers palette.

You changed the color of the type and created a drop shadow by using the Add a layer style button on the Layers palette.

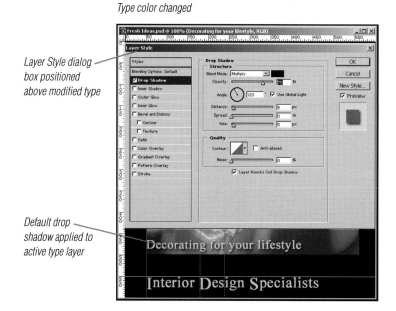

Layer Style dialog box positioned above modified type

Default drop shadow applied to active type layer

TABLE E-2: Drop Shadow Settings

setting	scale	explanation
Angle	0–360 degrees	At 0 degrees, the shadow appears on the baseline of the original text. At 90 degrees, the shadow appears directly below the original text.
Distance	0–30,000 pixels	A larger pixel size increases the distance from which the shadow text falls relative to the original text.
Spread	0–100%	A larger pixel size increases the width of the shadow text.
Size	0–250 pixels	A larger pixel size increases the blur of the shadow text.

Layer Style dialog box

Angle text box

Distance text box

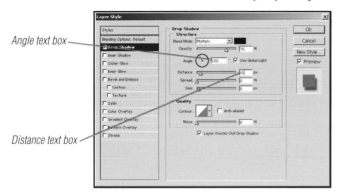

Drop shadow added to type layer

Drop shadow
appears behind text

Displays effect(s)
applied in layer

Modify drop shadow settings

1. Double-click the number in the Angle text box, then type **120**, if necessary.

   TIP You can also set the angle by dragging the dial slider in the Layer Style dialog box.

2. Double-click the number in the Distance text box, then type **10**, if necessary. See Figure E-12.

3. Click OK.

4. Click the triangle to the left of the Indicates layer effects icon on the Decorating for your lifestyle layer, as shown in Figure E-13.

5. Click the triangle to the left of the Indicates layer effects icon on the Decorating for your lifestyle layer to close the list.

6. Save your work.

You used the Layer Style dialog box to modify the default settings for the drop shadow.

APPLY ANTI-ALIASING TO TYPE

What You'll Do

 In this lesson, you'll view the effects of the anti-aliasing feature, then use the History palette to return the type to its original state.

Eliminating the "Jaggies"

In the good old days of dot-matrix printers, jagged edges were obvious in many print ads. You can still see these jagged edges in designs produced on less sophisticated printers. To prevent the jagged edges (sometimes called "jaggies") that often accompany bitmap type, Photoshop offers an anti-aliasing feature. **Anti-aliasing** partially fills in pixel edges with additional colors, resulting in smooth-edge type and an increased number of colors in the document. Anti-aliasing is useful for improving the display of large type in print media; however, this can cause a file to become large.

Knowing When to Apply Anti-Aliasing

As a rule, type that has a point size greater than 12 should have some anti-aliasing method applied. Sometimes, smaller type sizes can become blurry or muddy when anti-aliasing is used. As part of the process, anti-aliasing adds intermediate colors to your image in an effort to reduce the jagged edges. As a designer, you need to weigh the following factors when determining if you should apply anti-aliasing: type size versus file size and image quality.

Understanding Anti-Aliasing

Anti-aliasing improves the display of type against the background. You can use five anti-aliasing methods: None, Sharp, Crisp, Strong, and Smooth. An example of each method is shown in Figure E-14. The None setting applies no anti-aliasing, and can result in type that has jagged edges. The Sharp setting displays type with the best possible resolution. The Crisp setting gives type more definition and makes type appear sharper. The Strong setting makes type appear heavier, much like the bold attribute. The Smooth setting gives type more rounded edges.

QUICKTIP

You'll find that the appearance of type can help convey a message. Generally, the type used in your image should be the messenger, not the message. As you work with type, keep in mind that using more than two fonts in one document might be distracting or make the overall appearance look unprofessional.

FIGURE E-14
Anti-aliasing effects

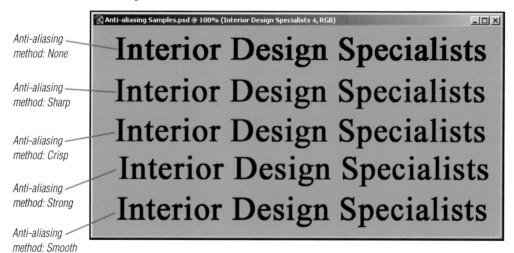

Anti-aliasing method: None

Anti-aliasing method: Sharp

Anti-aliasing method: Crisp

Anti-aliasing method: Strong

Anti-aliasing method: Smooth

Apply anti-aliasing

1. Double-click the layer thumbnail on the Interior Design Specialists layer.

2. Click the Set the font family list arrow, scroll up, then click Arial MT or Arial.

3. Click the Set the anti-aliasing method list arrow on the tool options bar. [Crisp ▾]

4. Click None, then compare your work to Figure E-15.

5. Click the Commit any current edits button on the tool options bar. ✔

You applied the None anti-aliasing setting to see how the setting affected the appearance of type.

Effect of None anti-aliasing

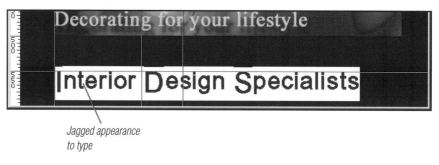

Jagged appearance to type

Placing Type in an Image

FIGURE E-16

Deleting a state from the History palette

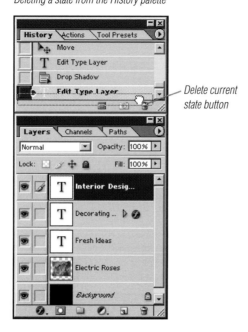

Delete current
state button

Undo anti-aliasing

1. Click the Edit Type Layer state in the History palette, then drag it to the Delete current state button, as shown in Figure E-16. 🗑

   TIP Various methods of undoing actions are reviewed in Table E-3.

2. Save your work.

You deleted a state in the History palette to return the type to its original appearance.

TABLE E-3: Undoing Actions		
method	description	keyboard shortcut
Undo	Edit ➢ Undo	[Ctrl][Z] (Win) [command][Z] (Mac)
Step Backward	Click Edit on the menu bar, then click Step Backward	[Alt][Ctrl][Z] (Win) [alt][command][Z] (Mac)
History palette	Drag state to the Delete current state button on the History palette	[Alt] 🗑 (Win) [option] 🗑 (Mac)

MODIFY TYPE WITH THE BEVEL AND EMBOSS STYLE

What You'll Do

In this lesson, you'll apply the Bevel and Emboss style, then modify the Bevel and Emboss settings.

Using the Bevel and Emboss Style

You use the Bevel and Emboss style to add combinations of shadows and highlights to a layer and make type appear to have dimension and shine. You can use the Layer menu or the Layers palette to apply the Bevel and Emboss style to the active layer. Like all Layer styles, the Bevel and Emboss style is linked to the type layer that it is applied to.

Understanding Bevel and Emboss Settings

You can use two categories of Bevel and Emboss settings: structure and shading. **Structure** determines the size and physical properties of the object, and **shading** determines the lighting effects. Figure E-17 contains several variations of Bevel and Emboss structure settings. The shading used in the Bevel and Emboss style determines how and where light is projected on

Filling type with imagery

You can use the imagery from a layer in one file as the fill pattern for another image's type layer. To create this effect, open a multi-layer file that contains the imagery you want to use (the source), then open the file that contains the type you want to fill (the target). In the source file, activate the layer containing the imagery you want to use, use the Select menu to select all, then use the Edit menu to copy the selection. In the target file, press [Ctrl] (Win) or [command] (Mac) while clicking the type layer to which the imagery will be applied, then click Paste Into on the Edit menu. The imagery will appear within the type.

the type. You can control a variety of settings, including the angle, altitude, and gloss contour, to create a unique appearance. The **Angle** setting determines where the shadow falls relative to the text, and the **Altitude** setting affects the amount of visible dimension. For example, an altitude of 0 degrees looks flat, while a setting of 90 degrees has a more three-dimensional appearance. The **Gloss Contour** setting determines the pattern with which light is reflected, and the **Highlight Mode** and **Shadow Mode** settings determine how pigments are combined. When the Use Global Light check box is selected, *all the type* in the document will be affected by your changes.

FIGURE E-17
Bevel and Emboss style samples

Add the Bevel and Emboss style and modify settings

1. Click the Fresh Ideas layer on the Layers palette.

2. Click Layer on the menu bar, point to Layer Style, then click Bevel and Emboss.

3. If necessary, move the Layer Style dialog box, shown in Figure E-18, so you can see the Fresh Ideas type.

4. Double-click number in the Angle text box, then type **120**, if necessary.

Some of the Bevel and Emboss settings are listed in Table E-4. You can use the Layer Style dialog box to change the structure by adjusting style, technique, direction, size, and soften settings.

(continued)

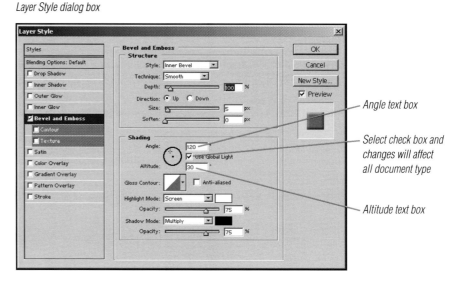

Angle text box

Select check box and changes will affect all document type

Altitude text box

TABLE E-4: Bevel and Emboss Structure Settings

sample	style	technique	direction	size	soften
1	Inner Bevel	Smooth	Up	5	1
2	Outer Bevel	Chisel Hard	Up	5	8
3	Emboss	Smooth	Down	10	3
4	Pillow Emboss	Chisel Soft	Up	10	3

*Bevel and Emboss
style applied to layer*

Bevel and Emboss style

5. Double-click the Altitude text box, then type **30**, if necessary.

6. Click OK, then compare your type to Figure E-19.

7. Save your work.

You applied the Bevel and Emboss style by using the Layer menu, then modified the default settings.

Warping type

You can add dimension and style to your type by using the Warp Text feature. After you select the type layer you want to warp, click the Horizontal Type Tool on the toolbox. Click the Create warped text button on the tool options bar to open the Warp Text dialog box. (If a warning box opens telling you that your request cannot be completed because the type layer uses a faux bold style, click the Toggle the Character and Paragraph palettes button on the tool options bar, click the Character palette list arrow, click Faux Bold to deselect it, then click the Create warped text button again.) You can click the Style list arrow to select from 15 available styles. After you select a style, you can modify its appearance by dragging the Bend, Horizontal Distortion, and Vertical Distortion sliders.

APPLY SPECIAL EFFECTS TO TYPE USING FILTERS

What You'll Do

 In this lesson, you'll rasterize a type layer, then apply a filter to it to change its appearance.

Understanding Filters

Like an image layer, a type layer can have one or more filters applied to it to achieve special effects and make your text look unique. Some filter dialog boxes have preview windows that let you see the results of the particular filter before it is applied to the layer. Other filters must be applied to the layer before you can see the results. Before a filter can be applied to a type layer, the type layer must first be **rasterized**, or converted to an image layer. After it is rasterized, the type characters *can no longer be edited* because it is composed of pixels, just like artwork. When a type layer is rasterized, the T icon in the layer thumbnail becomes an image thumbnail while the Effects icons remain on the type layer.

Creating Special Effects

Filters enable you to apply a variety of special effects to type, as shown in Figure E-20. Notice that none of the original type layers on the Layers palette displays the T icon in the layer thumbnail because the layers have all been rasterized.

> **QUICKTIP**
>
> Because you cannot edit type after it has been rasterized, you should save your original type by making a copy of the layer *before* you rasterize it, then hide it from view.

Producing Distortions

Distort filters let you create waves or curves in type. Some of the types of distortions you can produce include Glass, Pinch, Ripple, Shear, Spherize, Twirl, Wave, and Zigzag. These effects are sometimes used as the basis of a corporate logo. The Twirl dialog box, shown in Figure E-21, lets you determine the amount of twirl effect you want to apply. By dragging the Angle slider, you control how much twirl effect is added to a layer. Most filter dialog boxes have zoom in and zoom out buttons that make it easy to see the effects of the filter.

Using Textures and Relief

Many filters let you create the appearance of textures and **relief** (the height of ridges within an object). One of the Stylize filters, Wind, applies lines throughout the type, making it appear shredded. The Wind dialog box, shown in Figure E-22, lets you determine the kind of wind and its direction. The Texture filter lets you choose the type of texture you want to apply to a layer: Brick, Burlap, Canvas, or Sandstone.

Blurring Imagery

The Gaussian Blur filter softens the appearance of type by blurring its edge pixels. You can control the amount of blur applied to the type by entering high or low values in the Gaussian Blur dialog box. The higher the blur value, the blurrier the effect.

QUICKTIP

Be careful: too much blur applied to type can make it unreadable or cause it to disappear entirely.

FIGURE E-20
Sample filters applied to type

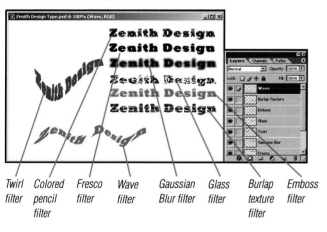

Twirl filter | Colored pencil filter | Fresco filter | Wave filter | Gaussian Blur filter | Glass filter | Burlap texture filter | Emboss filter

FIGURE E-21
Twirl dialog box

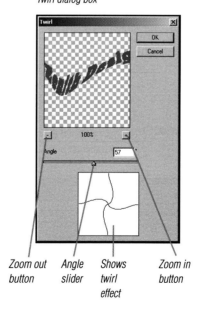

Zoom out button | Angle slider | Shows twirl effect | Zoom in button

FIGURE E-22
Wind dialog box

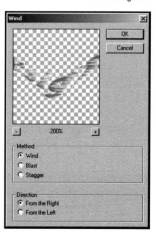

Rasterize a type layer

1. Click the Decorating for your lifestyle layer on the Layers palette.
2. Click Filter on the menu bar, point to Blur, then click Gaussian Blur.
3. Click OK to rasterize the type and close the warning box shown in Figure E-23.

   TIP You can also rasterize a type layer by clicking Layer on the menu bar, pointing to Rasterize, then clicking Type.

   The Gaussian Blur dialog box opens.

You rasterized a type layer in preparation for filter application.

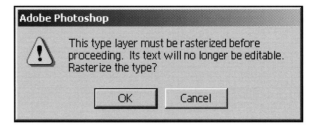

Using multiple filters

Sometimes, adding one filter doesn't achieve the effect you might have had in mind. You can use multiple filters to create a unique effect. Before you try your hand at filters, though, it's a good idea to make a copy of the original layer. That way, if things don't turn out as you planned, you can always start over. You don't even have to write down which filters you used, because you can always look at the History palette to see which filters you applied.

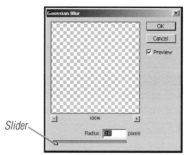

Slider

No longer a
type layer

Modify filter settings

1. Drag the slider in the Gaussian Blur dialog box until 0.8 appears in the Radius text box, as shown in Figure E-24.

2. Click OK.

3. Hide the rulers.

4. Save your work. Compare your blurred type to Figure E-25.

You modified the Gaussian Blur filter settings to change the blur effect.

Creating a neon glow

Want to create a really cool effect that takes absolutely no time at all, is super-easy, and works on both type and objects? You can create a neon glow that appears to surround an object. You can apply the Neon Glow filter (one of the Artistic filters) to any flattened image. This effect works best by starting with any imagery—either type or objects—that has a solid color background. Flatten the image so there's only a Background layer. Click the Magic Wand Tool on the toolbox, then click the solid color (in the background). Click Filter on the menu bar, point to Artistic, then click Neon Glow. Adjust the glow size, the glow brightness, and color, if you wish, then click OK.

A local flower shop, Beautiful Blooms, asks you to design its color advertisement for the trade magazine, *Florists United*. You have already started on the image, and need to add some type.

1. Open PS E-3.psd, then save it as **Beautiful Blooms Ad.**
2. Click the Horizontal Type Tool, then type **Beautiful Blooms** using a 48 pt Impact font in black.
3. Create a catchy phrase using an 18 pt Verdana font.
4. Apply a drop shadow style to the name of the flower shop using the following settings: Multiply blend mode, 75% Opacity, 120° angle, 5 pixel distance, 0° spread, and 5 pixel size.
5. Apply a bevel and emboss style to the catch phrase using the following settings: Inner Bevel style, Smooth technique, 100% depth, Up direction, 5 pixel size, 0 pixel soften, 120° angle, 30° altitude, and using global light.
6. Compare your document to the sample in Figure E-26.
7. Save your work.

FIGURE E-26
Completed Project 1

You are a junior art director for an advertising agency. You have been working on an ad that promotes milk and milk products. You have started the project, but still have a few details to finish up before it is complete.

1. Open PS E-4.psd, then save it as **Spilled Milk**.
2. Create a type layer above the Milk Glass layer using a catchy phrase, such as "Don't Cry".
3. Use the Eyedropper pointer to sample the white background color for the type layer. (*Hint*: You can use a location such as 40 H/150 V.)
4. Use a 60 pt Arial Black font for the catch phrase type layer. (If necessary, substitute another font.)
5. Create a bevel and emboss style on the "Don't Cry" type layer, setting the angle to 100° and the altitude to 30°.
6. Compare your document to the sample in Figure E-27.
7. Save your work.

FIGURE E-27
Completed Project 2

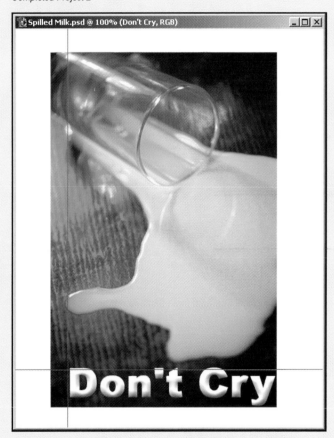

Placing Type in an Image

BONUS
SECTION

CREATING WEB DOCUMENTS

1. Learn about ImageReady.

2. Optimize images for Web use.

3. Create a button for a Web page.

4. Create slices in a document.

5. Create a rollover effect.

6. Create and play basic animation.

7. Add tweening and frame delay.

SECTION A
CREATING WEB DOCUMENTS

Using Photoshop for the Web

In addition to creating exciting images that can be professionally printed, you can use the tools in Photoshop to create images for use on the Web. Once you have a Photoshop image, you can use an additional program called Adobe ImageReady 7.0 to add the dimension and functionality required by today's Web audience. ImageReady is an integral part of Photoshop.

Understanding Web Graphics

With ImageReady you can tailor images and graphics specifically for the Web by creating buttons and other features unique to Web pages. Using these two programs, you can combine impressive graphics with interactive functionality to create an outstanding Web site.

QUICKTIP

ImageReady provides the capabilities for dividing one image into smaller, more manageable parts, and for creating more efficient Web-ready files.

Jumping Between Programs

Photoshop and ImageReady are designed to work together, so you can jump between the two programs to make changes in each program. Each program updates changes made in the other. This means you can work in ImageReady, return to Photoshop to tweak an image, then jump back to ImageReady to preview what your work will look like in your Web browser.

Tools You'll Use

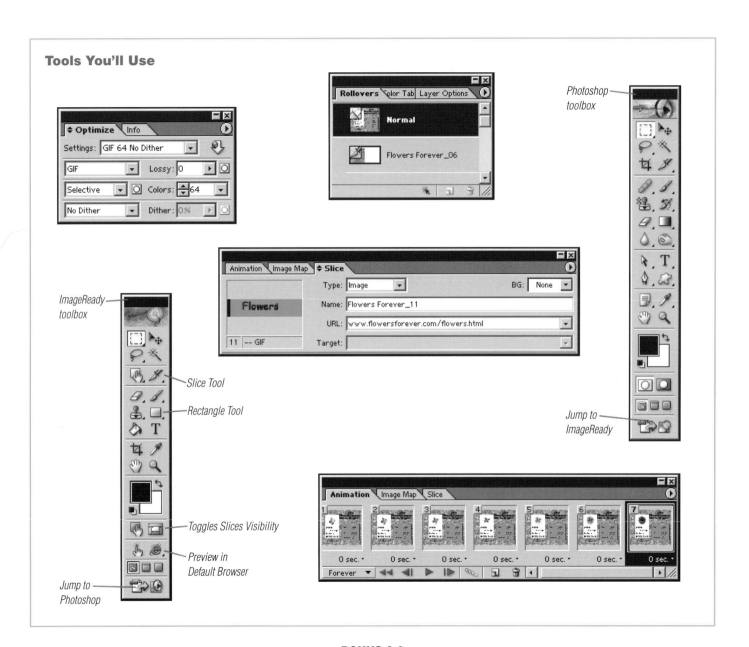

ImageReady toolbox

Slice Tool

Rectangle Tool

Photoshop toolbox

Jump to ImageReady

Toggles Slices Visibility

Preview in Default Browser

Jump to Photoshop

LEARN ABOUT IMAGEREADY

What You'll Do

 In this lesson, you'll open and rename a file in Photoshop, then use the Jump to feature to view the document in ImageReady. You'll also change your view of the document, exit ImageReady, then return to Photoshop.

Using Photoshop and ImageReady

Photoshop and ImageReady share similar tools and features, such as the toolbox, the tool options bar, and many palettes. Most features work identically, but some are found in different locations. For example, in Photoshop, the History palette appears above the Layers palette, but in ImageReady, the History palette is grouped with the Layers and Actions palettes. Figure A-1 shows the ImageReady workspace. You can use the Jump to ImageReady button (in Photoshop) or the Jump to Photoshop button (in ImageReady) to switch between the two programs.

Previewing Files for the Web

You can add many sophisticated Web effects to the files you create in ImageReady. To insert and view them in a Web page, you need to follow the procedures dictated by your HTML editor. HTML (Hypertext Markup Language) is the language used for creating Web pages. You can preview most Web effects directly in Photoshop or ImageReady. ImageReady also allows you to preview your files in your Web browser by clicking the Preview in Default Browser button on the toolbox (you can preview in Internet Explorer or Netscape Navigator).

QUICKTIP

Because monitor quality, operating systems, and Web browsers will vary from user to user, you should preview your images on as many different systems as possible before you finalize an image for the Web.

Updating Files

Each time you jump between Photoshop and ImageReady, the active program will automatically update the current file. This ensures that you always work with the most current version of the document.

QUICKTIP

A History state is created whenever Photoshop or ImageReady is automatically updated. This new state lets you know that an update occurred.

Creating Navigational and Interactive Functionality

You can divide a document you create for a Web site into many smaller sections, or slices. You use a slice to assign special features, such as rollovers, links, and animation, to specific areas within a document. A rollover changes an object's appearance when the pointer passes over (or the user clicks) a specific area of the document. An image sequence, or animation, simulates an object moving on a Web page. You can create an animation by making slight changes to several images, and then adjusting the timing between their appearances. When you convert a document to HTML, slices become cells in an HTML table, and rollovers and animations become files in object folders.

Jumping Between ImageReady and Other Programs

You can jump from ImageReady to other graphics programs or HTML programs, and then automatically update those files. To set up the programs that you want to jump to, click File on the menu bar, point to Jump To, click Other Graphics Editor or Other HTML Editor, then locate the program you want. To set up automatic file updating in Photoshop, click Edit on the menu bar, point to Preferences, click General, select the Auto-update open documents check box, then click OK. To set up automatic file updating in ImageReady, click Edit on the menu bar, point to Preferences, click General, select the Auto-Update Files check box, then click OK.

ImageReady workspace

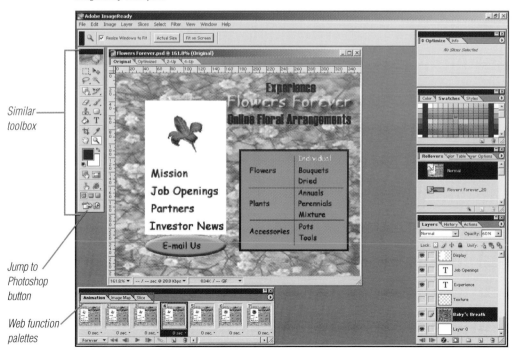

Similar toolbox

Jump to Photoshop button

Web function palettes

Jump to ImageReady

1. Start Photoshop, open PS Bonus A-1.psd, then save it as **Bloom Island**.

   TIP If you receive a message stating that some text layers need to be updated before they can be used for vector-based output, click Update (Mac).

2. Click the Default Foreground and Background Colors button on the toolbox. ▄▀

3. Display the rulers in pixels, if necessary.

4. Click the Jump to ImageReady button on the toolbox. 🖼️🔍

   Click the Toggle Slices Visibility button on the toolbox if the slices are not visible. 🔲 The Bloom Island document opens in ImageReady. Compare your screen to Figure A-2.

You opened a document in Photoshop, then jumped to ImageReady.

FIGURE A-2

Document in ImageReady

FIGURE A-3

Adjusted document view in ImageReady

Click button to change view

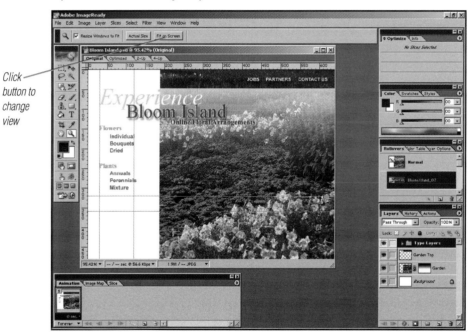

1. If necessary, click View on the menu bar, then click Rulers.

   TIP   Many commands, such as displaying rulers, and many shortcut keys are the same in ImageReady and Photoshop.

2. Click View on the menu bar, then deselect Extras, if necessary.

3. Click View on the menu bar, point to Show, then click Guides.

4. Click the Zoom Tool on the toolbox.

5. Verify that the Resize Windows To Fit check box is selected. ☐ Resize Windows To Fit

6. Click the Fit on Screen button on the tool options bar, then compare your document to Figure A-3.

7. Click File on the menu bar, then click Exit (Win) or click ImageReady on the menu bar, then click Quit ImageReady (Mac) to close the document in ImageReady and return to Photoshop.

   ImageReady closes, and you are returned to the Bloom Island document in Photoshop.

You adjusted your view of the document, then exited the program.

OPTIMIZE IMAGES FOR WEB USE

What You'll Do

In this lesson, you'll open a file in Photoshop, and then use the Save for Web command on the File menu to select a JPEG optimization format. You'll also jump to ImageReady and select a GIF optimization format, save the file as a GIF, then exit ImageReady. In Photoshop, you'll close the PSD version of the file, open the GIF version, drag it into the document, adjust the opacity setting of a layer, then rename it.

Understanding Optimization

You can create an awesome image in Photoshop and merge and flatten layers in the document, but still have a file so large that no one will wait for it to download from the Web. Both ImageReady and Photoshop contain features that let you precisely optimize an image. An **optimized** file is just as beautiful as a non-optimized file; it's just a fraction of its original size.

Optimizing a File

When you optimize a file, you save it in a Web format that balances the need for detail and accurate color against file size. Photoshop and ImageReady allow you to compare an image in the following common Web formats:

- JPEG (Joint Photographic Experts Group)
- GIF (Graphics Interchange Format)
- PNG (Portable Network Graphics)
- WBMP (a Bitmap format used for mobile devices, such as cell phones)

In Photoshop, the Save For Web dialog box has four view tabs: Original, Optimized, 2-Up, and 4-Up. See Figure A-4. The Original view displays the graphic without any optimization. The Optimized, 2-Up, and 4-Up views display the document in its original format, as well as other file formats. You can change the file format by

Exporting an image

You can export an image with transparency in Photoshop using the Export Transparent Image command on the Help menu. The Export Transparent Image Wizard guides you in selecting the area you want to be transparent. Most commonly, the background becomes transparent instead of white. By default, Photoshop saves the file as an Encapsulated PostScript (EPS) file.

Creating Web Documents

clicking one of the windows in the dialog box, then clicking the Settings list arrow. In ImageReady, a document opens in the optimization window, where you can change views and formats the same way you do in Photoshop. See Figure A-5.

QUICKTIP

You can also use the Photoshop Save As command on the File menu to quickly save a file under a different graphics format by using Photoshop's default settings.

Understanding Compression

GIF, JPEG, and PNG compression create compressed files without losing substantial components. Figuring out when to use which format can be a puzzle. Often, the decision may rest on whether color or image detail is most important. JPEG files are compressed by discarding image pixels; GIF and PNG files are compressed by limiting colors. GIF is an 8-bit format (the maximum number of colors a GIF file can contain is 256) that supports one transparent color; JPEG does not support transparent color. Having a transparent color is useful if you want to create a fade-out or superimposed effect. Because the JPEG format discards, or *loses*, data when it compresses a file, it is known as **lossy**. GIF and PNG formats are **lossless**—they compress solid color areas but maintain detail.

FIGURE A-4
Optimizing files in Photoshop

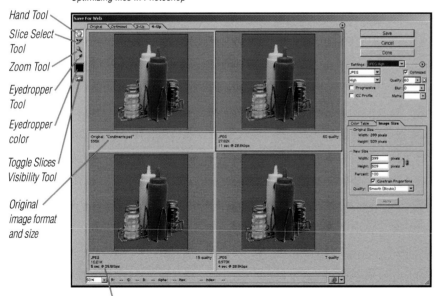

Hand Tool
Slice Select Tool
Zoom Tool
Eyedropper Tool
Eyedropper color
Toggle Slices Visibility Tool
Original image format and size

Settings indicate size and download time

FIGURE A-5
Optimizing files in ImageReady

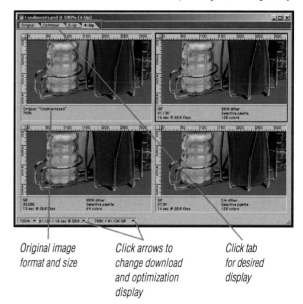

Original image format and size

Click arrows to change download and optimization display

Click tab for desired display

Comparing Image Types

Figure A-6 compares optimization of a photograph with a solid color background optimized in both GIF and JPEG formats. If you look very closely, you'll see that the GIF colors are streaky and broken-up, and the JPEG colors are crisp and appear seamless. Table A-1 lists optimization format considerations. Because you cannot assume that other users will have access to the latest software and hardware, it's a good idea to compare files saved under different formats and optimization settings, and preview them in different browsers and on different computers.

FIGURE A-6
Photograph optimization comparison

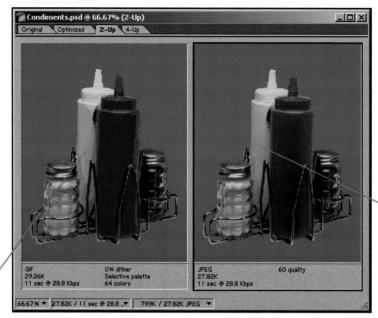

GIF (64 no dither) optimization

JPEG (high) optimization

TABLE A-1: Optimization Format Considerations

format	file format	use with
JPEG (very common)	All 24-bit (works best with 16 M colors)	Photographs, solid colors, soft edges
GIF (very common)	8-bit (256 colors)	Detailed drawings, sharp edges (logos, vector graphics), animation
PNG (less common)	24-bit (16 M colors)	Detailed drawings, logos, bitmap graphics
WBMP (less common)	1-bit (2 colors)	Cell phones and other mobile devices

FIGURE A-7

Save For Web dialog box

Outline
surrounds
optimal format

Your formats
may differ

Magnification
level

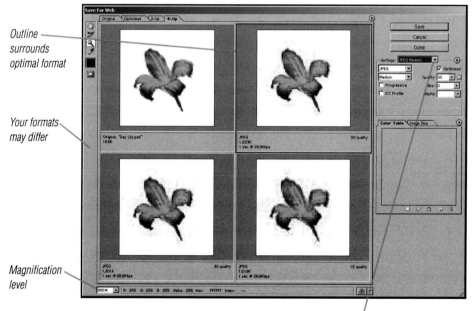

Click list arrow to
change format

1. Open Day Lily.psd.

   TIP Minimize the Bloom Island document if it gets in your way.

2. Click File on the menu bar, then click Save for Web.

3. Click the 4-Up tab, if necessary.

4. Click the Zoom Tool in the Save For Web dialog box.

5. Click the top-right image until all four images are enlarged to 300%.

   TIP The zoom level is displayed in the lower-left corner of the Save For Web dialog box. You can also click the Zoom Level list arrow and select a magnification.

6. Click the Settings list arrow, click JPEG Medium, then compare your dialog box to Figure A-7.

   Photoshop automatically selects the optimal format setting by highlighting it with a black border.

   TIP To optimize the file, click the desired format in the dialog box, click Save, enter a new name (if necessary) in the Save Optimized As dialog box, then click Save.

7. Click Cancel in the Save For Web dialog box.

You opened a file, used the Save for Web command on the File menu to open the Save For Web dialog box, then selected JPEG Medium as an optimization format.

Optimize an image in ImageReady

1. Click the Jump to ImageReady button on the toolbox.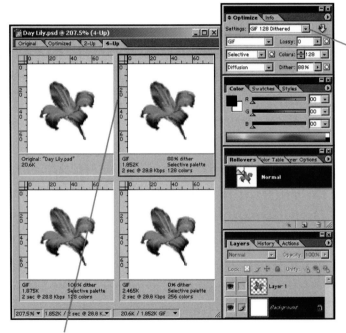

   The Day Lily document is opened in ImageReady.

2. Verify that the 4-Up tab is selected.

   > TIP To create a new view of the current image, drag any view tab to a new location in the workspace.

3. Click the Zoom Tool, if necessary.

4. Click Fit on Screen on the tool options bar.

5. Click the Settings list arrow on the Optimize palette, then click GIF 128 Dithered. Compare your image to Figure A-8.

   Did you notice that the optimized size of the file is 1.852K? The original file size was approximately 21K.

6. Click File on the menu bar, then click Save Optimized As.

7. Navigate to the folder where you want to save the file as **Day-Lily.gif**, then click Save.

   The optimized file is saved in the designated location.

8. Close ImageReady, then close Day Lily.psd in Photoshop without saving changes.

You jumped to ImageReady, saved an optimized file, then exited ImageReady. In Photoshop, you closed the PSD version of the Day Lily file.

FIGURE A-8
Document optimized in ImageReady

Click list arrow to change format

Outline surrounds optimal format

FIGURE A-9
Optimized image moved to document

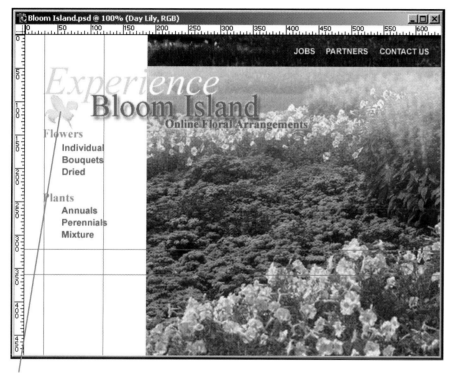

GIF image in
document

1. Verify that the Type Layers layer set is selected in the Bloom Island document.

2. Open Day-Lily.gif in Photoshop.

3. Click Select on the menu bar, click Color Range, then verify that the Image option button is selected and that the Fuzziness text box is set to 0.

4. Click the white background of the image in the Color Range dialog box, select the Invert check box, then click OK.

5. Click the Move Tool on the toolbox, then drag the selection to the Bloom Island document.

6. Drag the top of the day lily to 30 H/90 V.

7. Set the Opacity setting to 25% on the Layers palette.

8. Click the Layers palette list arrow, then click Layer Properties.

9. Type **Day Lily** in the Name text box, then click OK.

10. Make Day-Lily.gif the active document, then close this document.

11. Save your work, then compare your document to Figure A-9.

You opened an optimized file in Photoshop, dragged it into the Bloom Island document, adjusted the opacity setting, then renamed the layer.

CREATE A BUTTON FOR A WEB PAGE

What You'll Do

In this lesson, you'll create and name a layer in ImageReady, then use the Rounded Rectangle Tool to create a button based on the style you select on the tool options bar. You'll also add type to the button, apply a style to the type, and then link the type and button layers.

Learning About Buttons

A **button** is a graphical interface that helps visitors navigate through and interact with a Web site with ease. ImageReady provides several ways for you to create and use buttons. You can create your own shape, apply a preformatted button style, or import a button you've already created. You can assign a variety of actions to a button so that the button reacts to changes initiated by the visitor.

Creating a Button

You can create a button by drawing a shape with a shape tool, such as a rectangle, on a layer. After you create the shape, you can add interest to it by applying a color or style, and then you can add some text that will explain what will happen when it's clicked.

Saving a file for the Web and defining Web output

Before you can use Photoshop or ImageReady files on the Web, you must first convert them to the HTML format. You can convert all of the slices in ImageReady to HTML by clicking Edit on the menu bar, pointing to Copy HTML Code, and then clicking For All Slices. ImageReady stores the HTML code on the Clipboard so that you can then paste it into your Web page using an HTML editor. Photoshop and ImageReady use default settings when you save optimized images for the Web. You can specify the output settings for HTML format, your HTML editor, and the way image files, background files, and slices are named and saved. To change the output settings in Photoshop, click the Optimize Menu list arrow in the Save For Web dialog box, then click Edit Output Settings. In ImageReady, click an option you want to change from the Output Settings command on the File menu.

QUICKTIP

You can add a link to a button so that when you click it, a new Web page will appear.

Applying a Button Style

You can choose from 29 predesigned ImageReady button styles on the Styles palette, or you can create your own. To apply a style to a button, you must first create a button shape. After you create the button, double-click one of the button styles on the Styles palette, which appear as thumbnails, or click a style name from the Set style for new layer list arrow on the tool options bar. Figure A-10 shows the button styles on the ImageReady Styles palette. You can also modify a button with a style already applied to it by first clicking one of the shape tools, and then choosing a new style from the Styles palette.

QUICKTIP

Having both Photoshop and ImageReady open will significantly tax your computer's resources. When you're primarily working in ImageReady, it's a good idea to close any unnecessary programs (including Photoshop) and update your files frequently.

FIGURE A-10
Button styles in ImageReady

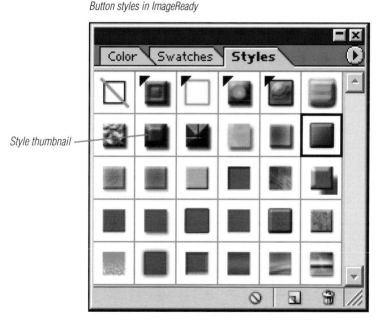

Style thumbnail

Create a button

1. Jump to ImageReady.

2. Click the Zoom Tool on the toolbox.

3. Click the Fit on Screen button on the tool options bar.

4. If necessary, display the rulers in pixels, and view Guides and Extras.

5. Click the Day Lily layer on the Layers palette, if necessary.

6. Click the Create a new layer button on the Layers palette.

   A new layer, Layer 1, appears at the top of the Layers palette.

7. Double-click the name Layer 1 on the Layers palette, type **QuickGift Button**, then press [Enter] (Win) or [return] (Mac).

8. Click the Rounded Rectangle Tool on the toolbox.

   | TIP Look under the Rectangle Tool if the Rounded Rectangle Tool is hidden.

9. Click the Set style for new layer list arrow on the tool options bar, then click Button-Stone, as shown in Figure A-11.

10. Drag the pointer from 30 H/320 V to 120 H/360 V.

    You created the shape that will be used for a button.

You jumped from Photoshop to ImageReady, verified settings, created a new layer, selected the Rounded Rectangle Tool, selected a button style on the tool options bar, and then created a button.

FIGURE A-11
Button style selected from style list

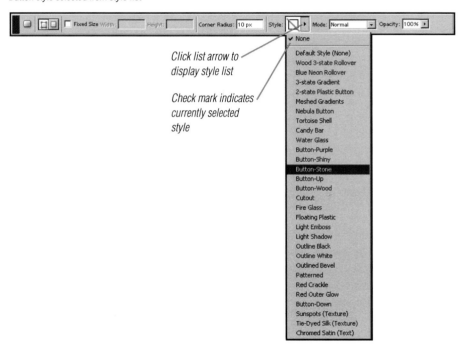

Click list arrow to display style list

Check mark indicates currently selected style

FIGURE A-12
Button created in document

Blue text baseline
indicates that
layer is active and
can be edited

Shape layer is linked
to type layer

1. Click the Type Tool on the toolbox. T
2. Click the button shape at approximately 40 H/345 V.
3. Click the Set the text color list arrow on the tool options bar, then select the third color swatch from the left in the third row from the bottom.
4. Click the Set the font family list arrow on the tool options bar, then click Arial, if necessary.
5. Click the Set the font size list arrow on the tool options bar, then click 18 px, if necessary.
6. Type **QuickGift**.
7. Click the Move Tool on the toolbox, then center the type on the button, if necessary.
8. Click the Add a layer style button on the Layers palette, then click Drop Shadow.
9. Click the Indicates if layer is linked button on the QuickGift Button (shape) layer. See Figure A-12.

   The type and button shape layers are linked.
10. Save your work.

You added type to a button, applied a style to it, and then linked the QuickGift type layer and the button shape layer.

CREATE SLICES IN A DOCUMENT

What You'll Do

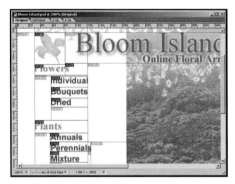

 In this lesson, you'll view the existing slices in the Bloom Island document, create slices around the Flowers and Plants type, resize a slice, and assign a Web address to the slice. You'll also use the New Layer Based Slice command on the Layer menu to create a new slice from the Day Lily layer on the Layers palette.

Understanding Slices

Using ImageReady, you not only have the ability to work with layers, but you can divide an image into unlimited smaller sections, or slices. ImageReady uses slices to determine the appearance of special effects in a Web page. A slice is a rectangular section of an image that you can use to apply features, such as rollovers and links, and can be created automatically or by using any marquee tool or the Slice Tool.

QUICKTIP

A slice is rectangular, even if you create it using an elliptical marquee.

Using Slices

ImageReady uses two kinds of slices: a **user-slice**, which you create, and an **auto-slice**, which ImageReady creates in response to your user-slice. You can use the Slice Tool to create a slice by dragging the pointer around an area. Every time you

Creating an image map

In addition to assigning a Web address (URL) to a slice, you can select an area in a document and assign it a Web address. This area, known as a hotspot, is invisible to the user, just as a slice is. When you click the hotspot, the browser opens a different Web page. The areas that link to different Web pages are known collectively as an **image map**. Unlike a slice, an image map can be a circle, rectangle, or polygon. You can create an image map in ImageReady by selecting the Rectangle Image Map Tool, the Circle Image Map Tool, or the Polygon Image Map Tool from the toolbox. Use any of these tools to create a selection, click the Image Map palette tab, then type a Web address in the URL text box. When you position the mouse over the hotspot in your browser, the Web address appears on the status bar.

create a slice, ImageReady automatically creates at least one auto-slice, which fills in the area around the newly created slice. ImageReady automatically numbers user- and auto-slices and updates the numbering according to the location of the new user-slice. User-slices have a solid line border, auto-slices have a dotted line border, and selected slices have a yellow border. A selected user-slice contains a bounding box and sizing handles. You can resize a slice by dragging a handle to a new location, just as you scale an image in Photoshop.

QUICKTIP

When two slices overlap, a **subslice** is automatically created.

Learning About Slice Components

By default, a slice consists of the following components:
- A colored line that helps you identify the slice type.
- An overlay that dims the appearance of the unselected slices.

- A number that helps you identify each individual slice.
- A symbol that helps you determine the type of slice.

Identifying and Adjusting Slice Attributes

You can adjust slice attributes by clicking Slices under the Preferences command on the Edit menu. Figure A-13 shows slice preferences. You can choose whether to display slice lines and numbers and symbols. You can also specify line color and

FIGURE A-13
Preferences dialog box

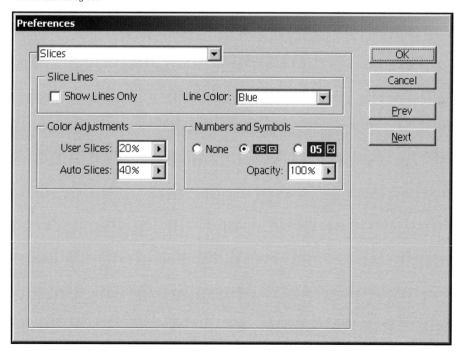

number and symbol opacity. Slice numbering changes as you add or delete slices. Each user-slice contains a symbol indicating if it is an image slice or a layer-based slice, if the slice is linked, or if it includes a rollover effect. See Table A-2 to see the symbols used to identify user slices.

QUICKTIP

It doesn't matter which layer, if any, is active when you create slices using the Slice Tool or the marquee tools.

Using a Layer-Based Slice
In addition to drawing a slice using the Slice Tool, you can use the New Layer Based Slice command on the Layer menu to create a slice from a layer on the Layers palette. This is an easy way of creating a slice *without* having to draw an outline.

Creating a Layer-Based Slice
Creating a layer-based slice automatically surrounds the image on the layer with a slice, which can be useful if you want to create a slice quickly or if you want a large slice. ImageReady updates the slice whenever you modify the layer or its content. For example, the slice automatically adjusts if you move its corresponding layer on the Layers palette, or you erase pixels on the layer.

QUICKTIP

To delete a layer-based slice, user-slice, or auto-slice, select the slice, then press [Delete] (Win) or [delete] (Mac) or click Slices on the menu bar, then click Delete Slice.

TABLE A-2: User Slice Symbols

symbol	used to identify
	Image slice
	Layer-based slice
	No image slice
	Slice containing a rollover

Using the Slice Palette

The Slice palette, shown in Figure A-14, is grouped with two other Web function palettes in ImageReady. You activate the palettes just as you do in Photoshop by clicking the tab of the palette you want to use. You use the features on the Slice palette to assign individual settings, features, and effects to the slices you've created in your document. For example, you could set a slice to initiate an action, such as opening another Web page or an e-mail response window when a user clicks the slide on a Web page.

Assigning a Web Address to a Slice

You can assign a Web page to a selected slice by typing its Uniform Resource Locater (URL) in the URL text box. The URL is the Web page's address that appears in the Address (Internet Explorer) or Location (Netscape) text box in your browser. You can designate how that Web page will be displayed in your browser by choosing one of the options on the Target list.

FIGURE A-14
Slice palette

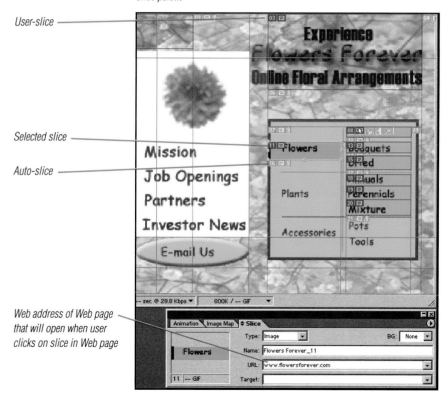

User-slice

Selected slice

Auto-slice

Web address of Web page that will open when user clicks on slice in Web page

Create a slice using the Slice Tool

1. Click the Zoom Tool on the toolbox. 🔍

2. Click the document at 50 H/200 V until the zoom percentage is 200%. 🔍

3. Click the Slice Tool on the toolbox. 🔪

   The existing slices in the document are visible, and the document colors appear faded.

   > TIP You can also create a slice by creating a selection with any marquee tool, clicking Select on the menu bar, then clicking Create Slice from Selection.

4. Drag the pointer around the Flowers type (from approximately 30 H/140 V to 120 H/160 V). 🔪

5. Drag the pointer around the Plants type (from approximately 30 H/235 V to 80 H/255 V), then compare your slices to Figure A-15. 🔪

You viewed the existing slices in the Bloom Island document, and created a slice for Flowers and a slice for Plants.

FIGURE A-15
New slices added to document

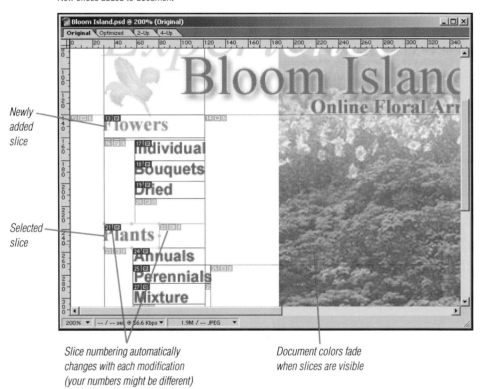

Newly added slice

Selected slice

Slice numbering automatically changes with each modification (your numbers might be different)

Document colors fade when slices are visible

FIGURE A-16
New layer-based slice

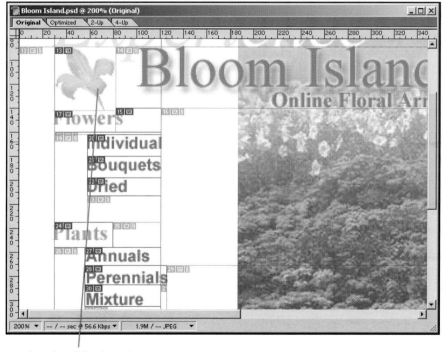

Layer-based slice does not
display sizing handles

1. Click the Day Lily layer on the Layers palette.
2. Click Layer on the menu bar, click New Layer Based Slice, then compare your slice to Figure A-16.

   A new slice surrounds the Day Lily layer object.

   > **TIP** You can also create a layer-based slice by right-clicking (Win) or [control] clicking (Mac) the layer, and then clicking New Layer Based Slice.

You made the Day Lily layer active on the Layers palette, then created a slice.

Resize a slice

1. Click the Slice Select Tool on the toolbox.

   TIP Look under the Slice Tool to find the Slice Select Tool. You can also press and hold [Shift], then press [K] to select the Slice Select Tool.

2. Click the Plants slice.

3. Drag the right-middle sizing handle to 120 H, compare your slice to Figure A-17, then release the mouse button. ←┃→

   TIP Because a layer-based slice is fitted to pixels on the layer, it does not contain sizing handles when you select it.

You resized the Plants slice.

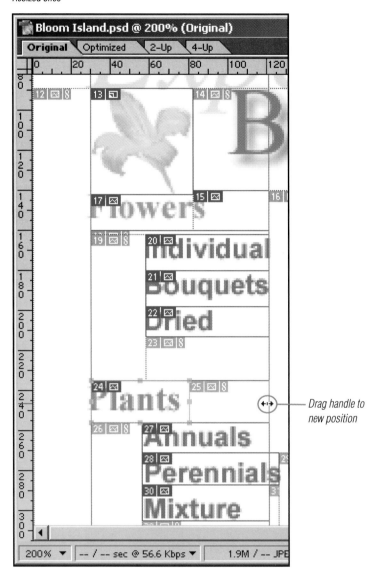

FIGURE A-17
Resized slice

Drag handle to new position

Web address assigned to slice

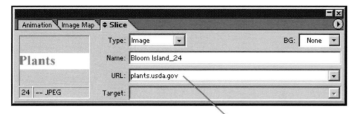

Type Web address here

FIGURE A-19
Deselected slices

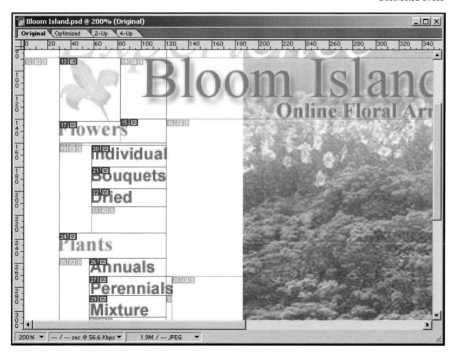

Assign a Web address to a slice

1. Click the Slice palette tab. [Slice]

2. Type **plants.usda.gov** in the URL text box, then compare your Slice palette to Figure A-18.

   I TIP   Your slice numbers might vary.

3. Click Select on the menu bar, then click Deselect Slices to deselect the Plants slice.

   TIP   To hide slices in your document, click the Toggle Slices Visibility button on the toolbox, or click View on the menu bar, point to Show, then click Slices.

4. Save your work, then compare your document to Figure A-19.

You assigned a Web address to a slice using the Slice palette, then deselected the slice.

Lesson 4   Create Slices in a Document

CREATE A ROLLOVER EFFECT

What You'll Do

In this lesson, you'll use the Slice Select Tool to select a slice, make the corresponding type layer active on the Layers palette, view the Rollovers palette, and then create a new Over state. You'll also change the font color of the Over state and preview the rollover effect in the document.

Learning About Rollovers

You might have noticed in your own Web surfing that user-initiated actions have become standard features in Web page design. Web sites that contain many interactive features are more interesting and useful to users. How you introduce and present your content is important to maintaining your visitors' interest, and ultimately, the amount of time they spend viewing your Web site. A rollover is one of the easiest features you can add to a Web page. You can use **rollovers** to respond to a user's action, such as clicking or pointing to (rolling on) an area in your Web page. The change in the Web page can serve as a navigational aid, or it can provide additional choices to the user.

Making Rollovers Happen

The activity of the pointer determines the appearance, or **state**, of the rollover. You can add and modify states on the Rollovers palette. The Rollovers palette is a live storyboard of the image's journey as you first position the pointer on the image, click it, then leave the image.

Learning About Rollover States

You can add the following states to the Rollovers palette: Normal, Over, Down, Click, Out, Up, and None. By default, every slice you create has a Normal state. The Normal state is how an image appears when it is inactive and without any user intervention. Most rollovers have Normal,

Over, and Down states. You can create a rollover out of images of almost any size, and you can control the appearance of each state by using tools and applying styles to its corresponding layer on the Layers palette. After a rollover is created, you can change the type of rollover effect by double-clicking the rollover state on the Rollovers palette. When you do this, the Rollover State Options dialog box opens. Click the type of rollover you want, then click OK. Figure A-20 shows several states on the Rollovers palette with different effects applied to them, and the Rollover State Options dialog box.

QUICKTIP

Because layer-based slices are automatically updated when you alter the layer, they offer the most flexibility when you use them to create rollovers.

Previewing Rollover Effects

You can preview the effects of a rollover in ImageReady or in your browser. To obtain immediate feedback on your rollover actions, click the Preview Document button on the toolbox, then move your mouse in the document, and observe the rollover behavior. For a complete review of how the rollover works, you can also click the Preview in Default Browser button on the toolbox. Your browser will open the document in an optimized format and display relevant HTML code in a box below the image. Exit your browser window when you have completed your rollover test. You can test the rollover in both Internet Explorer and Netscape Navigator, assuming you have both programs loaded on your computer.

FIGURE A-20
Rollover states

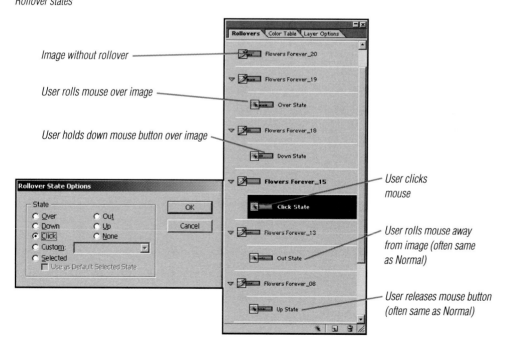

Image without rollover

User rolls mouse over image

User holds down mouse button over image

User clicks mouse

User rolls mouse away from image (often same as Normal)

User releases mouse button (often same as Normal)

Create a rollover state

1. Click the Hand Tool on the toolbox.
2. Drag the document down to the lower-left corner so that the Jobs type is visible.
3. Click the Slice Select Tool on the toolbox.
4. Click the Jobs slice.
5. Click the Indicates a layer set arrow for the Type Layers layer set on the Layers palette.
6. Click the JOBS layer on the Layers palette.
7. Click the Rollovers tab, if necessary.
8. Click the Create rollover state button on the Rollovers palette, then compare your Rollover and Layers palettes to Figure A-21.

   TIP When you create a rollover, you must select the layer on the Layers palette where you want the rollover effect to occur.

9. Click Layer on the menu bar, point to Layer Style, then click Color Overlay.

   The type in the Over state and in the document becomes the default color (red), or the last color selected in the Color Overlay palette.

10. Click the Set color of overlay list arrow on the Color Overlay palette, then click the sixth swatch from the left on the seventh row, as shown in Figure A-22.

You selected the Jobs slice and made the JOBS layer active on the Layers palette. You created a new Over state, and then changed its appearance by applying a new color to it.

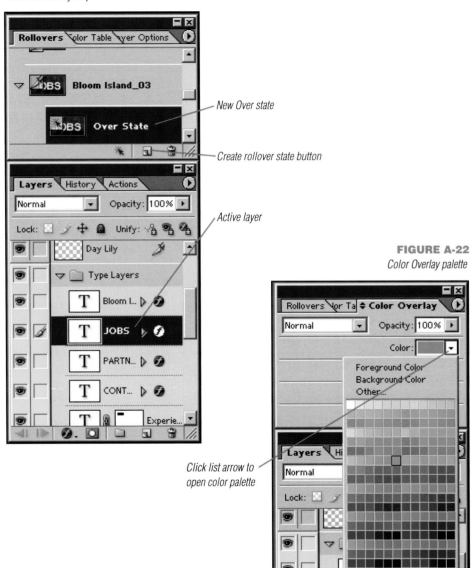

FIGURE A-21
Rollovers and Layers palettes

New Over state

Create rollover state button

Active layer

FIGURE A-22
Color Overlay palette

Click list arrow to open color palette

— New color of Over
   state type

Preview a rollover

1. Click the Rollovers tab, then compare your palette to Figure A-23.

2. Click the Zoom Tool on the toolbox. 🔍

3. Press and hold [Alt] (Win) or [option] (Mac), then click the document so that the zoom percentage is 100%. 🔍

4. Click the Toggle Slices Visibility button on the toolbox. 🔲

   The individual slices are no longer visible in the document.

   TIP   The Toggle Slices Visibility button remains on until you click it again to turn it off.

5. Click the Bloom Island_03 state on the Rollovers palette.

6. Click the Preview Document button on the toolbox. 🖑

7. Roll the mouse over Jobs in the document, then compare your document to Figure A-24. 🖑

   The Jobs type changes from white to green when the mouse rolls over it.

8. Click the Cancel Preview (Esc) button on the tool options bar. 🚫

9. Save your work, then close the Bloom Island document *leaving ImageReady open.*

You used the Preview Document button to preview the rollover effect in the document.

FIGURE A-24
Rollover preview in ImageReady

Type changes color
when mouse rolls
over it

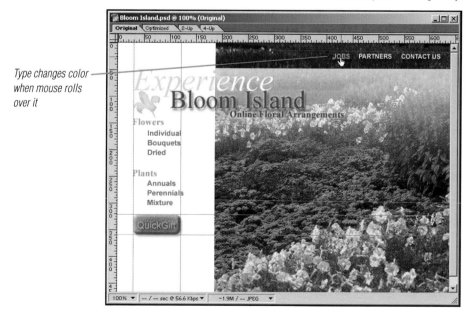

CREATE AND PLAY
BASIC ANIMATION

What You'll Do

 In this lesson, you'll create a rollover for the Rose layer. You'll also create animation frames. For each newly created frame, you'll modify the layers on the Layers palette by hiding and showing them, and changing their opacity, which will result in an animation sequence. You'll also play the animation in your document, and preview the animation in your browser.

Understanding Animation

You can use nearly any type of graphics image to create interesting animation effects in ImageReady. You can move objects in your document or overlap them so that they blend into one another. Once you place the images that you want to animate in a document, you can determine when and how you want the animation to play. If you want your users to initiate the animation, you can create different animations for each rollover state that you create on the Rollovers palette.

Creating Animation on the Animation Palette

Remember that animation is nothing more than a series of still images displayed rapidly. The Animation palette displays a thumbnail of the animation image in each frame. A **frame** is an individual image that is used in animation. When you create a frame on the Animation palette, you create a duplicate of the current frame, and can then modify it as desired. The layers that

are visible on the Layers palette appear in the selected frame, and thus, in the animation. Here's all that's involved in creating animation:

- Place images on layers in the document.
- Hide all but one layer.
- Duplicate the frame, turn off the displayed layer, then turn on the layer you want to see.

Animating Images

If you look at the Layers palette in Figure A-25, you'll see that there are images on two layers. The Animation palette contains two frames: one for each of the layers. When frame 1 is selected, the man appears in the document; when frame 2 is selected, the woman appears. When the animation is played, the images of the man and woman alternate in the document.

Moving and Deleting Frames

To move a frame to a different spot, click the frame in the Animation palette, and drag it to a new location. To select contiguous frames, press and hold [Shift], and then click the frames you want to include. To select noncontiguous frames, press and hold [Ctrl] (Win) or [command] (Mac), and then click the frames you want to include. You can delete a frame by clicking it in the Animation palette, then dragging it to the Deletes selected frames button on the Animation palette.

Looping the Animation

You can set the number of times the animation plays by clicking the Selects looping options list arrow on the Animation palette, then clicking Once, Forever, or Other. When you select Other, the Set Loop Count dialog box opens, where you can enter the loop number you want.

Previewing the Animation

You can preview the animation in a variety of ways:

- You can use the buttons on the bottom of the Animation palette. When you click the Plays/stops animation button, the animation plays.
- You can also view the animation as it occurs for the user by clicking the Preview Document button on the toolbox

and then initiating the animation based on the rollover state you selected.

- You can preview and test the animation as it functions in your browser by clicking the Preview in Default Browser button on the toolbox.

QUICKTIP

You can change the size of the Rollovers palette and Animation palette thumbnails by clicking the palette list arrow, clicking Palette Options, clicking a thumbnail size, and then clicking OK. You can select a different-sized thumbnail for each palette.

FIGURE A-25
Sample of basic animation

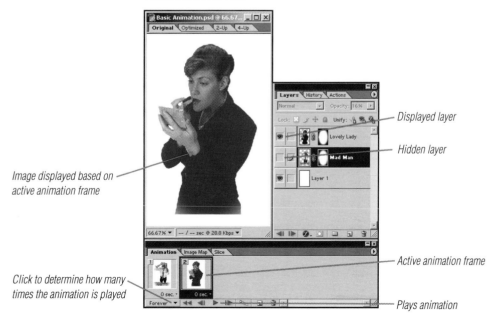

Displayed layer

Hidden layer

Image displayed based on active animation frame

Active animation frame

Click to determine how many times the animation is played

Plays animation

Create a rollover state

1. Open PS Bonus A-2.psd in ImageReady, then save it as **Rose Morph**.
2. Click the Indicates layer visibility button on the Stems layer on the Layers palette.
3. Click the Indicates layer visibility button on the Little Rose layer on the Layers palette.
4. Click the Toggle Slices Visibility button on the toolbox.
5. Click the Create rollover state button on the Rollovers palette.

   A new Over state is created on the Rollovers palette, as shown in Figure A-26.
6. Click the Toggle Slices Visibility button on the toolbox.

   TIP You can create different animations for each rollover state.

You created a new Over state on the Rollovers palette, and then used the Toggle Slices Visibility button to hide the slices.

FIGURE A-26

New Over state

FIGURE A-27

Frames created on Animation palette

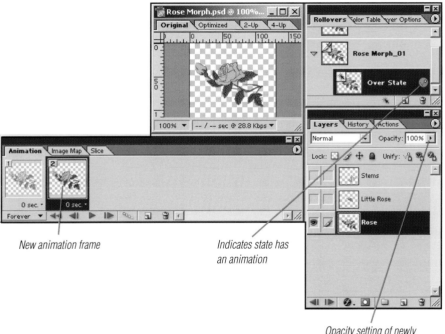

New animation frame

*Indicates state has
an animation*

*Opacity setting of newly
created animation frame*

1. Click the Animation palette tab.

   | Animation |

2. Adjust the opacity setting of the Rose layer to 50% on the Layers palette.

   The opacity of the active layer changes.

3. Click the Duplicates current frame button on the Animation palette.

   A new Animation frame is created and is now the active frame.

4. Adjust the opacity setting of the Rose layer to 100%, then compare your Animation palette to Figure A-27.

5. Click the Duplicates current frame button on the Animation palette.

6. Click the Indicates layer visibility button on the Rose layer on the Layers palette.

7. Click the Stems layer to make it active, then click the Indicates layer visibility button on the Layers palette for this layer.

   The content from the Stems layer appears in frame 3 of the Animation palette.

You created an animation frame, duplicated existing frames, and adjusted the visibility of the frames.

Adjust animation frames

1. Set the opacity setting of the Stems layer to 30%.

   The opacity of the active layer is changed to 30%.

2. Click the Duplicates current frame button on the Animation palette, then adjust the opacity setting of the Stems layer to 100%.

   The content of the new animation frame has an opacity of 100%.

3. Click the Duplicates current frame button on the Animation palette.

4. Click the Indicates layer visibility button on the Stems layer to hide it.

5. Click the Little Rose layer to make it active, then click the Indicates layer visibility button on the Layers palette for this layer.

6. Adjust the opacity setting to 50%.

7. Click the Duplicates current frame button on the Animation palette, then adjust the opacity setting of the Little Rose layer to 100%. Compare your screen to Figure A-28.

You adjusted the opacity of frames using the Layers palette.

FIGURE A-28
Completed animation frames

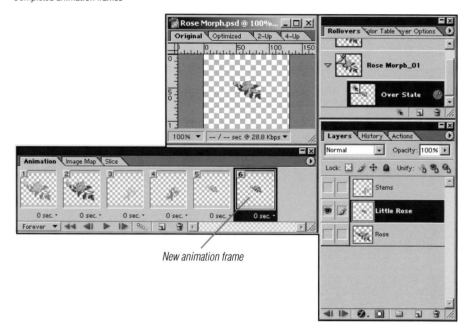

New animation frame

FIGURE A-29

Animation displayed in browser

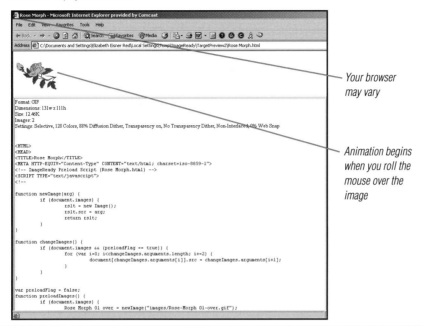

Your browser may vary

Animation begins when you roll the mouse over the image

TABLE A-3: Animation Tools

tool	tool name	description
Forever ▼	Selects looping options	Determines how many times the animation plays.
◀◀	Selects first frame	Makes the first frame in the palette active.
◀|	Selects previous frame	Makes the previous frame in the palette active.
▶	Plays/stops animation	Plays the animation.
■	Plays/stops animation	Stops the animation.
|▶	Selects next frame	Makes the next frame to the right in the palette active.
▦	Tweens animation frames	Creates frames in slight increments.

Lesson 6 Create and Play Basic Animation

Play animation in the document and browser

1. Click the Plays/stops animation button on the Animation palette. ▶

   The Plays/stops animation button changes its appearance depending on the current state of the animation. See Table A-3 for a description of the buttons in the Animation palette.

2. Click the Plays/stops animation button on the Animation palette. ■

   The animation stops, displaying the currently active frame.

3. Save your work.

4. Click the Preview Document button on the toolbox. 🖑

5. Move the pointer over the image, view the animation, then move the pointer off the document. 🖑

   The animation begins when you roll the mouse over the image and stops when you roll it off the image.

6. Click the Preview in Default Browser button on the toolbox, then compare your preview to Figure A-29. 🖳

7. Move the pointer over the image, then move the pointer off the image. 🖑

8. Close your browser.

   TIP The animation might play differently in ImageReady than in your browser, which is why it is important to preview your files on as many different systems as possible.

You played the animation in your document, then viewed it in a browser.

ADD TWEENING AND FRAME DELAY

What You'll Do

In this lesson, you'll add tweening to animation and adjust the frame delay for a frame on the Animation palette.

Understanding Tweening

To create animation, you assemble a series of frames, then play them quickly to create the illusion of continuous motion. Each frame represents a major action point. Sometimes the variance between actions creates erratic or rough motion. To blend the motion *in between* the frames, you can tween your animation. **Tweening** adds frames that change the action in slight increments from one frame to the next. In traditional animation (before computer-generated images), an artist known as an *inbetweener* hand-drew the frames that linked major action frames (at 24 frames per second!).

Using Tweening on the Animation Palette

You can add tweening to a frame by clicking the Tweens animation frames button on the Animation palette, and then entering the number of in-between frames you want in the Tween dialog box. You can choose whether you want the tweening to affect all layers or just the selected layer, and if you want the image to change position or opacity. You can also specify the frame on which you want the tweening to start, and specify the number of frames to add in between the frames (you can add up to 100 frames in a single tween). Figure A-30 shows a two-frame animation after five tween frames were added. The opacity of the man is 100% in the first frame and 0% in the last frame. Adding five tween frames causes the two images to blend into each other smoothly, or **morph** (metamorphose).

> **QUICKTIP**
>
> You can select contiguous frames and apply the same tweening settings to them simultaneously.

Understanding Frame Delays

When you create frames on the Animation palette, ImageReady automatically sets the **frame delay**, the length of time that each frame appears. You can set the delay time in whole or partial seconds by clicking the Selects frame delay time list arrow below each frame. You can set the frame delay you want for each frame, or you can select several frames and apply the same frame delay to them.

Setting Frame Delays

To change the delay for a single frame, click a frame, click the Selects frame delay time list arrow, then click a time. To select contiguous frames, press and hold [Shift], click the frames you want to include, and then click the Selects frame delay time list arrow on *any* of the selected frames. To select noncontiguous frames, press and hold [Ctrl] (Win) or [command] (Mac), click the frames you want to include, then click the Selects frame delay time list arrow on any of the selected frames.

FIGURE A-30
Animation palette

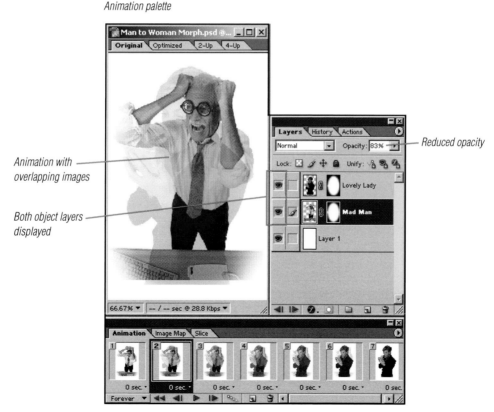

Animation with overlapping images

Both object layers displayed

Reduced opacity

Tween animation frames

1. Click the Cancel Preview (Esc) button on the tool options bar.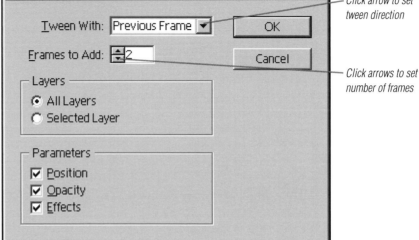

2. Click the Over State on the Rollovers palette.

3. Click frame 3 on the Animation palette.

4. Click the Tweens animation frames button on the Animation palette.

5. Adjust the settings in your Tween dialog box using Figure A-31 as a guide.

6. Click OK.

   Two additional frames are added after frame 2.

7. Click the Plays/stops animation button on the Animation palette, then view the animation.

8. Click the Plays/stops animation button on the Animation palette, then compare your palette to Figure A-32.

You used the Tweens animation frames button on the Animation palette to insert two new frames, then played the animation to view the results.

FIGURE A-31
Tween dialog box

Click arrow to set tween direction

Click arrows to set number of frames

FIGURE A-32
Tweening frames inserted

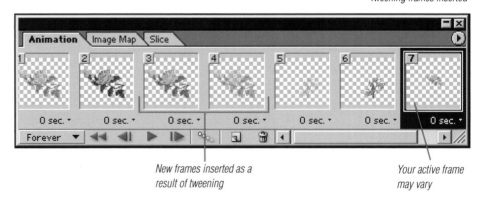

New frames inserted as a result of tweening

Your active frame may vary

Set frame delay

1. Click frame 2 on the Animation palette.
2. Click the Selects frame delay time list arrow at the bottom of the selected frame. ▣
3. Compare your frame delay menu to Figure A-33, then click 0.2.

   The frame delay for frame 2 changes to 0.2.
4. Click the Plays/stops animation button on the Animation palette, then view the animation. ▶
5. Click the Plays/stops animation button on the Animation palette. ▣
6. Click the Preview in Default Browser button on the toolbox. ▣
7. Move the pointer over the image to see the effect of the rollover, then close your browser. ☞

   > **TIP** Frame delays behave very differently in your browser than in ImageReady—be sure to preview them in your browser to ensure that they play the way you intend them to play.
8. Save your work.

You changed the frame delay for frame 2, then previewed the animation in ImageReady and in your browser.

FIGURE A-33
Frame delay menu

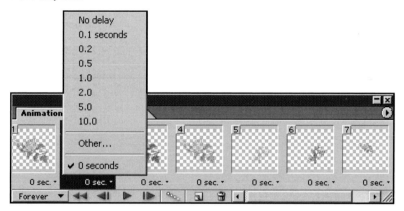

A local long-distance runners group is sponsoring a cross-country run for charity. The event will offer short cross-country races for all ages and fitness levels. You've volunteered to use your ImageReady skills to design an animation for their Web page that echoes the broad accessibility of the event.

1. Obtain the following images for the animation: an object that conveys the idea of movement and an obstacle it moves over, around, or through. You can also obtain a background and any other images, as desired. You can draw your own images, use the images that are available on your computer, scan print media, create images using a digital camera, or connect to the Internet and download images.

2. Create a new Photoshop document and save it as **Xtream Charity**.

3. Apply a color or style to the Background layer, then jump to ImageReady. (*Hint*: The Background layer in the sample has a Pattern Overlay style applied to it.)

4. Create at least two new states on the Rollovers palette.

5. Add animations to each of the states you created on the Rollovers palette. Make one a motion animation and the other a fade-out effect.

6. Tween each animation and add frame delays as necessary.

7. Preview the animation in your document and in your browser.

8. Save your work, then compare your screen to the sample shown in Figure A-34.

FIGURE A-34
Completed Project 1

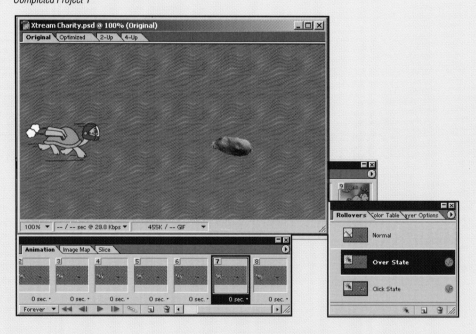

You've just been elected to the board of directors of a community access TV station. Each board member is expected to serve on at least one committee. You've chosen the Community Involvement Committee, and have been asked to design a snappy, numeric countdown animation that will introduce public service announcements.

1. Obtain images appropriate for a countdown. You can draw your own numbers, use the images that are available on your computer, scan print media, create images using a digital camera, or connect to the Internet and download images. You must include at least one other image, and can include any other images, as desired.

2. Create a new Photoshop document, then save it as **Countdown**.

3. Apply a color or style to the Background layer, add images as desired, and apply effects to them. (*Hint*: The Background layer in the sample has a Pattern Overlay style applied to it.)

4. Create at least three type layers with numbers for a countdown, and apply styles or filters to them as desired. (*Hint*: Each number in the sample has a duplicate with different opacities.)

5. Jump to ImageReady, then create a new rollover state.

6. Create an animation to the state you created on the Rollovers palette. Make the numbers move across the document and fade into one another.

7. Duplicate the last number so that it changes appearance at least twice.

8. Tween each animation and add frame delays as necessary.

9. Preview the animation in your document and in your browser.

10. Save Countdown as **Countdown Browser**, then adjust tweening and frame delays so that it plays perfectly in your Web browser.

11. Save your work, then compare your screen to the sample shown in Figure A-35.

FIGURE A-35
Completed Project 2

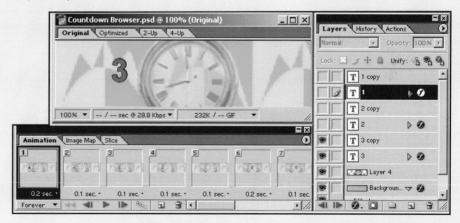

SECTION A

GETTING STARTED WITH ADOBE GOLIVE 6.0

1. Start GoLive and use the site window.

2. Understand the GoLive workspace.

3. Modify page properties.

4. Explore page views.

5. Publish a Web site.

6. Get Help.

SECTION A
GETTING STARTED WITH ADOBE GOLIVE 6.0

Introduction

Adobe GoLive is a Web site development tool that enables you to create Web pages and Web sites easily and manage them effectively. In addition to using GoLive to design, organize, and manage Web sites, you can use GoLive to create Web pages visually by dragging existing content into place and typing text where you want it to appear—GoLive writes the underlying HTML code for you.

Understanding Web Pages

Web pages are documents composed of **Hypertext Markup Language**—otherwise known as HTML code—that present text and images in a format that can be understood by a Web browser. The browser interprets a Web page's HTML and displays that interpretation in the browser window. When you see text on a Web page in a browser window, usually that text is actually contained in the Web page. When you see an image or other media, though, the page does not actually contain the image or media file—instead, it contains a reference to that file's location. Similarly, when you see a link on a Web page that takes

you to another Web page, the "link" is actually a reference in the HTML to the second page's location.

A Web site can contain multiple Web pages, with each page containing multiple file references and links. Keeping track of these relationships when you are developing a Web site can be a huge task. GoLive keeps this task manageable through the use of the site window, your main site organizational tool. Using the site window to move and rename a file will update all references to that file and in that file so that relationships remain intact.

Before pages can be viewed on the Web, the pages—and all of the linked pages and image files the pages reference—must be uploaded to a Web server. The path from a Web page to its referenced files must not change when it is uploaded to the Web server, or the references to images and linked pages will not work. Just as the site window maintains the relationships between files as you develop and edit your Web site, it also maintains those relationships for you when transferring files between the development site and a Web server.

Tools You'll Use

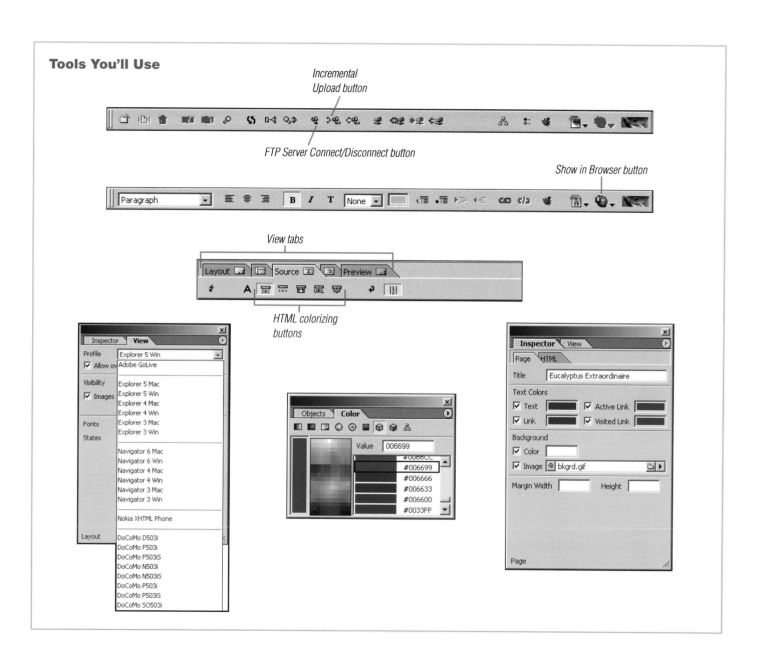

Incremental Upload button

FTP Server Connect/Disconnect button

Show in Browser button

View tabs

HTML colorizing buttons

START GOLIVE AND USE THE SITE WINDOW

What You'll Do

In this lesson, you'll start GoLive, open a Web site, review the site window, then open the home page of a Web site from the site window.

Starting GoLive and Viewing the Site Window's Files Tab

When starting GoLive, you are presented with options for opening a new page, a new site, or an existing GoLive page or site. When you open an existing GoLive site file (with the filename extension ".site"), the **site window** opens, with the **Files tab** in front. The Files tab in the site window is the tool you use to organize your Web site. By developing a habit of accessing your Web files through the Files tab in the site window, you will eliminate hours of tedious site management tasks.

Understanding the Site Window

The site window opens with the Files tab selected, listing all of the files in the site, including all of the Web pages that make up the site and any image and media files referenced in them. The home page of a site is in bold; in Figure A-1, the home page is the "index.html" file. The Status column displays either a check or a "bug" next to each Web page. A check indicates that all references to other pages and files in that page are intact. A **bug** indicates that there is at least one broken reference in the page. A file that is linked, directly or indirectly, to the home page is indicated by a diamond in the Used column. The Files tab also includes columns listing the file sizes, modification dates, and types of files.

A plus sign next to a folder indicates that the folder has files and/or folders within

it, similar to Windows Explorer and the folder arrows in Mac OS. Clicking the plus sign next to a folder will display the folders and files within it, hierarchically, while double-clicking the folder will display the contents of only that folder on the Files tab.

QUICKTIP

Web pages commonly use the extension ".htm" or ".html". GoLive defaults to the ".html" extension.

FIGURE A-1
Site window

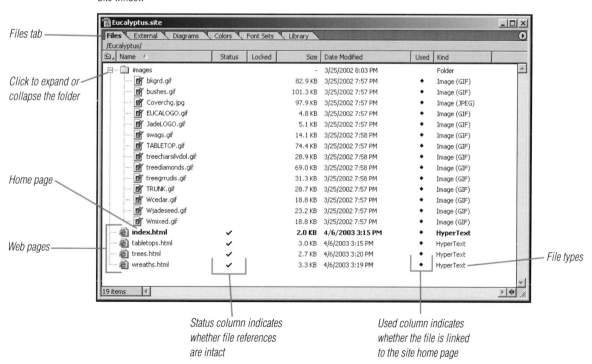

Open a GoLive site

1. Using the file management tool provided with your operating system, navigate to the drive and folder where your data files are stored, then copy the SectionA folder to the drive and folder where you are storing your work for this section.

   It is important to keep original copies of the data files for each section separate from your working data files, in case you need to start again from scratch while working through the lessons and exercises.

2. Click the Start button on the taskbar, point to Programs, point to the Adobe GoLive 6.0 (ENG) folder, then click Adobe GoLive 6.0 (ENG), as shown in Figure A-2.

   TIP If you are starting GoLive on a Macintosh, double-click the hard drive icon, double-click the Adobe GoLive 6.0 folder, then double-click the Adobe GoLive 6.0 program icon.

3. Click Open in the GoLive Open options dialog box, as shown in Figure A-3.

4. Navigate to the drive or folder where you are storing your work for this section, open the newly copied SectionA folder, then open the SiteA-1 folder.

5. Click Eucalyptus.site, as shown in Figure A-4, then click Open.

   TIP You can also open a site file by clicking File on the menu bar, then clicking Open.

You started GoLive, then opened an existing site.

FIGURE A-2
Starting GoLive 6.0 (Windows)

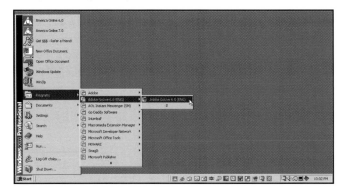

FIGURE A-3
Open options

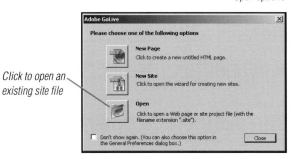

Click to open an existing site file

Site file

FIGURE A-4
SiteA-1 folder contents

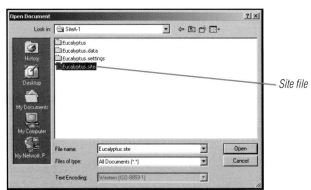

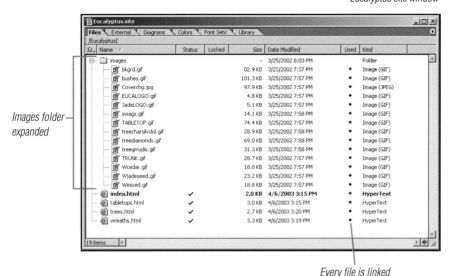

Images folder expanded

Every file is linked or referenced

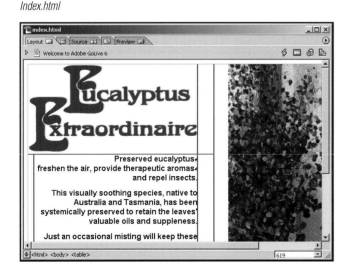

Explore the site window

1. In the site window, click the "+" sign (Win) or arrow (Mac) next to the images folder to expand the folder, as shown in Figure A-5.

2. Resize the window to view all of the Eucalyptus site files.

   Note that there is a diamond (Win) or circle (Mac) in the Used column for each image file, indicating that every file is used in the site.

3. Click the "-" sign (Win) or arrow (Mac) next to the images folder to collapse the folder.

You viewed the contents of a site using the site window.

Open the home page from the site window

1. Double-click index.html, the site's home page, in the site window. Compare the index.html document window that opens to Figure A-6.

You opened the site's home page from the site window.

UNDERSTAND THE GOLIVE WORKSPACE

What You'll Do

In this lesson, you'll customize the GoLive workspace.

Navigating the Workspace

The GoLive **workspace** includes the site window, a document window for each open Web page, and a variety of palettes for creating and editing your site. Within the document window for each Web page you'll find the Layout Editor. The **Layout Editor** is the environment in which you visually create and modify your Web pages. Figure A-7 shows the Layout Editor within the document window. The document window also includes tabs for the **Source Code Editor**, where you can directly edit or view the HTML of a Web page you are working on, and the **Layout Preview** view, where you can see how the page you are working on will appear in a browser.

The entire GoLive workspace is dynamic, in that palettes and toolbars respond to your selections as you work on a Web page. The toolbar at the top of the screen contains buttons and pop-up menus that change according to which window is open, how you are viewing a document, and what is selected within a document. For example, the toolbar changes depending on whether the site window or a document window is active. **Palettes** are windows that contain groups of properties (such as colors, or browser view types) that you can use to modify objects or views. They can be opened or closed from the Window menu, rearranged for a customized workspace, and hidden and displayed as you need them. By default the workspace contains the Inspector, the View palette, the Objects palette, and the Color palette, as shown in Figure A-7.

The **Inspector** is used to modify any object in the Layout Editor. Selecting an object causes the Inspector to display the properties of that object. For example, clicking the Page icon in the upper left corner of the Layout Editor causes the Inspector to become the Page Inspector. The **Page Inspector** enables you to edit the properties of the page. Similarly, selecting an image in the document window turns the Inspector into the **Image Inspector** for modifying the image's properties. The **View palette** enables you to simulate how your page will appear in different browsers. The **Objects palette** enables you to add objects such as tables, images, and text boxes to your page. The **Color palette** contains color libraries from which you can select colors to use in your Web page.

FIGURE A-7
GoLive workspace

Layout tab
Source tab
Preview tab

Objects palette
Color palette
Inspector
View palette

Document window

Customize the GoLive workspace

1. Click the Window menu, then click Eucalyptus.site to see changes in the toolbar.

2. Click the document window to return to the Layout Editor.

3. Click the Eucalyptus Extraordinaire logo on index.html to display the Image Inspector.

4. If necessary, click the Color tab in the small window at the top right of your screen to view the Color palette.

5. Click the Color tab and drag the Color palette to the Inspector window. Release the mouse button to place the Color palette in the Inspector window, as in Figure A-8.

   When the palette is dragged over a window, it has a rectangular outline, indicating you can drop it inside the window.

   > TIP Depending on which button is depressed on the Color palette toolbar, the appearance of your color palette may be different.

(continued)

FIGURE A-8
Color palette in the Inspector window

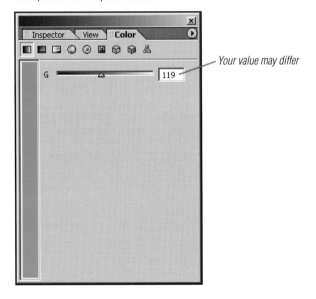

Your value may differ

6. Close the small window that contains the Objects palette.

7. Click and drag the Color tab outside of its window to the right side of the program window (Win) or screen (Mac) until you see the tab outline become vertical and positioned against the right edge of the window. Release the mouse button, then compare your screen to Figure A-9.

   The Color palette is now hidden.

8. Click the Color tab to show the Color palette, as in Figure A-10. Click it again to hide the palette.

9. Click Window on the menu bar, point to Workspace, then click Default Workspace to return the workspace to its original setup.

You customized the workspace, then returned the workspace to its default setup.

FIGURE A-10
Color palette visible

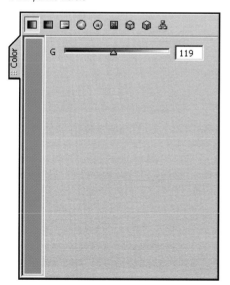

MODIFY PAGE PROPERTIES

What You'll Do

 In this lesson, you'll modify the page properties of a Web page. You will change the page title, modify the text colors on the page, change the page's background color, and add a background graphic.

Modifying Page Properties Using the Workspace

Web pages have properties that apply to the entire page, including title, background appearance, and text colors. You can use the Page Inspector, as shown in Figure A-11, to modify these properties.

The title of a Web page is the title displayed in the title bar when the page is being viewed. A page's title is not the page's filename (e.g., index.html)—it is embedded in its HTML code. In GoLive, you can change the title of a page in the Layout Editor or the Page Inspector, and the title embedded in the code will change as a result. The page title is important because it is the default name of a **bookmark** created in a browser when someone creates a Favorite (Internet Explorer) or a Bookmark (Netscape Navigator) while viewing the page on the Web. In addition, some Web search engines use page titles for ranking search results, where pages that include a searched word in the title are ranked above others.

Site colors

You can view the colors being used in a site by using the Site Color List in the Color palette (click the Site Color List button ⬚ to display the Site Color List). The Site Color List lists colors that have already been used and saved in your pages. Using colors that are on this list as you develop your Web site helps you maintain a consistent color scheme across the site. The Colors tab in the site window also lists site colors along with additional information, such as whether a color is Web safe and if it is currently being used. You can name colors in the site window for easy reference. To name a color using the site window Colors list, double-click the name of a listed color, then type the new name.

When creating a new Web page, you can set the default color of text, links, active links (text link color when being clicked), and visited links. Doing this simplifies page editing and keeps the colors on your page consistent, with less work on your part. Default page text colors can be overridden throughout your page, so you can still add other text colors where desired.

Web pages can contain a background color or graphic to visually enhance the page. The background color of a Web page in GoLive is white unless another color is specified, which can be done using the Color palette. While GoLive offers many color libraries, you will always want to use **Web colors** in your pages. Web colors (there are 216 of them) appear exactly the same

when viewed in any browser on any operating system; by only using Web colors, you maintain control over the colors seen by others on your Web site. In HTML code, colors are specified using an RGB value, such as #336699—but keeping track of six-digit RGB values is not a fun way to color! Fortunately, in GoLive, you can select colors from a color library's visual swatches as well as by RGB value.

When one of the 216 Web colors does not fit your needs for your Web site's background, you can use a background graphic instead. There are several considerations to use in choosing a background graphic, including file size and physical size. Background graphics should have a small file size so they do not stall the page's

loading. Background graphics physically smaller than the Web page will repeat, or tile, which is a feature you can use to reduce the file size of the background graphic and to create an interesting visual effect. For example, if you would like a background color that is not a Web color, you could use a single color graphic of just a few pixels as the background graphic, in any color you like. The graphic will tile the expanse of the page in the background. If you choose to use a background graphic, you should still select a background color in case the link to the graphic becomes broken, a browser is set not to view graphics, or someone with a slow connection gets to see "tiling" in action, with each graphic tile appearing one by one!

FIGURE A-11
Page Inspector

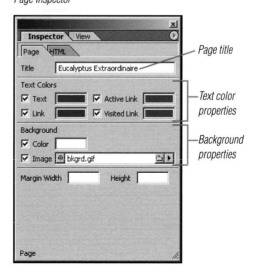

Modify the page title

1. Select the words "Welcome to Adobe GoLive 6" in the upper left corner of the Layout Editor.

2. Type **Eucalyptus Extraordinaire**, then compare your document to Figure A-12.

You changed the title of the Web page.

FIGURE A-12
Page title in Layout Editor

Page title

FIGURE A-13

Page Inspector with index.html page properties

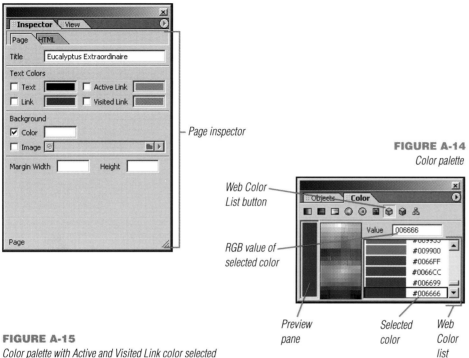

— Page inspector

FIGURE A-14

Color palette

Web Color List button

RGB value of selected color

Value 006666

#009955
#009900
#0066FF
#0066CC
#006699
#006666

Preview pane

Selected color

Web Color list

FIGURE A-15

Color palette with Active and Visited Link color selected

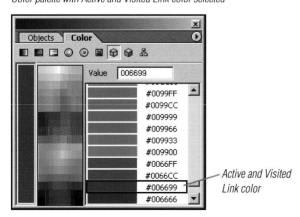

Value 006699

#0099FF
#0099CC
#009999
#009966
#009933
#009900
#0066FF
#0066CC
#006699
#006666

— Active and Visited Link color

1. If necessary, click the Color tab to show the Color palette.

2. Click the Page icon in the upper left corner of the document window. 📄

   The Inspector becomes the Page Inspector, as shown in Figure A-13.

   | TIP If the Inspector is not open or in front, double-click the Page icon.

   | TIP Macintosh users will see a ColorSync tab in the window in addition to the Inspector and View palette.

3. Click the Web Color List button to open the Web Color List on the Color palette. 🎨

4. In the Color Value field, type 006666, then press [Enter] (Win) or [return] (Mac). Compare your Color palette to Figure A-14.

5. Drag the color from the preview pane to the Page Inspector Text color field, then drag the same color to the Link color field.

6. In the Color palette, click the color just above the currently selected color, as shown in Figure A-15.

7. Drag the color from the preview pane to the Active Link color field, then drag the same color to the Visited Link color field.

You set the page text and link colors.

Change the background color of a page

1. Type **CCFFCC** in the Value field on the Color palette, then press [Enter] (Win) or [return] (Mac).

2. Drag the color from the Color palette preview pane to the Color field in the Page Inspector Background properties area. Compare your Page Inspector to Figure A-16.

3. Click the Color checkbox to deselect it and to return the background to white.

   TIP   In some browsers the default color is gray. To assure your background color is white in all browsers, specify the color white in the Inspector.

4. Scroll to the top of the Web Color List in the Color palette, click the white color swatch, then drag the new color from the Color palette preview pane to the Color field in the Page Inspector Background properties area.

You specified a new color for the background, and then reset the background color to white.

FIGURE A-16

Page Inspector with new background color

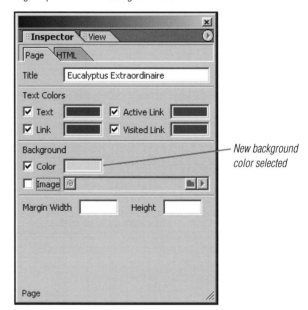

New background
color selected

FIGURE A-17

Page Inspector with index.html page properties modified

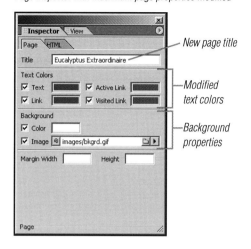

New page title

Modified text colors

Background properties

FIGURE A-18

Index.html with page properties modified

Page title

Background graphic

Text color

Link color

1. Click the Image checkbox in the Page Inspector.

2. Click the Browse button to the right of the image field.

3. Navigate to the drive and folder where you are storing your work for this section, open the SiteA-1 folder, open the Eucalyptus folder, open the images folder, then double-click bkgrd.gif.

   The image field displays the path from index.html to bkgrd.gif (images/bkgrd.gif), and an image of a eucalyptus tree is displayed in the background of index.html.

4. Compare your Page Inspector to Figure A-17 and compare your page to Figure A-18.

5. Click File on the menu bar, then click Save to save your changes.

You specified a background graphic, then saved the changes you made to the page properties.

EXPLORE PAGE VIEWS

What You'll Do

In this lesson, you'll preview index.html in various GoLive views and open it in a browser.

Previewing a Site with Layout Preview

Layout Preview, in the document window, displays your page in a way similar to a Web browser. In Layout Preview, you can test links and any animated graphics without opening your Web site in a browser. Clicking a link in Layout Preview will open the referenced page, allowing you to test links and to preview the entire site. Linked pages are opened in Layout Editor by default, just as pages are when opened from the site window. Since links are not active in Layout Editor, only Layout Preview, you can click the Preview tab to test a newly opened page's links.

QUICKTIP

The default page view can be changed in GoLive Preferences.

Previewing a Page with the View Palette

You can preview your page layout for several browsers, on several platforms and devices, in several versions, using the View palette in the Layout Editor (see Figure A-19). Although these views may not be exact, they are an approximation that may affect your pages' layout. Over the past few years, Web browsers have become much more consistent (thank goodness!), but there may still be differences. In addition, now there are browsers for wireless devices, which look very different from traditional Web browsers and are also included in the View palette. GoLive does a wonderful job of creating standardized HTML that keeps your pages consistent. Still, it is so simple to check how your page will appear using Layout Preview and the View palette, it's worth a look.

Viewing the Source Code

You can view the HTML source code generated in GoLive for a Web page by clicking on the Source tab in the document window. Although it may look scary at first glance, HTML's structure is rather simple. All HTML code is enclosed in brackets (< >). The code enclosed in a bracket is a **tag**. Most tags are "closed," in that they consist of two tags, an opening and a closing tag surrounding the text to be affected. A closing tag is identical to its opening tag, except that it is prefixed with a forward slash (/), and does not include attributes. **Attributes** are properties of the Web page, the same properties that you set in the GoLive Inspector. For example, in HTML code, the page title of index.html looks like this:

```
<title>Eucalyptus
Extraordinaire</title>
```

The Title tag does not have attributes. The Body tag, which encloses all of the page content, includes page attributes, and may look like this:

```
<body background="bkgrd.gif"
bgcolor="white"> .... </body>
```

There are hundreds of HTML tags; because you are using GoLive, you don't need to learn them all. However, making an effort to understand HTML will give you increased control over your pages and help you to resolve any unexpected results. Table A-1 describes the essential tags you will find in any Web page. You can also learn new tricks by viewing the HTML of Web pages that you find on the Internet. A little experience writing HTML will quickly give you an appreciation for the efficiency you gain using GoLive!

QUICKTIP

An opening tag and a closing tag are referred to as a tag, both individually and collectively.

QUICKTIP

To view the HTML in Web pages on the Internet, click View on the browser menu bar, then click Source (Internet Explorer) or Page Source (Netscape Navigator).

FIGURE A-19
View palette

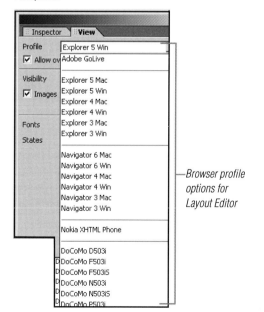

—*Browser profile options for Layout Editor*

TABLE A-1: Essential HTML tags

<html> ... </html>	The entire HTML document.
<head> ... </head>	The head of the HTML document contains information for the browser.
<title> ... </title>	The title of the HTML document, embedded in the HEAD tag.
<body> ... </body>	The content of the HTML document.
Attributes:	
Background	Background graphic
BGCOLOR	Background color
TEXT	Default text color
LINK	Default link color
ALINK	Default active link color
VLINK	Default visited link color
<p> ... </p>	A paragraph of text in the HTML document.

Viewing the source code in GoLive can be a little bit easier on the eyes if you use the colorizing buttons on the Source Code Editor toolbar, as shown in Figure A-20. The Colorize Detailed button is depressed by default when you open the Source Code Editor, showing all HTML items in color: for instance, tags are blue, attribute values are red, and hard returns are green. The Colorize Elements button enables you to see the code colorized by **element**, or type of HTML tag. Clicking the Colorize Media and Links button will colorize image file reference tags and page link tags. If you are checking links, you can click the Colorize

URLs button and all of the code will become black except the URLs (the paths to referenced files), which will be red. Clicking the Colorize Server Side Code button will highlight only code that performs a function on the server.

Viewing Your Pages in a Browser

You can confirm how your Web pages will look in the browsers installed on your computer before uploading them to a Web server. This is not quite as convenient as Layout Preview, but you can open a page in a browser without leaving GoLive using the

Show in Browser button. Clicking the Show in Browser button or list arrow enables you to open a page and one or more browsers in one step. Browsers installed on your computer can be added to the Show in Browser menu using GoLive Preferences.

QUICKTIP

If your pages include code not handled by Layout Preview (such as JavaScript or Shockwave animations), you must test this code in a browser to know if it works as planned.

FIGURE A-20
Source Code Editor

Colorize Detailed button

Colorize Elements button

Colorize Media and Links button

Colorize URLs button

Colorize Server Side Code button

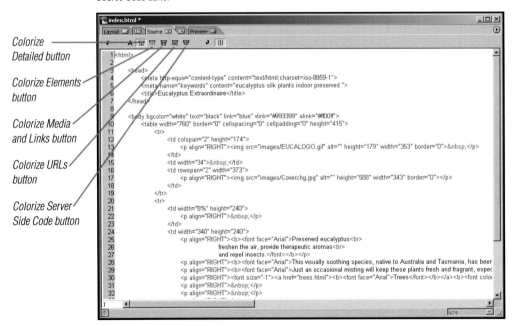

FIGURE A-21
Preview tab

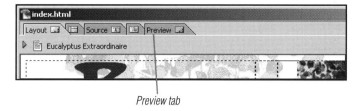

Preview tab

1. In the document window, click the Preview tab, as shown in Figure A-21.

2. Click on Wreaths & Swags at the bottom of the page.

   Wreaths.html opens in a new window and in Layout Editor view, as shown in Figure A-22.

   TIP Notice the text color change as the link becomes active.

3. Click the Close button in the document window to close wreaths.html.

You previewed the page in Layout Preview and tested one of the links on the page.

FIGURE A-22
Wreaths.html in Layout Editor

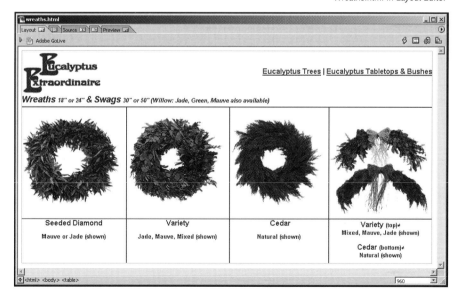

Lesson 4   Explore Page Views

Preview a page using the View palette

1. Click the Layout tab, as shown in Figure A-23, to return to the Layout Editor.

2. Click the View tab behind the Inspector palette to open the View palette.

3. Click the Profile list arrow on the View palette, then click Navigator 3 on the platform you are *not* using (Win or Mac). Compare your screen to Figure A-24 and notice how the text is different on an older browser.

4. Click the Profile list arrow again, then click Adobe GoLive.

You previewed your page in an older browser using the View palette.

Layout tab

Layout tab

FIGURE A-24
Text changes in older browsers

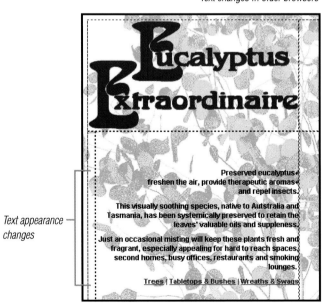

Text appearance changes

Source tab

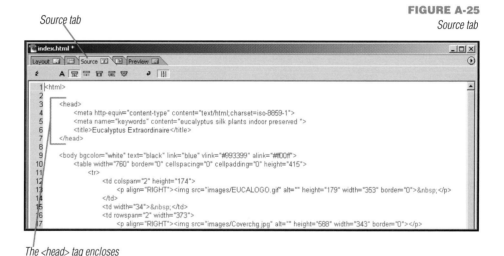

*The <head> tag encloses
information used by
browsers about the page*

1. Click the Source tab, as shown in Figure A-25, to view the HTML code for index.html.

2. Click the Colorize URLs button and notice how the appearance of the HTML code changes. ⊞

3. Click the Colorize Media and Links button and notice how the appearance of the code changes again. ⊞

4. Click the Colorize Detailed button to see HTML tags in blue and attribute values in red. ⊞

5. Find the opening and closing <head> tags at the top of the page, as shown in Figure A-25.

6. Click the Layout tab to return to the Layout Editor.

You viewed the HTML code for index.html, colorized the code for easier viewing, and located a set of HTML tags.

Add a browser to the Show in Browser menu

1. Click Edit on the menu bar, then click Preferences.

   TIP If you are not allowed to change your computer's Preferences, skip to the next set of steps.

2. In the left side of the window, click Browsers, as shown in Figure A-26.

   Click the Add button at the bottom of the window.

3. Navigate to a browser program file, click the file, then click Add to add it to the Show in Browser menu.

4. Click Done when you have finished adding browsers.

5. Click OK to close the Preferences window.

You added a browser to the Show in Browser menu.

FIGURE A-26

Preferences window

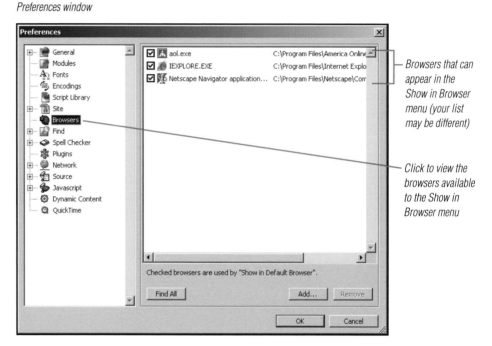

Browsers that can appear in the Show in Browser menu (your list may be different)

Click to view the browsers available to the Show in Browser menu

FIGURE A-27

Index.html in Internet Explorer

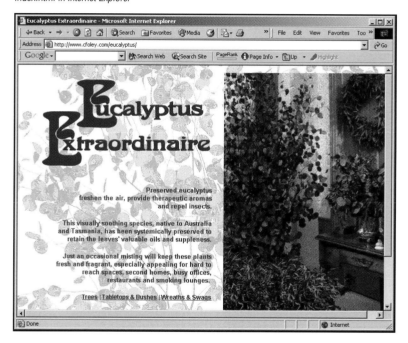

1. Click the Show in Browser list arrow. 🌐▾

   TIP If you click the Show in Browser button instead of the list arrow, the page will open in all of the browsers listed in the Show in Browser menu.

2. Click the name of one of the browsers on the menu to open index.html in that browser. Compare your screen to Figure A-27.

3. When you are through viewing the page, close your browser.

You viewed the Eucalyptus Extraordinaire page in a browser.

PUBLISH A WEB SITE

What You'll Do

 In this lesson, you will set up access to a Web server and upload the Eucalyptus site to that Web server.

Uploading Files to a Web Server

To make a Web site available to anyone browsing the Web, the site and all of its referenced files must reside on a Web server. A **Web server**, a computer dedicated to hosting Web sites, is connected to the Internet and configured with software to handle requests from browsers. Maintaining a Web server and its connections can be a complex and expensive endeavor. A large business or university may maintain its own server for hosting its Web site(s). Businesses that offer Web hosting provide services for the rest of us. Hosting services vary by the businesses that offer them. Your Internet Service Provider (ISP) may offer Web hosting as part of your Internet access package, giving you an account that allows you to upload files to a Web server it manages. An organization with a complex Web site or intranet might put its own server at a hosting company that would provide maintenance and network connections. Smaller Web sites can reside on a **virtual host**, where they share space on a Web server that a hosting company owns. In all cases, some method must be used to transfer—or upload— files from the development site to the Web server.

A standard method for transferring files from a development site to a Web server is through the use of **File Transfer Protocol (FTP)**. FTP is a "language" that enables you to access a remote server and send and receive files efficiently. The company hosting your Web site will provide you with an FTP server address and a username and password to use to gain access to the server. The hosting company may provide you with the path to the folder where your Web files should reside, or it is possible that submitting the username you are assigned may cause you to be directed automatically to the appropriate folder. Armed with this information, you can use FTP to upload Web files to the Web server, where the files can be viewed by anyone browsing the Web.

QUICKTIP

"Go live" and "publish" both refer to the first time a page or site is uploaded.

Connecting to the Server with GoLive

GoLive includes integrated FTP services. The FTP tab, found within the site window, is shown in Figure A-28. Although there are many FTP software packages available, there are advantages to using the GoLive FTP services for your GoLive sites. The most obvious reason is that you don't need to leave GoLive to access your server. The most important reason is that when you upload new files to your site on the Web server, GoLive will compare your site files' dates with the server files' dates, and upload only files that are new or modified since the last upload. Using this feature, called **incremental uploads**, will save you time and keep you organized. And if others are working on the same site, you won't accidently overwrite their files with your old ones!

You set up each server's FTP connection once in GoLive, and then you assign a site to a server connection. After that, incremental uploads are just a click away.

QUICKTIP

To FTP files created outside of GoLive, you can still use GoLive FTP services: click File on the menu bar, then click FTP Browser.

FIGURE A-28
FTP tab in the site window

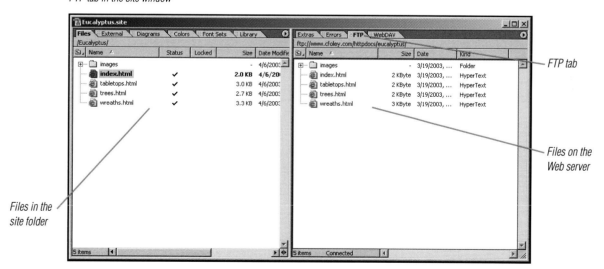

Files in the site folder

FTP tab

Files on the Web server

Set up an FTP connection to a Web server

1. Obtain the path to the folder where your Web site files should reside, and a username and password to use to gain access to the server; then continue with these steps.

2. Click Window on the menu bar, then click Eucalyptus.site to view the site window.

3. Click Edit on the menu bar, then click Servers.

   The Available Servers window appears.

4. Click the New Item button. █

   Clicking the New Item button makes the fields for FTP server information available.

5. Type a nickname for the server in the Nickname field.

   The nickname is a name you create to refer to the Web server within the GoLive environment.

6. Press [Tab] to move the insertion point to the Server field, then type the address to the server where your Web site will be hosted.

   | TIP   Don't forget to include "ftp://" at the start of the server address.

   (continued)

Working with WebDAV servers in GoLive

GoLive's FTP tools are excellent for keeping a development site on a local computer synchronized with a host server. For a development site that is located on a remote computer, GoLive 6 supports Web Distributed Authoring and Versioning, also known as WebDAV. WebDAV is an important technology in a world of increasing global collaboration, and GoLive enables you to take advantage of it!

If you are using a server with WebDAV capability as the location for your development site, GoLive will help you to synchronize the work done. WebDAV is a standard server technology that works similarly to the file management system on your computer or local network. Currently, WebDAV allows you to "lock" files you are working on, preventing more than one person from making changes to the files at once. In addition, when using WebDAV you can add properties to a file, such as the name of the author and the date last modified, to further keep track of changes to a document that may be worked on by a number of people over time. When a WebDAV file is selected or open in GoLive, you can use GoLive's File Properties Inspector to set and view file locks and add and view file properties. The file lock can be set for exclusive use or shared use; shared use allows multiple users to have editing privileges.

When using WebDAV, Web site developers can work directly with the files on the server, or they can download and upload a site to a WebDAV server using GoLive's synchronization tools (Setting up a connection to a WebDAV server with GoLive is the same as setting up a connection to an FTP server, except the server address will use the http:// protocol instead of the ftp:// protocol). When you are working directly with a file on a WebDAV server, it is locked to other editors. Working this way reduces the risk of overwriting newly updated files, and ensures that the server continuously has the most recent version of the file for other collaborators. The GoLive synchronization tools for WebDAV are similar in function to its FTP tools, in that GoLive detects edited files and changes in file structure between file locations. However, a WebDAV synchronization doesn't compare dates and times between local files and server files for deciding which file to upload or download, as differences in time zones could cause errors if this is done automatically. Instead, prior to synching, GoLive lists each file's synchronization action—that is, whether it will be uploaded or downloaded. You either confirm the action or change the action (to upload, download, skip, or delete) before starting the synchronization process.

FIGURE A-29

Available Servers window

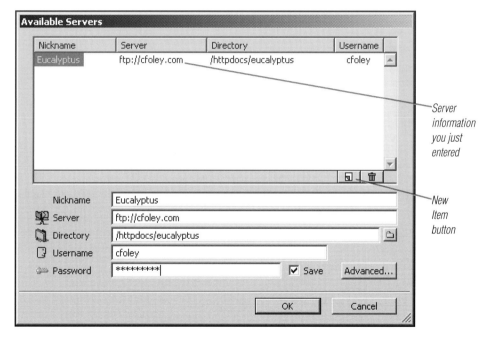

7. Press [Tab] to move the insertion point to the Directory field, then type the path of the folder for your Web files.

8. Press [Tab] to move the insertion point to the Username field, then type your username.

   | TIP   Keep in mind that usernames and passwords are often case sensitive.

9. Click the Save checkbox to select it and to activate the Password field, then type your password into the Password field. Compare your screen to Figure A-29.

   Each letter in your password will be represented onscreen by an asterisk (*) for security purposes.

10. Click OK.

You set up an FTP connection to a Web server.

Upload files via FTP to a Web server (if you have an Internet connection)

1. Click the FTP Server connect/disconnect button on the site window toolbar.

   The FTP tab appears in the right side of the site window and displays the Web server information.

   TIP If you receive a message warning you that you have not specified a server for this site, click OK, then from the Server list box in the Properties window, choose the server connection you just defined, then click OK.

2. Click the Incremental Upload button on the site window toolbar.

3. Click OK to accept the Upload Options default settings, as in Figure A-30.

4. Click OK to accept the list of files to transfer.

   This screen appears because the Show list of files to upload checkbox was checked in the Upload Options dialog box, as shown in Figure A-30. It allows you to select specific files to upload, if necessary.

5. Compare your site window to Figure A-31.

   The server files are shown in the right side of the site window in the FTP tab.

6. Click the FTP connect/disconnect icon to disconnect.

7. Click the double-arrow button in the bottom corner of the Files tab window to hide the FTP tab.

   (continued)

FIGURE A-30
Upload Options dialog box

FIGURE A-31
Eucalyptus site uploaded

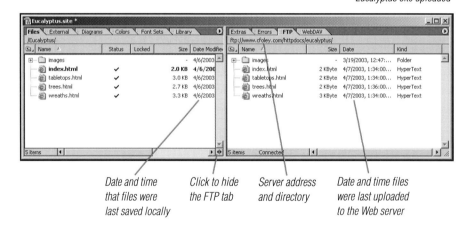

Date and time that files were last saved locally

Click to hide the FTP tab

Server address and directory

Date and time files were last uploaded to the Web server

FIGURE A-32

Eucalyptus Extraordinaire site on the Web

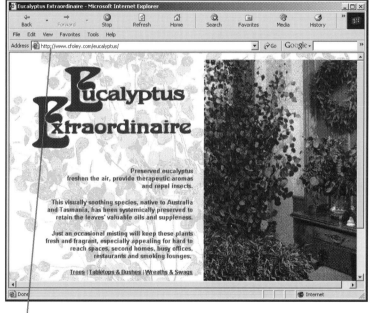

Web address of uploaded site

8. To view the current FTP server connection, click the Site Settings button on the site window toolbar, then click FTP and WebDAV Server on the left side of the window. The current FTP Server connection is shown on the right side of the window.

9. Click OK to close the Eucalyptus.site settings window.

You uploaded the Eucalyptus Extraordinaire site to a server.

View the site in a browser (if you have an Internet connection)

1. Open your browser.

2. Type in the Web address of the site you uploaded, then press [Enter] (Win) or [return] (Mac). Compare your screen to Figure A-32.

3. Close your browser after exploring the site.

You viewed the Eucalyptus Extraordinaire site on the Web using a browser.

GET HELP

What You'll Do

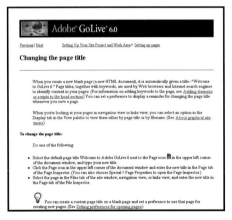

In this lesson, you'll view GoLive Help and find information using Contents, Index, and Search.

Opening GoLive Help

When you install GoLive, you also install an HTML-based help system on your computer that includes the complete *GoLive User's Guide* and some additional information, such as keyboard shortcuts. When you open GoLive Help, it opens in your default browser. You can use the Contents, Index, or Search features of Help to locate information. The GoLive CD also includes a PDF of the help system for printing.

QUICKTIP

You must have JavaScript active in your browser to search Help.

Navigating Help

GoLive Help has three basic methods for locating a topic: Contents, Index, and Search. Contents is useful for finding content at the subject level. First you locate the general subject of information you are looking for, and then you can drill down into the subject to find a related topic. The Index lists topics alphabetically and works well when you know your specific topic name. Search is useful when you know terms related to the topic, but are unsure of the topic under which helpful instructions might be located. Search will find pages that include all of the words you type into the Search text box. All three methods display pages with links to related topics.

FIGURE A-33

Help topic: Changing the page title

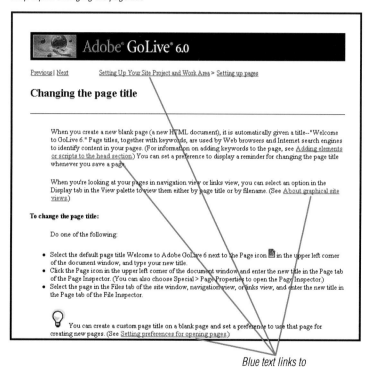

Blue text links to
related topics

1. Click Help on the menu bar, then click GoLive Help.

    TIP   If you are using Windows XP, Help may not open this way. If not, you can open GoLive Help using just your browser. To do this, open your browser, then open the help.html file in the Help folder located in the folder on your computer where GoLive is installed.

2. In the left frame of the browser window, click Setting Up Your Site Project and Work Area.

3. In the right frame of the browser window, click Setting up pages.

4. Click Changing the page title, then compare your window to Figure A-33.

You opened a topic using the Contents feature of GoLive Help.

Find information using the Help Index

1. Open Help if necessary, then click Index in the left frame of the browser window.

2. Click P in the alphabet at the top of the frame.

3. Scroll, if necessary, to the heading "page titles," then next to the subheading "changing," then click [1]. Compare your screen to Figure A-34.

You used an alphabetical index to view a Help topic.

FIGURE A-34
Help Index

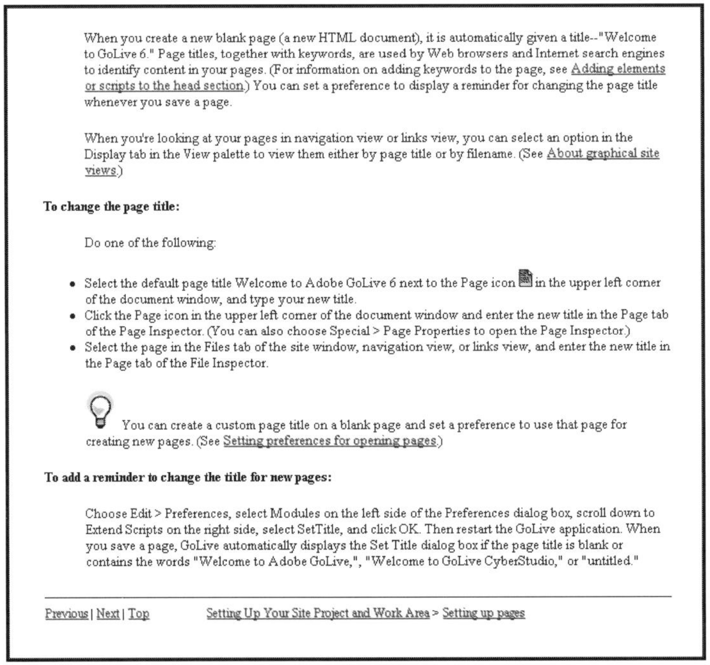

When you create a new blank page (a new HTML document), it is automatically given a title--"Welcome to GoLive 6." Page titles, together with keywords, are used by Web browsers and Internet search engines to identify content in your pages. (For information on adding keywords to the page, see Adding elements or scripts to the head section.) You can set a preference to display a reminder for changing the page title whenever you save a page.

When you're looking at your pages in navigation view or links view, you can select an option in the Display tab in the View palette to view them either by page title or by filename. (See About graphical site views.)

To change the page title:

Do one of the following:

- Select the default page title Welcome to Adobe GoLive 6 next to the Page icon [image] in the upper left corner of the document window, and type your new title.
- Click the Page icon in the upper left corner of the document window and enter the new title in the Page tab of the Page Inspector. (You can also choose Special > Page Properties to open the Page Inspector.)
- Select the page in the Files tab of the site window, navigation view, or links view, and enter the new title in the Page tab of the File Inspector.

💡 You can create a custom page title on a blank page and set a preference to use that page for creating new pages. (See Setting preferences for opening pages.)

To add a reminder to change the title for new pages:

Choose Edit > Preferences, select Modules on the left side of the Preferences dialog box, scroll down to Extend Scripts on the right side, select SetTitle, and click OK. Then restart the GoLive application. When you save a page, GoLive automatically displays the Set Title dialog box if the page title is blank or contains the words "Welcome to Adobe GoLive,", "Welcome to GoLive CyberStudio," or "untitled."

Previous | Next | Top   Setting Up Your Site Project and Work Area > Setting up pages

FIGURE A-35
Help search results

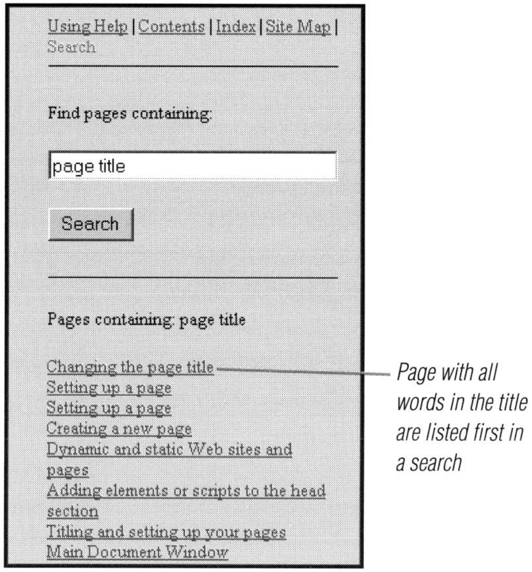

Using Help | Contents | Index | Site Map |
Search
_____

Find pages containing:

[page title   ]

[Search]
_____

Pages containing: page title

Changing the page title ———————————— *Page with all*
Setting up a page   *words in the title*
Setting up a page   *are listed first in*
Creating a new page   *a search*
Dynamic and static Web sites and
pages
Adding elements or scripts to the head
section
Titling and setting up your pages
Main Document Window

Find information in Help using Search

1. Open Help if necessary, then click Search in the left frame.

2. Type **page title**, then click Search. Compare the left side of your screen with Figure A-35.

   Search finds all pages that include the words "page" and "title" anywhere in the page, where pages with more occurrences are ranked near the top. Pages that include matches in their titles are ranked first.

   TIP Click Using Help in the left frame for more information on using Help.

3. When you are finished with Help, close your browser to close Help.

4. Click File on the menu bar, then click Close to close index.html.

   TIP Click Yes in the dialog box that appears to save any changes to index.html since you last saved the file.

5. Click File on the menu bar, then click Close to close the site window.

6. Click File (Win) or GoLive (Mac) on the menu bar, then click Exit (Win) or Quit GoLive (Mac) to exit GoLive.

You searched for a Help topic, closed all open windows, and exited GoLive.

Uncle Louie, the owner of a local pizzeria, would like his Web page to give visitors a better feel of the environment in his restaurant. As a Web page creator and a loyal customer, you offer to add a brick background to his home page in exchange for a Brick Oven Pizza every Friday night this month. He agrees. While you are linking the background graphic, you notice a few other improvements you can make to the page.

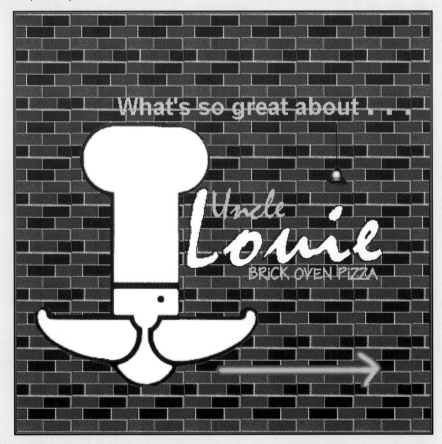

1. From the drive and folder where you are storing your work for this section, open the SiteA-2 folder, open UncleLouie.site, then open the Uncle Louie home page.
2. Set the page background to use brick.gif (*Hint*: this image is in the UncleLouie/images folder).
3. Change the page title to Uncle Louie Brick Oven Pizza.
4. Set the Text and Link colors to FFFF00.
5. Set the Active and Visited Link colors to FFFF99.
6. Save the page, then compare your screen to Figure A-36.

Your garden designer, Jayme, owns Grow Up Landscape Design. Her garden design theory insists on a variety of fresh and fun colors with a "clear, connecting thread throughout."

Jayme has come to you for some help with her Web site. She would like her site to be more reflective of the gardens she designs. She is satisfied that her Web pages project a consistent design element throughout, but she does not feel the pages include a variety of fresh and fun colors.

Jayme has asked you to select background colors for each of her Web pages. She also suggested that the default text color should be white, to brighten the pages.

1. From the drive and folder where you are storing your work for this section, open the SiteA-3 folder, then open GrowUp.site.
2. Open the five Web pages that make up the GrowUp site from the site window.
3. Review the GrowUp pages, paying special attention to the graphic at the bottom of each page that describes the design value of a color.
4. Change the default text color on each page to white.
5. Assign a background color to each page from the Web Color List, using a color that complements the existing text colors and the color described in the graphic.

6. Preview the changes you've made to the pages in Layout Preview.

7. When you are satisfied with your pages, save them and save the site. Compare your work with the example in Figure A-37.

FIGURE A-37
Completed Project 2

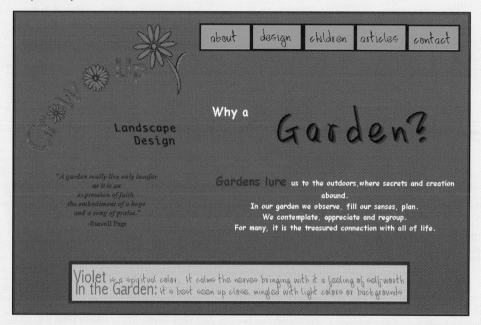

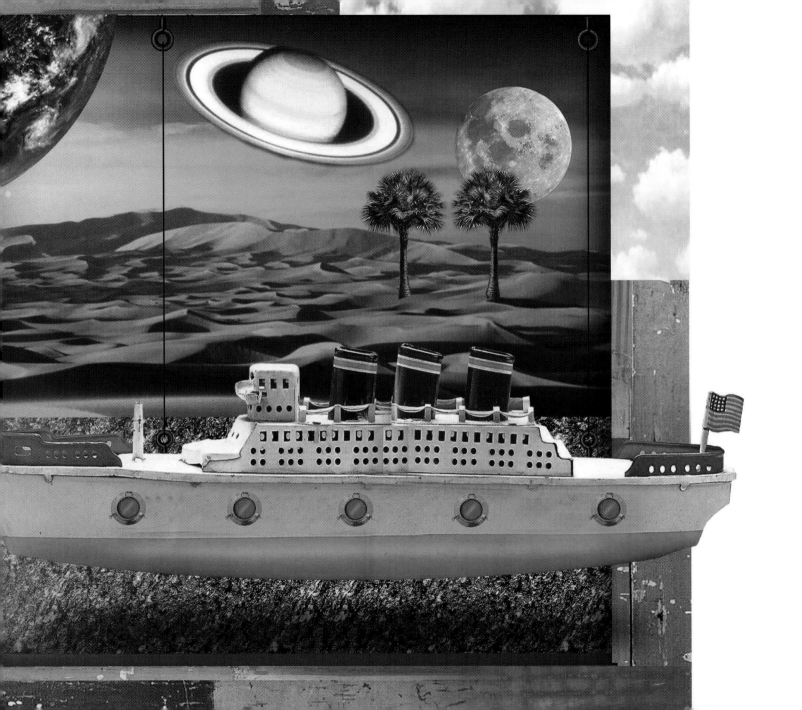

SECTION B
ADDING AND MODIFYING IMAGES

1. Create a new GoLive site.

2. Add a layout grid to a page.

3. Add images.

4. Modify image attributes.

5. Add and modify a Smart Object.

SECTION B
ADDING AND MODIFYING IMAGES

Creating a GoLive Site

Creating a GoLive site is the first step to building a great Web site using GoLive. A GoLive site consists of a project folder that contains all of the components for developing, managing, and controlling Web site files. Although it is possible to develop a Web site without using the site management tools GoLive provides, it is much easier to develop a Web site using them. Creating and working with a GoLive site enables you to track each file and file reference used in the site, to reference image and object files by dragging them onto a page, to organize files by moving or renaming them without breaking references, to delete any files that are not marked as used, and to upload only files changed since the last upload to the Web server.

Designing a Web Page

Web page design has come a long way since the debut of the Web. HTML has advanced through several versions, and technologies have evolved that enable exciting opportunities for adding interactivity to Web pages. Still, creating an effective Web page design by writing HTML code is an arduous process, like creating a brochure on an early word processor! HTML does not allow for white space or side-by-side placement of graphics and text. A Web page designer must use invisible graphics and tables, expanding graphics and merging table cells to ensure that objects of all shapes and sizes, in multiple locations on a page, work together visually.

Fortunately, GoLive simplifies page layout for you by providing easy-to-use design and image management tools. For instance, using the site window to add an image to a page causes GoLive to write the HTML that references the image—and all of its attributes—with just a couple of mouse-clicks. In addition, the Image Inspector can be used to modify image attributes quickly. And a tool called the layout grid enables you to arrange images and other objects within a defined area—without using invisible graphics or tables to control layout.

Tools You'll Use

Layout Grid object
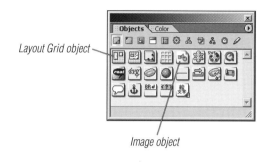

Image object

Click to generate a new site
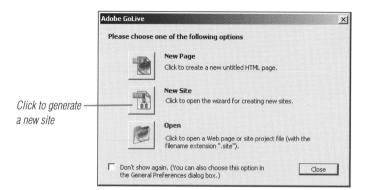

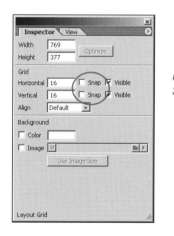

Point and Shoot button
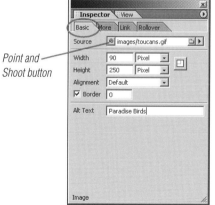

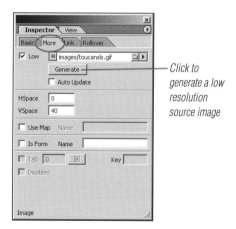
Click to generate a low resolution source image

Object position   Object size   Align and group tools

CREATE A NEW GOLIVE SITE

What You'll Do

In this lesson, you'll create a new GoLive site, review the contents of the new site project folder, and add a new folder to the site.

Understanding a GoLive Site

When you create a new site in GoLive, you are creating a project folder that holds all of the information needed by you and by GoLive to manage the site. There are four components to a GoLive site contained in the project folder: a site file (with the .site filename extension), a site folder, a data folder, and a settings folder.

The **site file** is a GoLive file that is used to manage all of the site components. When you open the site file, the site window opens displaying the contents of the site folder. The **site folder**, or root folder, holds all of the Web page and image files and any other source files that will be uploaded to the Web server when the site is published. The **data folder** holds site assets that you can reuse while working in GoLive, such as page templates. The **settings folder** holds site-specific GoLive setting information, including Web server connection information and upload instructions.

A new GoLive site includes a single blank page—index.html, the site home page—in the site folder. Using the site window, you can add new pages and folders to your site; you can also ensure that each new page links, either directly or indirectly, to index.html.

Using the Site Wizard

To create a new GoLive site, you use the site wizard. The **site wizard** asks you all the right questions about the basics of your Web site, then produces a site in the appropriate format based on your answers. As you progress through the site wizard, you can choose to create a single user site (for a GoLive site built solely on your computer), or a workgroup site (for a GoLive site being accessed by multiple developers on a remote workgroup server). You can create a blank site or a site based on templates, or import a site from another folder. You can even import a site from the Internet! The site wizard will ask you to name your site folder; that name will also serve as the root name of the project folder and the data and settings folders. It will also ask you to designate the location of your project folder.

FIGURE B-1

Open options dialog box

Click to create a new GoLive site

FIGURE B-2

Site wizard: Naming the new site

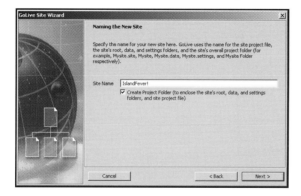

FIGURE B-3

Site wizard: Specifying the new site's location

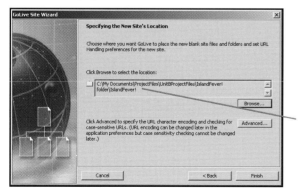

The location of the site folder for the new site (yours will differ)

Create a GoLive site

1. Start Adobe GoLive.

2. In the Open options dialog box (as shown in Figure B-1), click New Site to create a site using the GoLive site wizard.

   TIP If GoLive is already open, click File on the menu bar, then click New Site to create a new site.

3. In the site wizard, click Next to accept the Single User option.

4. In the Local Site Options section of the wizard, click Next to accept the Blank Site option.

5. In the Site Name field, select the text "New Site," then type **IslandFever!** in its place, as shown in Figure B-2.

   TIP You can use spaces in a site name, but you may find that a shorter, single word makes differentiating folders easier.

6. Click Next, click Browse to specify the new site's location, navigate to the drive and folder where you are storing your work for this section, then click OK (Win) or Choose (Mac). Compare your screen to Figure B-3.

7. Click Finish to create a new GoLive site folder and all of its components.

   When the wizard closes, the site window opens listing only index.html—the default content of a new, blank site created in GoLive.

You used the site wizard to create a new GoLive site and all of its components.

View a new site folder

1. Minimize (Win) or Hide (Mac) GoLive.

2. Using your file management tool, open the drive and folder where you are storing your work for this section, then locate and open the IslandFever! project folder (called "IslandFever! folder").

3. Note the contents of the project folder, as shown in Figure B-4: the three component folders, the IslandFever!.site file, and the Island Fever!Backup.site file.

   The Backup.site file is created when a site is opened, in case of a crash. When the site is closed, the Backup.site file disappears from the site folder.

4. Open the folder named IslandFever! (the site folder), noting that the folder contains a single file: index.html. Compare the folder content to that shown in Figure B-5.

5. Maximize (Win) or UnHide (Mac) GoLive.

You viewed the contents of the project folder and the site folder.

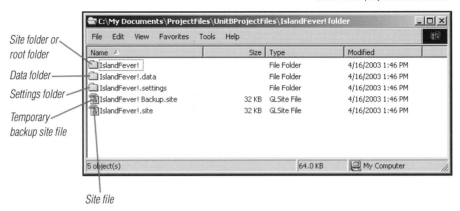

Site folder or root folder
Data folder
Settings folder
Temporary backup site file

Site file

IslandFever! site folder

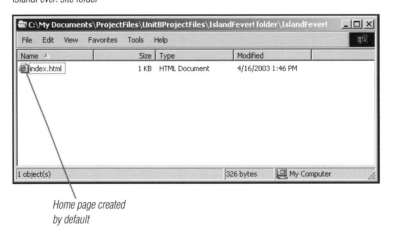

Home page created by default

Contents of new images folder

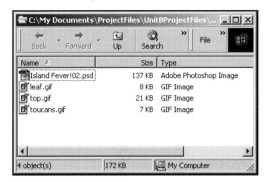

Site window with new image files

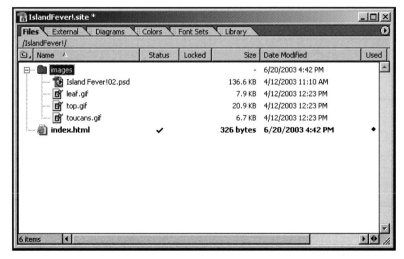

Create an images folder

1. On the site window toolbar, click the New Folder button to create a new folder in the site window and in the site folder. ⬚

2. Name the folder **images**, then press [Enter] (Win) or [return] (Mac).

3. Minimize (Win) or Hide (Mac) GoLive.

4. In your file management tool, note the new images folder in the IslandFever! site folder.

5. Navigate to the drive and folder where your data files are stored, open the SectionB folder, open the SiteB-1 folder, select all of the files in the SiteB-1 folder, then copy the files to the IslandFever! images folder. Compare the contents of the images folder to those shown in Figure B-6.

6. Maximize (Win) or UnHide (Mac) GoLive.

7. Click the Refresh View button to refresh the window. 🔁

8. Click the "+" sign (Win) or arrow (Mac) next to the images folder and resize the site folder, if necessary, to view its contents. Compare your site window to Figure B-7.

9. Save the IslandFever! site.

You added an images folder to the IslandFever! site folder.

ADD A LAYOUT GRID TO A PAGE

What You'll Do

 In this lesson, you'll start a home page for your site and add a layout grid to the page.

Building a Home Page

GoLive creates a home page called index.html for you when you create a new site. This makes sense because every site requires a home page to serve as a starting point. Of course, it's up to you to make your home page a helpful and visually impressive place—the home page GoLive initially creates for you, and any new page added to your site using GoLive, consists of just the required HTML for a basic, empty Web page. You can modify the page using either the Source Code Editor or the Layout Editor.

Determining Page Size

When considering the design of your Web pages, you may want to set some minimum standards to accommodate a specific audience profile—that is, the minimum configuration that a person visiting your site may have. This may include modem speed, browser version, and monitor size. If you assume your audience will have at least a 14" monitor size, then you should build pages that will look good design-wise

on that size of screen. A 14" monitor size translates to working within a page width of 580 pixels for the content of your page. In the Layout Editor, you can choose to view the page you are working on by different monitor sizes or pixel widths in order to make sure your page design works with your minimum standards.

Understanding the Layout Grid

The Layout Editor simplifies Web page arrangements for you with the layout grid. The **layout grid** is a GoLive object that allows you to place images and other objects freely on a page. The grid lines in the layout grid help you understand where objects are relative to other objects in the page. Technically, the grid is an HTML table with special attributes that make it visible in the Layout Editor and invisible in the browser. When you place objects into a page, the layout grid enables you to arrange the objects visually while GoLive simultaneously creates the necessary HTML to present that arrangement of the objects in a browser.

FIGURE B-8

Index.html source code

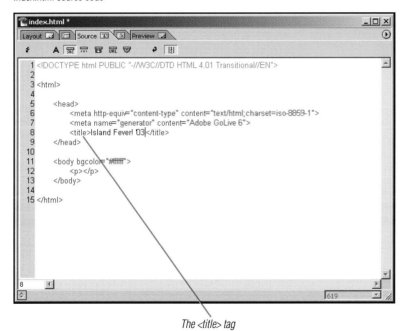

```
index.html *                                               _ □ ×
Layout        Source      Preview                              ►
 A

 1 <!DOCTYPE html PUBLIC "-//W3C//DTD HTML 4.01 Transitional//EN">
 2
 3 <html>
 4
 5    <head>
 6       <meta http-equiv="content-type" content="text/html;charset=iso-8859-1">
 7       <meta name="generator" content="Adobe GoLive 6">
 8       <title>Island Fever! '03</title>
 9    </head>
10
11    <body bgcolor="#ffffff">
12       <p></p>
13    </body>
14
15 </html>



 8                                                            619
```

The <title> tag

1. Double-click index.html to open the new, blank home page.

2. Click the Source tab to view the default HTML in a new GoLive page.

   A new page in GoLive contains the minimum required HTML tags, with white as the default background color and "Welcome to Adobe GoLive 6" as the default page title.

3. Within the <title> tag, select the text "Welcome to Adobe GoLive 6," then type **Island Fever! '03**, as shown in Figure B-8.

4. Click the Layout tab and note the new title.

You opened a blank home page and added a title to the page.

Add a layout grid

1. If the Objects palette is not open, click Window on the menu bar, then click Objects.

2. Drag the Layout Grid object from the Objects palette to the index.html document window.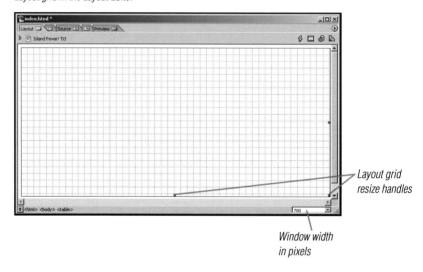

3. Close the Objects palette and the Inspector if necessary.

4. On the lower right corner of the document window, click the document window size list arrow, then click 780 (17" Monitor) to simulate the size of a browser window in a 17" screen.

5. Click the lower right corner of the layout grid, then drag to resize the layout grid to fill the window. Compare your window to Figure B-9.

(continued)

(continued)

FIGURE B-9
Layout grid in the Layout Editor

Layout grid resize handles

Window width in pixels

Adding and Modifying Images

6. Click the Preview tab to confirm that the layout grid is not viewable in a browser.

7. Click the Source tab to view the HTML for the layout grid, as shown in Figure B-10.

Because the layout grid is selected in the Layout Editor, when you switch to the Source Code Editor the code that applies to the layout grid is highlighted. The <table> tag attributes that include the word "grid" are attributes GoLive uses to manage the layout grid.

8. Click the Layout tab to return to the Layout Editor.

You added a layout grid to a page, resized the grid, previewed the page, then viewed the layout grid source code.

FIGURE B-10
Layout grid source code

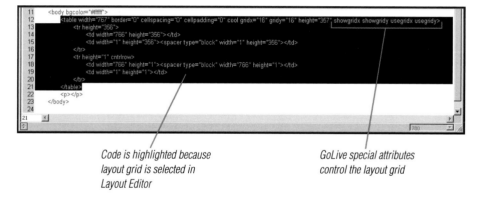

Code is highlighted because
layout grid is selected in
Layout Editor

GoLive special attributes
control the layout grid

ADD IMAGES

What You'll Do

 In this lesson, you'll arrange your workspace to work with images, add images to the layout grid, and align images on the layout grid.

Adding Images to a Page

GoLive greatly simplifies the task of working with images in a Web page. There are two ways to add images to a page in GoLive: by using the Point and Shoot button or by dragging the files onto the page.

The point-and-shoot feature requires you first to put a placeholder object on the page to locate where the image should be inserted. Like the layout grid, you drag the placeholder from the Objects palette to the Layout Editor. There is no need to resize this object, because the placeholder simply determines the placement of the upper left corner of the inserted image and is deleted once the image is placed. To assign an image or Smart Object to the placeholder, you drag from the Point and Shoot button next to the Image Inspector Source field to the file in the site window.

The upper left corner of the image is positioned on the upper left corner of the placeholder, and the HTML image tag is created with source and size attribute values obtained from the inserted file.

The dragging method of adding an image to a page does not require a placeholder. You simply drag an image or Smart Object from the site window to the location you want it to appear on the page in Layout Editor.

Both methods require some creative arrangement with your screen real estate, as you need the Layout Editor, site window, and possibly the Inspector all in view. Tiling windows, opening and closing palettes and the Inspector, and saving your workspace and naming it according to a specific task can all be helpful for adding images to a page.

Setting Layout Grid Attributes

As you work with images, the layout grid attributes can be modified to help you arrange them successfully. These attributes, which can be modified using the Layout Grid Inspector, include Snap, View, and the space between grid lines. Snap, a "magnetic force" put on the grid lines, helps you with the exact placement of images. As you first position an object in the layout grid near a grid line, the object is automatically placed with its edge aligned with the grid line. If you do not want images in your design to "snap" to gridlines, you can simply turn the Snap feature of the layout grid off. View allows you to hide and show vertical or horizontal grid lines. The space between grid lines affects the placement of the visual guide and alignments when you use Snap.

Aligning and Grouping Images

In addition to using layout grid attributes to help you arrange images on your Web page, you can also take advantage of the buttons available on the toolbar when an image is selected in the layout grid. The toolbar includes alignment buttons for aligning images relative to the layout grid: Align Left, Align Center (horizontal), Align Right, Align Top, Align Center (vertical), and Align Bottom. These buttons are active when an image is selected, but only if there is not another image blocking that alignment possibility. The Group and Ungroup buttons on the toolbar enable you to combine several images into one in order to maintain the relationship between those images as you move them around the Web page.

Using Snap

By default, when you add a layout grid object to a page the Snap feature of the grid is enabled. This means that when you move objects within the layout grid they will move in increments defined by the width between gridlines, and each object will be aligned to the grid lines to which it is closest. Objects "snapped" to the same gridline are perfectly aligned with each other; thus Snap enables you to have careful control of the alignment of the objects on the page. However, this gives you less control over where images end up when you move them because you are limited to the image locations defined by the layout grid lines. Turning off Snap enables you to move images anywhere on the page without regard to where the gridlines are. As you gain more experience building Web pages—and putting together different page designs—using the layout grid in GoLive, you will discover in which situations Snap is most helpful and which situations call for less grid line guidance.

Prepare your workspace for adding images

1. Click Window on the menu bar, point to Cascade and Tile, then click Tile Horizontally to view the site window and the document window.

2. If the content of the images folder is not viewable in the site window, click the "+" (Win) or arrow (Mac) next to the images folder to view the contents.

3. Resize the site window so that the last column showing on the right is the Date Modified column.

4. From the Window menu, open the Objects palette and the Inspector. Compare your screen to Figure B-11.

You arranged your workspace for adding images.

FIGURE B-11
Workspace arrangement for adding an image

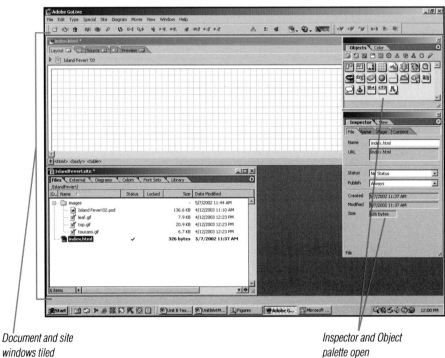

Document and site windows tiled

Inspector and Object palette open

FIGURE B-12
Point-and-shoot process

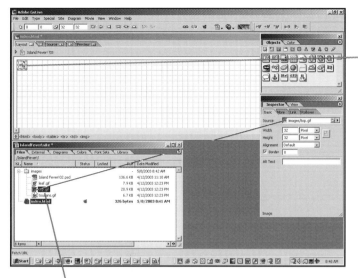

Image placeholder
selected and aligned
to the top and left of
layout grid

Drag the Point and Shoot button to
the image file in the site window

FIGURE B-13
<image> tag

```
<body bgcolor="#ffffff" leftmargin="0" marginheight="0" marginwidth="0" topmargin="0">
    <table width="781" border="0" cellspacing="0" cellpadding="0" cool gridx="16" gridy="16" height="433" showgridx showgridy>
        <tr height="432">
            <td width="780" height="432" valign="top" align="left" xpos="0"><img src="images/top.gif" alt="" width="667" height="148" border="0"></td>
            <td width="1" height="432"><spacer type="block" width="1" height="432"></td>
        </tr>
        <tr height="1" cntrlrow>
            <td width="780" height="1"><spacer type="block" width="780" height="1"></td>
            <td width="1" height="1"></td>
        </tr>
    </table>
    <p></p>
</body>
```

Image attributes
include source and
image size

Add an image using the Point and Shoot button

1. Drag the Image object from the Objects palette to the upper left corner of the layout grid so that the Image object's left and top edges are flush with the left and top edges of the layout grid.

    An image placeholder appears in the upper left corner of the layout grid.

2. Click the image placeholder in the layout grid to see its properties in the Image Inspector.

    The Source information for the image is "(EmptyReference!)," because an image has not been assigned to the placeholder.

3. Click the Point and Shoot button next to the Source text box on the Image Inspector then drag the pointer to "top.gif" in the site window, as shown in Figure B-12.

    The upper left corner of the selected image is positioned in the placeholder position. Note that the image source now referenced in the Image Inspector is "images/top.gif."

4. Close the Objects palette and the Inspector, then click the Source tab and view the image tag, as shown in Figure B-13.

    The source, height, and width attributes now contain information gathered from the inserted file.

5. Return to the Layout Editor.

You added an image to index.html using the point-and-shoot process.

Add an image by dragging from the site window

1. Scroll in the document window until you can see just the bottom edge of top.gif.

2. Drag leaf.gif from the site window to a location underneath the left and bottom edge of top.gif, then resize the document window so that you can see both images entirely.

3. Attempt to move leaf.gif so the left sides of both images are aligned.

   Snap is forcing the image to stay aligned with the grid line on the right side of the image and does not allow you to move the image.

4. Move the cursor over the left edge of the layout grid until you see a small box below the cursor, indicating you are positioned to select the layout grid.

5. Double-click to open the Layout Grid Inspector.

6. Click both the Horizontal and Vertical Grid Snap checkboxes to uncheck them and turn off Snap. Compare your Inspector to Figure B-14, then close the Layout Grid Inspector.

7. Position leaf.gif so that its left edge is aligned with that of top.gif and so that its top edge is flush with the bottom edge of top.gif.

8. Click the Preview tab to preview the results. Compare your document window to Figure B-15.

9. Return to the Layout Editor.

You added an image to index.html by dragging it from the site window.

FIGURE B-14
Layout grid Inspector with Snap turned off

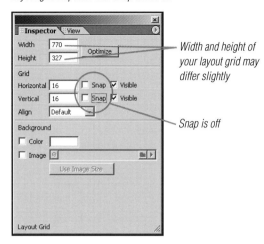

Width and height of your layout grid may differ slightly

Snap is off

FIGURE B-15
Leaf.gif positioned

top.gif

leaf.gif

FIGURE B-16
Image toolbar

Align Right button

FIGURE B-17
Toucans.gif aligned

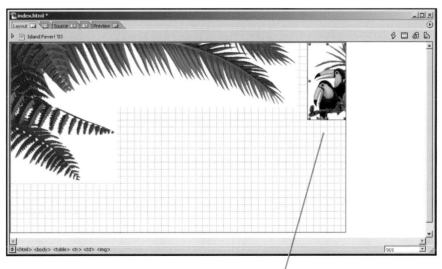

*Toucans.gif aligned to
the top and right of the
layout grid*

1. Drag the toucans.gif image from the site window to the right side of leaf.gif, then resize the document window so that toucans.gif is entirely visible.

2. Click once on the image to select the image and to display the image toolbar, as shown in Figure B-16.

3. Click the Align Right button to align the image to the right side of the grid.

   Before you clicked the Align Right button, only the Align Center (vertical) and Align Right buttons were available because the other alignment directions are "blocked" by other images. Clicking the Align Right button moves the toucans.gif image to the right edge of the layout grid; it also causes the Align Top and Align Center (horizontal) button to become available and the Align Right button to become unavailable.

4. Click the Align Top button. Compare your window to Figure B-17.

   TIP If the Align Top button is not available, it may be because there is not enough space between the right side of top.gif and the right side of the layout grid to fit the toucans.gif graphic. If so, make sure that top.gif is completely flush with the top and left edges of the layout grid, click the Align Right button again, then click the Align Top button.

You dragged an image to the layout grid, then aligned it with the right side and top of the layout grid.

MODIFY IMAGE ATTRIBUTES

What You'll Do

 In this lesson, you'll resize and restore an image, then modify other attributes of the image using the Image Inspector.

Understanding Image File Formats

Image files often have large file sizes that are inappropriate for Web pages because of the download time that would be needed by a browser to view them. Therefore, it's essential that image files in a Web page be in a compressed file format for faster downloading. A **compressed** file has been reduced in size through the removal of all the information in the file except that necessary to display it. Compressed file formats include GIF for illustrations with flat colors and crisp edges, and JPEG for photos.

It is a good idea to keep at least two versions of images: an uncompressed original image for modification, and a compressed image to reference from your Web page. Compressed files should not be resized or edited, because such changes compromise the quality of the modified images. Expanding a compressed image's size will cause the compressed image to pixillate (meaning that the pixels that make up the image become larger and more visible, causing reduced image clarity);

reducing the size of a compressed image may not affect its clarity, but the image will then be referencing a larger file than necessary. The best practice is to resize the original source image, then re-compress it.

Setting and Modifying Image Attributes

Once you have image files in a Web-ready compressed format, setting the image attributes in the Web page will ensure that your viewers will see what you intend for them to see.

When you place an image in a page, GoLive determines its height and width attributes based on the dimensions of the inserted image. The image size is displayed in both the Image Inspector (on the Basic tab, as shown in Figure B-18) and the image toolbar. Changing the size of an image can be done by dragging a selected image's resize handles or by changing the image size values in either the Inspector or the toolbar. As discussed earlier, resizing an image in a Web page is not a good idea—unless you are using a Smart Object (covered in Lesson 5). Should you resize an image, inadvertently or otherwise, the image in the Layout Editor will display a resize warning in the lower right corner of the image. You can easily return an image to its original size by clicking the Set to Original Size button in the Image Inspector.

QUICKTIP

Although image size attributes are not necessary for displaying an image, GoLive automatically includes them in the image tag as this helps the browser to calculate the page layout quickly.

You can add white space around an image using attributes available on the Image Inspector's More tab, as shown in Figure B-18. Adding vertical space (**vspace**) or horizontal space (**hspace**) adds white space that becomes part of the image and stays with it, should you move it or add a border. This attribute is critical to Web designers laying out pages—and creating space between images—without the benefit of a layout grid!

The low resolution and alternate text attributes of an image are for the benefit of viewers that have slow connections or hardware, or viewers that set their browser not to display graphics. Some graphics can be large and take time to download to the viewer's browser, even though they are compressed. Most browsers display an image placeholder while an image is loading. So that viewers of your page don't see this placeholder for long or at all, you can create a low resolution version of your graphic with reduced colors and a very small file size, then display this version while the larger image downloads. You can choose to have GoLive create this low resolution source file for you. In this case, the new file will have the same name as the original file, with an "ls" (low source) suffix.

For viewers that choose not to display graphics in their browser, or in the case of a broken reference, most browsers display a broken placeholder icon. You can set an image attribute for alternate text, so that in these cases the browser will display the alternate text in place of the image or placeholder. This is good practice, too, because even browsers that can view graphics do not always download them at the same time, and with alternate text showing your site's visitors will have an idea of what image to expect before it appears.

FIGURE B-18
Image Inspector Basic and More tabs

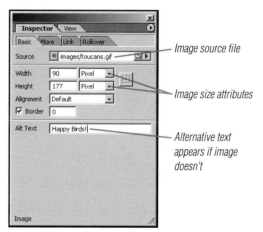

Image source file

Image size attributes

Alternative text appears if image doesn't

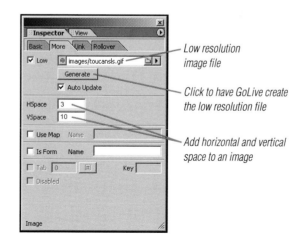

Low resolution image file

Click to have GoLive create the low resolution file

Add horizontal and vertical space to an image

Resize and restore an image

1. Click on the image of the toucans to select it, if it is not selected. If the Image Inspector is not open, open it.

2. Note the source and the size of the image in the Image Inspector, and the position and the size of the image in the image toolbar, as shown in Figure B-19.

3. Click the resizing handle on the bottom center of the toucans.gif image, then drag so that the height of the image is about 250 pixels. Compare your image to Figure B-20.

   The height shown in both the Inspector and the toolbar changes as you change the size of the image.

4. Note the pixillation of the image and the resize warning icon in the image.

5. Click the Set to Original Size button in the Image Inspector to restore the image to its original proportions.

You resized an image, viewed the effects of the resizing, then restored the image to its original size.

FIGURE B-19
Image toolbar

Object Position: pixels to the right of and pixels below the top left corner of parent object (grid)—your screen may vary

Object Size: width and height (in pixels)

FIGURE B-20
Toucans.gif image resized

Expanded image pixillates

Resize warning icon

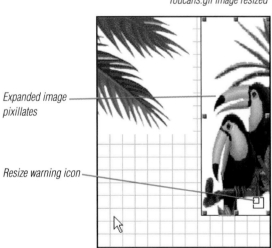

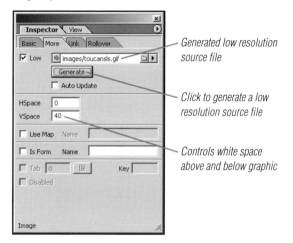

Generated low resolution
source file

Click to generate a low
resolution source file

Controls white space
above and below graphic

Modify image attributes with the Image Inspector

1. Click the More tab in the Image Inspector.

2. Type **40** in the Vspace text box, then press [Enter] (Win) or [return] (Mac).

3. Click the Low checkbox to include a low resolution source file for the image.

4. Click Generate. Compare your Image Inspector to Figure B-21.

   GoLive creates the low resolution source image (toucansls.gif), includes it in the HTML image tag, and saves the low resolution source image in the same folder as the selected image.

5. Click the Basic tab in the Image Inspector.

6. Type **Paradise Birds** in the Alt Text field on the Image Inspector.

7. Select all three images in the document window by holding down [Shift] and clicking on each image, then click the Group button on the image toolbar to group the images. 🖽

8. Click the Source tab, then locate the image tag for toucans.gif.

9. Return to the Layout Editor, compare your screen to Figure B-22, then save index.html.

You modified the vspace attribute of an image, created a low resolution source file for the image, added alternate text for the image, then grouped three images together.

FIGURE B-22

Toucans.gif with added vspace

Vspace
added

ADD AND MODIFY A SMART OBJECT

What You'll Do

 In this lesson, you'll add a Smart Object to the page, then position and resize the Smart Object.

Working with Smart Objects

GoLive Smart Objects simplify the task of managing multiple versions of an image created in an Adobe graphics program. A **Smart Object** is an Adobe non-compressed image file placed in a GoLive Web page. This feature works with original Photoshop, Illustrator, and LiveMotion image files, creating compressed images, called target files, when placed in GoLive.

When the uncompressed image file is added to a page, GoLive creates a target file. A **target file** is a Web-ready, compressed, resizable version of the original image. You can have multiple target files of an image, and you can manipulate the target files without affecting the uncompressed source file. A Smart Object can be resized and still look crisp, because GoLive regenerates the target file at the new size. Updating the source image will automatically update all of its target files and reapply the size and optimization settings used to compress the original target file.

Adding a Smart Object

When you add a Photoshop Smart Object to a page, a Save For Web dialog box opens, showing the visual appearance of the target file and listing its optimization settings. The Smart Object process, dialog boxes, and optimization settings change depending on the source program of the uncompressed file. Photoshop optimization settings include a choice of file formats that are recognized by the Web. The format you select will determine the other settings you can use to reduce the size of the target file and control the quality of the output. GoLive Help describes the settings for each file type in detail. You can leave these settings as is or change them when creating the target file. Altering the settings may affect the target file size and the estimated download time using a minimum modem speed; this information is shown at the bottom of the Save For Web dialog box.

To simplify image management further, you can use Smart Object variables. **Variables** are settings in the original image creation program that can be changed from target file to target file. In Photoshop PSD files, the topmost text layer is treated as a variable, as illustrated in Figure B-23. In Illustrator SVG files, text can be a variable, plus you can make any object in the SVG file visible or invisible in the target file. In Live Motion LIV files, text and styles, embedded links, and object colors, styles, and textures are all variables.

You add a Smart Object using the same methods as you would when adding an image by using the Point and Shoot button or by dragging. Each time you add a Smart Object to a page, the Variable Settings dialog box allows you to specify which items to set as variables and to specify their values in the compressed target file. This allows you to create multiple versions of a target file using a single source file. For example, you can create all of your site navigation buttons using a single Photoshop file, changing the text in each button when creating the target file. You can add these buttons as target files to every page in your site. If you later find that a button's text is not intuitive, you can change the button text in the target file right in GoLive, without any alterations to the source file, and all of the pages using that file will update at once!

Modifying a Smart Object

Resizing a Smart Object will generate a new, crisp compressed image, so you don't have to worry about pixillation or inefficiency as you would when resizing an already compressed image. The new target file is automatically compressed using the previous target file's variable and compression settings and the original source image is left intact. Double-clicking on a Smart Object in GoLive will open the source file in its native program for modifications. Saving the modified source file will update all of its target files to reflect any modifications.

FIGURE B-23

A Photoshop file...

...becomes a GoLive Smart Object

Top text layer becomes variable

Add a Smart Object

1. Click Window on the menu bar, point to Cascade and Tile, then click Tile Horizontally.

2. Drag IslandFever!02.psd, a Photoshop file, to the center of index.html.

3. In the Variable Settings dialog box, click the checkbox to the left of Topmost Textlayer to make the text box at the bottom of the dialog box active.

   The top layer of text in the added file is now editable.

4. Click in the text box, type **'03**, compare your Variable Settings dialog box to Figure B-24, then click OK.

   You changed the text in the top layer of the added file from '02 to '03 (though you don't see the graphic before the change is made). GoLive makes the change using the same color, size, and font (if the font is on your computer) as the text in the original file. It may take a few minutes.

   (continued)

FIGURE B-24
Variable Settings dialog box

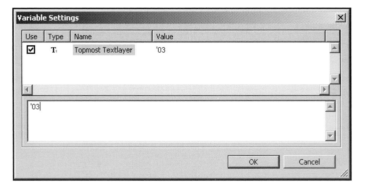

FIGURE B-25
Save For Web dialog box

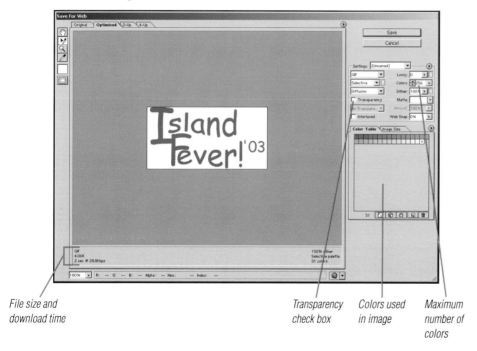

File size and download time

Transparency check box

Colors used in image

Maximum number of colors

5. In the Save For Web dialog box, note the file type, file size, and download time information listed at the bottom of the Optimized pane. Compare your screen to Figure B-25.

   This file, when saved with the current settings, will be a GIF file of 4.06 kilobytes, and take 2 seconds to download on a 28.8 Kbps modem connection.

6. In the Settings area on the right side of the window, click the Colors list arrow, click 8, then click the Transparency checkbox.

   Fewer colors reduces the file size and, possibly, the loading time. Transparency allows background colors to show through the bounding box.

7. Click Save, then in the Specify target file dialog box, navigate to the images folder within the Island Fever! site folder and click Save to save the GIF version of your image.

   The name of the new file is the name of the original file followed by an underscore, the variable text ("03"), and the ".gif" file extension.

You added a native photoshop file to a page as a smart object, changed its variable text, optimized it, then saved it in a file format for the web.

Position and resize the Smart Object

1. If necessary, resize the document window so that the entire layout grid is visible.

2. Click the Smart Object, then open the Inspector, if it is not open. Compare your Inspector to Figure B-26.

3. Move the logo so that it is flush against top.gif and leaf.gif. See Figure B-27.

   TIP If your logo is pink, it is overlapping another image. Move the logo so that it doesn't overlap any other image.

   An icon appears on the image to indicate it is a Smart Photoshop Object.

   TIP The appearance of your Photoshop Smart Object icon may vary depending on the version of Photoshop you have installed, or on whether you have Photoshop installed or not.

   (continued)

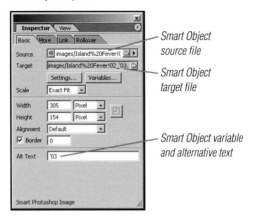

Smart Object source file

Smart Object target file

Smart Object variable and alternative text

FIGURE B-27
Smart Object logo positioned

Smart Photoshop Object icon

FIGURE B-28

Island Fever! '03 home page

4. Click on the bottom center resize handle and drag to make the image height close to 200 pixels.

   The resizing of the Smart Object may take a few moments.

5. Click the Preview tab to preview the layout of the page. Compare your window to Figure B-28.

6. Save and close index.html and IslandFever!.site.

You positioned and resized the smart object.

China Mist Gourmet Iced Tea company has hired you to start a new Web site for them, beginning with a home page. They would like their home page to contain just their logo and navigation buttons. They have an idea of what they would like their buttons to look like, but may change the text on the buttons as the site develops. In light of this possibility, you decide it would be best to use Smart Objects for buttons.

1. Create a new site named **China Mist**.
2. Create an images folder in the site folder.
3. Navigate to the drive and folder where your data files are stored, then copy the contents of the SiteB-3 folder into the images folder in the China Mist site folder.
4. Title the home page **China Mist Gourmet Iced Tea Company**.
5. Add a layout grid for a 14" monitor and turn off Snap.
6. Arrange the workspace for adding images to the layout grid.
7. Add the about.psd file to the page four times, changing the variable text for each respective Smart Object as listed in Table B-1 (including the line breaks as noted, which will be reflected in each image), then save the files in the China Mist images folder using the filenames listed in Table B-1.

8. Add horizontal space of 10 pixels and vertical space of 5 pixels to each button.
9. Align the buttons to the top of the grid and position them side by side. Group the buttons, then align them to the center of the grid horizontally.

FIGURE B-29
Completed Project 1

10. Add the file cmlogo.jpg to the page, then align it to the horizontal and vertical center of the grid.
11. Save the file.
12. Preview the file and compare it to Figure B-29.

TABLE B-1: Smart Object variable text and filenames

Variable text	Save as
China Mist [line break] Teas	cmteas.gif
Brewing [line break] Tea	brewtea.gif
Refreshing [line break] Recipes	recipes.gif
About [line break] China Mist	aboutcm.gif

Adding and Modifying Images

China Mist loves the home page you produced for them! They are ready to add a page that describes their teas. They would like this page also to be very graphical to communicate the lively flavors of their teas. They have asked you to lay out the page initially using only the graphics, as text will be added later.

1. Add a second page to the China Mist site you created in Project 1. (*Hint:* With the China Mist site open, click File on the menu bar, then click New Page.)
2. Title the page **China Mist Gourmet Iced Teas**, then save it as teas.html in the site folder.
3. Size Layout Editor for a 17" monitor, add a layout grid and resize it so it fills the document window (with the dimensions 770 × 500), then turn off Snap.
4. Add cmlogosm.gif to the page, positioned as shown in Figure B-30.
5. Add about.psd to the page using the variable text **China Mist**[line break]**Home Page**; add horizontal space of 10 pixels and vertical space of 5 pixels to the image.

6. Add the GIF files for the Brewing Tea, Refreshing Recipes, and About China Mist buttons to the page, then add horizontal space of 10 pixels and vertical space of 5 pixels to each. Position each of the buttons as shown in Figure B-30.

7. Add each file in the images/teas folder to the page and position each image as indicated in Figure B-30.
8. Preview, then save the page.

FIGURE B-30
Completed Project 2

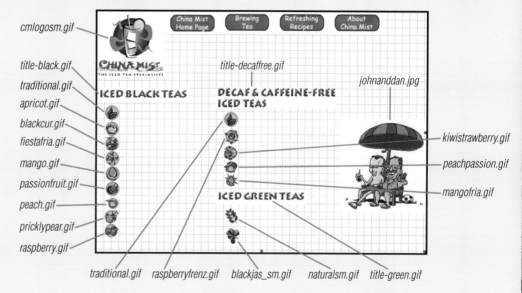

SECTION C

FORMATTING AND STYLIZING TEXT

1. Add and manually format text.

2. Apply element tags to text.

3. Create and modify an internal style sheet.

4. Create and modify an external style sheet.

5. Override styles.

6. Search text for errors.

SECTION C
FORMATTING AND STYLIZING TEXT

Introduction

Web pages are sometimes referred to as living documents because they have long lives and are often updated—not only in content, but also in style. Many businesses consider it imperative to keep their Web sites fresh, which can mean reworking the design of pages, and the text and images on those pages, many times during the life of a site. Because Web sites are complex, change often, and may be managed by different people over time, it is key for the process of managing changes to Web site content and style to be as streamlined as possible.

Formatting Text in Web Pages

Formatting the text in an HTML document can be done using in-line HTML tags within the source code for the document, or using a formatting toolbar, if working within a Web page editor such as the Layout Editor in GoLive. Manually formatting a document in this way is the equivalent of using the toolbar to format a document in a word processor. It requires no setup, but it can make a durable document difficult to maintain—if working in source code, tags must be entered individually wherever they are supposed to provide formatting; if working

in a Web page editor, text in the Web page must be selected individually and formatted using a series of toolbar buttons and list boxes. In both cases, the formatting process can be time-consuming, and even small changes to the resulting Web page can require lots of fixes to keep the document looking good.

Although for a short, basic Web page manual formatting may be your best bet, a more efficient and consistent approach to formatting text on complex Web pages and sites is to use styles and style sheets.

A **style** is a group of properties that can be applied to multiple instances of text on one page and/or across several pages. A collection of styles is called a **style sheet**, and a style sheet for an HTML document or documents is called a **cascading style sheet (CSS)**. Cascading Style Sheets were introduced to simplify the maintenance of Web pages, and they are the dominant method used to format text in the professional world of Web site development today. A CSS makes the formatting of text throughout a Web site a much more efficient process than one using manual formatting methods.

Tools You'll Use

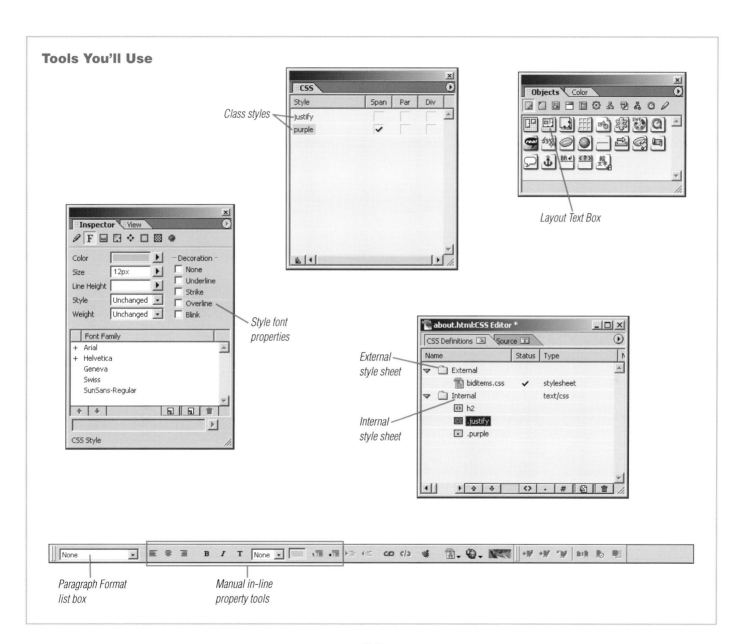

Class styles

Layout Text Box

Style font
properties

Inspector · View

Color
Size · 12px
Line Height
Style · Unchanged
Weight · Unchanged

Decoration
None
Underline
Strike
Overline
Blink

Font Family
+ Arial
+ Helvetica
Geneva
Swiss
SunSans-Regular

CSS Style

about.html:CSS Editor *

CSS Definitions · Source

Name · Status · Type
External
biditems.css · ✓ · stylesheet
Internal · text/css
h2
.justify
.purple

External
style sheet

Internal
style sheet

None

Paragraph Format
list box

Manual in-line
property tools

ADD AND MANUALLY FORMAT TEXT

What You'll Do

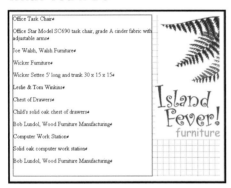

 In this lesson, you'll add text directly to a page, manually format text, and add text to a page using a text box.

Adding Text to a Page

In GoLive's Layout Editor, you can add text directly to a blank Web page, line by line as in a word processor, and the text will wrap to the margins of the page. Alternatively, you can position text anywhere on a layout grid using objects such as the Layout Text Box, Floating Box, and Table objects. Layout Text Boxes are the easiest way to include text in a page's layout, because text in a Layout Text Box wraps to the width of the box, while the width of a Floating Box or a Table will change to accommodate non-wrapping lines of text. Text can be typed, copied, or dragged from a word processor into the object; it can even be imported from a database, spreadsheet, or tab delimited file. Adding text to objects and positioning those objects in the layout grid enables you to easily control the appearance of your Web pages and thus create pages that are compelling to read.

Formatting Text Using the Toolbar and Type Menu

Once you have text in your Web page, you can manually format the text with in-line properties (such as bold, italic, font size, and font color) using the text tools in the toolbar and the Type menu on the menu bar. An **in-line property** is any property that is applied directly to selected text (unlike a style sheet, which can apply groups of properties to multiple instances of text).

To apply one in-line property to two instances of text, you must select each instance of text separately and use the toolbar or Type menu to format each one. See Figure C-1 for an example of text to which in-line properties have been applied. Formatting text in this way is immediate for each piece of selected text, but can take a lot of time if you have a lot of different pieces of text that need formatting on one page—or on multiple pages within a site.

When a property has been applied to selected text from within the Layout Editor, the HTML tags for that property appear around the text in the source code. See Table C-1 for a list of sample in-line properties, toolbar and Type menu options for applying the properties to text, and each property's corresponding HTML tag.

QUICKTIP

Properties of text in HTML documents are also known as "attributes."

FIGURE C-1
In-line properties applied manually

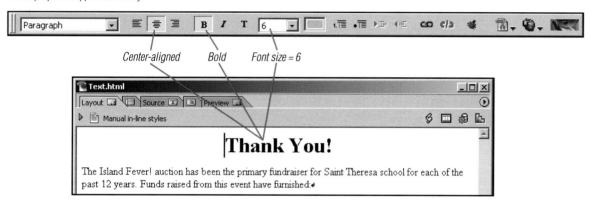

Center-aligned   Bold   Font size = 6

TABLE C-1: Sample manual in-line properties

Property	Toolbar	Type submenu	HTML tag
Font typeface	(None)	Font	\<font face="..."\>...\</font\>
Font size	Font size list box	Size	\<font size="..."\>...\</font\>
Font color	Font Color box	(None)	\<font color="..."\>... \</font\>
Bold	**B**	Style	\<b\>...\</b\>
Italicize	*I*	Style	\<i\>...\</i\>
Underline	(None)	Style	\<u\> ...\</u\>
Strikethrough	(None)	Style	\<s\>...\</s\> or \<strike\>...\</strike\>

Add text directly onto a page

1. Using the file management tool provided with your operating system, navigate to the drive and folder where your data files are stored, then copy the SiteC-1 folder to the drive and folder where you are storing your work for this section.

2. Start GoLive, then open IslandFever!.site from the SiteC-1 folder in the drive and folder where you are storing your work for this section.

3. Open about.html from the site window.

4. Click in front of the first word in the document ("The"), then press [Enter] (Win) or [return] (Mac) to create a blank line.

5. Using your keyboard arrows, move the cursor to the beginning of the first line, then type **Thank You!**. Compare your window to Figure C-2.

You typed text directly into the page.

FIGURE C-2
Text added to a blank page

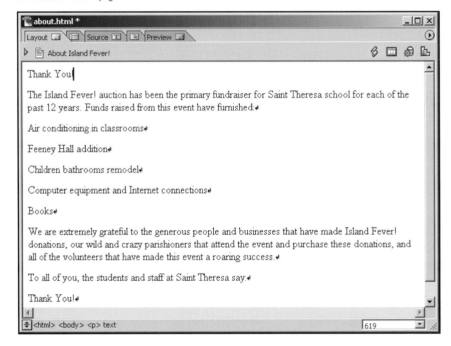

FIGURE C-3

In-line properties in source code

```
about.html *                                                    _ | □ | x |
Layout □   □   Source □ □   Preview □                              ⊙

ʃ    A  ☐ ☐ ☐ ☐ ☐    ↵  ⌷⌷

<!DOCTYPE html PUBLIC "-//W3C//DTD HTML 4.01 Transitional//EN">

<html>

    <head>
        <meta http-equiv="content-type" content="text/html;charset=iso-8859-1">
        <meta name="generator" content="Adobe GoLive 6">
        <title>About Island Fever!</title>
    </head>

    <body bgcolor="#ffffff">
        <p><font size="6" color="#ffcc33" face="Arial,Helvetica,Geneva,Swiss,SunSans-Regular">Thank You</font></p>
        <p>The Island Fever! auction has been the primary fundraiser for Saint Theresa school for each of the past 12
years. Funds raised from this event have furnished:<br>
        </p>
        <p>Air conditioning in classrooms<br>
        </p>

12                                                          ▶
                                                  619    ▼
```

In-line properties appear in the
same line of code as the text

1. Select the words "Thank You!" at the top of the page.

2. In the toolbar, click the Font Size list box, then click 6.

   In-line font sizes are expressed in relation to the browser's default size of 3. Thus, a font size of 6 is twice as big as the browser's default text size.

3. In the Color palette, click the Web Color List button if necessary, select the color FFCC33, then drag it from the Color palette preview pane to the Text Color box in the toolbar (to the right of the Font Size list box). ☒

4. Click Type on the menu bar, point to Font, then click Arial to apply the Arial font set to the text.

5. Click the Source tab, noting that the text Thank You! is enclosed by a <p> tag, which in turn encloses the <font> tag containing the applied font properties, as shown in Figure C-3.

6. Return to the Layout Editor, save the file, then close the file.

You formatted text using in-line properties and viewed the HTML code for those formats.

Add text to a Layout Text Box

1. Open furniture.html from the site window.

   The page is designed for a 14-inch monitor and consists of a grid, three grouped images, and a title.

2. Open the Objects palette if necessary, then drag the Layout Text Box object from the Objects palette to the top left corner of the layout grid.

3. Click and drag the lower right corner resize handle to make the text box as tall as the image and as wide as possible without overlapping the image, as shown in Figure C-4.

   (continued)

FIGURE C-4
Layout Text Box resized

*Drag resize handle to
enlarge text box as shown*

FIGURE C-5

Furniture.html text

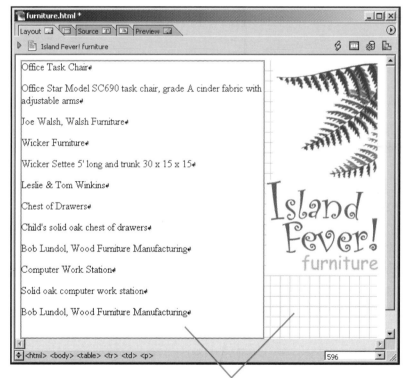

Text box and layout grid
lengthen to accomodate text

4. Click File on the menu bar, click Open, click the furniture.txt file in the SiteC-1 folder, then click Open.

The text file furniture.txt opens in a new window in GoLive.

5. Select and copy all of the text in furniture.txt, then close the file.

6. Click in the text box in furniture.html, then paste the text into the text box. Compare your window to Figure C-5.

> TIP The text box and layout grid lengthen to accommodate the added text, but their widths remain fixed.

You added a Layout Text Box to the page in the layout grid, then copied text into the text box.

APPLY ELEMENT TAGS TO TEXT

What You'll Do

Dance Classes

Gift Certificate for two dance classes a week for one month at
The Beat Performing Arts Studio and a T-shirt from the Beat

The Beat Performing Arts Studio

Brows and Lip Wax

Dino's Hair Design

Hair Styling and Make-Up Application

One hair-cut and style with a tylist and a make-up application
provided bythe Mane Attraction.

Mane Attraction

Photo Session

Island Fever! services

 In this lesson, you'll view existing elements, then apply element tags to text.

Understanding Elements and Element Tags

Elements are the building blocks of a Web page and are defined by the HTML tags in the source code of a document. Opening and closing tags identify the boundaries of an element and act as instructions for the browser about how to display that element. When you put a tag before and after text in the source code, you are applying an element tag or tagging an element.

HTML consists of structure elements, formatting elements, and text elements. Structure elements, such as head, title, and body elements, apply to the structure of the document as required by the browser and are automatically included in pages you create using GoLive. Formatting elements are tags that specify formatting properties (such as the in-line properties discussed in the previous lesson); they describe how the text looks. Text elements describe element content in a general way, as a heading type or a paragraph, for example, and you can apply styles by text element to format pages efficiently.

To format the text, you can use manual, in-line formatting elements—as you did in the previous lesson—or you can use cascading style sheets to apply styles to multiple text elements at once.

There are several standard HTML text elements. Each element has an opening and closing tag that encloses the text. The default formatting for each element is left-aligned, Times New Roman font. The heading elements are bold, and the higher the level, the smaller the size of the text. These eight text elements are paragraph text elements, in that they automatically add a line break and space below the closing tag. The default formatting is not very interesting and the serif font, Times New Roman, is not recommended for on-line reading. Therefore, text elements with default formatting cry out for new, more appealing styles!

Applying Element Tags

In GoLive, there are two ways to apply text element tags—by manually typing the tags in the source code around the text, or by using the Layout Editor's Paragraph Format list box in the toolbar. When you apply the paragraph format "Header 1" from the Paragraph Format list box to text in the Layout Editor, GoLive puts the appropriate tags, <h1>...</h1>, around the text in the source code, creating an <h1> element (or "Header 1 element"). The associated default

HTML element properties are automatically applied to the text in the element, as shown in Figure C-6.

If you create text for a Web site in a word processor using standard word processing styles, and export or save the file as HTML, you can copy text from the HTML document

into a GoLive document, and the text will already have element tags applied. This can be particularly helpful if the person assembling a Web site is different than the person writing the content. Content creators are better equipped to apply styles comprehensively throughout content.

FIGURE C-6
Paragraph text elements with HTML styles

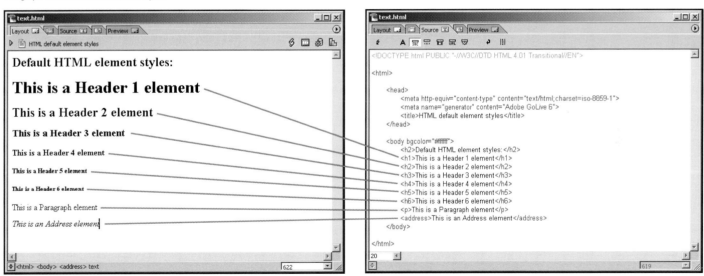

View elements

1. In furniture.html, put your cursor anywhere in the text Office Task Chair at the top of the text box.

   The current paragraph format indicated in the Paragraph Format list box on the toolbar is None, as shown in Figure C-7.

2. Click in any other text in the text box.

   The paragraph format indicated in the Paragraph Format list box is Paragraph.

3. Click the Source tab to view the source code.

4. Note that each line of text is enclosed by an opening and closing paragraph tag, <p>...</p>, with the exception of the text "Office Task Chair," as shown in Figure C-8.

   The line break, <br>, that precedes each line of text in the text file except the first line caused GoLive to tag each line as a <p> element (Paragraph element) when the text was pasted into the text box. Because there was no line break before the first line of text, it is not tagged as a <p> element.

You viewed Paragraph elements in the source code of a Web page.

FIGURE C-7
Paragraph Format list box

Paragraph Format list box

FIGURE C-8
Paragraph elements

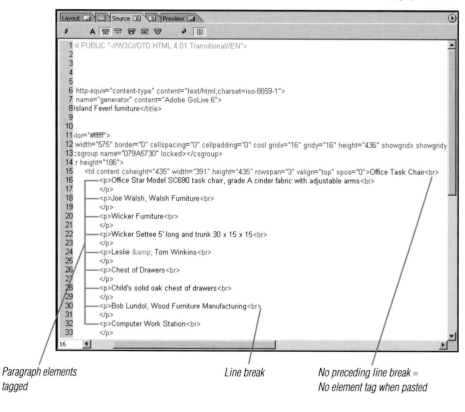

Paragraph elements tagged

Line break

No preceding line break = No element tag when pasted

FIGURE C-9
Furniture.html source code

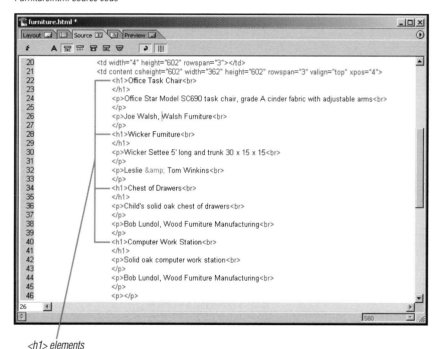

```
20        <td width="4" height="602" rowspan="3"></td>
21        <td content csheight="602" width="362" height="602" rowspan="3" valign="top" xpos="4">
22        <h1>Office Task Chair<br>
23        </h1>
24        <p>Office Star Model SC690 task chair, grade A cinder fabric with adjustable arms<br>
25        </p>
26        <p>Joe Walsh, Walsh Furniture<br>
27        </p>
28        <h1>Wicker Furniture<br>
29        </h1>
30        <p>Wicker Settee 5' long and trunk 30 x 15 x 15<br>
31        </p>
32        <p>Leslie &amp; Tom Winkins<br>
33        </p>
34        <h1>Chest of Drawers<br>
35        </h1>
36        <p>Child's solid oak chest of drawers<br>
37        </p>
38        <p>Bob Lundol, Wood Furniture Manufacturing<br>
39        </p>
40        <h1>Computer Work Station<br>
41        </h1>
42        <p>Solid oak computer work station<br>
43        </p>
44        <p>Bob Lundol, Wood Furniture Manufacturing<br>
45        </p>
46        <p></p>
```

<h1> elements

Apply element tags

1. Return to the Layout Editor, click in the text "Office Task Chair," click the Paragraph Format list arrow on the toolbar, then click Header 1.

   The text is now an <h1> element, and the text in the element is formatted with the default HTML Header 1 properties.

2. Click the Source tab, then in the source code. Note that Office Task Chair is now enclosed by the Header 1 tag, <h1>...</h1>.

3. In the Layout Editor, apply the Header 1 paragraph format to the text "Wicker Furniture," "Chest of Drawers," and "Computer Work Station."

   TIP The layout grid and text box lengthen to accommodate the larger text, but their widths remain fixed.

4. Click the Source tab, then in the source code, note that these paragraphs are no longer Paragraph elements enclosed by the <p> tag; they are now Header 1 elements enclosed by the <h1> tag, as shown in Figure C-9.

5. Return to the Layout Editor, click in the text "Joe Walsh, Walsh Furniture," click the Paragraph Format list arrow, then click Header 2 to change the text from a Paragraph element into a Header 2 element.

(continued)

6. Using the Paragraph Format list box, apply the Header 2 element format to the text "Leslie and Tom Winkins" and to the two instances of the text "Bob Lundol, Wood Furniture Manufacturing," then compare your screen to Figure C-10.

7. Click the Source tab to view the new element tags in the source code.

8. Return to the Layout Editor, then save and close furniture.html.

You tagged paragraphs with the Header 1 and Header 2 text element tags.

Add pre-tagged text

1. Open services.html from the site window.

2. Add a Layout Text Box object to the page, align it to the top left corner of the layout grid, then resize it so that it is about 380 pixels wide.

3. Click File on the menu bar, click Open, click servitems.htm in the SiteC-1 folder, as shown in Figure C-11, then click Open.

   Servitems.htm was created in Microsoft Word using standard Word text styles, and then saved as an HTML file.

4. Select and copy the text in servitems.htm, close the file, then paste the text into the services.html text box.

(continued)

FIGURE C-10
Furniture.html with element tags applied

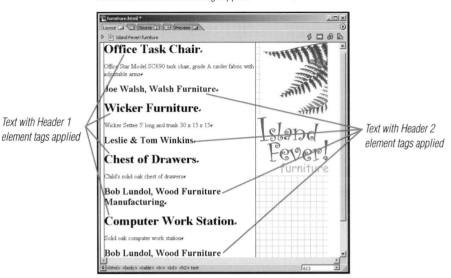

Text with Header 1 element tags applied

Text with Header 2 element tags applied

FIGURE C-11
Servitems.htm

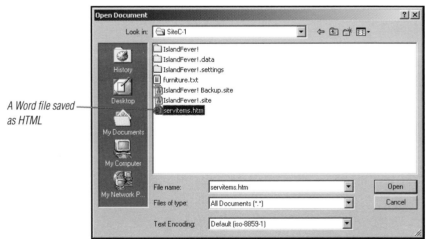

A Word file saved as HTML

5. Click in the text "Dance Classes," note that it is a Header 1 element, then click in other paragraphs, noting their element tags. Compare your window to Figure C-12.

The text was formatted in Microsoft Word using Word styles called "Heading 1" and "Heading 2." When you opened the HTML document in GoLive and copied the text into services.html, the Word styles were preserved as Header 1 and Header 2 element formats in the Layout Editor, and as elements bounded by <h1> and <h2> tags in the HTML source code.

6. Save services.html.

You added pre-tagged text to a Web page.

FIGURE C-12
Pre-tagged text

Heading 1 and Heading 2 styles in Word are Header 1 and Header 2 elements in Layout Editor

CREATE AND MODIFY AN INTERNAL STYLE SHEET

What You'll Do

Dance Classes

Gift Certificate for two dance classes a week for one month
at The Beat Performing Arts Studio and a T-shirt from the
Beat

The Beat Performing Arts Studio

Brows and Lip Wax

Dino's Hair Design

Hair Styling and Make-Up Application

One hair-cut and style with a stylist and a make-up
application provided by the Mane Attraction.

Mane Attraction

Photo Session

Photo session and One 16 x 20 master portrait

Hayes Button Image

Dental Visit for a Child

Child New Patient Visit includes complete oral exam,
charting, and evaluation; complete set of necessary
intraoral x-rays; professional teeth cleaning and hygiene
instructions; professional consultation with parent

 In this lesson, you'll create an internal style sheet.

Creating Element Styles and Style Sheets

Now that you have learned about applying element tags, it is extremely useful to know how to format multiple elements at once using styles and style sheets. As discussed earlier, when a standard HTML text element is created, it is automatically formatted with a default set of properties associated with that element. However, if only the default HTML styles were used for text in Web page designs, the Web would probably not be a very popular place to hang out! Fortunately, you can use styles and style sheets to override the default HTML styles in any Web site you create.

Style sheets are composed of element styles; an **element style** is a set of properties that applies to a designated element, such as a Header 1 element or a Paragraph element. An element style has the same name as the element to which it applies. For example, defining an element style called <h1> in a page's style sheet

Viewing style sheets with older browsers

Some older browsers do not recognize style sheets at all, and will display an element's default HTML formatting when the page loads. The formatting is not pretty, but the document will be readable. If your minimum standards require that the document be pretty in browser versions 3.0 and older, you can use manual in-line formatting to format the text on the page, but the formatting will usually override the style sheet in newer browsers.

instantly applies the <h1> element style to all <h1> elements (Header 1 elements) on that page. Similarly, defining an element style called <p> in a style sheet instantly applies the <p> style properties to all instances of a <p> element (Paragraph element) on that page.

In GoLive, you use the CSS Editor to create style sheets. When you are working within the CSS Editor, the Inspector becomes the CSS Style Inspector, as shown in Figure C-13; you use the CSS Style Inspector to specify the properties for each element style.

Understanding Style Sheet Types

Style sheets can be internal or external. An internal style sheet is embedded in a Web page's source code and applies only to that page. An external style sheet is a separate document and can be applied to multiple pages. The word "cascading" in cascading style sheets refers to the relationship between internal and external style sheets and is discussed further in the next lesson.

FIGURE C-13
Internal style sheet windows

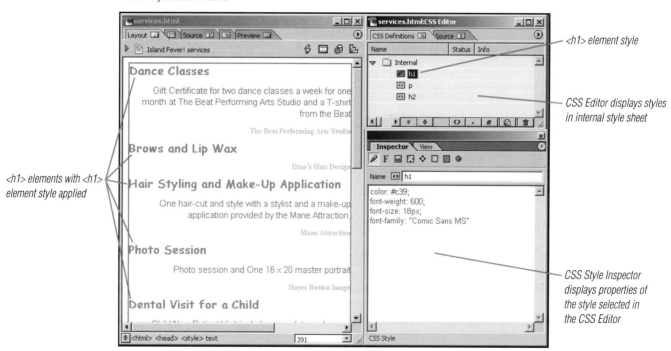

<h1> elements with <h1> element style applied

<h1> element style

CSS Editor displays styles in internal style sheet

CSS Style Inspector displays properties of the style selected in the CSS Editor

Create an internal style sheet

1. In services.html, click the Open CSS Editor button at the top of the Layout Editor to open the CSS Editor in a new window.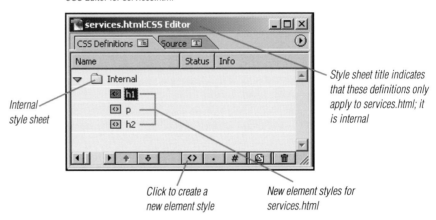

   Note that the CSS Editor has the name of the page in its title bar, because it includes information specific to the page.

2. In the CSS Editor toolbar at the bottom of the window, click the New Element Style button.

   An internal style sheet is created (as a folder called Internal) containing a new, unnamed element style.

3. Type **h1**, then press [Enter] (Win) or [return] (Mac) to create a style for all <h1> elements in services.html.

   You will define the style properties later.

4. Click the New Element Style button again, type **p**, then press [Enter] (Win) or [return] (Mac) to create a style for all <p> elements in services.html.

5. Click the New Element Style button again, type **h2**, then press [Enter] (Win) or [return] (Mac) to create a style for all <h2> elements in services.html. Compare your CSS Editor to Figure C-14.

You created an internal style sheet containing three element styles, without specified properties.

FIGURE C-14
CSS Editor for services.html

Internal style sheet

Style sheet title indicates that these definitions only apply to services.html; it is internal

Click to create a new element style

New element styles for services.html

1. Open the Inspector, if necessary, then click h1 in the CSS Editor to select the <h1> element style.

   When an element style is selected in the CSS Editor, the Inspector becomes the CSS Style Inspector. Note that the name of the element style selected in the CSS Editor (h1) is displayed in Name field of the CSS Style Inspector, as shown in Figure C-15.

   > TIP   If your CSS Style Inspector looks different from Figure C-15, click the Basic button on the Inspector toolbar. 🖉

2. In the Inspector, click the Font button to display the font properties of the h1 element style. **F**

3. Click the arrow next to the Color field, then click Fuchsia on the menu that appears.

   All <h1> elements in services.html become fuchsia.

4. In the Size field, type **18** to set the font size to 18 pixels (18px), then press [Tab] to apply the property.

   (continued)

FIGURE C-15
CSS Style Inspector

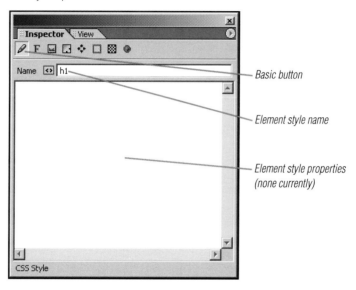

— Basic button

— Element style name

— Element style properties
(none currently)

5. Click p in the CSS Editor to show the properties for the <p> element style in the CSS Style Inspector.

6. Set the font color for the <p> element style to Green, set the font size to 14 pixels, type **25** in the Line Height field, then press [Enter] (Win) or [return] (Mac). Compare your Inspector to Figure C-16.

7. Click the Text button on the Inspector toolbar to view the text properties for the <p> element style.

   Text properties are properties that affect the appearance of text without directly changing the typeface.

8. Click the arrow next to the Alignment field, click Right, then compare your Inspector to Figure C-17.

(continued)

FIGURE C-16
Font properties

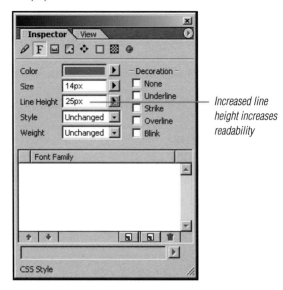

Increased line height increases readability

FIGURE C-17
Text properties

FIGURE C-18

<p> element style definition

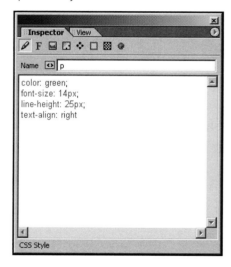

9. Click the Basic button on the Inspector tool-bar to see the property values of the <p> element style, reflecting the changes that you have made. Compare your Inspector to Figure C-18.

10. In the CSS Editor, click h2, then on the Inspector toolbar, click the Font button and set the font color to Yellow and the font size to 12 pixels. **F**

11. Click the Text button on the Inspector tool-bar, click the arrow next to the Alignment field, then click Right.

12. Save services.html.

   | TIP   Saving a page saves its internal style sheet.

You specified values for font and text properties in the <h1>, <p>, and <h2> element styles.

View CSS source code

1. In the CSS Editor, click the Source tab, then expand the window if necessary to see the source code for the internal style sheet.

2. In the document window, click the Source tab to see the style sheet where it resides in the source code for the page.

   The style sheet is enclosed in the <style> element, within the <head> element, as shown in Figure C-19. The comment tag (<!--...-->) around the style sheet causes older browser versions that don't recognize style sheets to ignore this information.

3. Return to the Layout Editor, then re-open the CSS Editor. 📖

   GoLive closes the CSS Editor when you click the Source tab in the document window.

You viewed the source code for services.html's internal style sheet in the CSS Editor and in the Web page source code.

FIGURE C-19
Internal style sheet

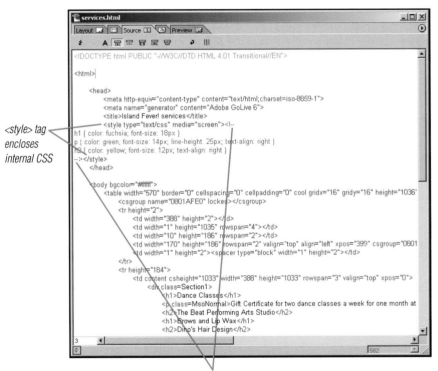

<style> tag encloses internal CSS

HTML comment element keeps the style sheet source code from appearing in older browsers

Formatting and Stylizing Text

**Arrange the workspace
for modifying internal
style sheets**

FIGURE C-20
Workspace for modifying CSS

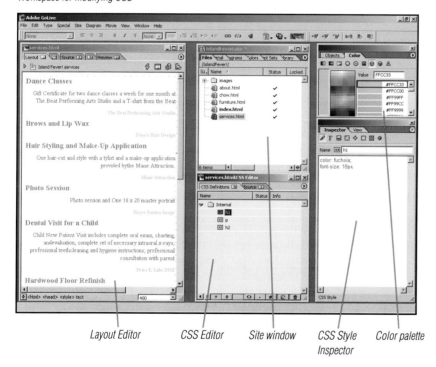

Layout Editor   CSS Editor   Site window   CSS Style
Inspector   Color palette

1. Open the Color palette Web Color List if necessary, then make sure that the Color palette and the Inspector are on the right side of the workspace, as shown in Figure C-20.

2. If necessary, move services.html to the left side of your workspace, and position the CSS Editor for services.html and the site window in the middle of the workspace, as shown in Figure C-20.

All of the tools you need for modifying the internal style sheet are now visible and accessible on the screen.

You arranged the workspace for modifying style properties in an internal style sheet.

Modify styles in an internal style sheet

1. In the CSS Editor, click the <h1> element style, then click the Font button in the Inspector to view the style font properties. **F**

2. In the Web Color List on the Color palette, select the CC3399 color, then drag the color from the preview pane to the font Color field in the CSS Style Inspector.

   The color of all of the Header 1 elements in services.html is updated.

3. In the Inspector, click the New Font button. 🔲

4. Click the arrow to the right of the FontName field, then click Comic Sans MS on the menu that appears.

   You have applied the font Comic Sans MS to the <h1> element style.

5. Click the list arrow next to the Weight field, then click 600. Compare your Inspector to Figure C-21.

   The thickness of a typeface is referred to as its weight.

   (continued)

FIGURE C-21
<h1> element style modified font properties

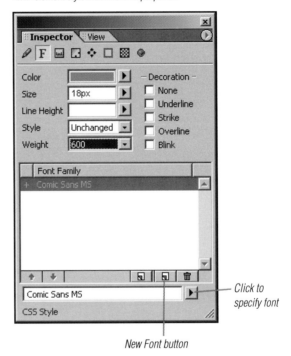

Click to specify font

New Font button

Click the <p> element style in the CSS Editor, click the New Font Family button (to the left of the New Font button) in the CSS Style Inspector, then click the second font family on the menu that appears (the Arial family). Compare your Inspector to Figure C-22.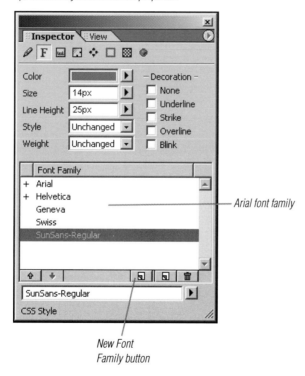

A font family is a set of similar fonts. When the browser loads the text element, it will display it in the first font in the font family that is found on the viewer's computer.

7. Click the Source tab in the CSS Editor window to view the style sheet.

8. Click the CSS Definitions tab, then save services.html.

You modified the font properties of the <h1> and <p> styles, and viewed the changes in the style sheet source code.

FIGURE C-22
<p> element style modified font properties

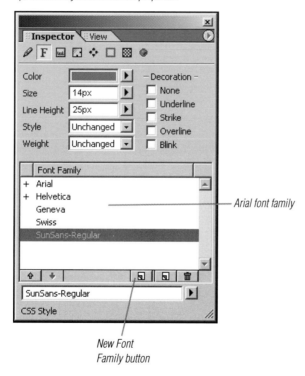

Arial font family

New Font
Family button

CREATE AND MODIFY AN EXTERNAL STYLE SHEET

What You'll Do

 In this lesson, you'll create an external style sheet, then apply the external style sheet to multiple pages within a site.

Understanding Cascading Style Sheets

As discussed earlier, an external style sheet is identical to an internal style sheet, but it is a separate document that is referenced by a page, rather than sitting within the code of the page itself. This way, multiple pages can reference one style sheet, and updating an element style in the external style sheet updates the element style in all of the pages that reference the style sheet.

It is important to understand why cascading style sheets are said to be "cascading:" this term refers to the fact that multiple style sheets can be in use at once for a Web page, and there is an order of precedence to those styles. Generally, the style closest to the affected text takes precedence. Thus, an internal style sheet within the source code for a page takes precedence over an external style sheet linked to that page.

For instance, if a page is linked to an external style sheet that contains <h1> and <h2> element styles, but has an internal style sheet embedded in its code that also contains <h1> and <h2> element styles, the <h1> and <h2> elements on that page will reflect the styles contained in the internal style sheet. If the <h1> and <h2> styles in the internal style sheet have undefined properties that are defined in the external style sheet, those properties will be set by the external style sheet. If the external style sheet has an <h3> element style, but the internal style sheet does not, any <h3> elements on the Web page will reflect the <h3> element style contained in the external style sheet. See Figure C-23 for an example of how an internal style sheet takes precedence over an external style sheet.

Creating an External Style Sheet

You can create a new external style sheet by clicking File on the menu bar, then pointing to New Special, then clicking Cascading Style Sheet. However, it is more likely, in application, that you will create a style sheet for a single page and then want to apply it to other pages. GoLive allows you to easily export an internal style sheet to an external style sheet. Using logical names for style sheets will help you to keep them straight in case you have several.

Unlike an internal style sheet, which is actually embedded in the page's source code, an external style sheet is a file that is referenced from a Web page's HTML header information. The reference includes the path from the page to the style sheet. In GoLive, you create the reference to an external style sheet using the Point and Shoot button, either to add the external style sheet to a single page's CSS Editor or to link an external CSS to a page or pages using the CSS palette and the site window.

FIGURE C-23
CSS precedence

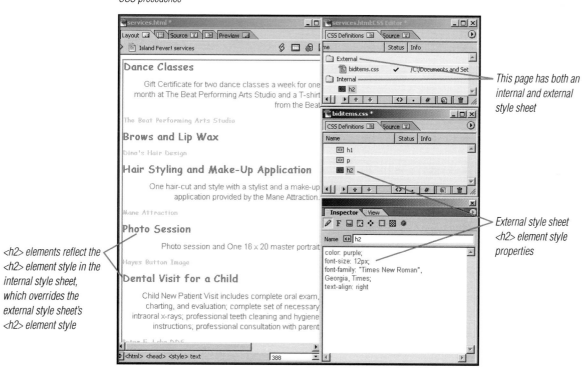

This page has both an internal and external style sheet

External style sheet <h2> element style properties

<h2> elements reflect the <h2> element style in the internal style sheet, which overrides the external style sheet's <h2> element style

Create an external style sheet

1. Click File on the menu bar, point to Export, then click Internal Style Sheet.

   TIP The CSS Editor must be open, with the CSS Definitions tab in front, in order for the Export command to be active.

2. In the Save As dialog box, type the filename **biditems.css**, then save the CSS file in the IslandFever! site folder, as shown in Figure C-24.

   The external style sheet, biditems.css, opens in a new window, as shown in Figure C-25.

   TIP The Save As dialog box will default to the last folder you saved to—be sure you are saving to the IslandFever! site folder! (The .html files are not displayed in the window because the style sheet file type is .css.)

3. Close biditems.css and services.html.

   The services.html CSS Editor closes with services.html.

You exported services.html's internal style sheet to an external style sheet named biditems.css.

FIGURE C-24
Save the external style sheet

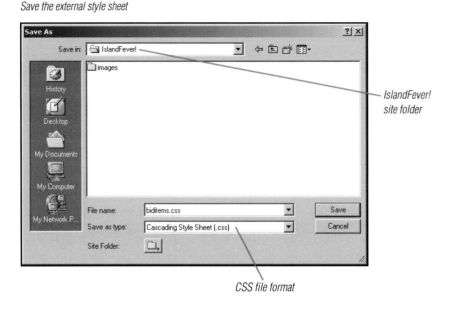

IslandFever! site folder

CSS file format

FIGURE C-25
External style sheet

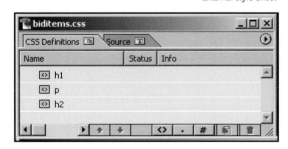

FIGURE C-26
External style sheet applied

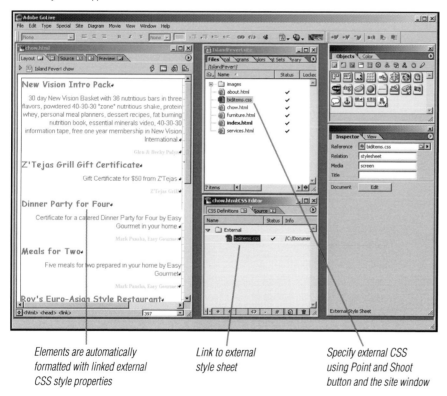

Elements are automatically
formatted with linked external
CSS style properties

Link to external
style sheet

Specify external CSS
using Point and Shoot
button and the site window

1. From the site window, open the document chow.html.

2. Open the Inspector if necessary, then click the Open CSS Editor button on the chow.html toolbar to open the CSS Editor for chow.html.

3. Arrange your workspace so that you have access to all open windows.

4. Click the New Link to External CSS button in the toolbar in the bottom of the CSS Editor window.

   An empty external style sheet reference is created in the CSS Editor, and the Inspector becomes the External Style Sheet Inspector.

5. Click the Point and Shoot button on the Inspector, then drag it to the biditems.css file in the site window to link the External Style Sheet Inspector Reference to biditems.css in the site window.

   Chow.html is instantly formatted with the style properties defined in biditems.css, and the chow.html:CSS Editor displays the link to the external style sheet, as shown in Figure C-26.

6. Save chow.html, then close chow.html and its CSS Editor.

   Saving a page saves its CSS Editor modifications.

You created a reference to an external style sheet in the CSS Editor for chow.html.

Apply an external style sheet using the CSS palette

1. Click about.html, hold down [Ctrl] (Win) or [shift] (Mac), click furniture.html, then click services.html in the site window to select all three files at the same time.

2. Click Window on the menu bar, then click CSS to open the CSS palette.

   The CSS palette can be used to apply an external style sheet to pages in the site window without opening the pages.

3. Click the Point and Shoot button next to the text box at the bottom of the CSS palette, point to biditems.css in the site window, then click Add. Compare your CSS palette to Figure C-27.

You added a reference to an external style sheet to the CSS palette for about.html, furniture.html, and services.html.

Modify a style in the external style sheet

1. Double-click on the biditems.css icon in the CSS palette to open the external style sheet editor, then close the CSS palette.

2. Click the <h2> element style in the CSS Editor, then view its font properties in the CSS Style Inspector.

3. From the Web Color List on the Color palette, select and drag the color FFCC33 from the Color palette preview pane to the <h2> font Color field. Compare your CSS Style Inspector to Figure C-28.

(continued)

FIGURE C-27
CSS palette

Click to assign a CSS to
multiple files in the site window

FIGURE C-28
CSS Style Inspector—<h2> element font properties

FIGURE C-29

Chow.html, furniture.html, and services.html with external style sheet applied

The biditems.css <h2> element style is overriden by an internal <h2> element style with the font color property Yellow

FIGURE C-30

Services.html without overrides

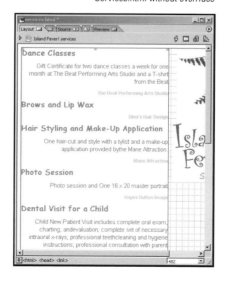

4. Save the style sheet.

5. Open chow.html, furniture.html, and services.html.

The <h2> elements are orange in chow.html and furniture.html, but not in services.html, as shown in Figure C-29. The color property defined in the internal style sheet for services.html is overriding the color property defined in the external style sheet.

You modified the font color property for the <h2> element style in the external style sheet, and viewed the effect of the update on three pages in the site.

Delete an internal style sheet

1. In services.html, click the Open CSS Editor button. 🔳

2. Click the h2 element style, then while holding down [Shift], click the other element styles in the Internal Style Sheet folder, then release [Shift] and click the Remove selected Items button on the CSS Editor toolbar to delete the internal style sheet. 🗑

Services.html is updated with the external style sheet styles, as shown in Figure C-30.

3. Save services.html, then close all pages.

You deleted the internal style sheet for services.html.

OVERRIDE STYLES

What You'll Do

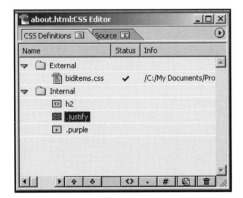

 In this lesson, you will view manual formatting overriding an external style sheet, override an existing external style sheet with an internal style sheet, and override element styles with class styles.

Overriding Styles

Applying consistent styles across a Web site aids reader comprehension and can be accomplished using external style sheets exclusively. However, there may be instances of a single page requiring a different element style than other pages in a site, and there may be instances of a single element requiring formatting that differs from the element style defined for it. This may be true in the case of a unique page in the site, or text within an element that needs highlighting. These cases don't justify the development of an additional external style sheet. Manual in-line properties can be used to format this text, because in-line properties override all styles. However, they must be applied to text selections one by one, so a set of properties cannot be quickly duplicated if it will be used more than once. The most efficient way to override external styles is with internal styles; similarly, the most efficient way to override properties of any element style is with a class style.

Using Class Styles

Similar to internal style sheets having precedence over external style sheets, class style properties have precedence over element style properties. If you have more styles than HTML elements (for instance, you would like to format <p> elements in

---

Overriding manually applied alignment properties

The GoLive alignment tools in the toolbar (the Align Right, Align Center, and Align Left buttons, and the Alignment submenu on the Type menu) are the exception to manual formats overriding styles. When you use these tools to align text, GoLive does not use in-line formatting tags as it does with the other tools. Instead, the Align tools create a division element with an alignment property, outside of the text element tags. Because the format closest to the text "wins" in cascading styles, manually applied alignment properties are overridden by alignment properties defined for element styles.

two different ways on your site), or if you want to override an element style (for instance, you would like to highlight a span of text within a <p> element), you can apply a class style to a paragraph element or span of text. A **class style** is a property or set of properties that overrides an element style. For example, a <p> element style with the font color Green will make all <p> elements green. A class style called ".gray" may have the font color property set to gray; when the class style is applied to a green <p> element (<p class="gray">... </p>), the gray font color in the .gray class style overrides the green font color in the <p> element style. You can assign a class style to multiple

element types. Using the example above, you can apply the class to an <h1> element (<h1 class="gray">... </h1>), and the class style will override the <h1> element style font color property, making that Header 1 element gray. See Figure C-31 for an example of class styles overriding element styles.

In GoLive, class styles are created in style sheets using a similar method to the one for creating element styles, and use the same properties in the Inspector as an element style. Applying class styles, however, is done using the CSS palette. The CSS palette allows you to apply the style to an entire element, to a span of selected text (a **span element**, with the tags

<span>...</span>), or to a selected block of text known as a "division." A **division element** (with the tags <div>...</div>) appears outside of a paragraph text element. As such, it does not override styles applied to text elements. Division elements can be used to apply properties to a block of text that are not specified in the text elements themselves.

QUICKTIP

You assign your own logical names to classes. A class style name is preceded by a period in a style sheet.

FIGURE C-31

Class styles applied to element styles

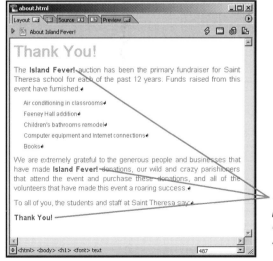

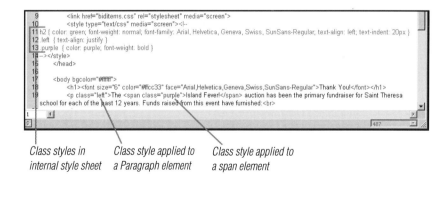

Class styles in internal style sheet

Class style applied to a Paragraph element

Class style applied to a span element

Class style properties override element style properties

View manual in-line style overrides

1. Open about.html, then click in the lines of text, noting that each is a <p> element.

   You applied the external style sheet to this page earlier through the site window, but the "Thank You!" font properties specified with in-line formatting tags (size, color, and font) are overriding the external style sheet. Properties not set by in-line tags, such as alignment, are inherited from the style sheet.

2. Click in the first line of text, "Thank You!," then click Header 1 on the Paragraph Format list in the toolbar.

   Because the alignment attribute for this element was not specified with in-line tags, nor was it specified for the <h1> element style in the external style sheet, the element is using the default Header 1 alignment attribute.

3. Click the Source tab, then compare your window to Figure C-32.

You viewed in-line style properties overriding style sheet properties and default style properties applying to text with no previously specified alignment properties.

FIGURE C-32

Style overrides

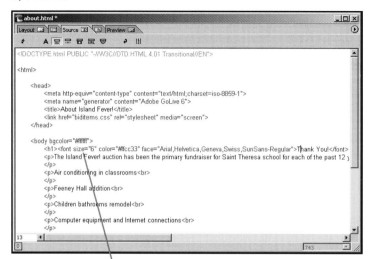

In-line properties override default HTML styles and <h1> element styles in internal or external style sheets

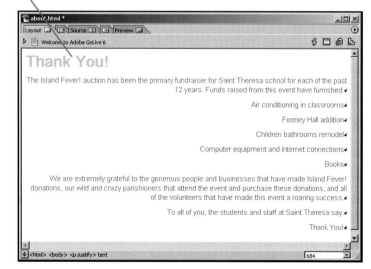

FIGURE C-33
Internal style sheet overrides external style sheet

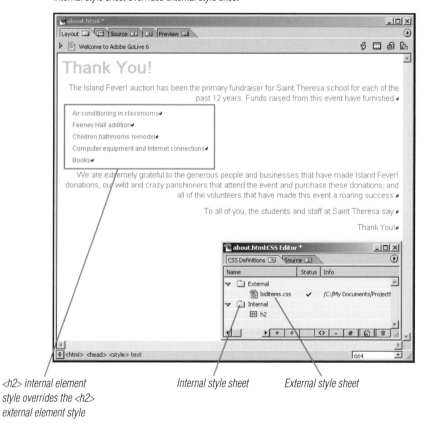

<h2> internal element
style overrides the <h2>
external element style

Internal style sheet   *External style sheet*

Override external style sheet properties with an internal style sheet

1. In the Layout Editor, select the text "Air conditioning in classrooms" and the four lines below it, then apply the Header 2 tag to this text.

   The elements pick up the <h2> style properties from the external style sheet.

2. Click the Open CSS Editor button, then click the New Element Style button.

   You created an internal style sheet with an unnamed element.

   TIP The New Element Style button is only active when the external style sheet is not selected.

3. Type **h2** to name the new element style, then press [Enter] (Win) or [return] (Mac).

4. On the CSS Style Inspector, click the Text button if necessary, then change the Alignment to Left and the Text Indent to 20 (pixels).

5. In the font properties area, change the Color to Green, the Weight to Normal, and the Font Family to the Arial family. F

6. Note the changes in about.html, then compare your screen to Figure C-33.

   The <h2> element style in about.html's internal style sheet overrides the external style sheet's <h2> element style.

You created an internal style sheet containing an element style that overrides an element style in an external style sheet.

Override an element style with a class style

1. In the CSS Editor, click the New Class Style button, type **justify**, then press [Enter] (Win) or [return] (Mac). [button]

2. Click the New Class Style button again, type **purple**, then press [Enter] (Win) or [return] (Mac). [button]

3. In the CSS Style Inspector font properties area, set the Color to Purple and the Weight to Bold.

4. Click .justify in the CSS Editor, then in the CSS Style Inspector text properties area, set the Alignment to Justify. [button]

5. Click Window on the menu bar, then click CSS to open the CSS palette.

6. Select the text "Island Fever!" in the second line of about.html, then in the CSS palette, click the checkbox to the right of "purple" and under "Span." Repeat this process for the other instance of "Island Fever!" on the page. Compare your screen to Figure C-34.

   You applied a class style to 2 different spans of text, overriding only the font color attribute from the element style.

   (continued)

FIGURE C-34
Class styles applied to about.html

New Class Style button   CSS palette

7. Select all of the text on the page except the first line, then in the CSS palette, click the checkbox to the right of "justify" and under "Par." Compare your screen to Figure C-35.

> TIP Sometimes class style formatting is not reflected in the Layout Editor. If this is the case for you, view the page in Layout Preview to see class styles applied.

8. Click the Preview tab to view the applied class styles.

9. Click the Source tab to view the source code for the new class styles.

   Note the <p> elements with the class attribute "justify" (<p class="justify">...</p>), and the <span> elements with the class attribute "purple" (<span class="purple">...</span>).

10. Save about.html and biditems.css, then close both files.

You created two class styles, then applied one to spans of text and the other to paragraph text elements.

FIGURE C-35

Class styles applied to <p> and <span> elements

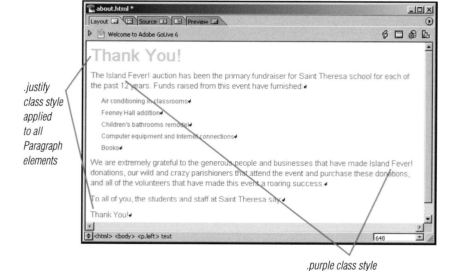

.justify class style applied to all Paragraph elements

.purple class style applied to spans of text

SEARCH TEXT FOR ERRORS

What You'll Do

In this lesson, you'll check the spelling throughout a site and find and replace text within the site.

Checking Spelling

You can check spelling of a single page or an entire site. When you check the spelling of a site, GoLive opens each page, then checks the text on the page, stopping for questionable words. For each questionable word, suggestions for correction are provided, along with options to ignore the word or to add it to the dictionary of words against which GoLive checks. When all of the text on a page has been checked, GoLive closes the page automatically.

You can choose to ignore all instances of the word during a spell check session (such as a proper name used throughout a site that GoLive thinks is a misspelling). You can also add such words to your GoLive dictionary, so that GoLive will ignore all instances of the word in future checks of any site or pages. You can edit your personal dictionary in Preferences.

QUICKTIP
GoLive will ignore HTML code and any text that appears in images in a spell check.

Finding and Replacing Text

The GoLive Find and Replace tools can be used to search a document, a site, or specified files. As living documents, Web pages will endure terminology changes, product versions, staff turnover, and event dates. The search tools in GoLive provide quick methods for updating a Web site to reflect such changes. You can also use the search tools for searching HTML source code. This feature can be useful for changing element tags and removing disruptive in-line styles in legacy Web sites.

FIGURE C-36

Check spelling dialog box

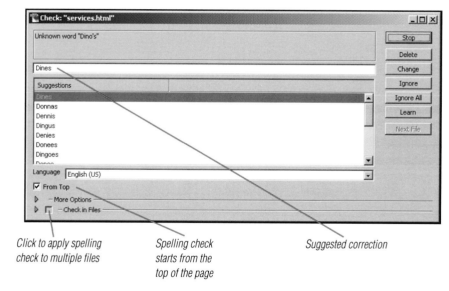

Click to apply spelling   Spelling check   Suggested correction
check to multiple files   starts from the
                                  top of the page

1. Open services.html. With your cursor anywhere in the services.html Layout Editor,
   click Edit on the menu bar, then click Check
   Spelling.

2. Click Start in the Check Spelling dialog box,
   then compare your screen to Figure C-36.

   > TIP   The From Top checkbox in the Check
   > Spelling dialog box is checked by default,
   > meaning that GoLive will start the spelling
   > check from the top of the document.

3. Click Ignore to allow the word Dino's to go
   unchanged.

4. When the text "tylist" is found, replace the
   suggestion "tallest" in the text box with
   stylist, then click Change.

5. When the text "bythe" is found, click Change
   to accept the suggested text "by the."

6. Continue checking the page, ignoring all
   suggestions except for missing spaces
   between words, until the top of the dialog
   box displays "No more misspellings found."

   It is important to check for missing spaces
   in pasted text, because changes in how text
   wraps in one document compared to another
   may eliminate spaces during the pasting
   process.

7. Close the Check Spelling dialog box, then
   save and close services.html.

You checked the spelling in a document.

Find and replace text

1. With just the site window open, click File on the menu bar, then click Save to save the site.

2. Click Edit on the menu bar, then click Find to open the Find dialog box.

   TIP If a window has been closed while on the left side of your workspace, it will open on the left side; move the Find dialog box to the right side of your workspace so it won't be covered by any files that open while finding and replacing text.

3. In the Find dialog box text box, type **Walsh**.

4. Click the arrow to the left of the word "Replace" in the dialog box to reveal the replace text box if necessary, then type **Welch** in the Replace text box.

5. Click the arrow to the left of the Find in Files checkbox if necessary, click the arrow next to Files from, then click IslandFever!.site to find and replace the indicated text in all files in the site. Compare your screen to Figure C-37.

   (continued)

FIGURE C-37
Find dialog box

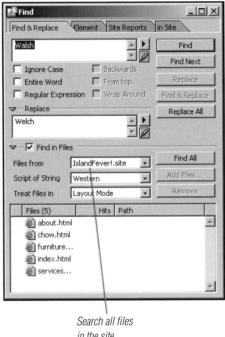

Search all files
in the site

FIGURE C-38

Find process completed

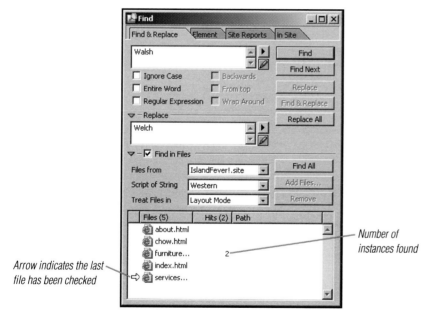

Arrow indicates the last file has been checked

Number of instances found

6. Click Find.

   The first instance is found in furniture.html; it opens with the text "Walsh" selected.

7. Click Find & Replace in the Find dialog box.

   The first instance is changed, and second instance of the text "Walsh" is selected.

8. Click Find & Replace in the Find dialog box, then compare your Find dialog box to Figure C-38.

   An arrow points to services.html, the last file in the Files list in the Find dialog box, indicating that all files in the list have been checked.

9. Close the Find dialog box, then save and close furniture.html and IslandFever!.site.

You searched and replaced text across the entire site.

China Mist Gourmet Iced Tea company is pleased with the pages you have designed for them so far. They would like to expand their Web site to include articles about tea that may be of interest to their customers. They have asked you to create a style that will make the articles easy and inviting to read on-line. They would like to use the style you create for future articles.

1. Navigate to the drive and folder containing your data files, then copy the contents of the SiteC-3 folder to the China Mist site folder you created in Section B.
2. Open the China Mist site, then open recipes.html. Apply <h1>, <h2>, <paragraph>, and <address> element tags to text within the page as seems appropriate.
3. Create an internal style sheet that includes styles for the <h1>, <h2>, <p>, and <address> elements, then modify each style's properties to make the page visually appealing.
4. Export the style sheet, then save it as **chinamist.css**.
5. Close all open pages, then apply the external style sheet to homebrew.html, recipes.html, and toatea.html.
6. Add an <h3> element style to the external style sheet.

7. Open homebrew.html, then define the <h3> element style properties in a way that makes the page visually appealing.
8. Modify the other element styles in the style sheet as appropriate to enhance the visual appeal of the page. Feel free to use Figure C-39 as a guideline.

9. Add a class style called **.indent** to the external style sheet that adds a 25 pixel indent, then apply the class style to the numbered items in the file. Compare homebrew.html to Figure C-39.

FIGURE C-39
Completed Project 1

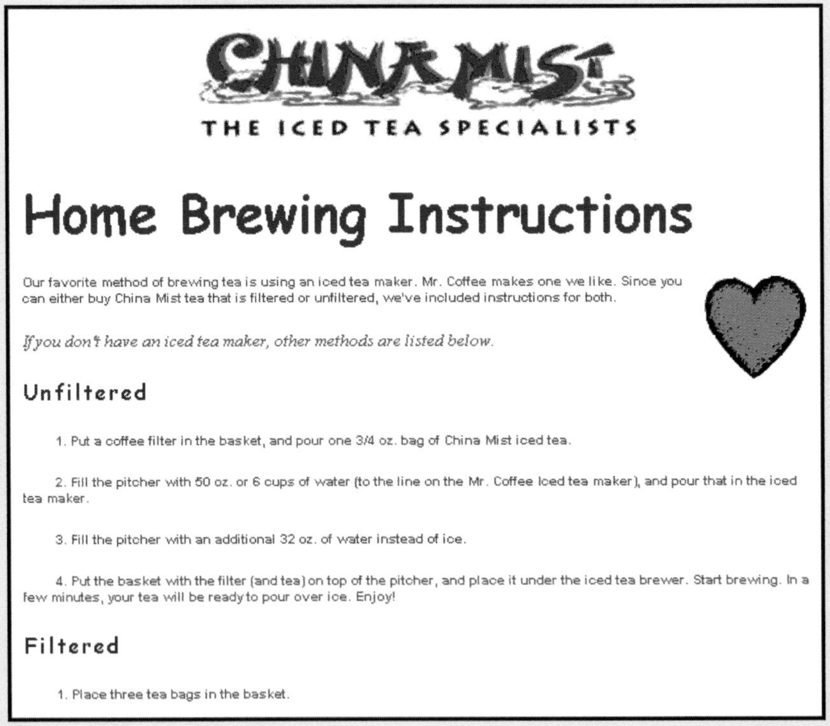

Home Brewing Instructions

Our favorite method of brewing tea is using an iced tea maker. Mr. Coffee makes one we like. Since you can either buy China Mist tea that is filtered or unfiltered, we've included instructions for both.

If you don't have an iced tea maker, other methods are listed below.

Unfiltered

1. Put a coffee filter in the basket, and pour one 3/4 oz. bag of China Mist iced tea.

2. Fill the pitcher with 50 oz. or 6 cups of water (to the line on the Mr. Coffee iced tea maker), and pour that in the iced tea maker.

3. Fill the pitcher with an additional 32 oz. of water instead of ice.

4. Put the basket with the filter (and tea) on top of the pitcher, and place it under the iced tea brewer. Start brewing. In a few minutes, your tea will be ready to pour over ice. Enjoy!

Filtered

1. Place three tea bags in the basket.

China Mist Gourmet Iced Tea Company is very pleased with the visual appearance of the page you designed for them listing their teas—it is fresh and flavorful. They have asked you to add the names of the teas to the page, keeping with the same fresh style for the text used on the page. They have provided some introductory text about their teas you can copy into the page, but the tea names will need to be typed in manually.

1. Navigate to the drive and folder containing your project files, copy the contents of the SiteC-4 folder to the China Mist project folder you created in Section B, then open China Mist.site.

2. Open teas.html, then add the tea names in text boxes next to each of the flavor icons, as shown in Figure C-40, tagging each tea name as an Address element. (*Hint*: Although you can experiment with combining tea names in a single text box, differences in line height handling by different browsers makes individual text boxes a more consistent method of aligning text to images.)

3. Add the text from teaintro.txt in a text box just under the navigation buttons. Tag this text as a Paragraph element, then create and define styles for the paragraph and address

elements in an internal style sheet so that the page is visually appealing. Feel free to use Figure C-40 as a guideline.

FIGURE C-40
Completed Project 2

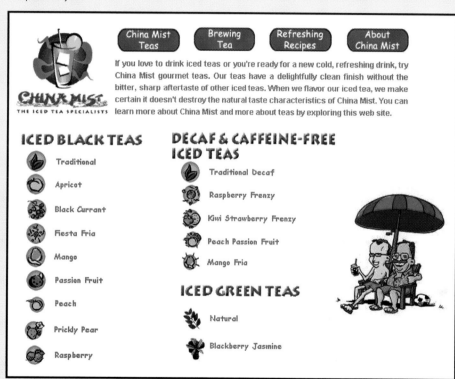

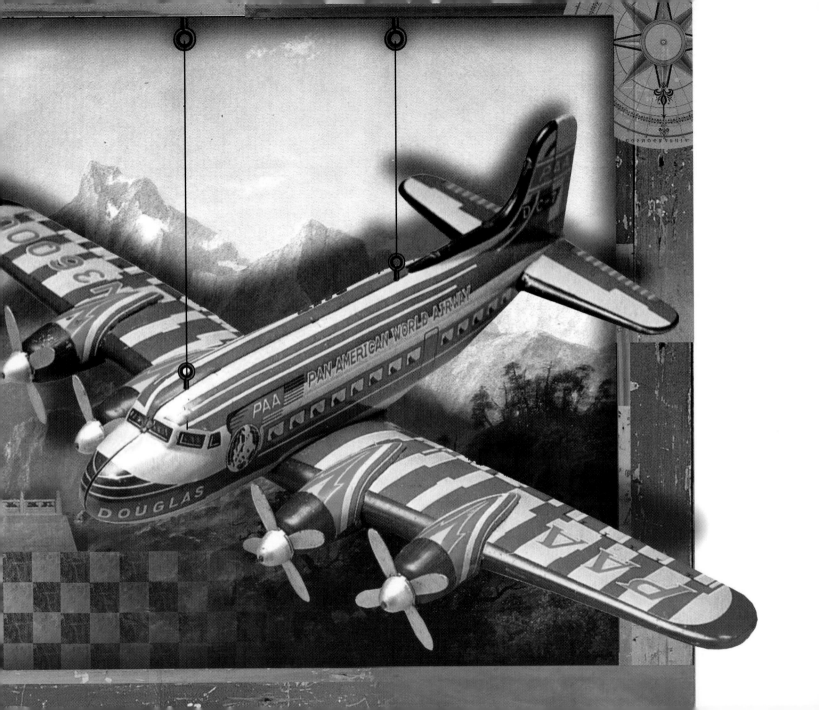

SECTION D

CREATING NAVIGATION LINKS

1. Create hyperlinks.

2. Enhance links with rollovers.

3. Store navigation links in a component.

4. Add links with an image map.

SECTION D
CREATING NAVIGATION LINKS

Introduction

Hyperlinks create the navigation system between the pages on your site and between your site and pages on other sites. A **hyperlink** is a Web page reference assigned to an image or selection of text; when that image or text is clicked, the referenced Web page opens. Because clicking on hyperlinks guides you from one Web page to another, hyperlinks are also called **navigation links**. This section will refer to navigation links as "links" for short (but keep in mind there are also other kinds of links, or "references," such as links from pages to images or from Smart Objects to their source files).

Visitors to a Web site want the site to be effective, responsive, and flexible: an effective site will allow a visitor to accomplish his or her objective at the site; sites that are responsive give lots of feedback with few surprises; and flexibility allows a visitor to move to a different page easily and consistently, wherever the person is in the site. You can create effective, responsive, and flexible sites by carefully evaluating your navigation links. Direct links to pages that target common visitor objectives, and that are named to describe the page's information or functionality, such as "Process Overview" or "Place Order," will go a long way towards making your site effective. You can assist a visitor to your site by adding responsiveness to your navigation links; for example, by having a link change appearance in response to visitor navigation actions. Continuously offering links to main topics on each page in a site offers flexibility, but you can sometimes guide a visitor by limiting the link options on a page. For example, it's a good idea to avoid navigation links on an order page, but including a Cancel button that returns to the previous page keeps it flexible. You can always ask a friend to visit your site to see how you've done!

Tools You'll Use

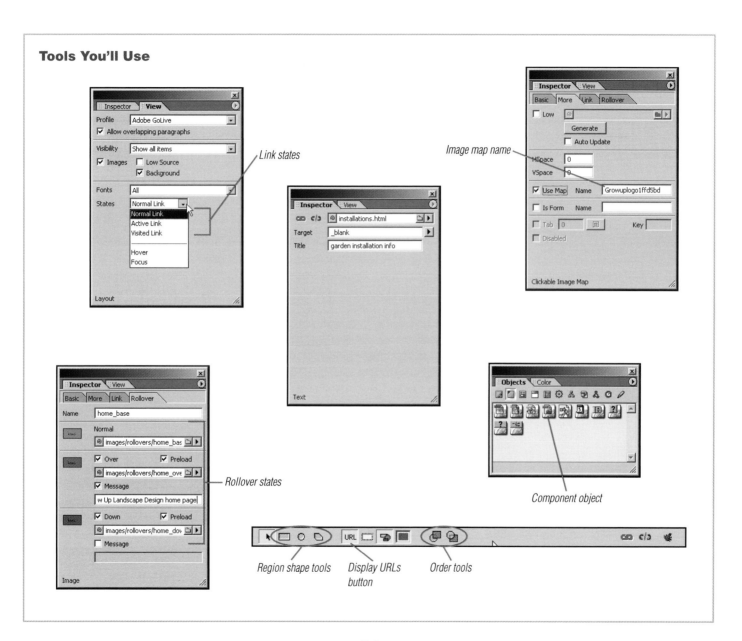

Link states

Image map name

Rollover states

Component object

Region shape tools

Display URLs button

Order tools

CREATE HYPERLINKS

What You'll Do

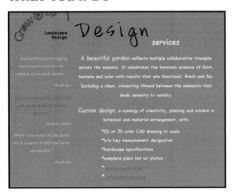

 In this lesson, you'll create hypertext links and image links to internal and external pages.

Understanding Image Links and Text Links

Hyperlinks in your Web pages are essential; they enable visitors to navigate to pages within your site, to Web pages in other sites, or even to an e-mail address you have designated for inquiries. Generally, Web users expect links to main topics to be images and links to supplemental information to be hypertext within the page text. This generality has evolved because main topics are more likely to stay the same throughout site development (thus enabling the use of images as stable design elements), while subtopics tend to be more dynamic. You can, however, use either text or images to present main topics or subtopics.

Image links provide great design flexibility and enable you to provide visitors with a visually interesting way to navigate through your site. Static image links are visually helpful, but they can also be made to be responsive using rollovers and actions. Rollovers and actions can be used to change an image visually in response to the visitor's mouse movements, providing specific information about the link or just giving the visitor confidence that clicking on the link will have an impact.

Text links are known as **hypertext**. Hypertext needs to be marked in some way so that the reader is aware that it is linked. Traditionally, hypertext has been blue and underlined.

Any consistent method of designating linked text will work, including altering the color, font, or weight of text. There is one important point to keep in mind when creating hypertext: the reader needs to recognize it as hypertext. Formatting hypertext in the same manner across a site, distinctive from non-hypertext, makes hypertext easily recognizable. For example, underlined hypertext is a great idea, but if non-hypertext headings are also underlined, the page is confusing. Careful consideration of the objective of your reader when creating hypertext words is important; using text that specifies the topic of the linked page is useful, while linked instructions, such as "click here," are distracting. Hypertext can make for very efficient reading, since it stands out on a page.

QUICKTIP
Hypertext is the foundation of the Web (hence **H**yper**t**ext **M**arkup **L**anguage).

Creating Hyperlinks

Hyperlinks are created within GoLive when you select the text or image in a page to link, then specify the address to which to link. You can specify the address in a couple of ways, both of which are very simple!

To create links to pages within your site, known as **internal links,** you can use the Point and Shoot button to link to a page in the site window, or you can drag a page from the site window to the selected text or image.

An internal link uses a relative address. A **relative address** is a path to a page that is based on the location of the page you are linking from. For example, a relative address for a link to a page located in a subfolder might look like "subfolder\newpage.html". A relative address for a link to a page located in a parent folder might look like "..\newpage.html" (".." indicates the parent folder). GoLive creates relative addresses for you and maintains them when you

use the site window to create links and rearrange files. You can use the site window to create all links to relative addresses because the site window gives you access to all of the files in your Web site.

On the other hand, you may want to point visitors to pages outside of your site for related information. To create links to pages outside of your site, known as **external links,** you type the address directly into the Inspector—you don't have access to the external files in the site window. An external link uses an **absolute address,** which includes the full path to the page address (e.g., http://www.course.com or mailto:info@course.com). Because their addresses are absolute, external links are not affected if you move a page.

Opening Linked Pages

When site visitors click a link, the linked page will open in one of two ways. The linked page can open in a new browser window, as shown in Figure D-1, or it can replace the contents of the existing browser window. Generally, it is preferable to have a linked page replace the contents of the browser window to prevent the development of a confusing stack of open windows. However, links to supplemental information, where the new page may not include navigation links or where the reader will likely want to return to the original page, may open in a new, additional browser window. For example, a link to an order form, definition, or bibliography entry might open in a separate window. You can specify a new window for the linked content, called a **target**, when creating a link. GoLive includes four target options in the Inspector: blank, _parent, _self, and _top. Specifying _blank as the target for a link will open the linked page in a new browser window. (The other three targets are used specifically for frames, a set of HTML elements that presents several pages in a single window.) If you do not specify a target for a link, the linked page will replace the existing page in the browser window. In Layout Preview, GoLive opens links to a new window in your browser, and links that replace window content in a GoLive window. You should always test your links in a browser for a better indication of their behavior.

FIGURE D-1

Linked page opens in a new window

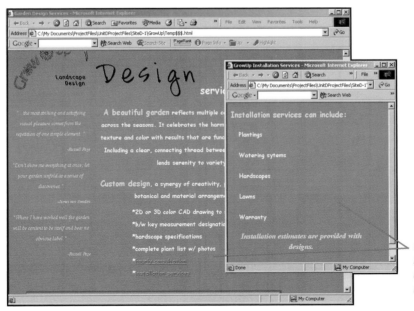

Clicking this link opened a new browser window; the window contains no links so it must be closed to continue

Understanding Link States

There are four states associated with text links: normal (visitor has not clicked it), visited (visitor has clicked it previously), active (visitor is in the process of clicking it) and hover (mouse is over the hypertext). The color of text in the first three of these states can be set using the Page Inspector (covered in Section A); all four can be modified using element styles. By default, hypertext is blue and underlined in its normal state.

The Open Window Action

If you want a link to open a page in a new window, consider using the Open Window action. The Open Window action, in addition to creating the link, will allow you to specify the new window's size, position, and properties. These can help your visitor to be aware that the previous window is still open. Turning off the new window's toolbar, menu, and status bar gives you more space for page content in a small window and can keep your visitor from getting confused about which browser navigation buttons to use, "forcing" him or her back to the original page. The Open Window action is covered in Section E.

Applying element styles to links

The element tag used to apply a link to text or an image is the <a> element (read "anchor element"). You can apply element styles to the four different link states (normal, active, visited, and hover) by creating <a:normal>, <a:hover>, <a:active>, and <a:visited> element styles in the CSS Editor. You will also find these elements on the CSS Editor menu (click the menu arrow ⊙, point to New Style, then click the appropriate element name). Element styles applied to links override page properties and paragraph element styles.

Arrange your workspace for creating links

1. Using the file management tool provided with your operating system, navigate to the drive and folder where your data files are stored, then copy the SiteD-1 folder to the drive and folder where you are storing your work for this section.

2. Start GoLive, open GrowUp.site from the SiteD-1 folder in the drive and folder where you are storing your work for this section, then open design.html.

3. Make sure the Inspector and Objects palette are open and appear on the right side of the workspace.

4. Click Window on the menu bar, point to Cascade and Tile, then click Tile Vertically to arrange your workspace for creating a hyperlink, as shown in Figure D-2.

You tiled the workspace windows vertically in order to prepare the workspace for easily creating links.

FIGURE D-2
Workspace for creating hyperlinks

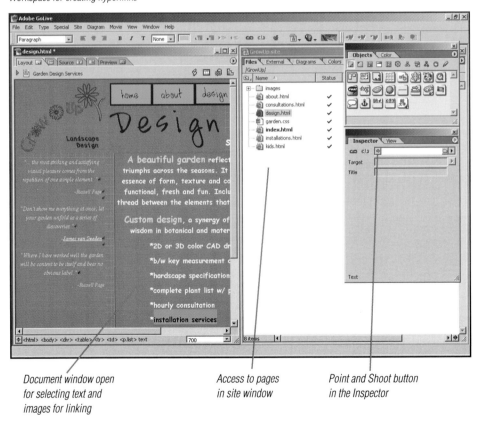

Document window open for selecting text and images for linking

Access to pages in site window

Point and Shoot button in the Inspector

FIGURE D-3

Installation services link

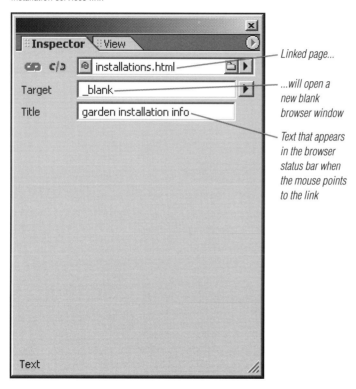

Linked page...

...will open a
new blank
browser window

Text that appears
in the browser
status bar when
the mouse points
to the link

1. In design.html, select the text "installation services" near the bottom of the page (do not select the "*").

   The Inspector becomes the Text Inspector.

2. In the Inspector, click and drag the Point and Shoot button to installations.html in the site window.

   The selected text on the page is now linked to installations.html, so that clicking on the text will open installations.html. The text is underlined, indicating that it now references a link.

   > TIP Once you have created a link, you can remove the link by clicking the Remove Link icon in the Inspector. c/ɔ

3. Click the arrow to the right of the Target field on the Inspector, then click _blank on the menu that appears to open the page in a new blank window.

4. In the Title field, type **garden installation info**, then compare your Inspector to Figure D-3.

   The link title will appear in the browser status bar when a page visitor's mouse hovers over the link.

You created and added a title to a hypertext link that will open the linked page in a new browser window.

Create a text link by dragging

1. In design.html, select the text "hourly consultation" (do not select the "*").

2. In the site window, click consultations.html, then drag the file to the selected text, as shown in Figure D-4.

   Note that clicking the file in the site window displays file information in the Inspector.

3. Click the selected text, then type **consulting services and pricing** in the Title field on the Inspector, leaving the Target field empty.

   The default value of the Target field assigns the linked page to the same browser window as the link, causing the linked page to replace the contents of the browser window when the link is clicked.

You created and added a title to a hypertext link that will replace the contents of the browser window with the linked page.

FIGURE D-4
Dragging a link

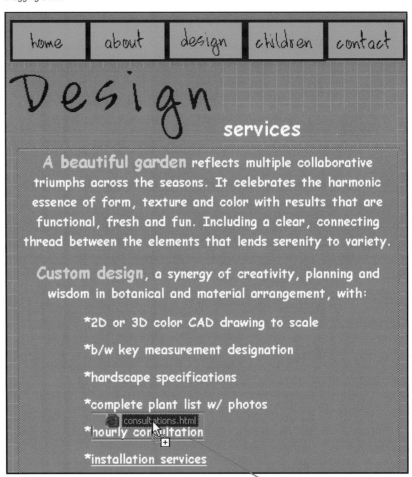

Dragging a page from the site window to text creates a link

FIGURE D-5
Link states on View palette

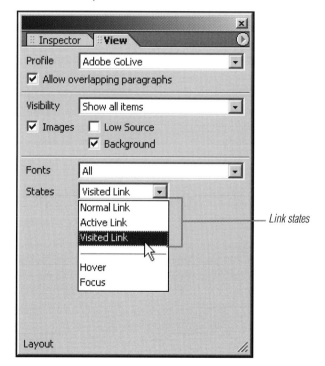

— Link states

1. In the Inspector, click the View tab and note that the States property is "Normal Link."

   Both instances of linked text on the page are formatted with the Paragraph element style, with an underline added to indicate the text is linked.

2. Click the States list arrow, then click Visited Link, as shown in Figure D-5.

   When the pages in the Grow Up site were developed, the Visited Link color in the Page Inspector was set to green. Thus, when you view the Visited Link state, the text appears green.

3. Click the Preview tab, then click installation services to test the link.

   The installations.html page opens in a new browser window.

4. Close the installations.html window.

5. Click hourly consultation.

   The consultations.html page opens in a new GoLive window in the Layout Editor, though the link was set to replace the browser window contents when clicked.

   (continued)

Lesson 1   Create Hyperlinks

6. Close the consultations.html window.

7. Click the Show in Browser button list arrow, then click a browser on the Show in Browser menu. 🐁▾

   TIP If you open the page using the same browser that opened when you earlier clicked the installation services link in Preview, the installation services hypertext appears in the visited state because it was previously "visited" by the browser.

8. Click installation services to test the link, then close the window.

   The installations.html page opened in a new window, as shown in Figure D-6.

9. Click hourly consultation.

   The consultations.html page replaces design.html in the browser window.

10. Close the browser.

You tested links in Layout Preview and in a browser.

FIGURE D-6
Link with _blank target opens in a new window

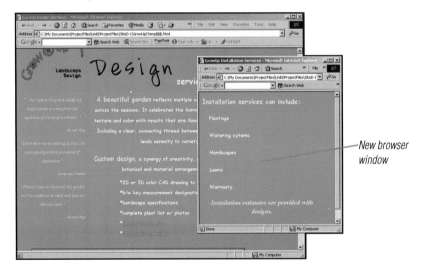

—New browser window

FIGURE D-7

Creating an image link

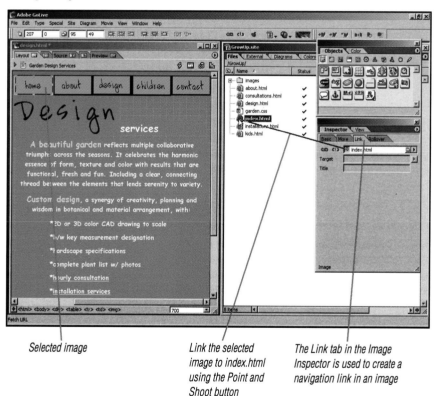

Selected image

Link the selected image to index.html using the Point and Shoot button

The Link tab in the Image Inspector is used to create a navigation link in an image

1. Return to the Layout Editor, then click the home image in the navigation bar at the top of the design.html page.

2. In the Inspector, click the Link tab to view the image's Link properties.

   TIP The information in the Source field on the Basic tab may look like a link, but it simply contains the source information for the image. There is no link information for the image yet.

3. Click the Point and Shoot button, then drag the pointer to index.html in the site window to link the image to index.html, as shown in Figure D-7.

4. In the Inspector, type **Grow Up home page** in the Title field.

5. In the Layout Editor, repeat Step 3 to link the about image to about.html, the design image to design.html, and the children image to kids.html.

6. Click the Preview tab, test each of the image links, then close the linked windows.

   TIP Clicking the Design link has no impact because you are already viewing the linked page: design.html.

7. Save design.html.

You created navigation links using images.

Create external links

1. In the Layout Editor, click the contact image in the navigation bar at the top of design.html.

2. In the Image Link Inspector link field text box, type **info@gugardening.com**, then press [Enter](Win) or [return](Mac) as shown in Figure D-8.

   GoLive inserts "mailto:" before an e-mail address in the link text box, which tells the browser to open a new message in an e-mail program, with the e-mail address in the To: field.

   | TIP   This is a fictitious e-mail address.

3. In the quotes column on design.html, select all of the text in the quote by James van Sweden. (Do not select the name "James van Sweden.")

4. In the Inspector link field, type the URL for a gardening Web site of your choice, then press [Enter] (Win) or [return] (Mac).

   GoLive inserts "http://" before a Web address in the link text box, which tells the browser this page is an external link using the http protocol.

   (continued)

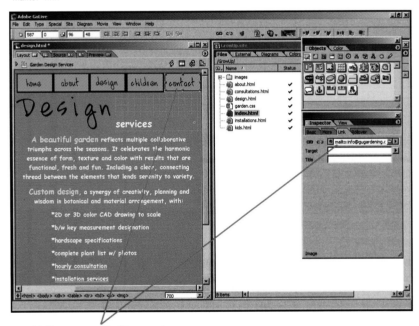

Linking to an e-mail address creates a "mailto:" link that opens a new e-mail message with the address in the To: field

FIGURE D-9

Inspector for external link in new window

External link uses an absolute address

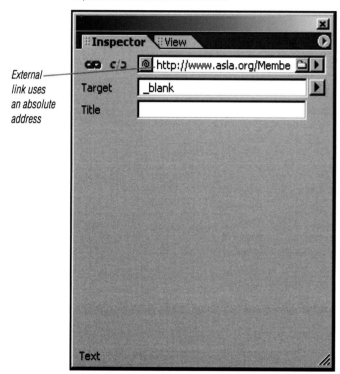

5. Click the arrow to the right of the Target field, then click _blank so that the linked page will open in a new window when the link is clicked. Compare your Inspector to Figure D-9.

6. Click the Preview tab, then test each link.

   The contact link opens a new message in an e-mail program (if associated), and the external link opens in a new browser window.

7. Close the browser and e-mail program, then save the page.

You created a link to an e-mail address and an external link to a Web page in another site.

ENHANCE LINKS WITH ROLLOVERS

What You'll Do

In this lesson, you'll enhance image links with rollovers.

Understanding Rollovers

Rollovers add interactivity to your image links, causing them to respond to a visitor's actions with a visual change. A rollover is a "cosmetic enhancement" to an image link, not a required functionality, but it is a valuable tool for providing responsiveness to your site. When the visitor rolls the mouse pointer onto a rollover image or holds the mouse button down on the image, the image changes its appearance in response. As is the case with hypertext, rollovers also have states: normal (visitor is not clicking it), over (visitor has the mouse pointer over it), and down (visitor is clicking it). Each state requires its own separate image; the over and down state images are usually a variation of the normal image. As with regular links, you can add a message to a rollover state that will display in the browser status bar when the visitor hovers over the image with the mouse or clicks it outright.

Using the GoLive rollover naming conventions will assign rollover images automatically to the over and down states, once you assign the normal image. This naming scheme requires that the normal image name have a suffix of _base (e.g., home_base.gif), the over image name be the same name but with the suffix _over (e.g., home_over.gif), and the down image name be the same with the suffix _down (e.g., home_down.gif). Specifying an image with the _base suffix as the source for an image on the Rollover tab will automatically create a rollover if images with the _over and _down suffixes exist in the same folder.

QUICKTIP

Adding rollovers to your image links will multiply the number of images on your site. Using the GoLive rollover naming conventions and sorting images into folders can help keep you organized and make creating rollovers a very efficient process in GoLive.

FIGURE D-10

Site window with _base, _over, and _down images

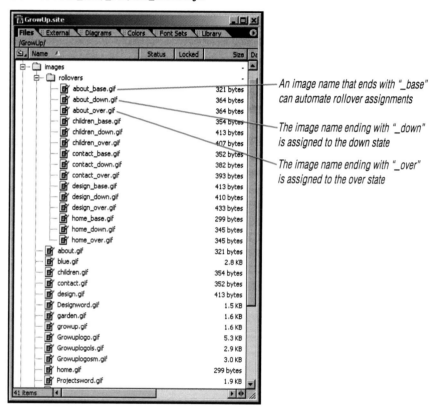

An image name that ends with "_base" can automate rollover assignments

The image name ending with "_down" is assigned to the down state

The image name ending with "_over" is assigned to the over state

Create rollovers

1. In the site window, expand the images folder, then expand the rollovers folder. Compare your site window with Figure D-10.

2. Return to the Layout Editor, then click the home image in the navigation bar.

3. In the Inspector, click the Rollover tab.

4. Click the Point and Shoot button in the Normal area, then drag the pointer to home_base.gif in the rollovers folder to link the home image to home_base.gif.

   The home_base image is a copy of home.gif. When a file with "_base" at the end of its filename is linked to an image, and files with the identical name (home) plus _over and _down suffixes exist in the same folder, the Over and Down states are automatically checked and linked to home_over.gif and home_down.gif, respectively.

   (continued)

5. Click the Message checkbox in the Over area of the Rollover Inspector, then type **Grow Up Landscape Design Home Page** in the text box, as shown in Figure D-11.

   The text "Grow Up Landscape Design home page" will appear in the browser status bar when the mouse hovers over the button.

6. Repeat Steps 4 and 5 for the about, design, children, and contact buttons to link each to its rollover counterpart with the respective messages: **About Grow Up**, **Design Services**, **Projects for Children**, **E-mail Jayme at Grow Up**.

   You created rollover actions for each navigation bar button.

FIGURE D-11
FIGURE D-11
Rollover setup

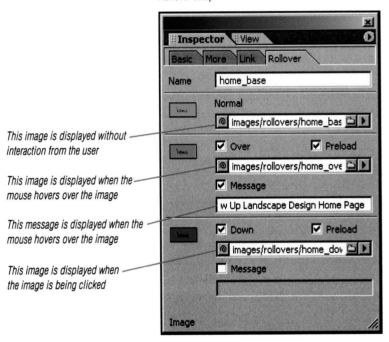

This image is displayed without interaction from the user

This image is displayed when the mouse hovers over the image

This message is displayed when the mouse hovers over the image

This image is displayed when the image is being clicked

FIGURE D-12
Over state

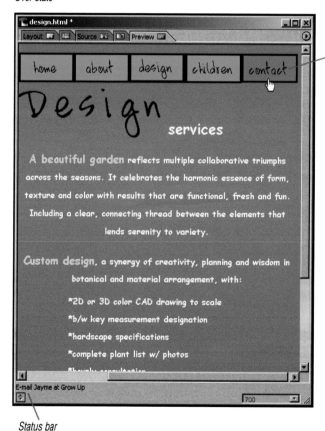

When the mouse pointer hovers over the image, contact_over.gif is displayed

Status bar message

Test the rollovers

1. Click the Preview tab, then hover the mouse over each button, noticing the messages in the status bar at the bottom of the window (Win only), as shown in Figure D-12.

   The _over image displays when the mouse hovers over the image.

2. Click each button, releasing the mouse button only when you've moved the mouse off of the image.

   The _down image displays when the image is clicked.

3. Save design.html, then return to the Layout Editor.

You tested the image rollovers in Layout Preview.

STORE NAVIGATION LINKS
IN A COMPONENT

What You'll Do

 In this lesson, you'll create a component containing navigation buttons, then add the component to multiple pages in a site.

Understanding Components

Once you've added a navigation bar to one page, it's hard to imagine going through the repetitive process of adding the same navigation bar to every single page in your site. If this were the only option, adding pages would be a chore and implementing changes to a navigation bar would be especially grueling!

Luckily, you can use GoLive to create a component that will help with this task. A **component** is a single source of content, including any combination of text, images, and GoLive objects, that can be reused on any page.

Components are a great example of the foundational theory of the markup languages. The theory, expressed in terms such as "reuse" and "single-source," is that documents, including HTML pages, consist of small and reusable pieces of data. Markup languages allow your documents to point to these pieces of data. This way, the data can exist in one place and be used in many documents. The result is more efficient composition and editing of documents. Specifically, HTML allows you to reference a single image in multiple pages, and any modifications to that image will be reflected in each page. Similarly, GoLive allows you to reference a component from any page in a site, meaning you only need to create the component once to make content available for use in multiple places.

A navigation bar is an especially good candidate for a component, as shown in Figure D-13, because creating one can be time consuming, with multiple images and links. Additionally, navigation bars may be updated often. However, you can use a component for any content in multiple pages, such as site credits or legal text. Using a component will help you to keep repeated content consistent in all of the pages that reference it, because editing a component will update each of the pages referencing it.

QUICKTIP

Components used in a page can be unlinked from their source file, if desired, so that changes to a component source file will be not be reflected on that page.

Creating Components

You create a component in a blank Web page. The component will consist of everything included in its <body> element in the source code. The size of the component is based on the size of objects within the <body> element. Using a layout grid, you can be specific about the size of the component in the Layout Editor, keeping in mind that GoLive will add 32 pixels of space (two horizontal grid lines using the layout grid's default spacing) under a component when added to a page.

Components are saved to the Components folder within the site's data folder. The data folder, and the folders within it, are used for sources of GoLive data. GoLive components are not a feature of the Web; rather, they are a feature for efficient development within GoLive. When you upload a page that references a component, GoLive embeds the component source code into the page source code. GoLive can accomplish this only if the component is stored in the Components data folder, which tells GoLive it needs to be handled as a component.

Using Components

A component is a GoLive Smart Object. To use a component, you first add a Component object to your page from the Objects palette, then link the Component object to the component file in the site window. You can locate the Components folder on the site window's Extras tab, where the site data folders are stored. Components can be added to any page or to any object, including a layout grid, layout text box, table, or floating box. Other objects on the page, or within the same parent object, will move to accomodate a component if necessary. It is a good idea to create enough room in a page or object prior to adding a component—remembering to account for the space added by GoLive—because an object that moves to accommodate the component will move according to a combination of its properties and of its parent object properties and can result in unexpected page layouts.

FIGURE D-13
Components

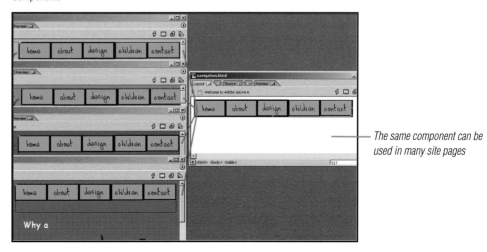

The same component can be used in many site pages

Create a component

1. Add a new, blank page to GrowUp.site.

2. Add a layout grid that is about 600 pixels wide.

3. Arrange your workspace windows so that both the top of design.html and the top of the new page are visible.

4. In design.html, hold down [Shift], click each of the buttons in the navigation bar across the top of the page to select them all, then drag the group of buttons to the new page, aligning them to the top left of the layout grid.

   TIP Be sure the layout grid has been deselected before dragging the buttons to the new page.

5. Close design.html.

6. Resize the layout grid in the new page to the width and height of the buttons, as shown in Figure D-14.

   When added to a new page, the size of a component is based on the size of the layout grid in the component.

   (continued)

FIGURE D-14
Completed component setup

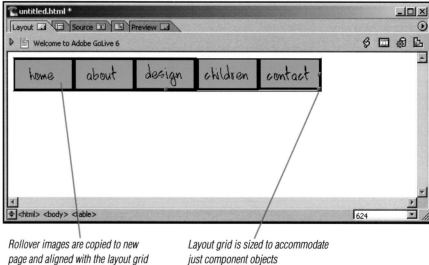

Rollover images are copied to new page and aligned with the layout grid

Layout grid is sized to accommodate just component objects

Saving a component

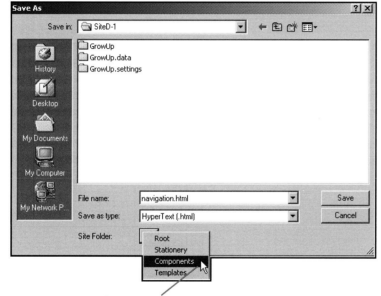

Click to save the component to
the Components folder in the site
data folder (GrowUp.data)

7. Click File on the menu bar, click Save As,
   click the Site Folder button at the bottom
   of the Save As dialog box, click Components
   on the Site Folder menu as shown in
   Figure D-15, type **navigation.html** in the
   File name text box (Win) or Save As text box
   (Mac), then click Save to save
   navigation.html in the site's Components
   folder. ☐

8. Close navigation.html.

*You created a GoLive component and saved it in
the site's Components folder.*

Arrange your workspace for working with a component

1. Open index.html.

2. Tile index.html and the site window horizontally, making sure the Inspector and the Objects palette are open.

3. In the site window, click the double-arrow button to show the right pane in the site window, with the Extras tab in front.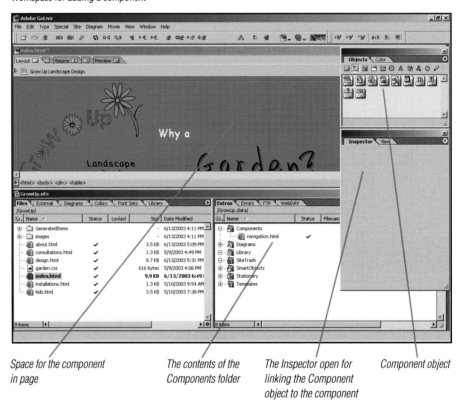

   The Extras tab displays the GoLive data folders, which contain any GoLive objects that will be converted when uploaded to the Web.

4. Expand the Components folder, if necessary, to see navigation.html, then compare your screen to Figure D-16.

You tiled the windows in the workspace and opened the right pane of the site window to prepare your workspace for adding a component.

FIGURE D-16
Workspace for adding a component

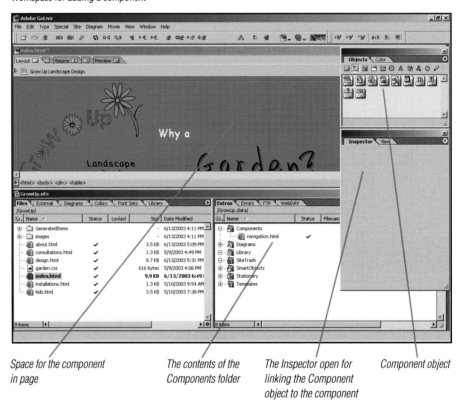

Space for the component in page

The contents of the Components folder

The Inspector open for linking the Component object to the component

Component object

1. In the Objects palette, click the Smart button to see the GoLive Smart Objects.

2. Drag the Component object from the Objects palette to just right of the Grow Up logo, then align it with the top of the layout grid.

    The Inspector becomes the Component Inspector, and displays "(EmptyReference!)" in the Page field.

3. With the Component object selected in index.html, use the Point and Shoot button in the Component Inspector to link the component to navigation.html in the site window, as shown in Figure D-17.

    The navigation component is added to index.html, with 32 pixels of space added below it.

4. Click the Preview tab, then test each of the image links in the component.

5. Save index.html, then click the double-arrow button to hide the right pane of the site window.

You added the navigation bar component to index.html.

FIGURE D-17

Adding a component

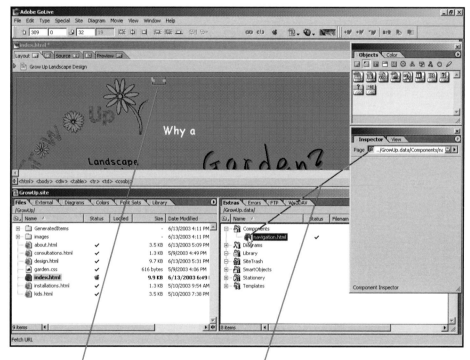

The Component object is placed on the page and selected

Use Point and Shoot to link the selected Component object to navigation.html

ADD LINKS WITH AN IMAGE MAP

What You'll Do

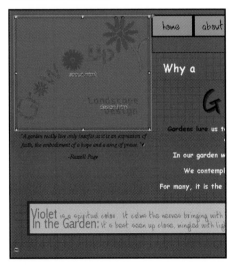

In this lesson, you'll add multiple linked regions to an image using an image map.

Linking an Image to Multiple Pages

As you gain experience developing Web pages and get more and more creative in creating navigation links, you may want to use a single graphic to link to several different pages. These days, in fact, it's possible to create a Web page that consists entirely of a single graphic!

These ideas were taboo in the early days of the Web, because downloading images was painfully slow. However, as bandwith has increased and affordable computers have become faster, the Web and browsers have gotten better at handling larger and more sophisticated graphics. These advancements allow graphic designers to be more involved in Web development, with less dependency on a technical counterpart. Still, you must consider your audience profile when deciding on the use of graphics in your site.

Designers of sites that can handle larger graphics will appreciate the interactivity that can be added to an image using an image map. An **image map** is a single image that contains regions that are linked, or "mapped," to actions or to other pages. Imagine a house plan image, where each room outline links to specifications for that room. Imagine an image of an appliance where each part of the appliance is linked to a closeup and description of the part. Imagine a group photo where each face is linked to a profile. The possibilities produced by the use of your own creativity with image maps will keep your Web sites dynamic and compelling!

Creating Image Maps

To create an image map, you first select the image and then click the Image Map checkbox in the Image Inspector's More tab. Doing so will create the source code for a map applied to the selected image and display a toolbar for specifying the linked regions. You can select a shape tool, then click and drag on the image to outline a region. Each region behaves as a separate image, in that each can be linked to a different page or action. To link an image map region, you click on it, then use the Inspector to link it—as you do with any normal image. You can also specify a title and target for each image map region using the Image Map Area Inspector.

Drawing regions in an image map can be a bit challenging with the limited shape tools, but you can draw rough shapes and then resize or reposition them. Shapes that overlap can be put in order using the Send Region to Back/Front button. The link a visitor goes to when an overlapping region is clicked is determined by the shape in front.

Viewing an Image Map

An image map with lots of linked regions can become complex. The image map toolbar offers viewing options that will help you to track the map regions and links in the Layout Editor. When you draw a shape to define a region, the region is highlighted in a transparent color. In addition, clicking the URL button in the toolbar displays a region's link address on the region. See Figure D-18 for an example of an image map. Though these indicators may at first seem to complicate the view, they are very useful when you revisit a map for modifications.

FIGURE D-18
An image map

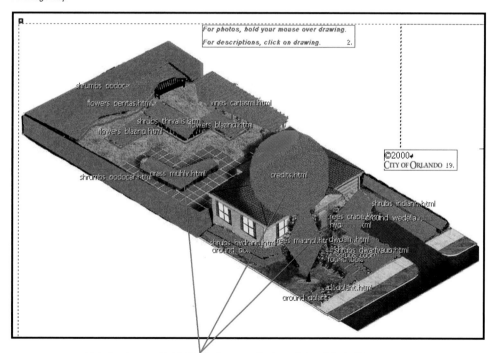

Linked regions are highlighted by transparent color and show linked addresses

Create an image map

1. In the Layout Editor, click the Grow Up logo image, then click the More tab in the Inspector.

2. In the Inspector, click the Use Map checkbox to select it, as shown in Figure D-19.

   GoLive created and named an image map element within the index.html source code; the toolbar changes to the Image Map toolbar for drawing map regions on the image.

3. In the toolbar, click the Create Rectangle button, then draw a rectangle around the words Landscape Design, as shown in Figure D-20. ▭

4. Use the Point and Shoot button in the Inspector to link the region to design.html.

5. Click the Create Rectangle button, then draw a rectangle around the entire Grow Up graphic. ▭

   > TIP To avoid resizing a graphic while drawing regions, draw a small region well inside the edges of the image, then resize the area. If you accidentally resize the Grow Up graphic, click Edit on the menu bar, click Undo Set Size, then try again.

6. Use the Point and Shoot button to link the selected area to about.html.

7. In the toolbar, click the Send Region to Back button to send the last shape you created to the back. ▣

   Sending the region "to the back" puts it behind the Landscape Design region. The area "in front" has precedence.

You created an image map by defining two linked regions in a graphic.

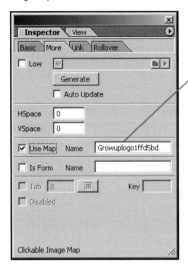

Image map element created and named by GoLive (yours will vary)

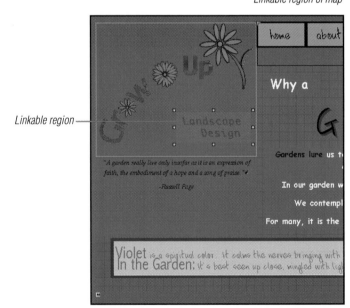

Linkable region

FIGURE D-21

URLs to which the image map links

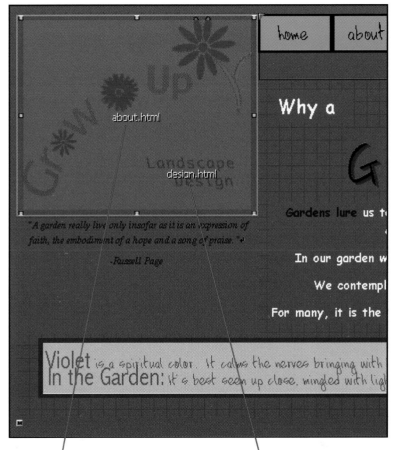

This region will open
about.html when clicked

This region (in front of the larger region)
will open design.html when clicked

1. Click the URL button on the toolbar to display the pages to which the image map's linked regions link, as shown in Figure D-21. URL

2. Click the Preview tab, then test both links.

3. Click the Layout tab in index.html, save and close the file, then save and close the site.

You tested the linked regions of an image map.

China Mist has approved all of your page creations, but would like the navigation bar you've created to be more interactive. You have decided to use rollover graphics to accomplish this task and have already created appropriate images for each button in Photoshop using the _base, _over, and _down suffixes. Now you need to create the rollover effects in the navigation bar. Given that you want the rollovers to appear on the navigation bar, and the navigation bar will appear on every page in the site, you plan to create a component of the navigation bar to reuse throughout the China Mist site.

1. Navigate to the drive and folder containing your data files, then copy the contents of the SiteD-3 folder into the images folder in the China Mist project folder that you created in Section C.
2. Open China Mist.site, then add a new page to the site containing a layout grid 600 pixels wide, with Snap turned off.
3. Drag each of the "_base" images from the images/rollovers folder in the site window to the blank page's layout grid. Add 10 pixels HSpace and 5 pixels VSpace to each image.

4. Align images to the top of the layout grid and side by side, in the same order from left to right as they appear in index.html. Select all of the images, then align the group of images to the left side of the layout grid. Resize the layout grid to the size of the image group.
5. Link each button to the following pages in the China Mist site, then add a message (as indicated below) that will appear on the status bar when the mouse hovers on the button:

	Link to:	Message:
brewtea_base.gif	homebrew.html	**Home brewing instructions**
cmteas_base.gif	teas.html	**List of China Mist teas**
recipes_base.gif	recipes.html	**Iced tea recipes**
aboutcm_base.gif	toatea.html	**Story of China Mist**

FIGURE D-22
Completed Project 1

6. Save the file as a component, naming the file **navigation.html**, then close the file.
7. Add the navigation.html component to the very top of each page in the China Mist site, making any adjustments necessary to the pages' layouts, as shown in Figure D-22. (*Hint*: Delete the existing buttons from both index.html and teas.html before adding the component to these pages.)
8. Save all open files.

Navigation.html component

PROJECT 2

The Public Relations Director for China Mist is impressed with the page you created to list the company's teas. He wants each tea to have its own page containing a description of that tea. He has asked you to link each tea to a simple page, to which they will add tea descriptions later.

1. Navigate to the drive and folder containing your data files, then copy the teapages folder in the SiteD-4 folder into the China Mist site folder.
2. Open teas.html. Link the name of each tea and its image to the corresponding page in the teapages folder. Save the file, then compare your screen with Figure D-23.

FIGURE D-23
Completed Project 2

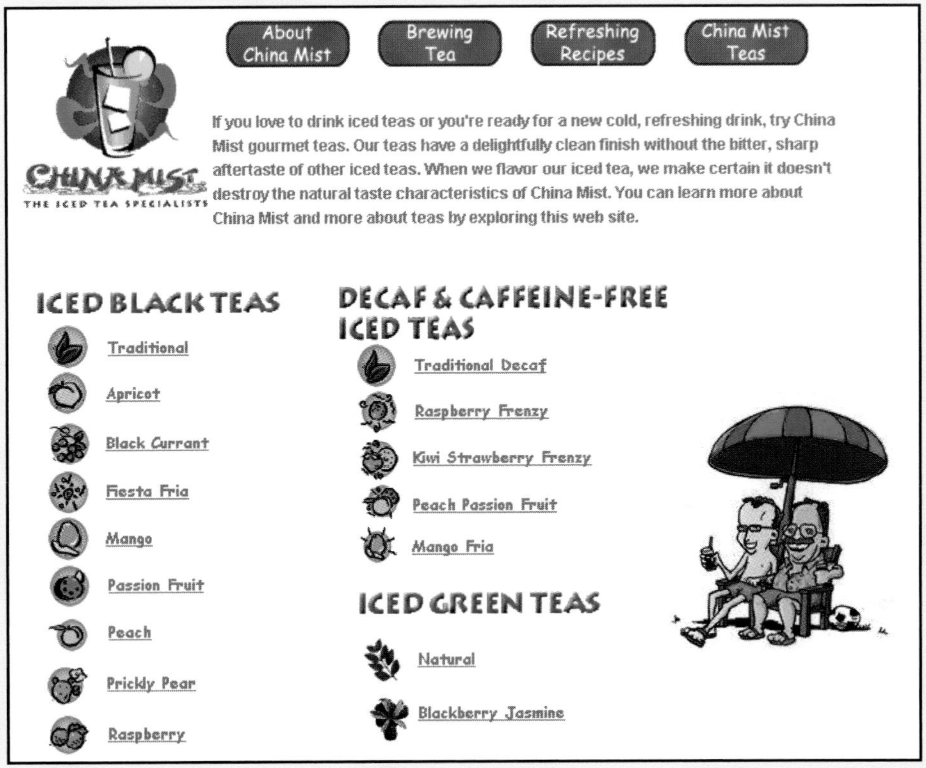

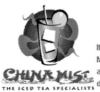

About China Mist
Brewing Tea
Refreshing Recipes
China Mist Teas
CHINA MIST
THE ICED TEA SPECIALISTS
If you love to drink iced teas or you're ready for a new cold, refreshing drink, try China Mist gourmet teas. Our teas have a delightfully clean finish without the bitter, sharp aftertaste of other iced teas. When we flavor our iced tea, we make certain it doesn't destroy the natural taste characteristics of China Mist. You can learn more about China Mist and more about teas by exploring this web site.
ICED BLACK TEAS
Traditional
Apricot
Black Currant
Fiesta Fria
Mango
Passion Fruit
Peach
Prickly Pear
Raspberry
DECAF & CAFFEINE-FREE ICED TEAS
Traditional Decaf
Raspberry Frenzy
Kiwi Strawberry Frenzy
Peach Passion Fruit
Mango Fria
ICED GREEN TEAS
Natural
Blackberry Jasmine

SECTION

USING NAVIGATION VIEW

TABLES, FORMS, AND ACTIONS

1. Import a Web site and work in navigation view.

2. Create a table.

3. Create a form.

4. Add actions.

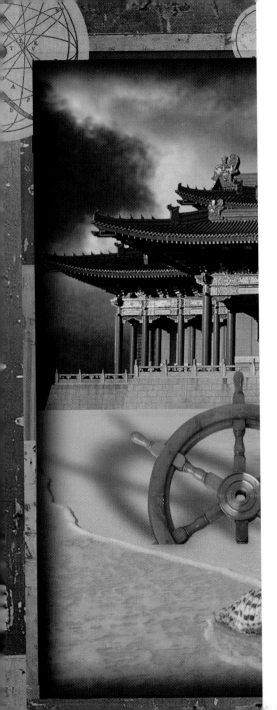

Introduction

As you have discovered by now, GoLive is long on features for creating modern, responsive Web sites. It handles basic Web pages as elegantly as it handles sophisticated sites. Still, as with any new software, the biggest challenge in learning GoLive is becoming familiar with all of its features. Web development software can be especially tricky to learn, because the capabilities of the Web are constantly changing. However, with an understanding of some additional, important GoLive features, you can further explore different ways to build responsive Web sites.

For instance, importing a Web site is a useful feature that you can use to convert an existing Web site into a GoLive site. Views that indicate the navigational structure of your site and how site pages are linked together provide valuable information and tools for communication with others about a site. The ability to create easy-to-read Web tables is a basic skill required by many data-rich pages and forms. And GoLive forms, while requiring a server script for processing, can easily be designed to be ready for scripts.

Actions, scripts that cause pages or objects to respond to events, will spur your imagination in creative ways and keep your visitors intrigued. GoLive includes an Action library, giving you the ability to add interactivity to pages that otherwise might require writing lots of code. As an imaginative designer, getting to know how to work with this library will help you make your site appealing to visitors in many exciting ways!

Tools You'll Use

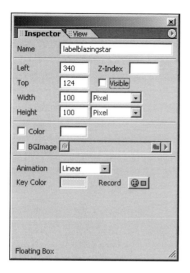

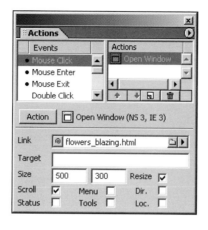

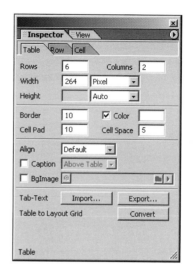

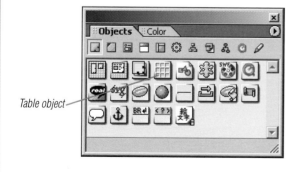

Table object

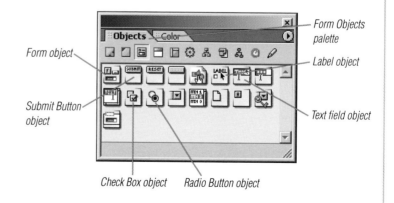

Form Objects palette

Form object

Submit Button object

Check Box object

Radio Button object

Label object

Text field object

IMPORT A WEB SITE AND WORK IN NAVIGATION VIEW

What You'll Do

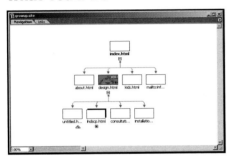

In this lesson, you'll import a Web site, then modify its navigation view.

Importing a Web Site

GoLive's site wizard enables you to import a Web site into the GoLive format from a folder on your hard drive, from an FTP site, or from an HTTP site. This powerful option allows you to download any Web site's text and media files to your computer, creating a GoLive site file and GoLive folders in the process. The ability to import a Web site is useful for exploring methods used by other developers, taking over the development of a site from another developer, or simply converting a site into the GoLive structure from another Web development tool.

QUICK TIP

Although it is easy to import a Web site, it is illegal to use someone else's work or copyrighted files in your own Web pages, without the originator's or copyright owner's explicit permission.

To import a Web site, you first indicate whether to import the site from a folder on your local hard drive or from a remote server. You can import a site from a remote FTP server or HTTP server. If you import the site using FTP, you need the FTP address, user name, and password. If you import a Web site from an HTTP server, you need only its Web address.

Once you have designated where the site should be imported from, you can choose how many levels (clicks away from the home page) of the site to import. If you are unfamiliar with a site, it may be difficult to know just how many levels it is. By specifying a limited number of levels, you can avoid downloading large numbers of files from an extensive site.

The imported site will be structured just like a site created from scratch in GoLive, and will include a site file and the three GoLive folders. The site folder will replicate the site content's folder structure. You can then rearrange the folders and files within the site folder using the site window, without breaking links.

Viewing Navigation View

The **navigation view** of a site is a graphical representation of its hierarchical structure, descending from the home page. If you are unfamiliar with the structure of a site you have imported, viewing the site using navigation view can be useful for understanding how the site is put together, such as which pages link to which other pages and how many levels are in the site. Even if you have

built a site from scratch in GoLive, navigation view offers another way to look at the relationship between pages that you have put into place.

QUICK**TIP**

Navigation views can be printed for use in site planning and discussion.

FIGURE E-1
Navigation view

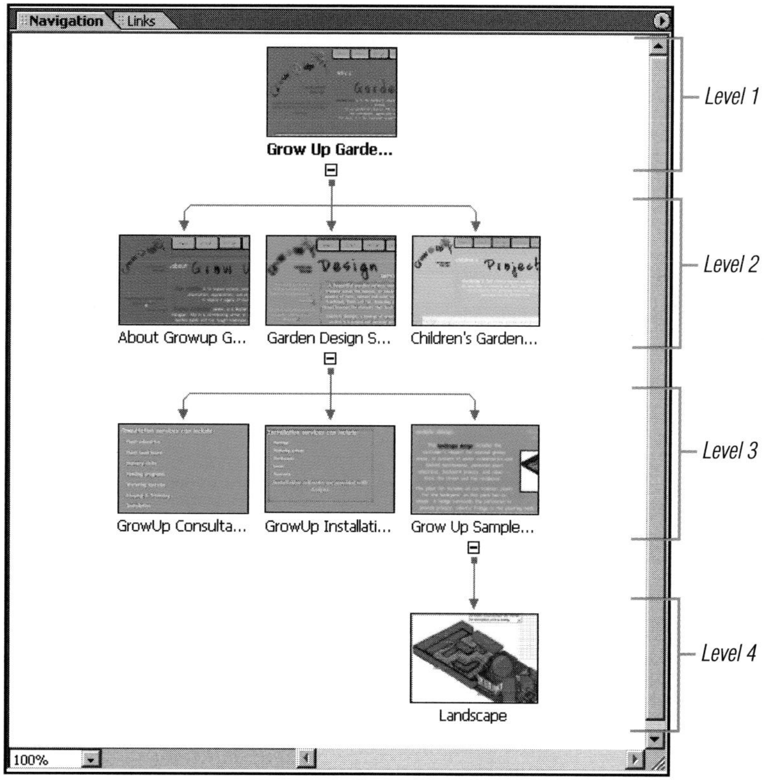

Navigation view displays a Web site in a hierarchical structure, as shown in Figure E-1; the home page is the first (top) level, and the first level is always a single file. Second-level pages, "children" of the home page, are pages linked to the home page. Similarly, third-level pages, children of second-level pages or grandchildren of the home page, are pages linked to pages in the second level. GoLive determines the level a page is on based on whether a page link is an image or hypertext. A page linked by an image is assumed by GoLive to be a child of the page that links to it. A page linked by hypertext is assumed to be a sibling (a page on the same level) of the page that links to it.

Changing Site Structure in Navigation View

If you want your site structure to appear different from GoLive's automatically developed hierarchy in navigation view, you can can rearrange pages in navigation view by dragging them from one level to another, and the integrity of the links between pages will not be affected. When you are in navigation view, you can use the options available in the View palette to modify the way pages appear in the view. For example, you can use the View palette's Display tab to label pages in navigation view with file names or with page titles, or to display pages as icons or as thumbnails.

You can add generic, blank pages to your site in navigation view using Diagram objects on the Objects palette. Adding a page this way will create a new, blank Web page in a NewFiles folder in the site window. You can then add content to the page, delete the page, or move it around in either navigation view or the site folder.

Links view

Links view provides yet another way to look at your site. Links view, like navigation view, displays site structure in a hierarchy, but it displays *all* files that are referenced in a page, including incoming and outgoing navigation links, images, rollover images, and style sheets. Links view becomes useful in long-term site maintenance or updating. For example, links view can be useful in resolving link errors. You can also use links view to find pages that use a component or a non-file item in the site window, such as a color or font set. Incoming navigation links and non-file items are listed to the left of the page in links view, while outgoing navigation links and other referenced files are listed to the right. Links view can also be modified to suit specific needs by using the View palette to change the page display or filter specific media types.

FIGURE E-2
Lndscp.html

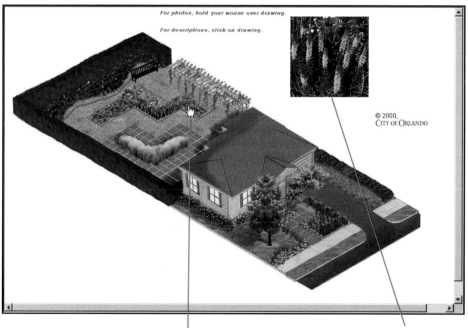

*Click the image to
open a page about
that plant*

*Photo of plant appears
when mouse is held
over the plant's image*

1. In your browser, go to *www.course.com/
   designprofessional/growup*.

2. Click design to open design.html, click CAD
   drawing to scale: 2D or 3D, color to open
   sampledesign.html, click landscape design
   to open lndscp.htm, then click on the house
   and some of the plant drawings, as shown in
   Figure E-2.

   There is a single path from the Design main
   page to the page containing the enlarged
   sample landscape design. The house links to
   a credits page with external links. Each plant
   drawing links to a page containing a description of the plant. Note that the plant images
   appear when moving the mouse over the
   landscape image.

3. Start GoLive, then click New Site in the Open
   options dialog box to open the site wizard.

   > TIP If GoLive is already open, click File
   > on the menu bar, then click New Site to open
   > the site wizard.

4. Click Next to accept Single User, click the
   Import from Server radio button, click Next,
   click the HTTP radio button, then click Next.

5. Type **http://www.course.com/designprofes-
   sional/growup/index.html**, the path to the
   home page, in the URL field, click the Get
   Entire Site radio button, then click Next.

6. In the Site Name field, type **growup**, then
   click Next.

(continued)

7. Click the Browse button, browse to the drive and folder where you are storing your work for this section, click OK (Win) or Choose (Mac), then click Finish.

GoLive imports the growup folder specified in the path and four additional folder levels. Be patient, this may take a few minutes. When the importing is complete, the site window opens.

> TIP If you receive a message that the growup folder already exists, click OK, browse to the drive and folder where you are storing your work for this section, click the Make New Folder button, name the new folder **SectionE**, click OK, then click Finish.

8. In the site window, open the designprofessional folder, then click the "+" (Win) or arrow (Mac) next to the growup folder and the landscape folder, noting the locations of design.html, sampledesign.html, and lndscp.html, as shown in Figure E-3.

These are the pages you navigated through on the Web. Index.html, design.html, and sampledesign.html are in the same folder (growup), and lndscp.html is in a different folder (landscape). Next you will view the navigation diagram, where the navigation hierarchy is *not* determined by the folder structure.

You viewed a Web site, imported the Web site, then viewed its folders in the site window.

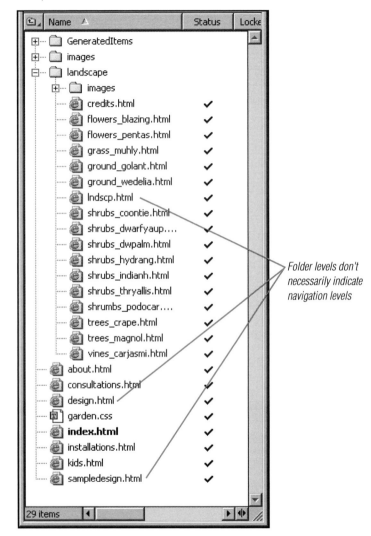

Folder levels don't necessarily indicate navigation levels

FIGURE E-4

Importing Files from a Folder site wizard screen

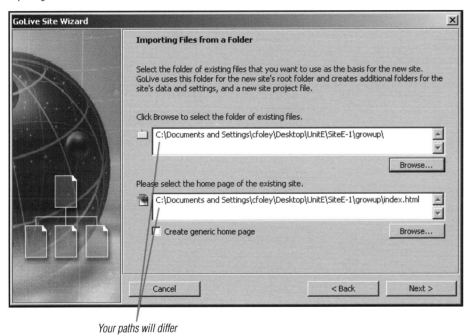

Your paths will differ

1. Using the file management tool provided with your operating system, navigate to the drive and folder where your data files are stored, then copy the SectionE folder to the drive and folder where you are storing your work for this section.

2. Start GoLive, then click New Site in the Open options dialog box to open the site wizard.

   TIP If GoLive is already open, click File on the menu bar, then click New Site to open the site wizard.

3. Click Next to accept Single User, click the Import from Folder radio button, then click Next.

4. Click the top Browse button, browse to the SectionE/SiteE-1/growup folder in the drive and folder where you are storing your work for this section, then click OK (Win) or Choose (Mac).

   The home page in that folder, index.html, is selected in the field below. Compare your screen to Figure E-4.

5. Click Next.

6. Click the Browse button, click Save to accept the SiteE-1 folder for the site location, then click Finish.

   GoLive creates a growup.site file in the growup folder, thus enabling you to manage this pre-existing site using GoLive and the site window. When the importing is complete, the site window opens.

   (continued)

7. In the site window, click the "+" (Win) or arrow (Mac) next to the landscape folder, noting the locations of design.html, sampledesign.html, and lndscp.html.

You imported the Web site from a local folder, then viewed its folders in the site window.

View a navigation diagram

1. Click the Navigation View button in the toolbar.

   A site window containing Navigation and Links tabs opens, displaying the home page, index.html.

2. Click the "+" under the home page to open the 2nd level.

   Because pages linked with hypertext are determined to be siblings, design.html, sampledesign.html, consultations.html, and installations.html all appear on the same level.

3. Click index.html, then click the Unfold All button on the toolbar to open all levels of the site, as shown in Figure E-5.

   Lndscp.html, in the same folder as the plant pages on the Files tab in the site window, is visually represented as the parent to the plant pages in navigation view because it links to the plant pages from images (an image map, specifically). Credits.html is a parent to four external links. The links are hypertext in the credits page, but the remote location of the links makes them children of the page, rather than siblings, in navigation view.

You opened a site in navigation view and then unfolded all levels in the navigation diagram of the site.

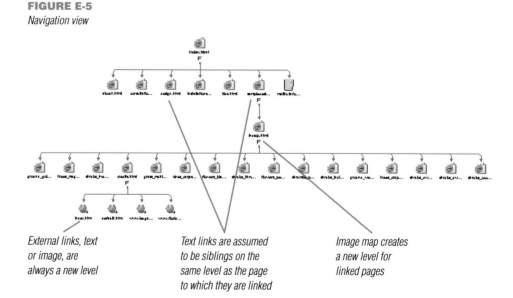

External links, text or image, are always a new level

Text links are assumed to be siblings on the same level as the page to which they are linked

Image map creates a new level for linked pages

FIGURE E-6

Navigation view with display properties modified

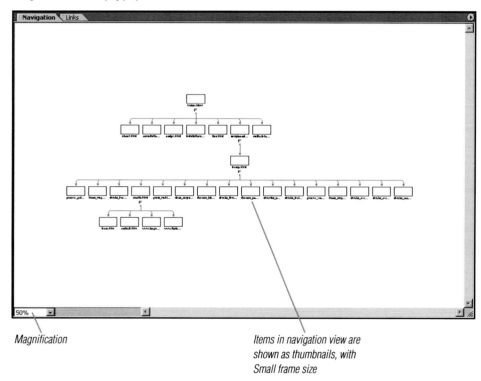

Magnification

Items in navigation view are shown as thumbnails, with Small frame size

1. Click the magnification list arrow in the lower left corner of the window, then click 50% to view as much of the diagram as possible; scrolling may still be necessary to see the whole thing.

2. Open the View palette if necessary, then click the Display tab if necessary.

3. Click the Thumbnails radio button under Show Items as.

4. Click the Frame Size list arrow, then click Small. Compare your screen to Figure E-6.

   Thumbnails display small images of pages, but not until the page has been edited in GoLive. Opening navigation view after completing this section will display content in the thumbnails for the pages you edit in these lessons.

You changed the magnification of navigation view, then used the View palette to show the items in navigation view as thumbnails, with Small frame size.

Modify a site in navigation view

1. Click the magnification list arrow in the lower left corner of the window, then click 100%.

2. Click the "–" below sampledesign.html to hide all child levels, so that only index.html and the second level are showing.

3. Drag sampledesign.html over the bottom part of design.html until a bar appears underneath design.html indicating that the moved page will be a child, then release the mouse button.

4. Repeat Step 3 with consultations.html and installations.html.

5. Click the "+" below sampledesign.html.

6. Drag lndscp.html to the left of sampledesign.html until you see a vertical bar on the left side of sampledesign.html, then release the mouse button.

7. Click sampledesign.html, click the Delete Selected Item button on the toolbar, click Yes (Win) or Move (Mac), then compare your navigation view window to Figure E-7. 🗑

   A bug is displayed under design.html, indicating that a link was broken.

8. Double-click design.html to open the page, select the line of text that begins "CAD drawing to scale:", then use the Point and Shoot button in the Inspector to link the text to lndscp.html in navigation view. ⊚

   The bug under design.html is gone.

You rearranged navigation view, deleted a page from the site, and modified a hypertext link.

FIGURE E-7
Modified navigation view

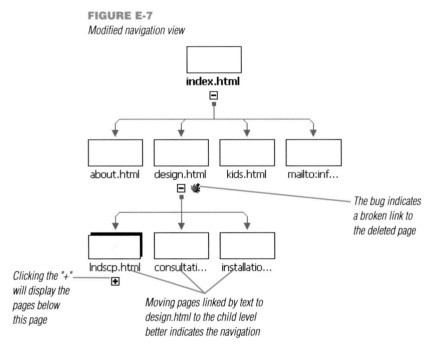

The bug indicates a broken link to the deleted page

Clicking the "+" will display the pages below this page

Moving pages linked by text to design.html to the child level better indicates the navigation

FIGURE E-8

New page in navigation view

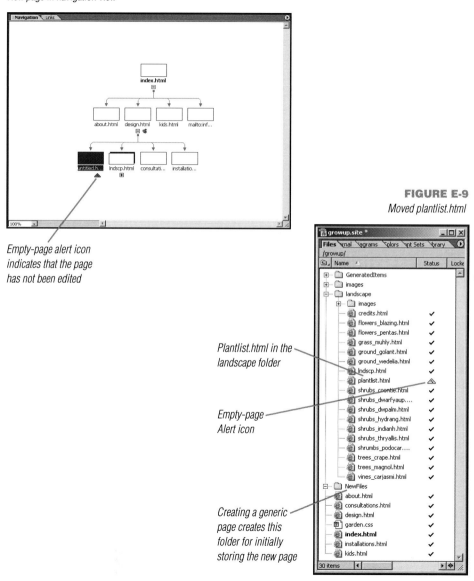

Empty-page alert icon
indicates that the page
has not been edited

FIGURE E-9

Moved plantlist.html

Plantlist.html in the
landscape folder

Empty-page
Alert icon

Creating a generic
page creates this
folder for initially
storing the new page

1. In the Objects palette, click the Diagram button. 🔲

2. Drag the Page object to navigation view, position it over the left side of lndscp.html until a bar appears to the left of lndscp.html, then release the mouse button. Compare your navigation view to Figure E-8. 🔲

3. In the site window, open the NewFiles folder that has been added to the site, rename the new html file as plantlist.html, then move the file to the landscape folder, as shown in Figure E-9.

   The plantlist.html file is marked in the Status column with the Empty-page Alert icon. △

4. In design.html, select the line of text "complete plant list w/ photos," then use the Point and Shoot button to link the text to plantlist.html in navigation view. 🔲

5. Close and save design.html.

   The design.html thumbnail is displayed in navigation view, because at this point it has been edited and saved.

6. Close the navigation view site window.

In navigation view, you added a page to the site, then linked hypertext to the new page.

CREATE A TABLE

What You'll Do

Plant List

Select the plants that interest you:

Blazing Star

Carolina Jasmine

Hydrangea

In this lesson, you will create a table and modify table, row, and cell properties.

Understanding Tables

As you develop a Web site, tables can come in handy for organizing text and images on a page. **Tables** are an arrangement of cells into a series of rows and columns, as shown in Figure E-10. A table is useful for creating a visible structure for similar or related data. For example, you may create a table where each row represents a product, and each cell in the row lists a property of the item (cost, volume, etc.). The table structure makes it easy to understand relationships at a glance. Table cells can contain text, images, or other (**nested**) tables. A table may also include a heading row and caption to define its contents better. Tables can be visually enhanced using borders, background colors, spacing between cells, and margins within cells. You can also make a table invisible if you are using it to arrange Web page elements.

Within a table, properties can be modified on the table level, the row level, or the cell level using the Table Inspector. Modifiable table properties include border width, color, cell pad, and cell width, and modifiable row properties include vertical

The layout grid is a table

The layout grid is technically a table, though you don't need to think about it as a table when you work with it. As you arrange objects on a layout grid, GoLive adjusts the table, row, and cell attributes to accommodate the layout. The layout grid is useful for randomly placing objects, helping you to control where disparate objects such as images and text are in relationship to each other.

alignment, row height, and color. Cell properties that can be specified include cell width and row properties that can be overridden on the cell level. In addition, you can specify that a cell span across multiple columns or rows.

The columns in Web tables do not have properties. Column properties are determined by the cells within the column. If the largest row in the table consists of five cells, then the table consists of five columns. If the largest cell in a column is 50 pixels wide, the column is 50 pixels wide.

QUICK**TIP**

Table Inspector properties can be saved as a table style using the Capture Table Style button on the Table palette, then applied to other tables for consistency.

Using Element Styles with Tables

In HTML, a table consists of a hierarchical structure containing a table (<table>) element, which encloses row (<tr>) elements, which in turn enclose cell (<td>) elements.

In addition to row and cell elements, a table element can also enclose a caption (<caption>) element that contains the table's title and a table header (<th>) element for a row that may appear as a header above other rows. Element styles for each table element can be added to Cascading Style Sheets to apply styles instantly to text in a table.

FIGURE E-10
Anatomy of a table

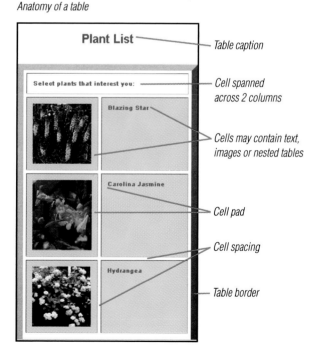

Plant List —————— Table caption

Select plants that interest you: ——— Cell spanned across 2 columns

Blazing Star ———— Cells may contain text, images or nested tables

Carolina Jasmine

—— Cell pad

Hydrangea —— Cell spacing

—— Table border

Create a table

1. Open plantlist.html from the site window.

2. Open the Objects palette if necessary, click the Basic button, then click and drag the Table object from the Objects palette to plantlist.html. ⬜ ⬜

   A table with 3 rows and 3 columns is added to the document, aligned to the top left corner of the page. The Inspector becomes the Table Inspector, displaying the table's properties.

3. Tile the windows horizontally in the work-space, open the landscape folder in the site window if necessary, open the images folder in the landscape folder, then open the PlantPics folder, as shown in Figure E-11.

You created a table and prepared your workspace for adding images to the table.

FIGURE E-11
Workspace for adding table images

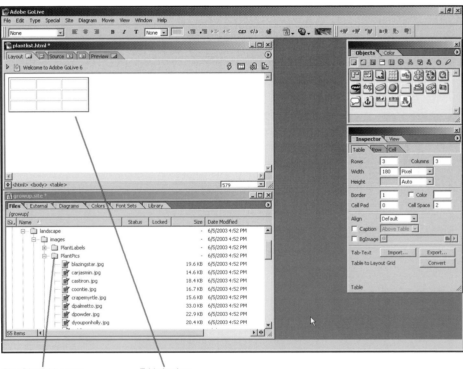

PlantPics folder open   Table in view

FIGURE E-12
Table with images

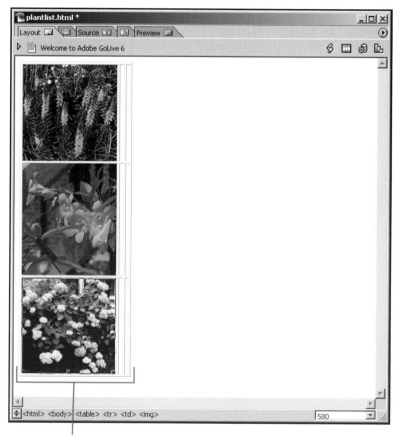

*Adding images resizes
the column, but leaves
the table width constant*

1. Drag blazingstar.jpg from the PlantPics folder in the site window to the first cell in the first column of the table.

   The cell resizes to accommodate the graphic, consequently resizing the column, while the overall table width remains fixed.

2. Repeat Step 1 with carjasmin.jpg and hydrangea.jpg, dragging them to the second and third cells in the first column of the table, respectively, as shown in Figure E-12.

3. Click in the first cell in the second column of the table, then type **Blazing Star**.

   The cell width grows enough to accommodate the longest word in the column without hyphenating, and the table width increases accordingly.

4. Click in the second cell in the second column of the table, type **Carolina Jasmine**, then click in the third cell in the second column and type **Hydrangea**.

You inserted images into the table by dragging them from the site window, then typed text directly into the table.

Modify table cell properties

1. Position the cursor over the top of the second column so that it becomes ↓, then click to select the column.

2. In the Table Cell Inspector, click the No Text Wrap check box.

   The text in each cell in the table now appears on one line only, and both the column and table widths increase.

3. Click the Width list arrow on the Inspector, click Pixel, double-click the Width text box, then type **150** to set the second column's cell width to 150 pixels.

4. In the first column, click and drag the bottom right corner handle of each plant image while holding down [Shift] to resize each image to a width of 100 pixels, using the Image Inspector to track the width. Compare your screen to Figure E-13.

   Holding down [Shift] keeps the image size changes proportional. The column resizes to accommodate the widest cell.

You modified the properties of cells in a table using the Table Inspector and modified the width of a column indirectly by changing the properties of images contained in the column.

Table with cell properties modified

FIGURE E-14

<td> element style font properties

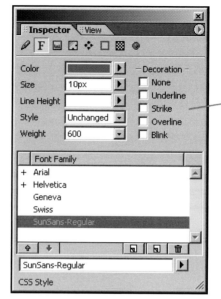

— *All text within a table cell will pick up the <td> properties*

FIGURE E-15

Table reflecting new <td> element style

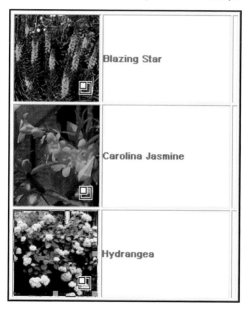

Blazing Star

Carolina Jasmine

Hydrangea

Apply styles to table elements

1. Open the plantlist.html CSS Editor. 📇

2. Click the New Element Style button, type **td**, then press [Enter] (Win) or [return] (Mac). <>

   A <td> element is a table cell element ("td" stands for "table data"). Every cell in the table in plantlist.html is bound by <td> element tags in the HTML source code.

3. In the Inspector, set the <td> element style font properties to Green font color, font size of 10 pixels, 600 weight, Arial font family, as shown in Figure E-14.

   The text in each table cell is formatted using the <td> element style. Should text be added to the first and third columns, that text would also use the <td> element style. Compare your table to Figure E-15.

4. Click the New Element Style button, type **caption**, then press [Enter] (Win) or [return] (Mac). <>

5. In the Inspector, set the <caption> element style font properties to Green font color, font size of 20 pixels, Bold, Arial font family.

   Nothing changes in the table because you have not added a caption to it yet.

You created an internal style sheet for plantlist.html that contains two table element styles, and you modified the properties of the element styles.

Arrange table cells

1. Click the right side of the second cell in the first row to select the cell.

   The Inspector displays the cell's properties, and the Add and Delete Row/Column buttons are active, as shown in Figure E-16.

2. Click the Add Row Above button to add a row above the selected cell.

3. Select the first cell in the last row, then click the Add Row Below button twice to add two rows below the last row.

4. Select any cell in the third column, then click the Delete Column button once.

5. Select the first cell in the row you added at the top of the table, double-click the Column Span field in the Table Cell Inspector, type **2**, then press [Tab] to indicate that the cell should span 2 columns, as shown in Figure E-17.

(continued)

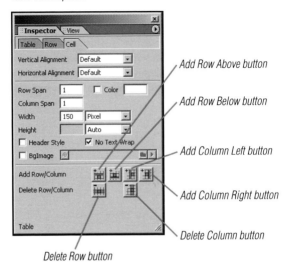

Add Row Above button

Add Row Below button

Add Column Left button

Add Column Right button

Delete Column button

Delete Row button

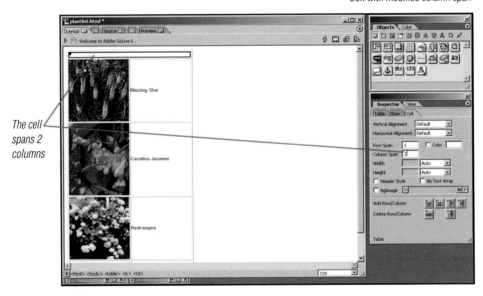

The cell spans 2 columns

Using Navigation View, Tables, Forms, and Actions

FIGURE E-18

Plant List table

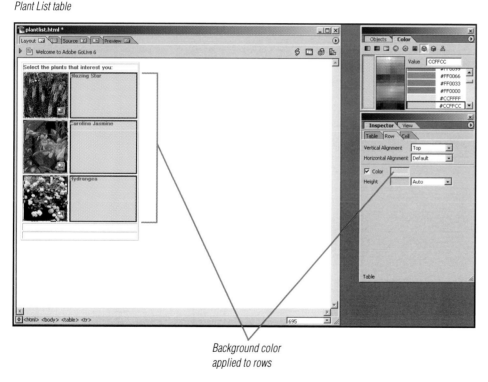

Background color
applied to rows

6. Repeat Step 5 for the first cell in the other two empty rows.

7. Click in the spanned cell at the top of the table, then type **Select the plants that interest you:**.

8. Position the cursor to the left of the first row containing a plant image until you see ➡, then click and drag down to select all three rows with plant images.

9. Click the Row tab in the Table Inspector, then set the Vertical Alignment to Top and the Color to CCFFCC. Compare your table to Figure E-18.

You added rows to the table, deleted a column, and modified cell and row properties.

Modify table properties

1. Position the cursor over the top left corner of the table so that the cursor becomes ⬁▫, then click to select the table.

2. In the Table Inspector, set the table Border to 10 (pixels), the Color to White (#FFFFFF), the Cell Pad to 10, and the Cell Space to 5, as shown in the Inspector in Figure E-19.

   The table border surrounds the outside of the table; an invisible border (border value = 0) can be used to hide the fact that you are using a table from people who visit your site. Cell Pad is the distance between the edge of the cell and the content of the cell, which provides for readability. Cell Space is the distance between cells.

3. Click the check box to the left of Caption to add a caption above the table, then click above the table and type **Plant List**.

   | TIP   There is only one caption (and only one <caption> element) in each table.

4. Click the Preview tab in the document window to preview the table, then compare your table to Figure E-20.

You modified the table border, table color, cell space, and cell pad, added a caption to the table, and previewed the table.

FIGURE E-19
Table properties

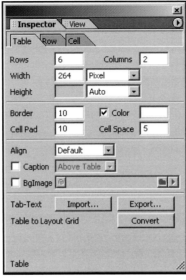

FIGURE E-20
Plant List table

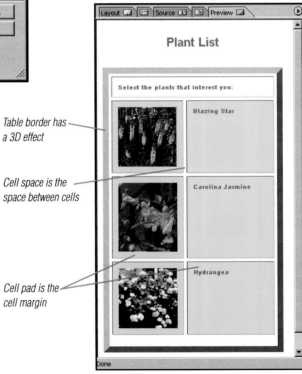

Table border has a 3D effect

Cell space is the space between cells

Cell pad is the cell margin

FIGURE E-21
Table source code

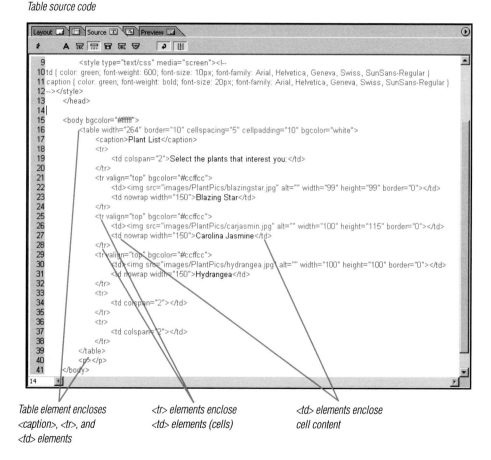

```
 9          <style type="text/css" media="screen"><!--
10 td { color: green; font-weight: 600; font-size: 10px; font-family: Arial, Helvetica, Geneva, Swiss, SunSans-Regular }
11 caption { color: green; font-weight: bold; font-size: 20px; font-family: Arial, Helvetica, Geneva, Swiss, SunSans-Regular }
12 --></style>
13      </head>
14
15    <body bgcolor="#ffffff">
16          <table width="264" border="10" cellspacing="5" cellpadding="10" bgcolor="white">
17              <caption>Plant List</caption>
18              <tr>
19                  <td colspan="2">Select the plants that interest you:</td>
20              </tr>
21              <tr valign="top" bgcolor="#ccffcc">
22                  <td><img src="images/PlantPics/blazingstar.jpg" alt="" width="99" height="99" border="0"></td>
23                  <td nowrap width="150">Blazing Star</td>
24              </tr>
25              <tr valign="top" bgcolor="#ccffcc">
26                  <td><img src="images/PlantPics/carjasmin.jpg" alt="" width="100" height="115" border="0"></td>
27                  <td nowrap width="150">Carolina Jasmine</td>
28              </tr>
29              <tr valign="top" bgcolor="#ccffcc">
30                  <td><img src="images/PlantPics/hydrangea.jpg" alt="" width="100" height="100" border="0"></td>
31                  <td nowrap width="150">Hydrangea</td>
32              </tr>
33              <tr>
34                  <td colspan="2"></td>
35              </tr>
36              <tr>
37                  <td colspan="2"></td>
38              </tr>
39          </table>
40          <p></p>
41    </body>
```

Table element encloses
<caption>, <tr>, and
<td> elements

<tr> elements enclose
<td> elements (cells)

<td> elements enclose
cell content

View the source code for a table

1. Click the Source tab to view the HTML code for the table, click the Colorize Elements button if necessary, then compare your code to Figure E-21. ▦

2. Note that the entire table is enclosed in the <table> tag.

3. Note that the table contains a <caption> element, and table row elements (<tr> elements) that enclose table data elements (<td> elements).

   Table data elements contain cell content.

4. Return to the Layout Editor and save the file.

You viewed the HTML structure of the table.

CREATE A FORM

What You'll Do

Plant List

Select the plants that interest you:

☐ Blazing Star

☐ Carolina Jasmine

☐ Hydrangea

email address: [_____]

○ existing customer
○ new customer

Order Plant Report

In this lesson, you'll add various form input elements to a table, then you'll add the table to a form element.

Understanding Forms

Forms provide a way to gather information from visitors in a Web page and to send the information to a Web server. For example, a Web form can be used to send product orders, software registrations, or hotel reservations. The receiving Web server contains a script, or small program, that processes the form information in some way; for example, it might store the information in a database, format it and send it in an email, or display it on a Web page.

Creating a Form

To create a form, you add form input elements from the Objects palette to a Web page. Form **input elements** are fields that accept input from the visitor such as text fields, radio buttons, check boxes, and buttons, as shown in Figure E-22. When you add input elements to a page, you assign each element a unique name and define its properties, such as a default value or maximum number of characters, using the Inspector. The name of each input element

is important to the script that processes it, as it identifies the data being input for processing. For example, an address form may include a text field for entering a company name. By naming the text field "companyname," the script can include instructions for storing the "companyname" value in a specific place in a database. The company name entered into the form, such as "Course Technology," is the **value** of the "companyname" field in that form.

The input elements you include in a form depend on the input you expect. A **radio button** is used to give users a choice of only one option in a group of two or more options. Rather than naming each radio button, you give each button a value and name the Group of radio buttons; selecting one radio button in the group will deselect any others in the same Group.

Check boxes are used to provide users with one or multiple options, when any number of those options can be selected. These don't need to be in a Group because the status of one check box does not affect other check boxes. Text fields, list boxes, and pop-up menus are also available to use as input elements. Labels are used to identify the field for the visitor and do not affect the input element's name or value. A **Submit button** is used specifically to submit form data to a script; other buttons can be used to reset all of the form elements to their original value, or to invoke another script related to the form.

Input elements are added to a page using GoLive form objects.

All input elements included in a form must be enclosed by a form element (<form>) in order for the input to be processed by the script. You add a form element to a page by dragging the Form object from the Objects palette, then putting the input elements into the form element. The developer of the form's script should provide you with the location of the script; you enter this

location into the form element properties using the Form Inspector. The Form Inspector can provide you with a printed inventory of a form's elements to help you communicate your script needs to your script developer. This inventory ensures that the script developer will have the correct information for processing or storing the form data, including field name syntax and field value properties.

FIGURE E-22
Anatomy of a form

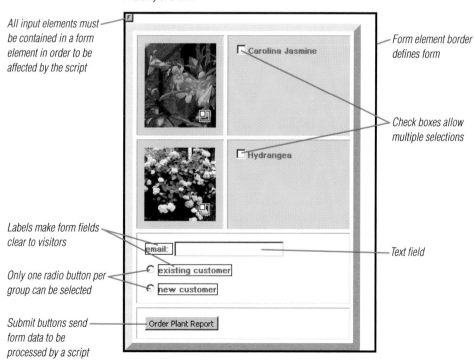

All input elements must be contained in a form element in order to be affected by the script

Form element border defines form

Check boxes allow multiple selections

Labels make form fields clear to visitors

Text field

Only one radio button per group can be selected

Submit buttons send form data to be processed by a script

Add a text field to a cell

1. Open plantlist.html if necessary, make sure you are in the Layout Editor, then in the Objects palette, click the Forms button to access Form objects.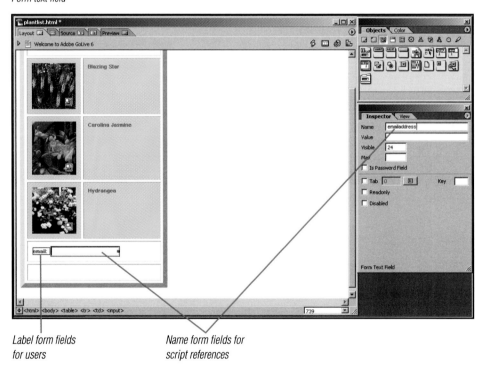

2. Drag the Label object to the second-to-last row of the table, select the word "Label," then type **email:** followed by a space.

3. Drag the Text Field object to the right of the label.

4. With the text field selected, in the Form Text Field Inspector, change the Name of the text field to **emailaddress**. Compare your screen to Figure E-23.

   Naming fields is important to server scripts that will receive input from the form; using a single word for field names makes them universally acceptable.

You added a text field and label to a table cell, then named the text field.

FIGURE E-23
Form text field

Label form fields
for users

Name form fields for
script references

Form Radio Button Inspector

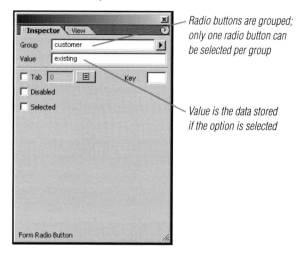

Radio buttons are grouped;
only one radio button can
be selected per group

Value is the data stored
if the option is selected

FIGURE E-25
Plant List form

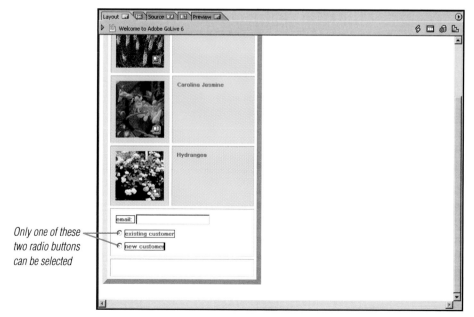

Only one of these
two radio buttons
can be selected

Add radio buttons to a cell

1. Click to the right of the text field, then press [Enter] (Win) or [return] (Mac) to add a blank line to the table cell.

2. Drag a Radio Button object from the Objects palette to the new blank line.

3. In the Form Radio Button Inspector, type **customer** in the Group field, type **existing** in the Value field, then compare your Inspector to Figure E-24.

   If this radio button is selected, the form will send the value "existing" for the "customer" input element.

4. Drag a Label object from the Objects palette to the right of the radio button, select the word "Label," then type **existing customer**.

5. Click after the "existing customer" label, press [Enter] (Win) or [return] (Mac) to add a new blank line to the table cell, then drag a Radio Button object to the new blank line.

6. In the Form Radio Button Inspector, click the Group field list arrow, click customer on the list that appears to select the group you just created, then type **new** in the Value field.

   If this radio button is selected, the form will send the value "new" for the "customer" input type.

7. Drag a Label object to the right of the new radio button, select the word "Label," then type **new customer**. Compare your window to Figure E-25.

You added radio buttons and labels to the table cell.

Add check boxes

1. Drag a Check Box object from the Objects palette to the immediate left of the text "Blazing Star" in the table. 🖼

2. In the Form Check Box Inspector, change the Name to **blazingstar**, and change the Value to **yes**.

   If this check box is checked, the form will send the value "yes" for the "blazingstar" input element.

3. Drag a Check Box object to the immediate left of the text "Carolina Jasmine" in the table, then in the Form Check Box Inspector, change the Name to **carolinajasmine** and the Value to **yes**. 🖼

4. Drag a Check Box object to the immediate left of the text "Hydrangea," then change the Name of the check box to **hydrangea** and the Value to **yes**. Compare your form to Figure E-26. 🖼

You added check box elements to the table, setting their names and values.

FIGURE E-26
Plant List form with check boxes

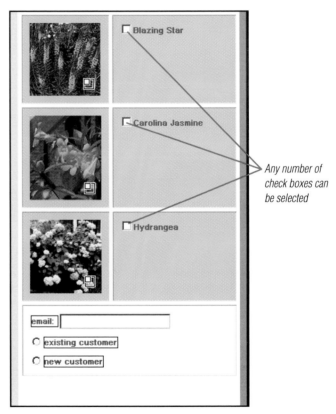

Any number of check boxes can be selected

FIGURE E-27
Plant List form with Submit button

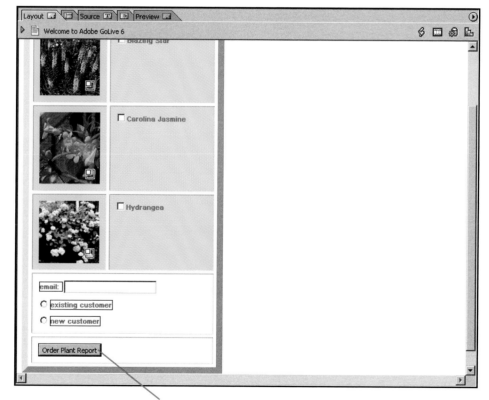

Label the Submit button so
the user knows exactly what
will happen when clicked

1. Scroll to the bottom of the table, then drag a Submit Button object from the Objects palette to the last cell in the table. 🔳

2. In the Input Button Inspector, change the Name to **plantreport**.

   This name is used to activate the script that processes the form.

3. Click the Label check box in the Inspector, then type **Order Plant Report** in the Label field to indicate to the user exactly what clicking the button will do functionally.

   The label appears as text on the button, as shown in Figure E-27.

You added a Submit button to a table cell and modified its label.

Add a form element to a page

1. Drag the Form object from the Objects palette to the left of the table, so that there is a solid black line outlining the whole page, as shown in Figure E-28, then release the mouse button. 🖳

    Since the table is in the first line of the body of the page, dragging the form to the left of the table ensures that the form is before the table. When you release the mouse button, the form element is inserted above and wider than the table, as shown in Figure E-29.

    > TIP If the form element is not wider than the table, it is in the table. Click the Form icon in the upper left of the form to select it, delete the form, then try again. **F**

2. Position the cursor over the top left corner of the table so that the cursor becomes ▶□, click to select the table, then drag the table into the form.

3. Click the Form icon in the document window to select the form and see the Form Inspector, then in the Form Inspector, change the Name of the form to **formPlantlist**. **F**

    > TIP If you had the location information for a script to process the form information, you would enter it into the Action field in the Form Inspector. You would also need to enter the Method: Get or Post.

You added a form to the page, then moved the table into the form element.

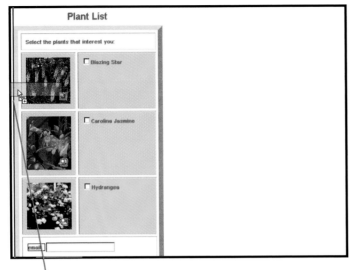

The solid line surrounding the page indicates that you are positioning the form in the page, not in the table

FIGURE E-29
Form element in page

The form element is above the table

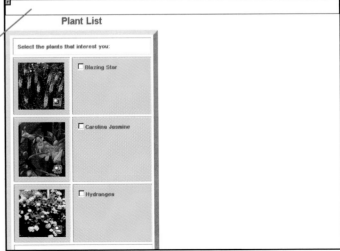

FIGURE E-30
Form inventory

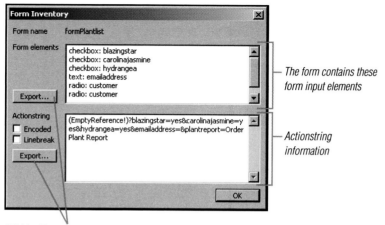

— The form contains these form input elements

— Actionstring information

Clicking Export will create a text file of the form input elements or actionstring

FIGURE E-31
Form source code

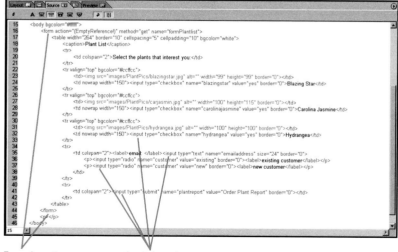

The Form element encloses the table and all input elements

Input elements

1. In the Form Inspector, click the Inventory button.

   The Form Inventory dialog box opens, listing the form input elements, as shown in Figure E-30. Exporting this list creates a text file of the inventory that you could submit to the person developing the script that will process the form information.

2. Click OK in the Form Inventory dialog box, then click the Source tab in the document window and compare your window to Figure E-31.

   Note that the opening and closing <form> tags enclose the entire table. Note the four types of input elements: text, radio, check box, and submit.

3. Click the Show in Browser button, select a browser, then test the form elements by selecting each one.

   TIP Clicking the Order Plant Report button will display an error page, as you have not specified an Action for this form. Once you specify an Action string, and a method, and provide a working script, the form becomes usable.

4. Close your browser, then save the file.

You viewed the form's inventory and its source code, then tested its elements in Preview.

ADD ACTIONS

What You'll Do

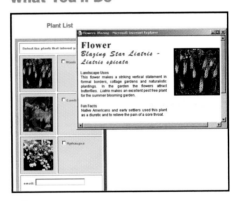

Plant List

 In this lesson, you will add actions to images that show and hide a floating box and open a floating box in a new window.

Understanding Actions

GoLive provides an easy method to add advanced interactivity to your pages without involving a programmer or script writer. **Actions**—small, prewritten scripts included in GoLive—can be assigned to an event. An **event** is an action trigger that may be caused by something a user does with the mouse or keyboard, by a browser, or by a timeline.

For example, an action can be triggered by the mouse pointer moving over an object or clicking on an object. For example, you can set up an action (specifically, a ShowHide action) to display, then hide, an image or text anywhere on the page when the mouse pointer is over, or has just left, an object. You can also create a navigaton link that opens a new window using an Open Window action; using an action to do this enables you to specify the properties of the new browser window, including its size and which of its toolbars are visible.

Creating an Action

To create an action that is triggered by the user's mouse in relation to an object, you first click the New Link button with the object selected; this allows an action to be linked to the object. Then, using the Actions palette, you associate an event with the action, specify the action, then set the values of the action. GoLive includes a library of pre-scripted actions; more information about these actions can be found in GoLive Help. The Adobe GoLive Web site offers links to additional action scripts.

QUICKTIP

Keep in mind that actions were introduced with most browsers' version 4; you should test actions in plenty of browsers on a variety of platforms before publishing your site.

Understanding Floating Boxes

Using floating boxes with actions can enable you to create some fun multimedia effects. **Floating boxes** are GoLive objects that can be of any size, can contain any object, and can be positioned anywhere on a page. When you add a floating box to a page, it is initially positioned on the left margin of a text object (page, text box, table, or floating box), and its **anchor,** a small yellow box, is selected, displaying the floating box properties in the Inspector. To select a floating box in Layout Editor, click the anchor. You can position the floating box anywhere, and the anchor remains in its original position. You can use floating boxes for hiding, layering, or positioning any object in a Web page.

Using Floating Boxes with Actions

A floating box can come in particularly handy when you create multimedia actions because of its flexibility in positioning, its visibility property, and the fact that its name property makes it controllable by an action, as shown in Figure E-32. For instance, with an action you can show a floating box (and its contents) when the user puts the mouse pointer over a specific object, or you can move a floating box in response to the movement of the mouse pointer. Floating boxes are added to a Web page using the Floating Box object on the Objects palette. Once added, you can then position the floating box and modify its properties, including its name, visibility, and size.

FIGURE E-32

Floating box action [and] Floating box properties

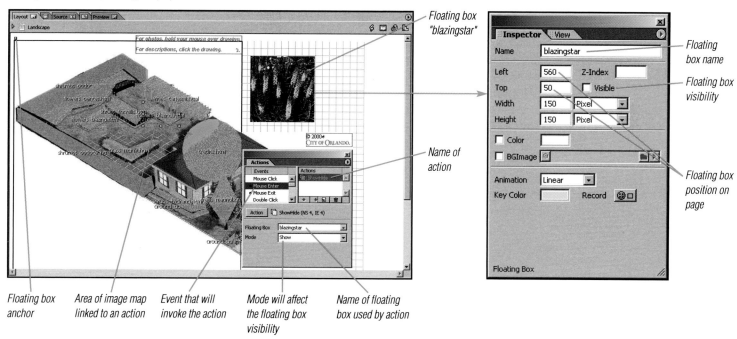

Floating box "blazingstar"

Name of action

Floating box name

Floating box visibility

Floating box position on page

Floating box anchor

Area of image map linked to an action

Event that will invoke the action

Mode will affect the floating box visibility

Name of floating box used by action

Add images to floating boxes

1. Tile the windows horizontally in the workspace, then in the site window, open the PlantLabels folder, as shown in Figure E-33.

2. Click the Basic button on the Objects palette, then drag a Floating Box object to the right of the table. 🔲 🔲

   Dragging the Floating Box object to the right of the table positions the floating box after— and therefore below—the table in the page. The floating box is labeled "1." and its anchor is left-aligned to the page.

3. Position the cursor over the edge of the floating box until it becomes 🖑, then drag the floating box to the right of the Blazing Star row, to a position of 340 from the left margin.

   > TIP You may have to release and reselect the floating box to read its position in the toolbar or the Floating Box Inspector.

4. In the Floating Box Inspector, change the Name to **labelblazingstar**, then uncheck the Visible check box, as shown in Figure E-34.

   (continued)

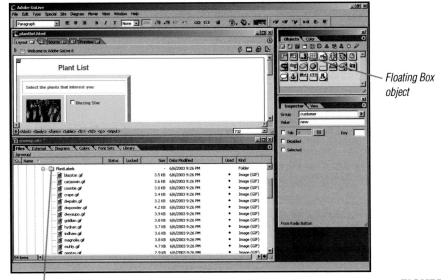

Floating Box object

PlantLabels folder contains images

FIGURE E-34
Floating Box Inspector

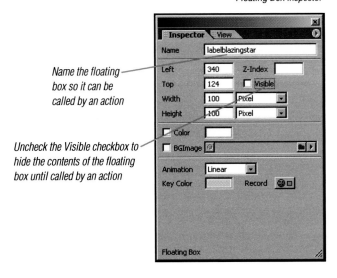

Name the floating box so it can be called by an action

Uncheck the Visible checkbox to hide the contents of the floating box until called by an action

Using Navigation View, Tables, Forms, and Actions

Floating box with image

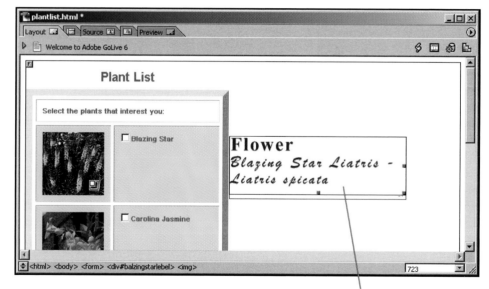

The floating box
resizes to accomodate
the image

5. Drag blazstar.gif from the site window (located in the PlantLabels folder) to the floating box, then compare your Layout Editor to Figure E-35.

6. Drag a second Floating Box object to the page, position it to the right of the Carolina Jasmine row at 340 pixels from the left margin, change the Name of the floating box to **labelcarjasmin**, then uncheck the Visible check box.

   Browsers handle the exact alignment of floating boxes differently. Consistency in placement (such as putting each floating box 340 pixels from the left margin), however, will keep your layout clean.

7. Drag carjasmin.gif to the floating box.

8. Add one more floating box to the page, position it to the right of the Hydrangea row at 340 pixels from the left margin, change the Name of the box to **labelhydran**, uncheck the Visible check box, then drag hydran.gif to the floating box.

You added three floating boxes to the page, positioned each next to the table, and dragged images into each floating box.

Add rollover actions to images

1. Click Window on the menu bar, then click Actions to open the Actions palette.

2. Click the Blazing Star plant image, then click the New Link button on the toolbar. 🔗

   The events that can be associated with the object appear in Actions palette; each can be linked to an action.

3. In the Actions palette, click Mouse Enter under Events, then click the New Item button to add a generic action. 🔲

   A generic action, "? None", appears in the Actions list, as shown in Figure E-36.

4. In the Actions palette, click the Action button, point to Multimedia, then click ShowHide.

   The ShowHide action properties appear. You indicate which floating box to affect in the Floating Box field, and what effect to apply to the floating box in response to the event in the Mode field.

   TIP If you make a mistake, click the Remove selected Items button to remove the action. 🗑

5. Next to the Floating Box field, click the list arrow, then click labelblazingstar.

   (continued)

FIGURE E-36
Generic action assigned to Mouse Enter

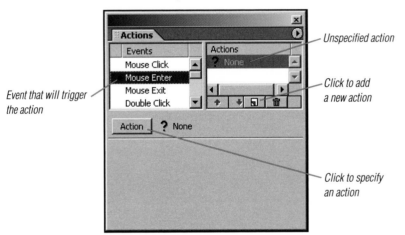

Unspecified action

Click to add a new action

Event that will trigger the action

Click to specify an action

6. Click the list arrow next to the Mode field, click Show, then compare your screen to Figure E-37.

6. Click the list arrow next to the Mode field, click Show, then compare your screen to Figure E-37.

   TIP The Toggle mode switches the Mode from Show to Hide on each Mouse Enter event, a bit different than the response we are creating here.

7. Click Mouse Exit in the Events list, click the New Item button to add a new action, click the Action button, point to Multimedia, then click ShowHide. 🖳

8. Click the Floating Box field list arrow, click labelblazingstar, click the Mode field list arrow, then click Hide.

9. Repeat Steps 2-8 for the Carolina Jasmine image and the Hydrangea image.

   TIP Be sure first to click the New Link button after selecting each image to link to an action. 🔗

10. Click the Show in Browser button, select a browser, then move the mouse pointer on and off of each image to test the actions. 🔍

11. Close your browser, then save the file.

You added user-triggered actions to each of the plant images.

FIGURE E-37
ShowHide action with Show mode specified

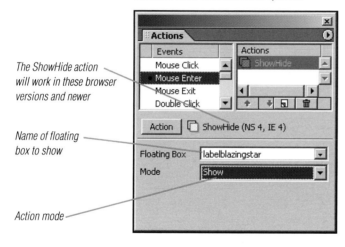

The ShowHide action will work in these browser versions and newer

Name of floating box to show

Action mode

Add an Open Window action to an image

1. In the Layout Editor, select the Blazing Star image, click Mouse Click under Events in the Actions palette if necessary, then click the New Item button to add an action.

2. Click the Action button, point to Link, then click Open Window.

   A new set of Action properties, related to the Open Window action, appears in the Actions palette.

3. Use the Point and Shoot button in the Actions palette to change the Link field to flowers_blazing.html in the landscape folder in the site window.

4. Type **500** in the first Size field and **300** in the second Size field to set the size of the window that opens to 500 by 300 pixels.

5. Unclick the Menu, Dir., Status, Tools, and Loc. check boxes, then compare your Actions palette to Figure E-38.

   Unchecking these boxes will cause the new window to open without a browser menu bar, directory bar, status bar, toolbar, or address bar.

6. Click the Show in Browser button, select a browser, then click the Blazing Star image to test the action, as shown in Figure E-39.

7. Close your browser, then save the page.

   (continued)

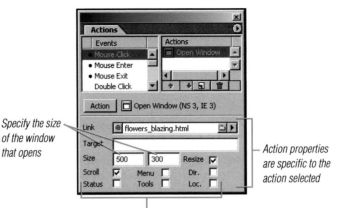

Specify the size of the window that opens

Action properties are specific to the action selected

Turn off window attributes to control user actions and unclutter the view

FIGURE E-39
Open Window action

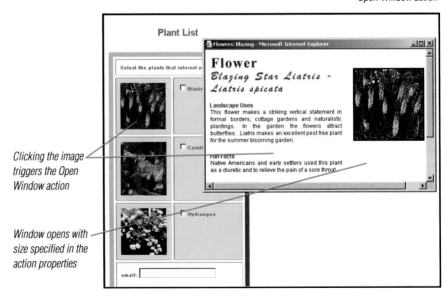

Clicking the image triggers the Open Window action

Window opens with size specified in the action properties

Using Navigation View, Tables, Forms, and Actions

8. Click the site window title bar, save the site, click the Navigation View button on the tool-bar. Then click the "+" signs under index.html and design.html if necessary. Compare your window to Figure E-40.

Navigation view now shows page content in the thumbnail for plantlist.html. The bug below plantlist.html indicates a broken reference, because the form element is not linked to an action. Also note that, although the Open Window action in plantlist.html links to a new window, it is not indicated as a link in navigation view.

9. Close the site and exit GoLive.

You added an Open Window action to an image, then viewed the site in navigation view to note changes.

FIGURE E-40
Navigation view of modified site

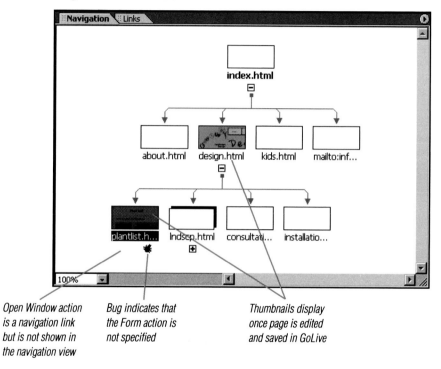

Open Window action
is a navigation link
but is not shown in
the navigation view

Bug indicates that
the Form action is
not specified

Thumbnails display
once page is edited
and saved in GoLive

China Mist has decided that they would like to offer on line ordering services. You have suggested that they keep their site simple and direct by making their tea page an order form. They love your thinking and have asked you to do just that.

1. Open China Mist.site from the last saved China Mist project folder you used in Section D.
2. Open the page teas.html.
3. Add a check box to the left of the representative image for each tea, naming the check box the name of the tea and giving each check box a Value of **yes**. (*Hint*: If there is not enough room left of the tea images for check boxes in your page, drag to select all of the images and tea names in a column, then hold down the [Alt] key (Win) or [option] key (Mac) while pressing the keyboard arrows to move the objects one pixel at a time.)
4. Add a text box underneath johnanddan.jpg containing the following text: **"To order tea for home brewing, just select your flavors, then click the button below."** Apply the Address Paragraph Format to the text, then modify its style.
5. Add a Submit button named **teaorder** under the text box with the following label: **Prepare to checkout!**
6. To put the fields in a form element, add a Form object to the page, then cut and paste the layout grid into the form element. (*Hint*: Save the file before moving the layout grid into the form element.)
7. Preview the page, then compare the page to Figure E-41.

FIGURE E-41

Completed Project 1

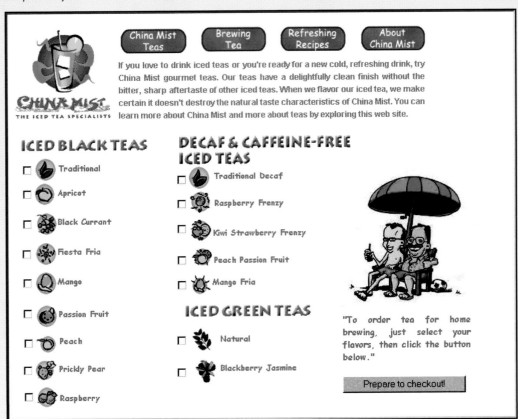

China Mist has released its Web site and has already recieved feedback from several customers. The word is that many visitors clicked on the teas in tea.html for additional information, but did not know how to return to the tea page. They have asked if you could open tea detail pages in a smaller window so visitors could still see the tea page when a tea detail page is open. This way they can add tea pricing and other ordering information without cluttering the tea page, and visitors can easily close the detail page in order to access the tea page again. You have decided to add actions to the decaffeinated and caffeine-free teas in order to test the opening of the detail pages.

1. Open China Mist.site from the China Mist project folder, then open teas.html.
2. Add Open Window actions triggered by Mouse Click events to a each tea image in the Decaffeinated and Caffeine-free Iced Teas group on the page. The window that opens should contain the corresponding page from the teapages folder, and it should be resized to 200 by 100 pixels with no page elements showing. (*Hint*: Break the link from the image to the corresponding tea page before adding the action to each image.)
3. Test your actions, then compare your screen to Figure E-42.

FIGURE E-42
Completed Project 2

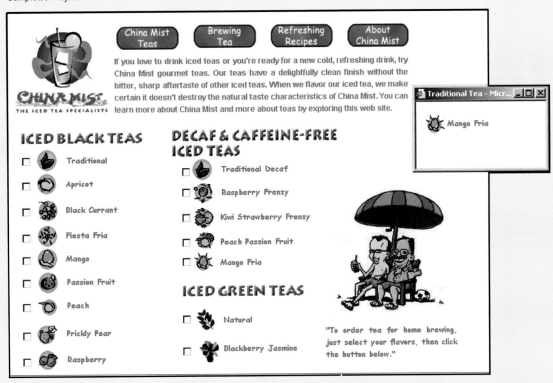

SECTION A

GETTING STARTED WITH ADOBE LIVEMOTION 2.0

1. Start LiveMotion and open a new composition.

2. Examine the LiveMotion window.

3. Create basic objects.

4. Modify an object.

5. Apply a basic style and rollover.

6. Get Help.

SECTION A
GETTING STARTED WITH ADOBE LIVEMOTION 2.0

Introduction

Have you ever visited a Web site that captivated you with its animation of pictures, shapes, or text? Maybe you have been to a Web site that responded to the movement of your mouse when you rolled over a button, a tab, or some text? Well, it's just that kind of movement and interactivity that Adobe LiveMotion is designed to create. **LiveMotion** is a design and development tool that enables you to create both stationary and interactive content for multimedia presentations and online Web pages. In addition to interactive animations and rollovers just described, you can use Live Motion to design 3D layered buttons, decorative backgrounds, navigation bars, or other Web navigation elements.

LiveMotion enables you to bring Web page content to life. You can develop your own content using LiveMotion's tools and palettes or you can import images and other items from other programs. Use LiveMotion to create dynamic animations and interactive behaviors that can be exported to a Web site development program, such as Adobe GoLive, and used to build a Web page or site. The final step in creating a LiveMotion file is to export it for use on the Web, and you are given a number of export options to choose from including: Flash (SWF), GIF, Animated GIF, QuickTime Video, and JPEG. So, whether you want to develop a button, a navigation bar, content for an entire Web page, or a Flash animation, LiveMotion can handle the job.

Tools You'll Use

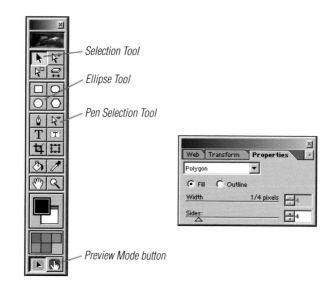

Selection Tool

Ellipse Tool

Pen Selection Tool

Preview Mode button

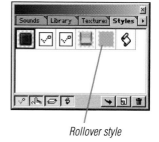

Rollover style

START LIVEMOTION AND OPEN A NEW COMPOSITION

What You'll Do

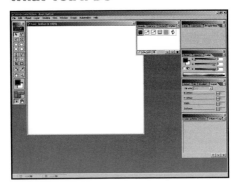

 In this lesson, you'll start LiveMotion, open a new composition, and then save the composition with a new filename.

Learning the Basics

LiveMotion is an object-based program—this means that every element you work with in LiveMotion, whether it is created in LiveMotion or imported, is an object. Each **object** is a single element that has distinct attributes and characteristics, which can be formatted and manipulated without affecting other objects. Some examples of objects include text blocks, drawn shapes, and imported pictures. All objects that you create or import are placed in a **composition**—the basic LiveMotion document that you create when you open a new file, which has the file extension ".liv". Using LiveMotion's tools, you can design different objects, such as rectangles, ellipses, freeform shapes, and lines, and then format them to attain just the look you want.

LiveMotion has a number of formatting attributes and effects that you can apply to an object to adjust how it appears. Among the editable properties are object color, texture, shading, brightness, lighting, contrast, and tint, as well as object size, rotation, and position on the composition.

Making Your Composition Come Alive!

Once you have finished creating and formatting the objects of your composition, you can apply a rollover to an object or animate it. A **rollover** is an interactive behavior that causes an object to change on the screen when you click it or move your mouse over it. An example of a simple rollover behavior is a color change or a change in shape. Typically, you apply a rollover to a button, a tab, or a piece of text that you want to highlight on a Web page when a person visiting your site moves the mouse pointer over it. Highlighting Web elements invites the user to click on those elements to link to another page or to open a related list.

Animation in LiveMotion is the movement of one or more objects from one side of the screen to the other, or the changing of the color or opacity of an object over time. Applying rollovers and animation to objects in a composition is what makes the components of your Web page or multimedia presentation enjoyable and engaging to the viewer.

Starting LiveMotion and Opening a Composition

When you start LiveMotion, the LiveMotion window opens. Figure A-1 shows the default LiveMotion window (viewed with a monitor resolution of 1024 by 768). Six small windows are displayed that contain tools and object properties, each of which

can be used to create and modify objects in a composition.

When you open a new composition in LiveMotion, the Composition Settings dialog box opens. The Composition Settings dialog box allows you to modify the size of the composition and the frame rate, which determines the quality of the animation in the composition. The **frame rate** is the rate an animation plays in frames per second. The higher the frame rate, the smoother the animation plays back. The default composition size is 550 pixels wide

by 500 pixels high with a default frame rate of 12. If you are designing a full Web page, you will need a larger composition size than if you are designing an individual Web page component. The largest composition size is 1024 by 1024 pixels. A frame rate of 12 or 15 is usually sufficient for most Internet connections. An animation with a high frame rate will require a fast Internet connection to be displayed properly. After clicking OK in the Composition Settings dialog box, the Composition window opens, and you're ready to begin!

FIGURE A-1
LiveMotion window

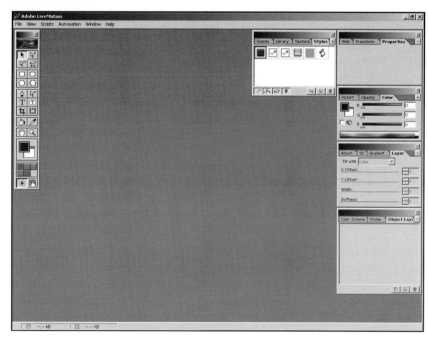

Start LiveMotion

1. Click the Start button on the taskbar, point to Programs, then click Adobe LiveMotion 2.0, as shown in Figure A-2.

   TIP If you are starting LiveMotion on a Macintosh, double-click the hard drive icon, double-click the Adobe LiveMotion folder or Applications folder, then double-click the Adobe LiveMotion program icon.

2. Click File on the menu bar, then click New Composition.

   The Composition Settings dialog box opens.

3. Click OK.

You started LiveMotion and then opened a new, blank composition.

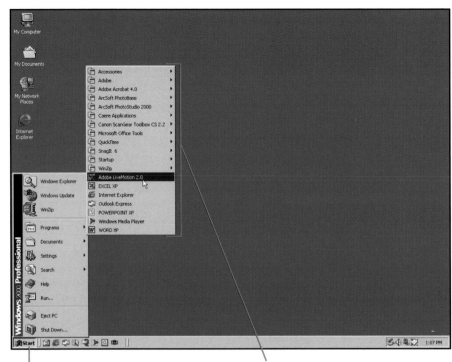

Start button

Your Programs menu may differ

Producing good Web content

What is it about a Web page that captures your attention and holds it? It is probably a cool animation, an interesting background, or a simple, yet effective, presentation of the Web page content. Keep in mind when you are designing content for a Web page that your goal is to draw the user into your Web site quickly and easily. To do this effectively, Web page content should be simple to read and understand and easy to navigate. A good Web site should also be interactive and enjoyable to view. However, be careful not to overanimate your composition. A good Web page does not over-power viewers with too much activity.

Save As dialog box

New file name

Save a new composition

1. Click File on the menu bar, then click Save As.

2. Type **basic_button** in the File name text box (Win) or Save As text box (Mac), navigate to the drive and folder where you are saving your work for this section, then compare your Save As dialog box to Figure A-3.

3. Click Save, then compare your screen to Figure A-4.

You used the Save As command on the File menu to save the file with a new name.

FIGURE A-4

Basic button composition

Composition name

New composition

LiveMotion window

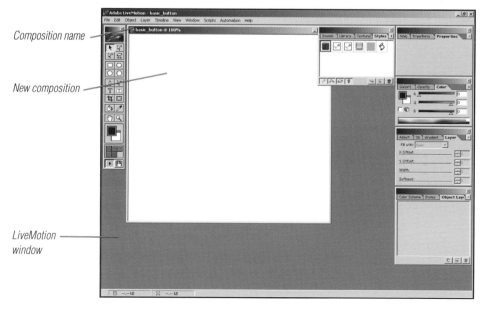

EXAMINE THE LIVEMOTION WINDOW

What You'll Do

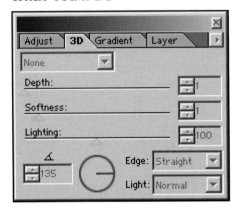

 In this lesson, you'll examine the LiveMotion window and its components, learn how to show and hide palettes, and change a palette display.

Identifying LiveMotion Components

The LiveMotion work area includes all of the space within the program window from the program title bar on top of the screen, which displays the program name, to the bottom of the screen. LiveMotion has two toolbars: the Status bar, which appears in the program window (Win) or the Composition window (Mac), and the Standard toolbar, which is hidden by default but can be viewed by clicking View on the menu bar, pointing to Toolbars, then clicking Standard. The Status bar displays the file size and other relevant information about the current composition. The Standard toolbar contains buttons whose functions are common to most software programs, such Open, Save, Cut, Copy, Paste, and Print. Directly below the program title bar is the menu bar, which con-

tains all of LiveMotion's command menus. Some menu commands display **shortcut keys** on the right side of the menu that provide a way to access the command quickly using the keys on your keyboard. Menu commands that are dimmed or grayed out are not available to use.

Within the program window itself by default are five palettes that help you create and modify objects. At the screen resolution of 1024 by 768, all of the palettes appear in the program window as shown in Figure A-5 (at a different screen resolution the palettes might be positioned differently). LiveMotion **palettes** are small windows that contain groups of adjustable properties (such as colors, or opacity); you can use each palette to modify objects. Palettes are docked, or arranged together, on the right side of the screen in palette groups, as shown in Figure A-5.

A palette within a palette group can be displayed or hidden as you need it by clicking the tab containing the name of the palette. You can reposition a palette group within the work area by dragging its title bar, and you can shuffle a palette within its existing palette group by dragging its tab within the palette window. You can also separate a palette from its original group by dragging its tab to another part of the program window to create a new palette group. Many palettes have a palette menu, which provides additional palette options or views. Palette positions are saved when you exit LiveMotion and appear in the same positions when you re-start the program.

QUICKTIP

To return palettes to their default settings and screen position, click Window on the menu bar, then click Reset To Defaults.

FIGURE A-5

LiveMotion work area

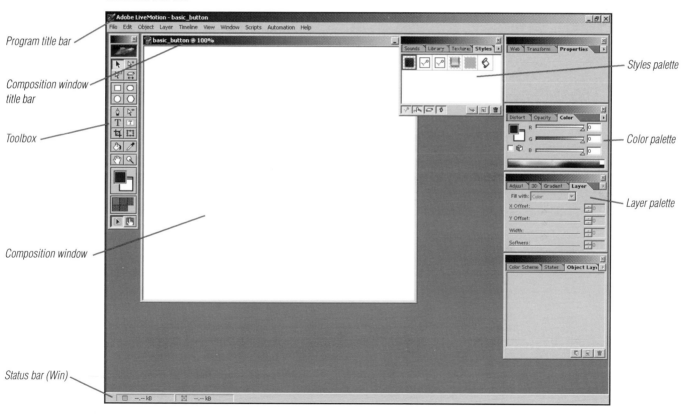

Program title bar

Composition window title bar

Toolbox

Composition window

Status bar (Win)

Styles palette

Color palette

Layer palette

The LiveMotion **toolbox** contains 18 tools you can use to create, select, and edit objects. All of the tools on the toolbox display a graphic icon that represents the function of the tool. For example, the Type Tool displays a letter "T" on its face. You can identify a tool in the toolbox by moving your mouse over a tool to display its ScreenTip. A **ScreenTip** identifies the name of the tool and its corresponding shortcut key. To use a shortcut key command for a tool, simply place your mouse in a composition and press the appropriate key command on your keyboard.

The large window in the center of the program window is the Composition window, which is empty in Figure A-5. The name of the composition shown in the Composition window appears in the window's title bar.

Setting Preferences and modifying the Composition window

You have the option of customizing certain program settings, which changes the way LiveMotion appears and acts. To change these preferences, click Edit (Win) or LiveMotion (Mac) on the menu bar, then click Preferences to open the Preferences dialog box. You can adjust the behavior of the Arrow Tool to revert to the Selection Tool automatically after any single use of another tool, or customize how gridlines appear in the Composition window. Changes made in the Preferences dialog box are applied to the existing composition and to new compositions. You can also adjust the size of an existing composition by opening the Composition Settings dialog box while you are working within a composition. Click Edit on the menu bar, then click Composition Settings to open the Composition Settings dialog box. Change the composition size or frame rate depending on your needs.

Result of closing the Layer palette

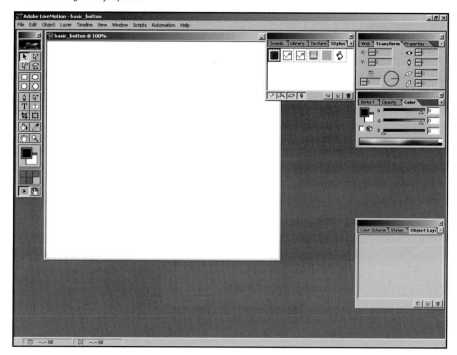

Change the palette display

1. Click Window on the menu bar, then click Layer to close the Layer palette as shown in Figure A-6.

   Check marks in the Window menu appear next to the palettes that appear at the front of each palette group.

   TIP   Press [Shift] [Tab] (Win) to show or hide all open palettes except the toolbox. Press [tab] (Mac) to show or hide all open palettes including the toolbox.

2. Click Window on the menu bar, then click Layer to reopen the Layer palette.

3. Click the Gradient tab to display the Gradient palette, then click the 3D tab to display the 3D palette, as shown in Figure A-7.

4. Click the Layer tab to re-display the Layer palette.

   TIP   You can move a palette from one palette group to another by dragging its tab to the desired palette group window.

You closed and opened the Layer palette and displayed the Gradient and 3D palettes.

FIGURE A-7
3D palette displayed

3D palette tab —

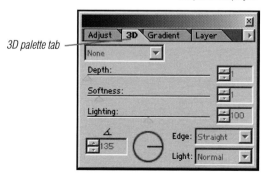

Move a palette and open a palette menu

1. Click the Color tab, if necessary, then drag the Color palette title bar to the center of the Composition window.

   TIP If you drag a palette tab by mistake, drag the palette tab back to the palette group window or click Window on the menu bar, then click Reset To Defaults.

2. Click the Color palette menu button, then click HSB View, as shown in Figure A-8, to view the hue, saturation, and brightness of the current color. ▶

3. Click the Color palette menu button, then click RGB View to reset the Color palette back to its original state. ▶

4. Click Window on the menu bar, then click Reset To Defaults to reposition the Color palette.

You moved the Color palette, displayed a different palette view using the palette menu button, and then restored your palettes to their default settings.

FIGURE A-8

Color palette with its palette menu displayed

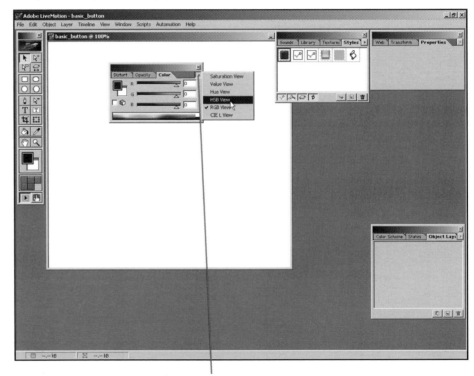

Color palette menu button

FIGURE A-9

Polygon Tool ScreenTip displayed

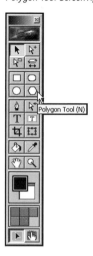

Select a tool

1. Place your mouse over the Polygon Tool button to display its ScreenTip and corresponding shortcut key, as shown in Figure A-9. ⬡

2. Click the Polygon Tool on the toolbox. ⬡

    TIP   You can press and hold a tool's shortcut key to use the tool without selecting that tool. The tool will remain active until you release the shortcut key.

3. Click the Properties tab, if necessary, to view the properties of the Polygon Tool, as shown in Figure A-10.

    Each tool in the toolbox has its own set of properties.

4. Click the Type Tool on the toolbox to view its properties. T

5. Press [V] on your keyboard to select the Selection Tool in the toolbox.

You displayed the Polygon Tool's ScreenTip, selected the Polygon Tool and the Type Tool, and pressed the shortcut key for the Selection Tool.

FIGURE A-10

Polygon Tool properties

Lesson 2   Examine the LiveMotion Window

ADOBE LIVEMOTION A-13

CREATE BASIC OBJECTS

What You'll Do

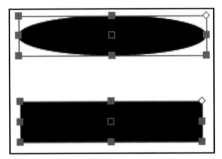

▶ *In this lesson, you will learn to create and select basic geometric objects.*

Learning about LiveMotion Objects

There are three basic objects in LiveMotion: geometric, text, and image objects, as shown in Figure A-11. A **geometric** object is an object that you create with one of the LiveMotion drawing tools, such as the Rectangle Tool or the Ellipse Tool. A **text** object is a word or words that you create using the Type Tool or the Text Field Tool. An **image** object is an imported bitmap object from an image editing program like Photoshop. There is a fourth type of object, a **sound** object (.wav), which is an audio file that you import from your hard drive or the Web. Sounds are unique in that they are not editable objects within LiveMotion and do not appear in the Composition window.

LiveMotion objects are made up of layers, which enhance your ability to create vivid effects. For instance, if an object has two layers, you can create a floating three-dimensional look by blurring the outside edge of the bottom layer. When you first create an object in a composition, you are creating the first layer of the object. One object can have up to 99 additional layers added to it. Using LiveMotion menu commands and palette properties, objects

A vector program
LiveMotion is a vector program. In a vector program, the shapes of objects are developed using mathematical coordinates instead of individual pixels as in a raster (or bitmap) program like Adobe Photoshop. One advantage that a vector program like LiveMotion has over a raster program is that changes to objects created in such a program maintain their quality at any resolution in the composition. Another advantage is that an object's properties can be changed many times without affecting the quality of the object. A third advantage is that vector graphics are often smaller than corresponding bitmap graphics.

and object layers can be moved, scaled, rotated, skewed, restacked, aligned, distributed, grouped; or assigned a 3D effect, contour, opacity, color, gradient, or texture. So, as you can see, your options for transforming an object in LiveMotion are limited only by your imagination!

Selecting Objects

Like other object-based programs, objects must be selected first before they can be moved, grouped, or edited. LiveMotion offers several different selection tools; choosing which one to use depends on exactly what you want to select. The Selection Tool provides the most common way of selecting an entire object by clicking anywhere on the object. This method of selection selects the object or group of objects and all associated layers. The Drag Selection Tool enables you to drag a bounding box, called a **marquee**, around objects to select them. This tool is useful to select objects that are hidden behind or in front of other objects that you don't want to select. The Subgroup Selection Tool selects individual objects within a grouped object. A **grouped object** consists of two or more objects joined together to form one object using the Group command. Each time you click a grouped object using this tool, a different object in the group is selected. You can also use the Pen Selection Tool to select an object. When you select an object with this tool, you can reshape the object's sides.

When an object is selected, a **selection border** appears around it containing several blue squares, called **handles**, as shown in Figure A-11. Handles are used to resize or reshape an object. The hollow handle in the middle of the object is the object's default **anchor point**—a fixed point on or around the object. Transformation actions, such as rotating or skewing, are performed in relation to an object's anchor point. The top right handle (hollow circle), is used to rotate the object using the Selection Tool.

FIGURE A-11
Sample objects

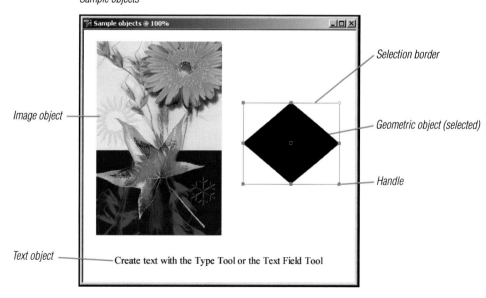

Image object

Text object

Selection border

Geometric object (selected)

Handle

Create simple objects

1. Click the Ellipse Tool on the toolbox and notice its properties in the Properties palette.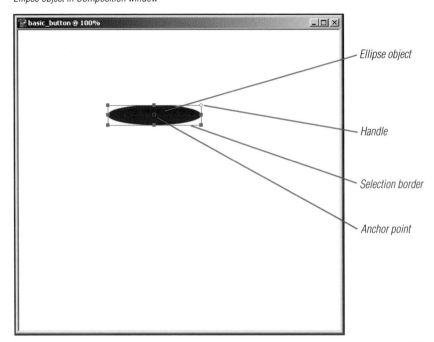

2. Drag a small ellipse in the Composition window similar to the one in Figure A-12.

   > TIP Press [Shift] as you drag to draw an object proportionally. Press [Alt] (Win) or [Option] (Mac) as you drag to draw the object from the center out.

3. Click the Rectangle Tool on the toolbox, then drag a small rectangle about the size of the ellipse directly under the ellipse.

   The rectangle object remains selected until you select another object or click off the rectangle in the Composition window.

You created an ellipse object and a rectangle object.

Select an object

1. Click the ellipse object in the Composition window to select it.

   > TIP You can select all objects in the composition by clicking Edit on the menu bar, then clicking Select All.

2. Click the Drag Selection Tool on the toolbox, then drag a marquee around the ellipse object and the rectangle object to select both objects, as shown in Figure A-13.

3. Click in a blank area of the composition to deselect the objects.

   > TIP You can deselect all selected objects in the composition by clicking Edit on the menu bar, then clicking Deselect All.

(continued)

FIGURE A-12
Ellipse object in Composition window

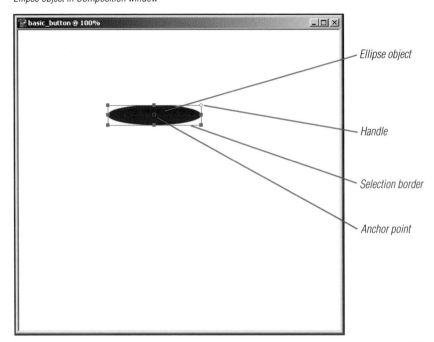

Ellipse object

Handle

Selection border

Anchor point

FIGURE A-13
Objects selected with the Drag Selection Tool

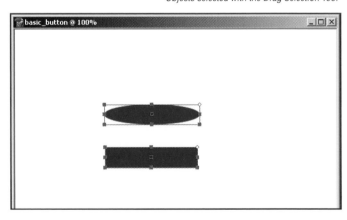

Object selected with the Pen Selection Tool

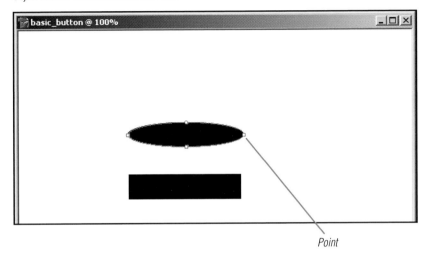

Point

FIGURE A-15

Result of deleting the ellipse object

4. Click the Pen Selection Tool on the toolbox, then click the ellipse object to display its points, as shown in Figure A-14.

5. Click the rectangle object to display its points, then click the Selection Tool on the toolbox.

You selected objects using the Selection Tool, the Drag Selection Tool, and the Pen Selection Tool.

Delete an object

1. Click the ellipse object to select it.

2. Click Edit on the menu bar, then click Cut.

   The ellipse object is deleted from the composition and is placed on the Clipboard until you cut or copy another object.

   > TIP Click Edit on the menu bar, then click Undo or History to undo previous actions.

3. Compare your Composition window to Figure A-15.

4. Click File on the menu bar, then click Save to save the composition.

You selected the ellipse object and deleted it from the composition.

MODIFY AN OBJECT

What You'll Do

 In this lesson, you will learn how to change object properties and then resize and move an object with the Selection Tool.

Working with Object Properties

All objects you create or import in LiveMotion have specific properties, which appear in the Properties palette. The Properties palette changes depending on what kind of object is currently selected. For example, when a geometric object, such as a polygon, is selected in the composition, the Properties palette looks similar to Figure A-16. Using the Properties palette, you can transform a geometric object's shape to one of four other shape styles by selecting one of the options in the Shapes list, and you can switch between showing an object's fill or outline.

You can also use the Properties palette to change the number of sides a polygon object contains, or to increase or decrease the radius of the round corners of a rounded rectangle object. Text objects have their own unique properties. When you type text in a composition, the Properties palette changes to look similar to Figure A-17. Notice that the Properties palette shows all of the text characteristics you can change, such as the font type or font style. If you import an image into a composition, the Properties palette changes again and looks similar to Figure A-18. Use the Properties palette to modify an imported image.

Other ways to move objects

You can also use the Transform palette to rotate an object or move an object to an exact location in the composition along the X (horizontal) axis or the Y (vertical) axis. Moving an object using the Transform palette moves the entire object. In addition, move individual layers of an object can be moved using the Layer Offset Tool. Whichever layer is selected in the Object Layer palette is the layer that moves when you drag an object with the Layer Offset Tool. You can also enter precise offset values in the Layer palette to move an object layer.

QUICKTIP

Editing objects in LiveMotion is nondestructive—meaning that the properties and characteristics of an object can be restored to their original state even after saving a composition. Simply change the properties of the object back to what they were before you edited the object.

Resizing Objects

As you progress through the design process, you will undoubtedly need to resize objects you have created. All three types of LiveMotion objects can be resized, or scaled, by dragging one of the object's handles. To resize an object horizontally and vertically at the same time, drag one of its corner handles (except for the top right corner handle, which will rotate the image if you drag it). To resize an object horizontally or vertically, drag one of the object's side handles. Note that resizing raster (bitmap) image objects you import from other programs will cause a loss of quality in the image. Generally, the loss of quality is not noticeable when you reduce the image; however, when you enlarge the image, it can become fuzzy, or pixelated.

Rotating and Moving Objects

You can rotate any object by dragging its top right corner handle (hollow circle). All objects rotate in a 360-degree circle around their anchor point. If you add layers and effects to the object before you rotate it, the layers and effects are rotated with the object. In addition to rotating them, being able to move objects around the composition is important, especially when the object needs to be precisely positioned in a certain location. The easiest way to move an object is to select it and then drag it to a new location within the composition. If you need to move an object a tiny distance, you can use the arrow keys on the keyboard to move, or nudge, the object one pixel at a time. You can also move hidden or nested objects by selecting the object with the Drag Selection Tool and then moving the object. A **nested** object is an object that is contained within another object, such as a small object on top of a large object.

FIGURE A-16
Properties palette when a geometric object is selected

FIGURE A-17
Properties palette when typing text

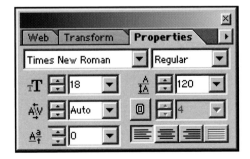

FIGURE A-18
Properties palette when an image object is selected

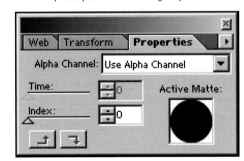

Reshape an object

1. Click the rectangle object, then click the Properties tab to display the Properties palette, if necessary.

2. Click the Shapes list arrow, then click Ellipse as shown in Figure A-19.

   TIP Reshaping an object using the Properties palette preserves any formatting, effects, or layer effects previously applied to the object.

3. Click the Outline option button in the Properties palette to display the outline of the ellipse. Compare your Properties palette to Figure A-20.

   The width of an object's outline is measured in ¼-pixel increments. Notice that the width of the ellipse outline is 4 in the Properties palette, which is equal to 1 pixel.

   TIP You can click the Width slider or the Width Up arrow or the Width Down arrow to change the width of the object outline.

4. Click the Fill option button in the Properties palette.

You modified the properties of a rectangle object using the Properties palette.

FIGURE A-19
Properties palette

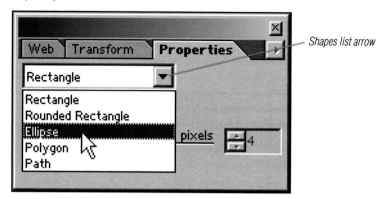

Shapes list arrow

FIGURE A-20
Properties palette with Outline option button selected

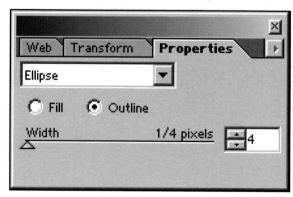

Resized ellipse

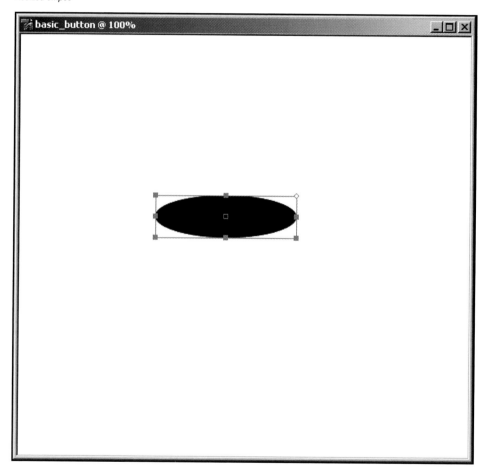

Resize an object

1. Position your pointer over the bottom right corner handle of the ellipse.

2. Drag the handle down and slightly to the right to enlarge the ellipse, as shown in Figure A-21. Don't worry if your figure looks different than the one in Figure A-21.

3. Drag the object's bottom center handle up slightly to change the height of the ellipse.

4. Drag the object's bottom left handle to the right slightly to change the length of the ellipse.

> TIP Press [Alt] (Win) or [option] (Mac) while you drag an object's handle to resize it from the handle instead of from the object's anchor point.

You resized an ellipse using the object's handles.

Rotate an object

1. Position your pointer over the top right corner handle of the ellipse.

2. Drag (don't let go of the mouse button) the handle to the left until the ellipse is rotated about 90 degrees from its original position, as shown in Figure A-22, then release the mouse button.

3. Click Edit on the menu bar, click Undo Rotate, then click in a blank area of the composition.

   The ellipse returns to its original position and is no longer selected.

You rotated an ellipse object by dragging its top right corner handle, and then you used the Undo command to return the ellipse to its original position.

FIGURE A-22
Rotated ellipse object

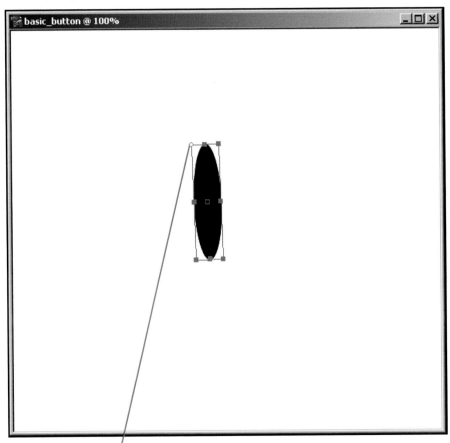

Drag this handle to rotate the object

FIGURE A-23
Moved ellipse object

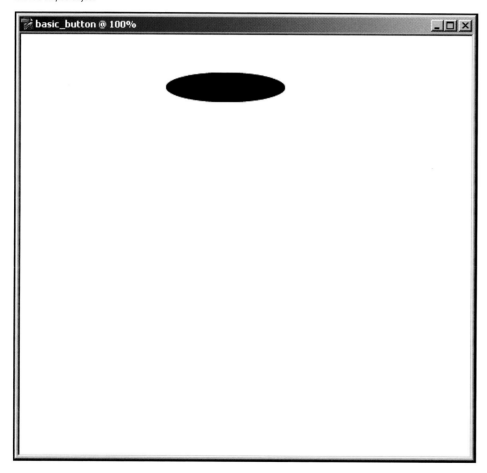

1. Click the ellipse object to select it.
2. Position your pointer over the ellipse, then drag it to the top of the composition, as shown in Figure A-23.

   TIP   To constrain the movement of an object to the horizontal or the vertical axes, press and hold [Shift] while dragging.

3. Press [←] on the keyboard two times to move the object to the left by 2 pixels.
4. Press [Shift][←] once to move the object to the left 10 pixels, then press [Shift][→] once to move the object to the right 10 pixels.
5. Click in a blank area of the composition.
6. Save your work.

You moved the ellipse object by dragging it with the Selection Tool and then moved it using the arrow keys on the keyboard.

APPLY A BASIC STYLE AND ROLLOVER

What You'll Do

 In this lesson, you'll learn how to apply predefined LiveMotion styles.

Understanding Styles

LiveMotion comes with six predefined styles in the Style palette: two styles with animation; one style with a rollover; two styles with object layers; and one style with a script, as shown in Figure A-24. A style is a saved set of attributes that you can apply to objects. A style can include attributes like layer color, opacity, texture, 3D effects, distortion, and other palette settings. A style can also contain multiple layers, animation directions, and a rollover. Attributes that a style can't contain include the type of object, such as

geometric, text, or image; the shape of an object, such as a rectangle or a polygon; or any settings from the Transform or Web palettes. Applying a predefined style to an object changes the object's attributes to those of the style. Once you apply a style to an object, the previous layers and layer attributes of the object are removed and the object takes on the layers and attributes of the style. You can apply one or more predefined styles to any of the three LiveMotion objects. LiveMotion's predefined styles offer a sample of the types of effects and behaviors you can create.

Remote rollovers

Remote rollovers are interactions between two or more objects. A remote rollover begins when the mouse hovers over or clicks an object, known as the trigger, which causes one or more target objects to be affected. The target objects have custom states that are linked to the trigger rollover state. For example, you could click a trigger object such as a button that had a rollover state that changed the appearance of the button, which in turn triggered a target object, such as a menu, to appear in another part of the composition. Remote rollovers can be a little complex in their design, but they are very effective and powerful tools on Web pages.

Whether you create your own styles or use the predefined LiveMotion styles, make sure you use them consistently in your Web site.

Learning About Rollovers

A rollover is a change that occurs to an object in response to a mouse action. An example of a typical rollover is a button that changes color when you move the mouse over it. In this simple example, the button has a rollover state applied to it that the mouse "triggers" to produce the resulting color change. A **state** is a collection of attributes that affect the way an object appears after being triggered by a mouse action or a script. Practically any object attribute that you can change can be applied to a rollover state. Attributes like object color, opacity, layer offset, softness, or fill, texture, 3D effects, and gradients can be applied to a rollover state to produce visually engaging results. Rollovers are important because they can function as navigational tools that provide Web users visual clues about where to click to get further information or to be linked to another Web page or Web site. As mentioned, LiveMotion has one predefined style that includes a rollover.

FIGURE A-24
Styles palette

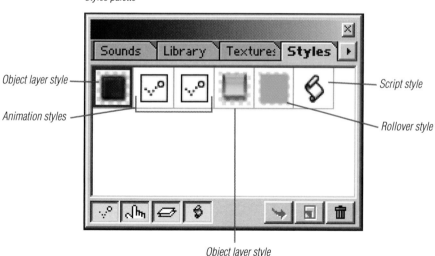

Object layer style

Animation styles

Script style

Rollover style

Object layer style

Apply a predefined rollover style

1. Click the ellipse object to select it.

2. Click the Styles tab to open the Styles palette, if necessary.

    > TIP   If the Styles palette is not visible, click Window on the menu bar, then click Styles.

3. Click the green swatch in the Styles palette to select it, as shown in Figure A-25.

4. Click the Apply Style button at the bottom of the Style palette. ➦

    Notice that the ellipse fill color has changed to green, which is the color of the rollover style. Also, notice that the layers in the Object Layers palette now reflect the three object layers of the newly applied rollover style.

5. Click the Preview Mode button on the toolbox. 🖐

    Preview mode allows you to preview interactive elements such as rollovers and animations, displaying how the elements will look in a browser. Notice that in Preview mode all of the palettes are hidden from view.

6. Position your mouse over the ellipse, as shown in Figure A-26. 🖑

    The ellipse changes color, indicating that a rollover state has been activated.

7. Click the ellipse to activate the other rollover state, as shown in Figure A-27.

8. Click the Edit Mode button on the toolbox. ▶

You applied a predefined rollover style to an object and then previewed it.

FIGURE A-25
Rollover style selected in Styles palette

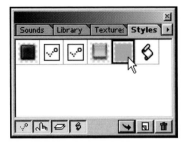

FIGURE A-26
Ellipse showing first rollover state

Ellipse changes color in Preview mode when the pointer is moved over the object

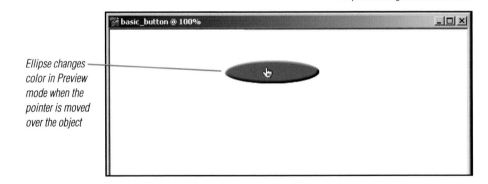

FIGURE A-27
Ellipse showing second rollover state

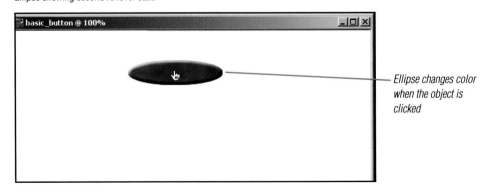

Ellipse changes color when the object is clicked

FIGURE A-28
Object layer style selected in Styles palette

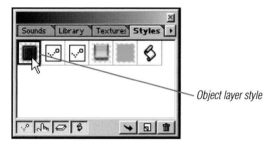

Object layer style

FIGURE A-29
Ellipse with new object layer style

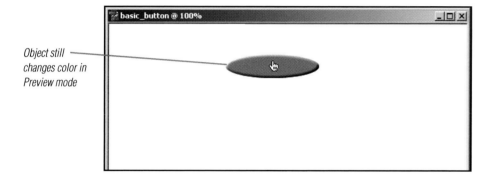

Object still
changes color in
Preview mode

FIGURE A-30
Ellipse showing second rollover state

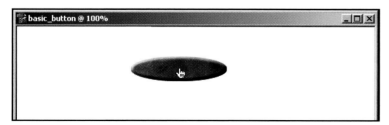

Apply an object layer style

1. Click the red/blue object layer style swatch in the Styles palette, as shown in Figure A-28.

2. Click the Apply Style button at the bottom of the Style palette.

   The ellipse layers change to match the applied layer style.

3. Click the Preview Mode button on the toolbox, then position the pointer over the ellipse, as shown in Figure A-29.

   Notice that the previously applied rollover state is still intact. Applying the object layer style changed the object layers of the object and not its rollover style.

4. Click the ellipse to activate the other rollover state, as shown in Figure A-30.

5. Click the Edit Mode button on the toolbox.

6. Save your work.

You applied a predefined object layer style to an object and then previewed it.

GET HELP

What You'll Do

 In this lesson, you'll view LiveMotion Help and find information using Contents, Index, and Search.

Understanding LiveMotion Help

LiveMotion Help is an HTML-based help system that is automatically installed on your computer system when you install LiveMotion. LiveMotion Help includes the complete *LiveMotion 2.0 User Guide* and some additional information, such as keyboard shortcuts and some procedure details. The help system provides information on LiveMotion tools, commands, and features for both Windows and Macintosh operating systems. When you open Help by clicking the LiveMotion Help command on the Help menu, a separate window opens in your default browser as shown in Figure A-31. You can use the Contents, Index, or Search features to locate information. The LiveMotion CD also includes a PDF of the help system for printing.

QUICK TIP

You must have JavaScript active in your browser to search Help.

Navigating Help

LiveMotion Help has three basic methods for locating a topic: Contents, Index, and Search. Contents allows you to find information by subject matter. First you locate the general subject of information you are looking for, and then you click the specific subject. The Index lists topics alphabetically and works well when you know your specific topic name. Use the Search feature when you know words related to the help topic for which you are interested. Search finds Help topics that contain all of the words you type into the Search text box. All three methods display pages with links to related topics.

FIGURE A-31

Topic in the Contents section of Help

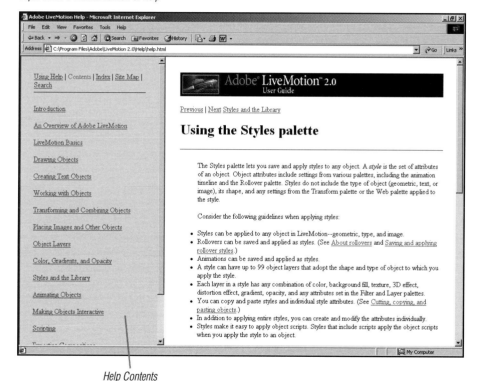

Help Contents

1. Click Help on the menu bar, then click LiveMotion Help.

   TIP You can also open the Help window by pressing [F1] (Win).

2. In the left frame of the browser window, click Styles and the Library.

3. In the right frame of the browser window, click Using the Styles palette.

4. Compare your window to Figure A-31.

You opened a topic using the Contents feature of LiveMotion Help.

Find information using the Help Index

1. Click Index in the left frame of the browser window.

2. Click R in the alphabet at the top of the frame.

3. Scroll, if necessary, to the heading "rollovers," then click the [1] next to the subheading "defined." Compare your screen to Figure A-32.

You used an alphabetical index to view a Help topic.

FIGURE A-32
Help Index

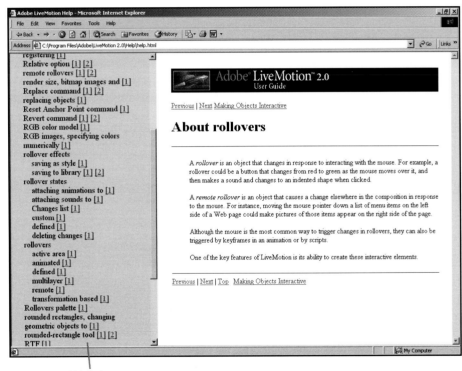

Help Index

FIGURE A-33
Help search results

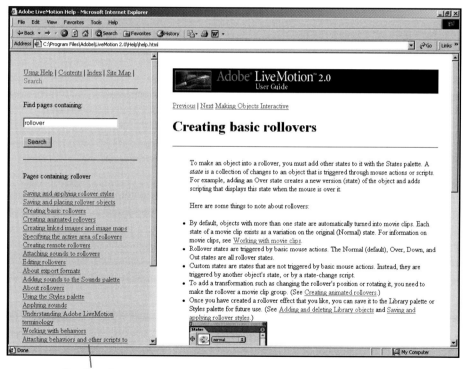

Search results

1. Scroll to the top of the page if necessary, then click Search in the left frame.

2. Type **rollover** in the Find pages containing text box, then click Search.

   Search finds all pages that include the word "rollover" anywhere in the page. Pages with more occurrences are listed at the top of the list; pages that include matches in their titles are ranked first.

   | TIP   Click Using Help in the left frame for more information on using Help.

3. Click Creating basic rollovers in the left pane. Compare your screen to Figure A-33.

4. In your browser, click File on the menu bar, then click Close to close LiveMotion Help.

5. In LiveMotion, click File on the menu bar, then click Close to close the basic_button file.

6. Click File on the menu bar, then click Exit (Win) or Click LiveMotion on the menu bar, then click Quit LiveMotion (Mac) to exit LiveMotion.

You searched for a Help topic, closed the basic button file, and exited LiveMotion.

The LiveMotion Help system provides a wealth of information for you to view and print. Designing elements for the Web can be challenging when deciding what colors to use, so you decide to learn more about color.

1. Open the LiveMotion Help window.
2. Click the Contents link, if necessary.
3. Click the Color, Gradients, and Opacity link in the left panel.
4. Click the About using color link, then read the information presented.
5. Once you have read the topic, click the Using the Color palette link under Related Subtopics, then read the information presented.
6. Once you have read the topic, click the Next link at the bottom of the page. The About color models topic appears.
7. Read the information presented, then print out the topic. Compare your results to Figure A-34.

FIGURE A-34
Completed Project 1

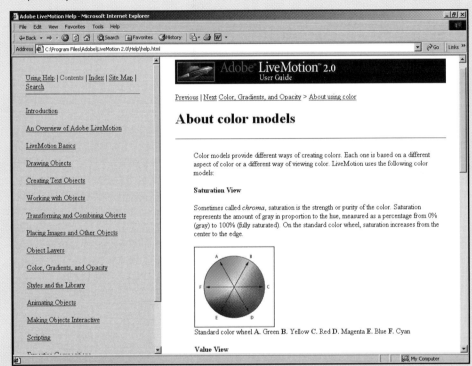

You are one of the designers at Conceptual Designs, a Web development and advertising company. Part of your job is to present clients with prospective designs for their Web page elements. You have determined from discussions with your latest client that they are interested in having an interactive navigation bar on the home page of their Web site that links Internet users to other pages and other Web sites. You decide to create a series of differently shaped and interactive buttons to preview to the client.

1. Create a new composition, then save it as **client1_buttons**.
2. Create two objects using each of the four object tools in the toolbox (Rectangle Tool, Rounded Rectangle Tool, Ellipse Tool, and Polygon Tool), for a total of eight objects.
3. Use the objects' handles to resize the objects so they are all about the same size.
4. Select and move the objects as necessary to arrange them in an orderly manner.
5. Apply the red/blue object layer style to one object in each pair of object shapes.
6. Apply a rollover style to the rectangle and ellipse objects that did not have the red/blue object layer style applied to them.

7. Apply both the light blue object layer style and the rollover style to each of the remaining two objects.
8. Preview the composition in Preview mode.
9. Save the page, then compare your screen to Figure A-35.

FIGURE A-35
Completed Project 2

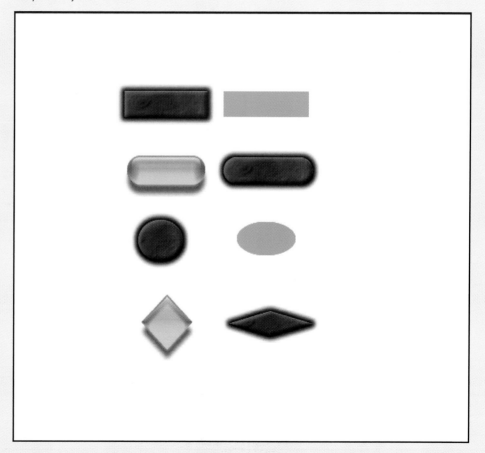

SECTION B

WORKING WITH OBJECTS AND TEXT

1. Draw and edit an object with the Pen Tool.

2. Transform objects.

3. Create object duplicates and aliases.

4. Align, distribute, and group objects.

5. Create a text object.

6. Edit a text object.

SECTION B
WORKING WITH OBJECTS AND TEXT

Introduction

Whether you are creating navigation tools, such as buttons or tabs, or a Flash animation, objects formulate the basis for your composition. Once you create or import an object, it probably will need to be modified in some way to look exactly the way you want. All three LiveMotion objects (geometric, text, and image) can be modified easily using the tools in the toolbox or by changing the properties of the object in a palette. For example, LiveMotion objects can be resized larger or smaller, reshaped, repositioned to an exact spot on the composition, or rotated to a different angle. You can transform or change the way an object appears by adjusting one of its handles or by changing the object's properties in the Transform palette. You can also duplicate objects easily and align, distribute, and arrange them in a specific order.

Creating Text

Like other Adobe (and most object-based) programs, you add text in LiveMotion by selecting a text tool from the toolbox. The text tool that you use in LiveMotion to create a word or a small phrase in a composition is the Type Tool. The Type Tool can also be used to create a bounding box (by dragging the mouse) into which you enter text. Text objects can be modified by changing the usual font properties, such as size, type, and style, and also object properties, such as layers, rotation, and skew. Remember, text in LiveMotion is an object and therefore can be treated and modified as such to create just the look you want.

Tools You'll Use

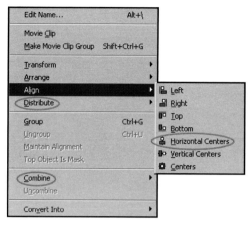

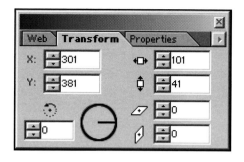

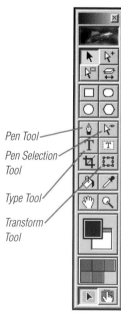

Pen Tool

Pen Selection Tool

Type Tool

Transform Tool

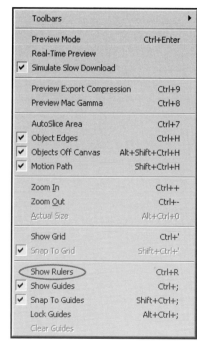

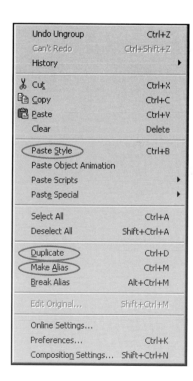

DRAW AND EDIT AN OBJECT WITH THE PEN TOOL

What You'll Do

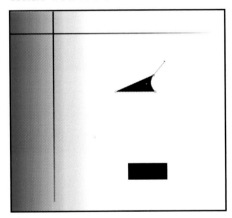

 In this lesson, you'll open an existing composition and then draw and edit an object created with the Pen Tool.

Understanding the Pen Tool

Here's an interesting challenge for you. Let's say you are designing a Web site for a local golf course and you want to incorporate some irregular shapes in the design that look like a putting green or maybe a sand trap. How would you create these shapes? The drawing tools in the toolbox (Rectangle, Ellipse, Rounded Rectangle, and Polygon) allow you to draw regular geometric shapes, but do not allow you to create irregular or curved shapes. The tool you need to accomplish this task is the Pen Tool.

The Pen Tool creates objects called **paths**, which are freeform objects made up of one or more straight or curved segments. Each end of a segment in a path is designated by a **control point**. You can change the shape of a path by modifying one of the object's control points. There are two different types of control points—corner points and smooth points. A **corner point** is a point where the path suddenly changes direction like a corner in a hallway. A corner point

can connect both straight and curved segments. A **smooth point** only connects curved segments and is used to create a flowing curve. When you select a smooth point it displays a **direction line** with **direction points** at either end of the line. The angle and length of the direction line determines the shape and size of the curve. Dragging a direction point adjusts the size and shape of a curved segment. Figure B-1 shows a path with a smooth point selected. A corner point does not have a direction line or direction points.

QUICKTIP

If you are having trouble drawing the shape you want with the Pen Tool, you can draw an object using one of the geometric tools, then select the object with the Pen Selection Tool to edit its control points.

Drawing Segments

If you are new to the Pen Tool, don't let it intimidate you! With a little understanding of how the tool works—and some practice—you can create some incredible-looking shapes and lines. To create a straight line using the Pen Tool, simply position your pointer where you want the segment to begin, click your mouse, then move your mouse and click where you want the segment to end. To continue adding segments to the path, continue clicking your mouse. Each time you click the mouse a new corner point is added to create a path of straight segments. Now, drawing a curved segment can be a little tricky, but after you have practiced a few times, you'll get the hang of it. Honest! To draw a curved segment, position your pointer where you want the segment to begin and then drag, creating a direction line in the process, as shown in Figure B-2 and Figure B-3. The length of a direction line determines the height or depth of a curve. To complete the curve, position the

pointer where you want the segment to end, and then drag in the opposite direction of the previous direction line to create a C-shape curve or in the same direction as the previous direction line to create an S-shape curve.

You can create an open or closed path. An open path consists of segments that don't close the shape, like an arc. In an open path the starting and ending control points are called **endpoints**. A closed path consists of segments that form a closed shape, like a circle. To close a path, simply click on the first control point you created.

Working with Control Points

When the shape of an existing path you have created is not looking quite right, you can add, delete, move, or convert control points. To add a control point, use the Pen

Tool to select the path you want to edit and then click the path segment to add a corner control point, or drag to add a smooth control point. To delete a control point, select the path with the Pen Tool and then click on the control point you want to delete. You can move a control point by selecting a path with the Pen Selection Tool and then dragging the control point to a new position. Sometimes it might be helpful to convert a control point from a corner point to a smooth point or vice versa. To convert a smooth point to a corner point, select the path with the Pen Selection Tool, press [Alt] (Win) or [Option] (Mac) and then click the smooth point you want to convert, or drag the corner point you want to convert. Paths can be filled with color or outlined. Figures B-2 and B-3 show paths that are outlined.

FIGURE B-1
Path with smooth point selected

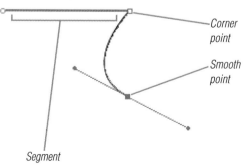

FIGURE B-2
S-shaped curved path

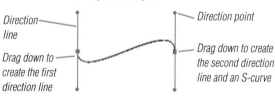

FIGURE B-3
C-shaped curved path

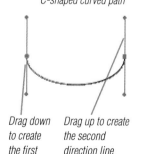

Create an object with the Pen Tool

1. Start LiveMotion, click File on the menu bar, click Open, navigate to the drive and folder where your data files are stored, click LMB-1.liv, then click Open (Win) or Choose (Mac).

2. Click File on the menu bar, click Save As, navigate to the drive and folder where your data files are stored, then save the file as **navbar_1**.

3. Click Window on the menu bar, then click Reset To Defaults.

4. Click the Pen Tool on the toolbar, then position the cursor in the middle of the Composition window.

5. Click (do not drag) to place the first control point (hollow red circle) of the path in the composition.

6. Move the pointer about a half-inch to the right, then click.

   A selected line appears between the two corner control points.

7. Position the pointer about a half-inch directly above the right control point, then drag up and to the right as shown in Figure B-4 to create a smooth control point.

   TIP   If your path is not filled with color as shown in Figure B-4, click the Properties tab if necessary, then click the Fill option button.

8. Click the Selection Tool in the toolbox.

You opened an existing LiveMotion file, then created an object using the Pen Tool.

FIGURE B-4
Path object created with the Pen Tool

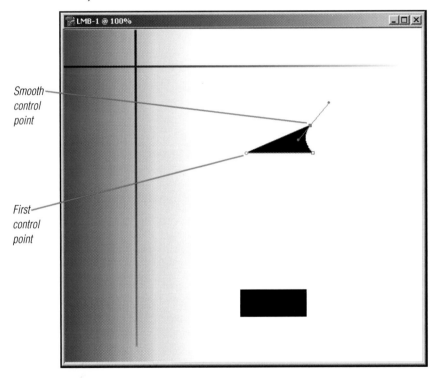

Smooth control point

First control point

FIGURE B-5

Path with new control points

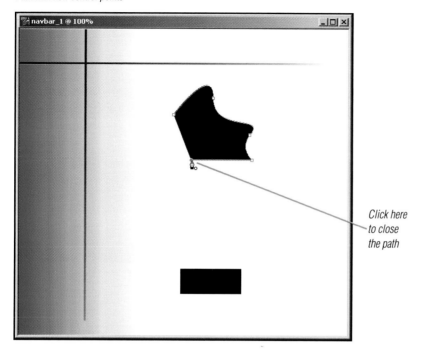

Click here to close the path

FIGURE B-6

Path without new control points

Add and delete control points

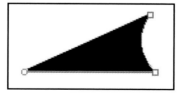

1. Click the Pen Tool in the toolbox, click the path object if it is not selected, position your pointer anywhere above the path object, then to place a new smooth control point.
2. Click to the left of the path object to place a corner control point.

   Notice that this corner point joins a curved segment and a straight segment.
3. Click the original control point to close the path as shown in Figure B-5.

   TIP Your closed path is likely to look different than Figure B-5, depending on where you put the control points in the composition.
4. Click the original control point again to delete the last segment you added.
5. Click the two control points you added in Steps 1 and 2 to delete them.

   The path should look similar to Figure B-6.

You added and deleted control points on an existing path object.

Format the path

1. Click the Pen Selection Tool in the toolbox, then click the path object to show its control points.

2. Click the top control point, then drag the bottom direction point to a point just to the right of and above the original control point, as shown in Figure B-7.

   Notice the curved segment change shape.

3. Click the Selection Tool in the toolbox.

4. Click the Styles tab if necessary, click the Styles palette menu list arrow, then click Preview View.

   (continued)

FIGURE B-7
Adjusted path object

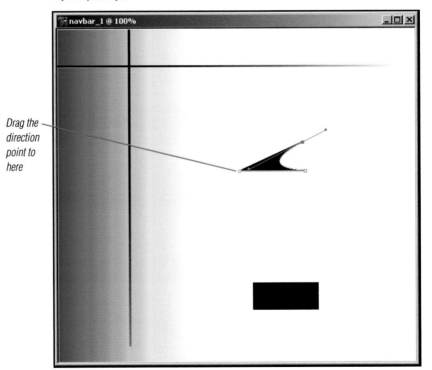

Drag the
direction
point to
here

Formatted path object

Move the path
object here

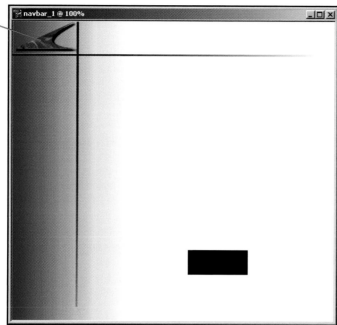

5. Click the Logo Wave style in the list box, then click the Apply Style button. ↘

   TIP If the Logo Wave style does not appear in the Styles palette, you can either add it to the LiveMotion Styles folder on your hard drive or use the 01_EmbossGradTexture style in the Styles palette instead. For information on how to add a style to the Styles folder, see the sidebar entitled "Adding a style to the LiveMotion Styles folder."

6. Drag the path object to the top left corner of the composition, as shown in Figure B-8.

   TIP If the top of the object is cut off when repositioned, use one of the resize handles to resize the object so that the entire object is visible.

7. Save your work.

You changed the shape of a path object by dragging a direction point, applied a style to the object, then moved the object.

Adding a style to the LiveMotion Styles folder

In order for a style to appear in the Styles palette, it must be installed in the Styles folder on your computer's hard drive. To access the Styles folder using Windows, use Windows Explorer to access your hard drive (usually "Local Disk (C)"), then open the Program Files/Adobe/LiveMotion 2.0/Styles folder. To access the Styles folder using a Mac, double-click the hard drive icon on the Desktop, navigate to the drive and folder that contains the Adobe LiveMotion 2 folder (usually found within the Applications folder), open or expand the Adobe LiveMotion 2 folder, then open the Styles folder that appears within the list of folders. Locate the Logo Wave style in your data files for this section, then copy the Logo Wave style from your data files into the Styles folder. The Logo Wave style will now appear in the Styles palette in LiveMotion. If LiveMotion is running when you perform this operation, click the Styles palette menu button, then click Refresh to see the new style.

TRANSFORM OBJECTS

What You'll Do

 In this lesson, you'll use the Transform palette and the Transform command to modify an object.

Working with the Transform Palette

LiveMotion has a variety of transforming tools that you can use to change radically the way objects appear in your composition. You already performed some basic object transformations in Section A when you resized and rotated an object by its handles. The Transform palette, shown in Figure B-9, offers you another way to transform an object easily by changing the object's properties in the palette. In the Transform palette you can resize, rotate, move, and skew an object with precision by entering specific values in the appropriate text boxes.

Each object in LiveMotion is in a specific position on the horizontal and vertical axes, identified by coordinates in the X and Y text boxes of the Transform palette. Thus, moving an object to a specific spot along the composition's horizontal axis or vertical axis is easily done by entering specific values in the X text box or the Y text box. This feature is useful because many times in Web page design elements need to be placed in an exact position in the composition. You can also resize an object precisely by entering values in the Height and Width text boxes. This feature is great to use when an object, such as a photograph, needs to be a specific size. You can also slant or **skew** the horizontal or vertical sides of an object in the same manner by entering values in the Horizontal Skew or Vertical Skew text boxes. And finally, you can rotate an object by entering a value in the Rotation text box

Changing an object's anchor point

Transformation actions are performed in relation to a fixed point called an anchor point, which by default is the center of the object. You can change the anchor point of an existing object by dragging it with the Transform Tool. ⬚ To reset the anchor point, click Object on the menu bar, point to Transform, then click Reset Anchor Point.

or by dragging the Rotation wheel. You should use the palette to rotate an object (instead of the object's top right corner handle) when you know exactly how many degrees you want to rotate it.

Learning Other Ways to Transform Objects

You can also transform an object by using certain commands on the Object menu and by using the Transform Tool in the toolbox. One of the transforming commands found on the Object menu, but not found in the Transform palette, is the Flip command. Flipping an object, horizontally or vertically, produces a mirror image of the object. The Transform Tool in the toolbox enables you to rotate an object by dragging any one of its four corner handles. You can also use the Transform Tool to skew an object horizontally or vertically by dragging any one of its middle handles.

QUICKTIP

If you want to undo all transformations applied to an object, select the object, click Object on the menu bar, point to Transform, then click Clear Transforms.

Combining Objects

Combining objects creates a new object from two or more selected objects. Combining is a little like grouping but with a twist. When you group objects, the objects are joined together to form one object, which can then be modified and transformed as one object. Combining objects allows you to join objects together in a group to create a particular effect in the area where the objects overlap or don't overlap. You can combine objects five different ways: Sectione, Sectione with Color, Minus Front, Intersect, and Exclude, as shown in Figure B-10. Sectione joins the outer edges of the objects together to create a single

merged object. The layers and layer properties of the backmost layer are preserved and applied to the new object. Sectione with Color joins the objects together to form one object while maintaining their individual attributes. The objects won't look different but they will only have one layer. Minus Front creates one object by subtracting the selected frontmost objects from the backmost object. The frontmost objects literally cut out the backmost object. Intersect creates one object from the overlapped area shared by the objects. All non-overlapped areas of the objects are deleted. Exclude creates one object by knocking out the area where one object overlaps another. Overlapping areas become transparent. If there are more than two objects that overlap, the overlap is made transparent where there is an even number of objects and filled where there is an odd number of objects.

FIGURE B-9
Transform palette

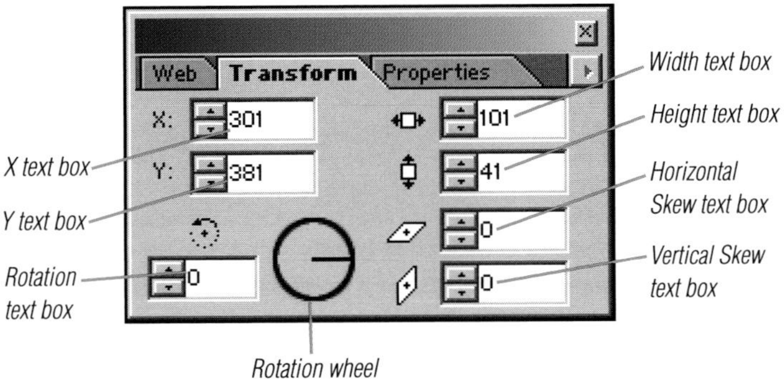

Width text box
Height text box
Horizontal Skew text box
Vertical Skew text box

X text box
Y text box
Rotation text box
Rotation wheel

FIGURE B-10
Sample combined objects

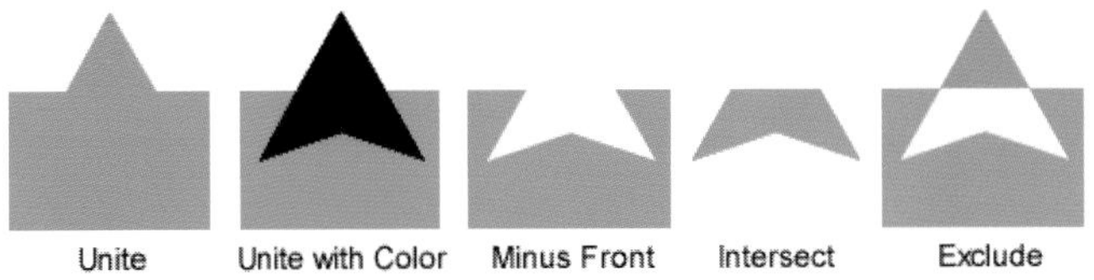

Unite   Unite with Color   Minus Front   Intersect   Exclude

Transform an object

1. Click the Selection Tool in the toolbox if necessary, click the rectangle object, click Edit on the menu bar, click Copy, click Edit on the menu bar, then click Paste. ▶

2. Click the Transform palette tab, then click the Width down arrow until 95 appears, as shown in Figure B-11.

3. Click the Height down arrow until 40 appears.

4. Select the number in the X-axis box, type **125**, select the number in the Y-axis box, type **420**, then press [Enter] (Win) or [return] (Mac).

   The new rectangle object moves to a new location in the composition.

You copied a rectangle object, then changed its size and position in the composition using the Transform palette.

FIGURE B-11
Transform palette

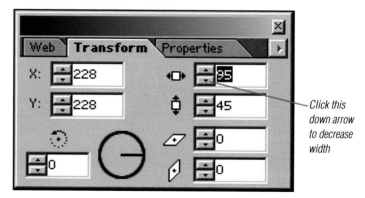

Click this down arrow to decrease width

Transform palette

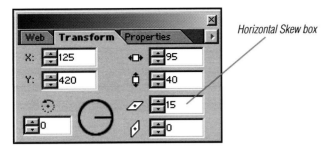

Horizontal Skew box

Skew an object

1. Click the Transform Tool on the toolbox, then position the pointer over each of the selected rectangle object's handles.

   Notice that the pointer changes to the rotate pointer on the corner handles and the skew pointer on the center handles.

2. Position the skew pointer over the bottom center handle, then drag to the left until a number around 15 appears in the Horizontal Skew box on the Transform palette.

3. If the number 15 is not displayed in the Horizontal Skew box, click the Horizontal Skew up or down arrow until the number 15 appears, as shown in Figure B-12.

4. Compare your composition to Figure B-13.

You used the Transform Tool to skew the rectangle object.

FIGURE B-13
Skewed rectangle object

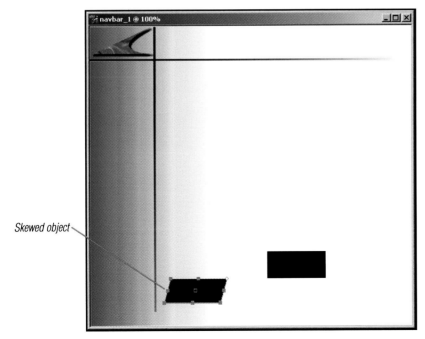

Skewed object

Combine objects

1. Click the Polygon Tool on the toolbox, then draw an object that measures 50 wide by 45 high.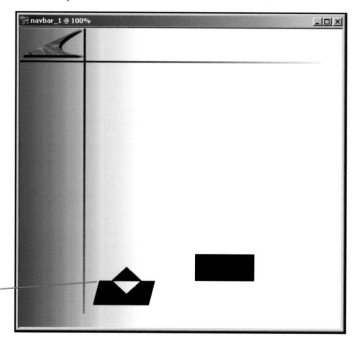

2. In the Transform palette, type **159** in the X-axis text box, type **398** in the Y-axis text box then press [Enter] (Win) or [return] (Mac).

   The polygon object moves and overlaps the top of the skewed rectangle.

3. Click the Drag Selection Tool, then drag a selection marquee around both objects so both objects are selected.

   TIP If you accidentally select more objects than intended, click in a blank area of the composition, then try again.

4. Click Object on the menu bar, point to Combine, click Exclude, then click in a blank area of the composition.

   The overlapping portion of the polygon and rectangle objects is "excluded" and becomes transparent, as shown in Figure B-14.

   You created a small polygon object, moved it over top of the skewed rectangle, and then combined the two objects.

FIGURE B-14
Combined objects

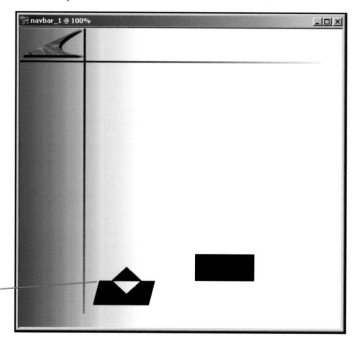

Polygon and rectangle combined

Rotate and flip an object

1. Click the Selection Tool on the toolbox, click the combined object, then type **180** in the Rotation box on the Transform palette.

   TIP To rotate an object quickly while viewing the degrees rotated in the Rotation box, drag the line in the Rotation wheel.

2. Click Object on the menu bar, point to Transform, then click Flip Vertical.

   The object is flipped back over as shown in Figure B-15.

3. In the Transform palette, type **45** in the Width text box, type **30** in the Height text box, move the object to the bottom left corner of the composition, then click in a blank area of the composition.

4. Compare your composition to Figure B-16.

5. Save, then close the file.

You rotated, flipped, and resized the combined object, then repositioned the object.

CREATE OBJECT DUPLICATES AND ALIASES

What You'll Do

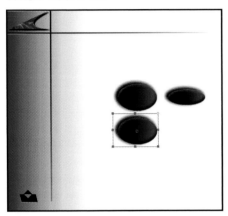

 In this lesson, you will learn to duplicate objects, create object aliases, and paste object attributes.

Duplicating Objects and Creating Aliases

When you need to create a number of the same Web elements, you can duplicate the objects or create aliases. **Duplicating** an object makes an exact copy of the selected object, as shown in Figure B-17. The duplicated object is independent from the original object, so changing the attributes of the original object has no effect on the duplicated object. When you duplicate an object, the duplicated object is placed directly over the top of the original object, and can then be moved and modified. Duplicating an object can be a quick way to create an exact copy of an object, but you might find creating an object alias to be a preferable method for duplicating objects. An object **alias** looks similar to an object that has been duplicated, but only on the surface. Actually, an object alias is a linked duplicate of the original object, so changes you make to the original or any alias object created from the original will be reflected in the other(s). This is a great advantage when you have a number of

objects that you need to modify in the same way. Object aliases are useful in other ways as well because they minimize the composition file size, reduce the time to redraw like objects, and speed up the editing process. And if you want to modify an object independently from the other object aliases, you can break the alias link.

Pasting Object Attributes

You might be wondering why there is a section on pasting objects, since the copy/paste action is fairly basic. Well, LiveMotion has a unique set of pasting features found on the Edit menu that are worthy of some attention. In LiveMotion you can copy and paste object attributes such as color, texture, layers, transformations, animations, scripts, and the current, or active, matte. On the Edit menu there are four Paste commands: Paste Style, Paste Object Animation, Paste Scripts, and Paste Special. The Paste Style command copies the style (color, texture, layers, etc.) from one object to another. Think of this feature as "painting" the format of one object onto another object. The Paste Object Animation command pastes the animation settings of an object to another object. If you are using scripts in your composition, you can paste them to other objects using the Paste Scripts command. The Paste Special command has a submenu with eight commands you can use to paste a particular object attribute, including Paste Image, Paste Texture, Paste Active Matte, Layer, Transformations, Fill, Effects, and Properties. Use the Paste Image command to copy an image object to a selected object. The image is cropped and resized to fit within the object. The Paste Texture command applies the copied object as a texture to a selected object or the composition background. The Active Matte command is used to apply the shape of the copied object to the selected image object. Use the Layer command to apply the attributes of a selected layer of the copied object to a selected object. The Transformations command is used to copy the rotation and skew of a copied object to another object. Use the Fill command to copy the fill color, image, texture, tint, gradient, and background of a copied object to a selected object. The Effects command applies the 3D and Distort palette settings from a copied object to a selected object. And lastly, the Properties command is used to apply the Properties palette settings of a copied object to a selected object.

FIGURE B-17
Duplicated objects

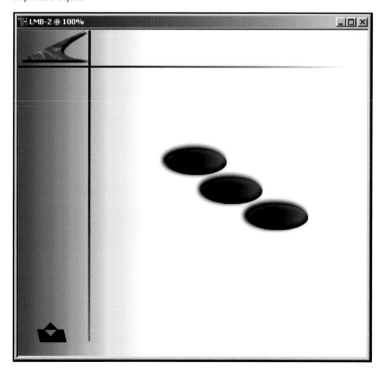

Duplicate an object

1. Open LMB-2.liv, then save it as **navbar_2**.

2. Click the Selection Tool on the toolbox if necessary, then click the ellipse object in the composition. ▶

3. Click Edit on the menu bar, then click Duplicate.

   An exact copy of the ellipse object appears, placed on top of the first object.

   > TIP   You can also right-click an object (Win), or press [control] and click an object (Mac), then click Duplicate in the shortcut menu, or press [Alt] (Win) or [option] (Mac) and drag to create a duplicate.

4. Drag the selected object to the right of the first object, as shown in Figure B-18.

   You created a duplicate copy of the original ellipse object.

Make an alias

1. Click the original ellipse object, click Edit on the menu bar, then click Make Alias.

   An exact copy of the ellipse object appears, placed on top of the first object.

   > TIP   You can also right-click an object (Win) or press [control] and click an object (Mac), then click Make Alias in the shortcut menu to create an object alias.

2. Drag the new object alias down off of the original object.

   (continued)

FIGURE B-18
Duplicate copy of the ellipse object

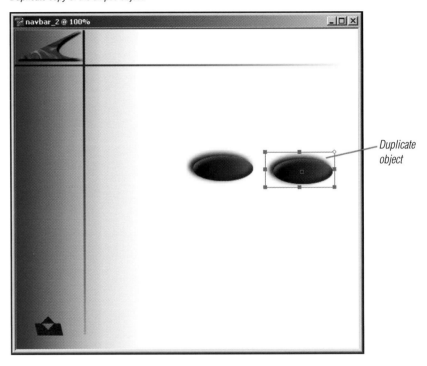

Duplicate object

Working with Objects and Text

FIGURE B-19
New alias object

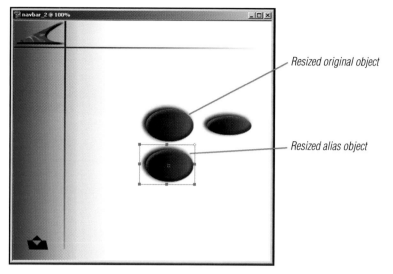

Resized original object

Resized alias object

FIGURE B-20
Object with pasted style attributes

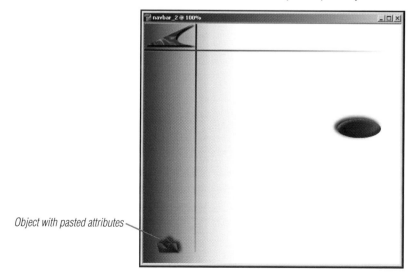

Object with pasted attributes

3. Drag the bottom right handle of the new
   object alias down to reshape the alias.

   Notice that both aliases change shape, as
   shown in Figure B-19.

4. Press [Ctrl] (Win) or [shift] (Mac), click the
   other alias ellipse, click Edit on the menu
   bar, then click Clear.

*You created an object alias from the original ellipse
object, formatted the alias objects, then deleted
both alias objects.*

Paste object properties

1. Select the ellipse object, click Edit on the
   menu bar, then click Copy.

2. Select the small object in the bottom left
   corner of the composition, click Edit on the
   menu bar, then click Paste Style.

   The object takes on all of the layer style
   characteristics of the ellipse object.

3. Compare your Composition window to
   Figure B-20.

4. Save your work.

*You selected the ellipse object, copied it, then
pasted the style attributes of the ellipse to the
combined object.*

ALIGN, DISTRIBUTE AND GROUP OBJECTS

What You'll Do

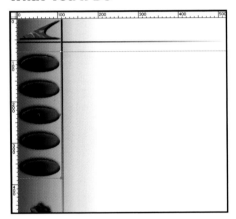

In this lesson, you will learn how to align, distribute, and group objects.

Aligning Objects

Some elements that you create in LiveMotion, such as buttons, tabs, and text blocks, need to be organized or aligned in a specific location in the composition. One way to accomplish this is to drag the objects manually to specific points, which can be time consuming. The best and quickest way to align objects in a composition is to use the Align command on the Object menu. The **Align** command aligns objects relative to the horizontal or vertical axis or specific points on the axis. The Left, Right, and Horizontal Centers commands align objects along the vertical axis, while the Top, Bottom, and Vertical Centers commands align objects along the horizontal axis. The Left, Right, Top, and Bottom commands align objects relative to the edge of the farthest object. For example, if you are aligning three objects to the left, the objects are aligned along the left edge of the selected object that is farthest left. The Horizontal Centers and Vertical Centers commands align the centers of the selected objects. The Centers command aligns the collective horizontal and vertical centers of all of the selected objects, causing the objects and their anchor points to overlap.

Object stacking order

LiveMotion stacks each new object that is created or imported above the previous object, no matter where it is in the composition. The stacking order of objects determines how objects are displayed when they overlap. You can change the stacking order any time by selecting one of the Arrange commands on the Object menu. The Bring to Front command brings an object or group to the front of the entire stack of objects. The Bring Forward command and the Send Backward command move an object one level forward or backward. The Send to Back command moves an object all the way to the back of the stack of objects.

Distributing and Grouping Objects

Even spacing between objects is an important way to keep a Web page's design looking professional. **Distributing** objects spreads them out evenly along the horizontal or vertical axis of the objects by adding equal amounts of space between them, as shown in Figure B-21. Distributing objects provides an accurate way to balance the space between three or more objects. Once you have aligned and distributed objects, you can group them together to preserve their alignment and spacing. A **grouped** object is treated as one object and is moved or transformed as a group. Even though a grouped object is treated as one object, the individual objects in the group do not lose their identity and can be formatted using the Subgroup Selection Tool. Multiple objects that are stacked in a certain order and then grouped maintain their original stacking order.

Using Rulers, Guides, and Grids

When you need to measure an object exactly or place an object in a certain place in the composition, the LiveMotion rulers can help simplify the task. When you display the rulers, one ruler appears along the top and one ruler appears along the left side of the Composition window. The ruler origin is the upper left point, where the rulers display 0. Object position on the horizontal and vertical axes is measured from the ruler origin. You can display rulers by selecting

Show Rulers on the View menu. When rulers are displayed, you can place ruler guides in the composition, which can help you position objects in precise locations. These are non-printing guides and are not exported with your composition. Objects can "snap" to guides, which forces the edge of the object to align on the guide, when they are dragged within 8 pixels of the guide. In order for you to see a guide, you first need to make sure that the Show Guides check box is selected on the View menu. Then to place a guide in the Composition window, simply drag from the horizontal or vertical ruler. You can also move, lock, and delete guides. To move a

guide, simply select it and move it to a new location. If you want to lock a guide to avoid accidentally moving it, select the Lock Guides command on the View menu. When you want to delete a guide, drag it back to the ruler. The grid, a series of connected boxes (like graph paper), is another feature you can use to position objects in the composition. An object's bounding box snaps to the grid, which makes positioning objects very easy. To show the grid, click View on the menu bar and then click Show Grid. As you work with objects in LiveMotion, you'll find the rulers, guides, and grid helpful and necessary to accomplish your tasks quickly.

FIGURE B-21
Objects vertically aligned and distributed

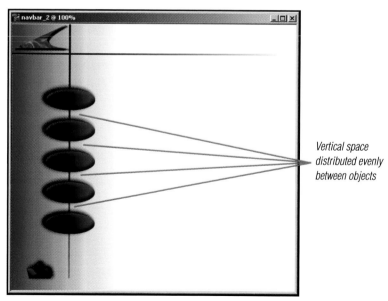

Vertical space distributed evenly between objects

Align, distribute, and group objects

1. Open LMB-3.liv, then save it as **navbar_3**.

2. Click the Drag Selection Tool if necessary, then drag to select all of the ellipse objects.

3. Click Object on the menu bar, point to Align, then click Horizontal Centers.

   The ellipse objects are aligned vertically based on the horizontal center of the top ellipse.

4. Click Object on the menu bar, point to Distribute, then click Vertical.

   An even amount of space is placed between each ellipse.

5. Click Object on the menu bar, then click Group.

6. Compare your composition to Figure B-22.

You selected all of the ellipse objects, aligned them vertically, and then distributed and grouped them.

FIGURE B-22
Grouped ellipse objects

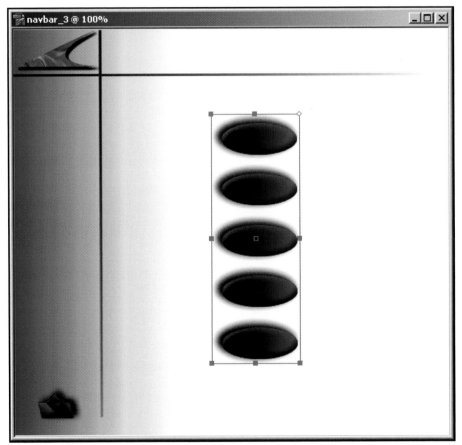

navbar_3 @ 100%

Composition window showing guides

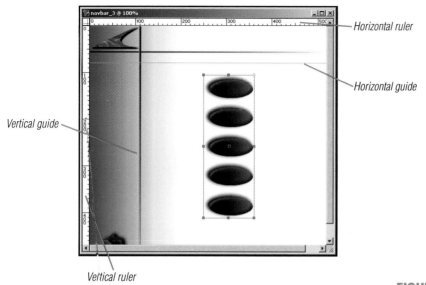

Horizontal ruler

Horizontal guide

Vertical guide

Vertical ruler

FIGURE B-24

Object positioned using guides

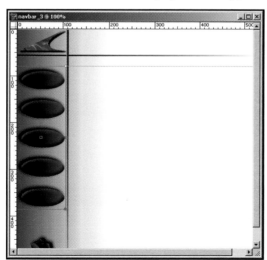

Use rulers and guides

1. Click View on the menu bar, then click Show Rulers.

2. Position the pointer over the vertical ruler, then drag to the middle of the Composition window.

   A vertical green guide appears as you drag.

3. Position the pointer over the guide, then drag the guide to the left edge of the vertical black line.

4. Drag a horizontal guide down to the 80 pixel mark on the vertical ruler, as shown in Figure B-23.

5. Drag the grouped ellipse objects to the left side of the vertical guide, then drag the grouped object up to meet the horizontal guide, as shown in Figure B-24.

   The grouped object snaps to both guides.

   TIP If the top and right sides of the selection border of the grouped object do not overlap the guides, move the object slowly to the left of the vertical guide and up to the horizontal guide until it "snaps" into place.

6. Click Edit on the menu bar, then click Deselect All to deselect the ellipse objects.

7. Position the pointer over the horizontal guide, drag it to the horizontal ruler, then drag the vertical guide to the vertical ruler.

8. Click View on the menu bar, then click Show Rulers to hide the rulers.

9. Save your work.

You displayed rulers, used guides to position the grouped ellipse object, then hid the rulers.

Lesson 4   Align, Distribute, and Group Objects

ADOBE LIVEMOTION B-23

CREATE A TEXT OBJECT

What You'll Do

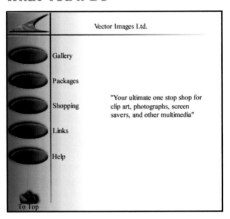

 In this lesson, you'll learn how to create a text object.

Learning about Text in Web Design

If you are experienced with word processors, or with using text in graphic design, you may think there is little you need to know about text and how to use it on the Web. However, there are some issues that you should keep in mind when creating text specifically for the Web. First of all, without getting into all the gruesome details, fonts are organized into type categories, such as serif, sans serif, monospaced, script, and decorative, as shown in Table B-2. Within each font category are the individual font types, such as Arial and Times New Roman, which you use when you create text in a document or composition. The font type you decide to use in your composition can help or hurt the look of your Web page. Keep in mind that your Web content is primarily viewed online and not in printed form, which poses different challenges to designing text. When deciding which font type to use for your Web page, you want to choose a font that is easy to read like serif and sans

TABLE B-2: Font type categories

Category	Sample
Serif	Bookman is a serif font.
Sans Serif	Arial is a sans serif font.
Monospaced	Courier is a monospaced font.
Script	NuptialScript is a script font.
Decorative	Comic Sans MS is a decorative font.

serif fonts. The size of your font is also important. If you are creating a large block of text, you want to use a font size of 10 to 15. For headings and titles, you can use a much larger font, depending on the overall look you are trying to achieve. Another point to keep in mind is how you are going to identify hypertext links in your text. Traditionally, hypertext links were identified by underlining; however, you can also bold the text, increase the text size, or create a rollover effect. If you have a large amount of text, you want to design your site's paragraph column width so it is manageable and easily readable. A wide, lengthy column with small point text is difficult to read on screen. Finally, be careful when using effects and color. You can detract from the legibility of text if you enhance it with too many effects. Make sure that the color of the font you use matches the overall design of your Web page. And, of course, the best test of the quality of your Web content is to preview it in your Web browser.

Adding Text to a Composition

In a LiveMotion composition, you can use the Type Tool to add two types of text: point text and paragraph text. **Point text** is a word or string of characters you create by selecting the Type Tool, clicking in the composition to set the insertion point, and then typing text. Point text appears in a bounding box but does not automatically wrap inside the box; the text determines the size of its bounding box. **Paragraph text**, as the name suggests, is multiple sentences that make

up a paragraph. You can create paragraph text by selecting the Type Tool, dragging a bounding box in the composition, and then typing text, as shown in Figure B-25. The text stays within the boundaries of the bounding box and wraps accordingly. A text

overflow handle (solid black box) appears in the lower right corner of the box if the amount of text is too large for the box. To increase the size of the bounding box, simply drag one of its handles.

FIGURE B-25
Text object created with the Type Tool

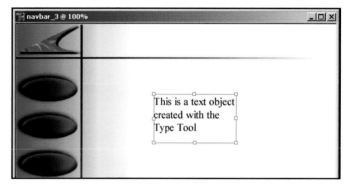

Text fields

If you find that you are using a large amount of text in your composition or plan to export your composition as a Flash file (SWF), you'll want to use the Text Field Tool to create text. Text created with the Text Field Tool produces a smaller file size than text created with the Type Tool and is searchable on the Web using JavaScripts or search engines. You can either drag a bounding box or click in the Composition window to create a text field. Once you create a text field, there are several options you can change in the Properties palette (such as allowing users to input information in the text field or exporting the text field as HTML) to define the text field's behavior.

Create point text

1. Click the Type Tool in the toolbox, then position the pointer in the middle of the composition. 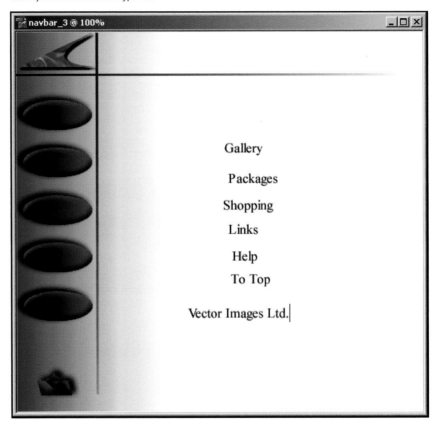T|

2. Click the mouse, then type **Gallery**.

   > TIP   If you make a mistake while typing, press [Backspace] (Win) or [delete] (Mac), or click to insert the I-beam pointer, select the incorrect text, then type again.

3. Move the pointer below the text object, click the mouse, then type **Packages**.

4. Type the five remaining text objects shown in Figure B-26.

You created seven text objects.

FIGURE B-26
Text objects created with the Type Tool

Paragraph text object

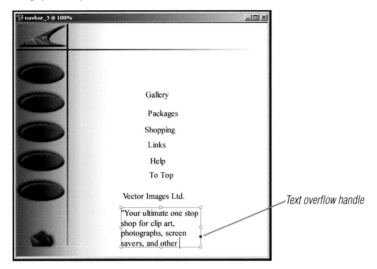

Text overflow handle

FIGURE B-28
Positioned text objects

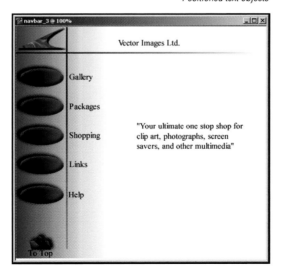

Create paragraph text

1. Below the last text object, drag a bounding box about 3 inches wide by 2 inches high.

2. Type **"Your ultimate one stop shop for clip art, photographs, screen savers, and other multimedia"** (include the quotes), as shown in Figure B-27.

   The sentence wraps inside the boundaries of the text box. Depending on the size of the bounding box, some text may be hidden from view.

3. Drag the bottom right handle to the right to enlarge the text box so the text fits on three lines.

4. Click the Selection Tool, drag each text object to the position in the composition shown in Figure B-28, then click in a blank area of the composition.

5. Save your work.

You created a paragraph text object, then moved all of the text objects in the composition.

EDIT A TEXT OBJECT

What You'll Do

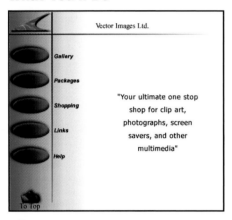

 In this lesson, you'll format the text in a text object.

Formatting Text

Any object you create usually needs to be modified or changed in some way before you can call it final. Text is no exception; in fact, it's vital that text in your composition look good and communicate the message you want it to. Not only does Web page text communicate a specific message, but it also communicates a tone and personality. With LiveMotion you have the ability to format the type, size, color, spacing, and many other aspects of text using the Properties palette.

When you create a text object, the Properties palette looks similar to Figure B-29. The current font type you are using is identified in the Font Type list box. You can change the font of paragraphs, sentences, or individual words and characters by selecting the appropriate set of text and applying a font type to it. To enhance the look of your text, you can change its font style to italic, bold, or bold italic by clicking the Font Style list arrow. Since text is a vector object, which means the object remains clear at any resolution and is stretchable, you can change the size of a text object simply by dragging one of its handles. This is a very cool feature! However, if you want to size text precisely, click the Point Size

Converting text objects

You may find it necessary at times to convert a text object into individual character text objects. The individual characters retain their original alignment and kerning and are completely editable. Converting text becomes vital when you want to animate individual characters of words, for example. You can also convert a text object into a vector image; however, in this case, the object is no longer editable using LiveMotion's text tools or properties. To convert a text object, select the text object, click Object on the menu bar, point to Convert Into, then click Objects or Group of Objects.

list arrow on the Properties palette and select a font point size.

Adjusting the space between adjacent text baselines can really improve the look of your text. The space between text lines is known as **leading**, or line height. You can adjust the leading of text by clicking the Leading text box on the Properties palette and entering a new number. Not only can the space between lines of text be important, but the space between letters within words as well. You can adjust the spacing between selected letters, or **tracking**, by clicking the Tracking list arrow in the Properties palette and changing the setting. The Tracking list arrow appears in the palette only when the text object is selected using the Selection Tool. Tracking applies a uniform amount of space between characters and can dramatically change the look of your text. Each letter in a text object takes up a different amount of space, depending on its width. This space is known as **proportional spacing**. **Kerning** controls the individual (proportional) space between specific letter pairs. You normally change the kerning of text when you need to make minor spacing adjustments between specific letter pairs. For example, you might want to close up the space between letters in a word you want to stand out. To change the kerning of letters in a word, select the word, then click the Kerning list arrow in the Properties palette to change the setting. The Outline button in the Properties palette changes the text and displays it as outlined. The Baseline Shift property, also found in the Properties palette, allows you to change how far selected text is off the baseline (for making superscripts and subscripts). You can also align the text four ways: left-align, right-align, center-align, and justify using the appropriate buttons on the Properties palette.

QUICKTIP

By default LiveMotion turns on anti-aliasing for text. **Anti-aliasing** is the addition of pixels around the edges of letters, which reduces the jaggedness that appears around text. To turn anti-aliasing off or to set a different anti-aliasing option, open the Properties palette menu.

FIGURE B-29
Properties palette

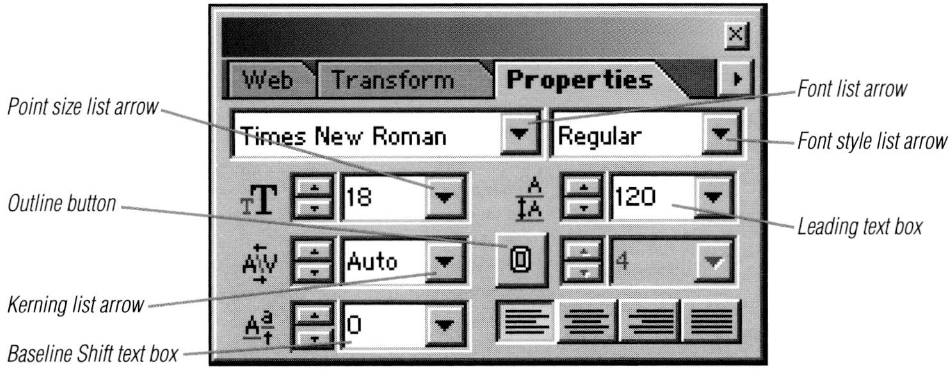

Point size list arrow
Font list arrow
Font style list arrow
Outline button
Leading text box
Kerning list arrow
Baseline Shift text box

Modify font type, style, and size

1. Click the Drag Selection Tool in the toolbox, then drag to select all of the point text objects that are to the right of the ellipse objects.

2. In the Properties palette, click the Font list arrow, then click Arial.

3. Click the Font style list arrow, then click Bold Italic.

4. Click the Font size list arrow, click 14, then click in a blank area of the composition.

   TIP   You can also change the font size by clicking the Font size up or down arrow.

5. Compare your composition to Figure B-30.

You changed the font type, style, and size of all of the point text objects.

FIGURE B-30
Formatted text

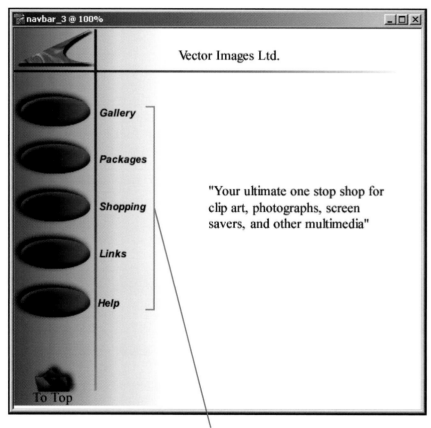

Formatted text objects

FIGURE B-31

Formatted paragraph text object

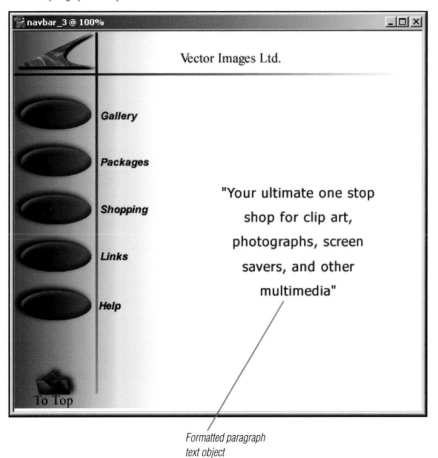

*Formatted paragraph
text object*

1. Click the Selection Tool in the toolbox, then click the paragraph text object.

2. Click the Font list arrow, click Tahoma, click the Tracking list arrow, then click 5.

   > TIP   If Tahoma is not on your font list, choose a different font.

3. Click the Leading list arrow, then click 180.

   The text moves below the boundaries of the text box and is hidden from view.

4. Click the Type Tool in the toolbox, then drag the bottom center handle of the paragraph text object down until all of the text is visible. T

5. Click the Center align text button in the Properties palette.

6. Click the Selection Tool, click in a blank area of the composition, then compare your composition to Figure B-31.

7. Save your work, then close the file.

You changed the font style, font size, tracking, leading, and alignment of the paragraph text object.

The Conservatory Theater you work for has decided to update its Web site to showcase the plays for the current season. You have been selected to create the new look for the Web site. You have recently started learning LiveMotion and are ready to use your skills to create the elements for an interactive banner. Using the skills you have learned so far, create a composition that looks similar to Figure B-32.

1. Create a composition 400 pixels wide by 300 pixels high, then save it as **theater**.
2. Use the Pen Tool to create the "stage light" shape (the black shapes in Figure B-32), then use the Pen Selection Tool to modify the shape. (*Hint*: The "stage light" shape is created using one corner point and one smooth point.)
3. Create the ellipse shape (the white shapes shown in Figure B-32), use the arrow keys to position the ellipse within the "stage light" shape, then combine the two objects.
4. Make additional "stage light" shapes by making aliases.
5. Create the black bar shape, then use the rulers and guides to position the "stage light" shapes on the bar.

6. Rotate each "stage light" shape.
7. Create text objects for each text block in the composition, positioned as shown in Figure B-32.
   - Format the composition heading: 24 point, Arial Black, with a tracking of 5.
   - Format each of the play names: 16 point, bold, Times New Roman, with a tracking of 5.

- Format the bottom paragraph: 12 point, bold, Times New Roman, with a tracking of 0 and a leading of 100, centered in the text object.
8. Save the file, then compare your results to Figure B-32.

FIGURE B-32
Completed Project 1

You are a Web designer in a small Web design company. You have recently been given a job to design a Web site that provides detailed historical information about the American Civil War. You have compiled a lot of the information and photos that are going into the site, and you are now ready to create an interactive navigation bar. Use Figure B-33 to help you create the navigation bar.

1. Open the file LMB-6, then save it as **webbar**.
2. Rotate the rectangles 90 degrees (*Hint*: Reposition them as necessary to make them easy to work with), then transform each rectangle to a width of 40 and a height of 138.
3. Use the rulers and guides to place the top of each rectangle on the Y-coordinate of 82, as shown in Figure B-33.
4. Create a black line 550 pixels long and 2 pixels wide, then position it on the Y-coordinate of 36.
5. Use the Type Tool to create all of the text objects.
    - Format the composition heading: 30 point, bold, Times New Roman, with a tracking of 0, then center it in the composition above the black line.
    - Format the date text box: 24 point, bold, Times New Roman, with a tracking of 0, then center it in the composition below the black line.

- Format the button text: 16 point, bold, Times New Roman, with a tracking of 0, then position each text object in a colored button.
- Format the paragraph text: 16 point, Arial, with a tracking of 5, a leading of 100, and justified alignment, then center in the composition with the top of the object on the Y coordinate of 184.
6. Select all of the button text objects, then align their bottom edges.
7. Use the Pen Tool to create the small shapes in the buttons as shown in Figure B-33.

FIGURE B-33
Completed Project 2

(*Hint*: Create a large shape first, format the object to the correct shape, then decrease its size. This path uses four control points: three corner points and one smooth point.)
8. Duplicate the path object three times, place each object in a button then align the center of each path object with the center of the text object next to which it appears.
9. Then group all of the button elements together.
10. Hide guides and rulers, save the file, then compare your screen to Figure B-33.

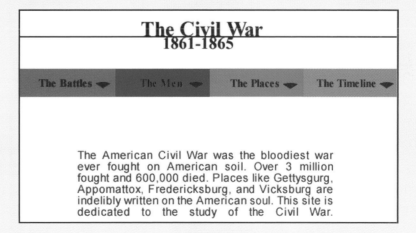

WORKING WITH IMPORTED IMAGES AND OBJECT LAYERS

1. Place an image in a composition.

2. Work with images.

3. Create and work with object layers.

4. Change layer opacity.

5. Modify object layers.

Understanding Imported Images

Most Web designers today use some sort of image, whether it be a photograph, an illustration, or a piece of clip art, to add character to a Web page. You can acquire images for use in LiveMotion from a variety of sources, including a digital camera, a scanner, the Web, or CDs. Bitmap or vector images created or modified in image-editing or drawing programs such as Adobe Photoshop or Adobe Illustrator can be placed easily in a LiveMotion composition. When you place an image in a composition, you are actually placing a copy of the image in the composition, not the original. The original image remains intact and unaffected by any modifications done in LiveMotion.

Understanding Object Layers

In LiveMotion, objects are created in layers like the layers of a cake. Whether you create an object in a composition or place it from another source, you are initially working with the first or topmost layer of the object. Each object has one layer when you draw or place it in a composition, and can have up to 99 additional layers. Each layer in an object has its own attributes, such as color, softness, or opacity, that belong specifically to the layer. Unlike a Photoshop layer, an object layer in LiveMotion matches the dimensions of the object and not the entire composition. When you add a layer to an object, the new layer is added as a copy of the object and is placed directly underneath the first layer of the object. Because each layer of an object can be modified independently from other layers, you can use object layers to create shadow, offset, three-dimensional, and embossed effects, to name just a few. Object layers allow you to create unique effects with very little effort. To create new object layers or modify existing ones, you use the Object Layers palette.

Tools You'll Use

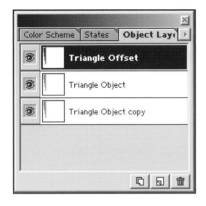

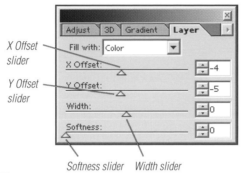

X Offset slider

Y Offset slider

Softness slider   *Width slider*

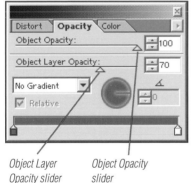

Object Layer Opacity slider   *Object Opacity slider*

New Composition...   Ctrl+N
New Script   Ctrl+Alt+N
Open...   Ctrl+O

Close   Ctrl+W
Save   Ctrl+S
Save As...   Shift+Ctrl+S
Revert   F12

Place...   Ctrl+I
Place Sequence...   Alt+Shift+Ctrl+I
Place As Texture...
Replace...   Shift+Ctrl+I

Export Settings...   Alt+Shift+Ctrl+E
Export   Ctrl+E
Export As...   Shift+Ctrl+E
Export Selection...

Preview In   ▶

File Info...
Workgroup   ▶

Print Setup...   Shift+Ctrl+P
Print...   Ctrl+P

1 C:\LIVEMO~1\UNITC~1\LMC-6
2 C:\LIVEMO~1\UNITC~1\excursion
3 C:\LIVEMO~1\UNITC~1\design1
4 C:\LIVEMO~1\UNITC~1\LMC-2

Exit   Ctrl+Q

PLACE AN IMAGE IN A COMPOSITION

What You'll Do

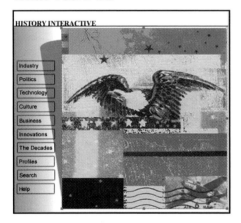

In this lesson, you'll place a Photoshop image in a composition.

Learning about Images

Without a doubt, an appropriate image enhances a Web page better than most anything else. How you decide to use images in your composition is significant to the composition's overall design and should therefore play an important part in the entire development process. You can place both bitmap (raster) and vector images in a composition, which gives you a multitude of images from which to choose. A vector image has an advantage over a bitmap image in that it can be resized larger or smaller without losing image quality. Keep in mind, however, that most stock images that you can buy or download from the Internet are bitmap images, and you may want to enhance the image in an image-editing program like Photoshop before you place it into a composition. Table C-1 describes some of the common types of images that you can place in a LiveMotion composition.

Before you place an image in a composition, there are a few issues that you should keep in mind. When you place a compressed bitmap image in a composition it retains its compression, which reduces the overall file size of the composition. If you

Placing images as a sequence

You can place a set of images as an animated sequence using the Place Sequence command. Each image is converted into one frame of the animation, so the filenames of the images must be consistently named, in sequential order (for example, Rocket1.jpg, Rocket2.jpg, Rocket3.jpg, etc.), and located in the same folder. The frames of the animation are placed in order according to their filenames, so the filename with the first number is the first frame of the animation. The length of the animation is the total number of frames divided by the frame rate setting in the Composition Setting dialog box.

are developing a large Web site with multiple pages, image compression may be an important consideration. Another issue to keep in mind is that the better the quality, or resolution, of the image you use in LiveMotion, the better the quality of the image when you export it. This is true regardless of the file format of the image. Images don't have to be a certain resolution to be seen on the Web; however, images on the Web currently appear at 72 dpi (dots per inch). So, it makes little sense to place images in your composition that have a higher resolution than 72 dpi (unless you need to enlarge the image once it's in LiveMotion). Finally, before you use an image, especially one that is downloaded off the Web, make sure you have the legal right to use the image. In most cases, if an image is protected by copyright laws, you will need permission to use it in your composition. There are many royalty-free images on the Web that you can use any way you like; you just have to find them!

QUICKTIP

To place an Illustrator 9 or Illustrator 10 file into a composition, it must be saved using the Create PDF Compatible File command in Illustrator.

Placing Images

When it's time to place an image into a composition, you have a few options from which to choose. You can place the object into your composition using the Place command, which embeds a copy of the

TABLE C-1: Common importable image formats

File Format	Description
.GIF	Graphics Interchange File. Format for saving graphics for display over the Web.
.JPEG	Joint Photographic Experts Group. Format for saving bitmap images at varying degrees of compression.
.PNG	Portable Network Graphics. Format used for compressing and saving images on the Web.
.BMP	Bitmap. An image composed of pixels in a grid, known as a raster image.
.EPS	Encapsulated PostScript. Uncompressed format for bitmap and vector images.
.PICT	Macintosh picture format. Format for bitmap and vector images.
.PDF	Portable Document Format. An Adobe format developed to compress a file while preserving its format.
.PSD	Photoshop Document. Bitmap image saved in Photoshop.

object as an image object, as shown in Figure C-1. You can place both vector and bitmap objects that are created in other programs and other LiveMotion compositions using this method. If the dimensions of the image exceed those of the composition, LiveMotion will resize the image to fit the composition. Alternatively, you can use the Place as Texture command to place an image to the composition background or to the fill of a selected object's layer. And if LiveMotion and the program where the

image is located are both open, you can use the Copy and Paste or Paste Special commands to place the image into your composition, or simply drag and drop the image from the image-editing program into the LiveMotion composition.

QUICKTIP

If you want to restore the size of a placed image that has been resized to fit the composition, click Object on the menu bar, point to Transform, then click Clear Transforms.

You can use the Replace command to place an image within the bounding box of a selected object, such as a geometric object or an image object. When you replace an image, LiveMotion resizes the replacement image to match the selected object by cropping the image if necessary. Replaced images match the transformation settings and style of the selected image object.

FIGURE C-1
Placed image object

Image object

FIGURE C-2
Placed image object

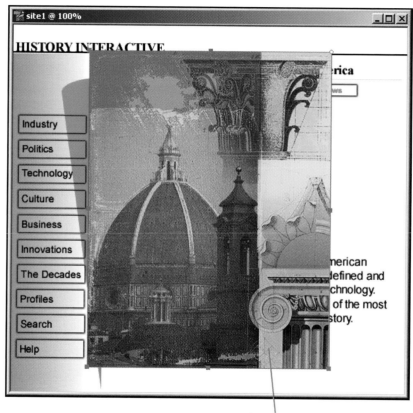

Image object

1. Open LMC-1.liv, then save it as **site1**.
2. Click Window on the menu bar, then click Reset To Defaults.
3. Click File on the menu bar, then click Place.
4. Navigate to the drive and folder where your data files are stored for this section, click Buildings.jpg, then click Open (Win) or Choose (Mac).
5. Compare your composition to Figure C-2.

   An image appears in the center of the composition.

You placed an image file into a composition.

Resize and position an image

1. Click the Transform palette tab.

2. Select the number in the Width text box, type **425**, select the number in the Height text box, type **450**, then press [Enter] (Win) or [return] (Mac).

   The image increases in size.

3. Select the number in the X text box, type **122**, select the number in the Y text box, type **42**, then press [Enter] (Win) or [return] (Mac).

4. Compare your composition to Figure C-3.

   The image moves to the lower right corner of the composition.

You resized and positioned the image object.

FIGURE C-3
Resized and repositioned image

FIGURE C-4
Replaced image object

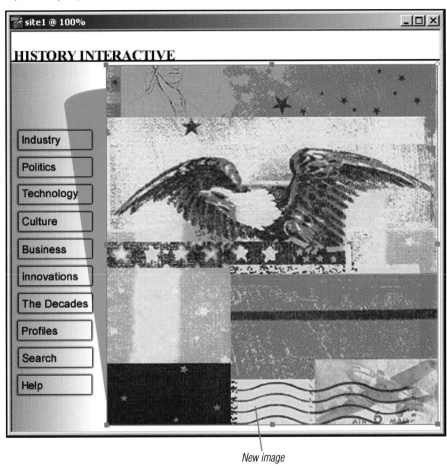

New image

1. With the image object selected, click File on the menu bar, then click Replace.

2. Navigate to the drive and folder where your data files are stored for this section, click Patriotic.jpg, then click Open (Win) or Choose (Mac).

   The original image object is replaced with a different image object; the size and position settings remain the same.

3. Compare your composition to Figure C-4.

You replaced the original image object with a different image object using the Replace command.

WORK WITH IMAGES

What You'll Do

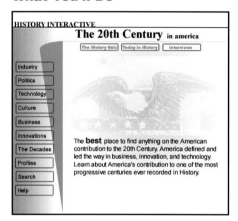

In this lesson, you'll learn how to edit image objects.

Understanding Image Object Editing

So how do you transform an image object? That's right...in the same way you would transform any other LiveMotion object. An image object, once selected, can be moved, flipped, rotated, skewed, and resized using the commands on the Object menu or by changing the object's properties in the Transform palette. (But don't forget that when you are working with a bitmap image, resizing it will degrade the quality of the image.) You can also apply effects to both vector and bitmap image objects using the Layer, 3D, Adjust, Opacity, and Distort palettes.

How you edit an image object depends on how you are going to use it. If the image object is to be used as a background where other elements, such as text, are placed over the image, then you most likely will need to soften or lighten the image in order to see the other elements on top of the image. On the other hand, if the image is to be used as a focal point on the Web page, say in a Web page header or banner, you might want to distort or add a 3D effect to the image object to distinguish it from other elements. You can accomplish most basic editing tasks in LiveMotion using LiveMotion commands and palettes; however, when LiveMotion is unable to perform the right editing task on an image, you can edit the image using either Adobe Photoshop or Adobe Illustrator (assuming, of course, that you have access to those programs). Use the Edit Original command on the LiveMotion Object menu to open vector images in Illustrator or bitmap images in Photoshop. Changes you make to an image using this editing method are made on the LiveMotion copy of the image, so the original image remains unaffected.

Modifying an Image Object

In LiveMotion you have access to different techniques that allow you to customize image objects. Two such techniques are cropping and applying a matte. Cropping is a simple technique that reduces the visible portion of an image object by changing the object's selection border. Let's say that you have an image of a sailboat tied up to a dock in a beautiful South Pacific setting. The only problem is that there are a couple of boats tied up to the other end of the dock that you don't want displayed. Using the Crop Tool, you can **crop**, or hide, the portion of the image—in this case the boats at the end of the dock—that you don't want to display. The hidden parts of the image are preserved, not deleted, and can be un-cropped at any time using the Crop Tool. The Crop Tool also allows you to move a cropped image within an object's selection border or matte. A **matte** is simply the background or shape that defines the visible area of an image. For example, an image can have a simple rectangular shape or it can have the shape of an object like a tree, an animal—or any other shape. Applying a matte to an image is like cropping it, but instead of changing the selection border of the image, you change the shape of the image. So, whatever part of the image is within the matte's visible area is displayed and whatever part of the image is outside the matte's visible area is not seen, as shown in Figure C-5. A matte that is applied to an image object is called an **active matte**. Other techniques you can use to customize an image object include changing its opacity and applying an opacity gradient to the object. The **opacity** of an object is the measurement of how transparent an object is in relation to its background. An **opacity gradient** gradually blends (or fades) the object or the color of the object with the background object or color.

FIGURE C-5
Active matte applied to an image

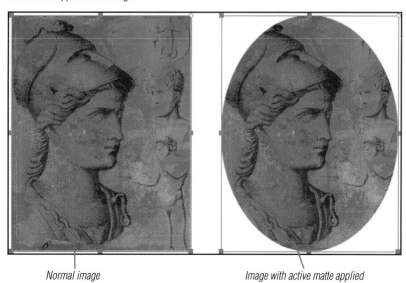

Normal image   Image with active matte applied

QUICKTIP

Objects that have been cropped become a bitmap when exported to SWF (Flash). Use a matte to reduce the size of the visible area of a vector image if you want to maintain the image as a vector.

Alpha channels

Channels store information about the colors that make up an image. An **alpha channel** is a grayscale image that is added to the color channels that make up a given image. If an image has an alpha channel, you can create and store a matte whose shape is defined by the image object. You can use an alpha channel to mask or hide parts of an image, as shown in Figure C-6. Let's say, for example, that you have a picture you created in Photoshop of a businessman walking along a busy street. You want to use this picture in a composition but you want to drop the street background so you can place the businessman on a textured background. All you need to do is select the businessman in Photoshop, save the selection (the businessman) as an alpha channel, save the file, and then place the image in LiveMotion. Once the image is in your composition, make sure you select the Use Alpha Channel option from the Properties palette and LiveMotion will drop the street background from the photograph.

FIGURE C-6
Example of an image using an alpha channel

Other portions of the image are hidden from view

Image background is transparent

Original Image

Image with an Alpha Channel

FIGURE C-7
Edited image object

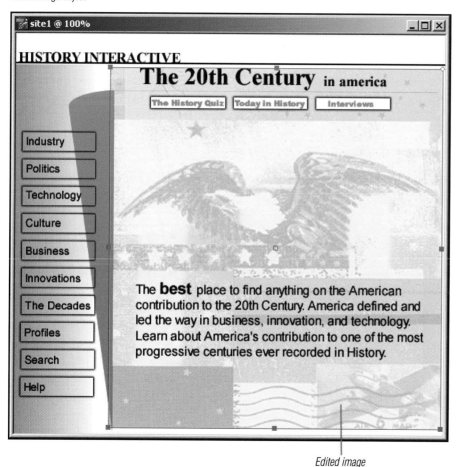

Edited image

1. Click the Selection Tool in the toolbox, then click the image object, if necessary. ⬧

2. Click Object on the menu bar, point to Arrange, then click Send to Back.

   The image object moves behind all of the other objects in the composition.

3. Click the Opacity palette tab.

4. Drag the Object Opacity slider until the number 25 appears in the Object Opacity text box.

   TIP   Use the Object Opacity up or down arrow to set the object opacity precisely to 25 if necessary.

5. Compare your composition to Figure C-7.

You used the Arrange command to send the image object to the bottom of the object stack and changed the opacity of the image.

Crop and matte an image

1. Click the Crop Tool on the toolbox, then position the pointer over the bottom center handle of the image object. 🔲

2. Drag the bottom center handle of the image object up to the bottom of the last line of the paragraph text.

3. Click the Selection Tool on the toolbox. 🔺

4. Click the Properties palette tab.

5. Click the Alpha Channel list box, then click Active Matte.

   The active matte, which is an ellipse shape, is applied to the image.

6. Compare your composition to Figure C-8.

You used the Crop Tool to crop the bottom portion of the image object and then you applied an active matte to the image.

FIGURE C-8
Cropped and matted image

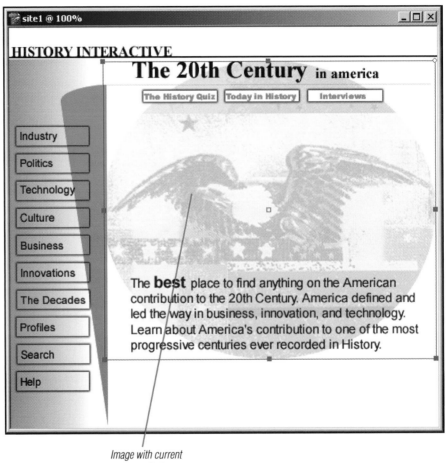

Image with current
matte applied

1. Click the Opacity tab, if necessary.

2. Click the Gradient list box, then click Radial.

   LiveMotion gradually blends the image object with the composition background.

3. Click in a blank area of the composition, then save the composition.

4. Compare your composition to Figure C-9.

You used the Gradient list box to apply the Radial gradient to the image layer.

FIGURE C-9
Gradient applied to the image

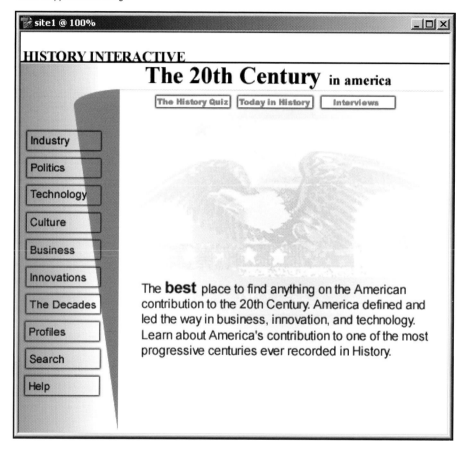

Lesson 2   Work with Images

CREATE AND WORK WITH OBJECT LAYERS

What You'll Do

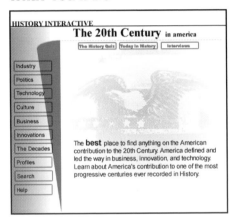

 In this lesson, you will learn to create and work with object layers in the Object Layers palette.

Understanding Object Layers

When you begin to use object layers in LiveMotion, you'll find that the creative possibilities for designing dynamic Web elements are endless. Adding layers to an object—any object—and then changing the properties of those layers allows you to create depth and definition that is difficult to create any other way. Layers function independently from each other, so they can be offset from each other and have different attributes, such as color, opacity, softness, and so on. Just for a moment, let's say that you have created a red geometric shape using the Ellipse Tool and you want to give the object some depth using a soft shadow. To create a shadow behind this object you would create a second object layer and apply the appropriate effects to the second layer.

In the event that you have more than one object in the composition selected, the Object Layers palette shows the layer of the topmost selected object. Before you can apply any formatting to an object layer, you first need to make it active by selecting it in the Object Layers palette, as

shown in Figure C-10. Only one layer can be selected at a time, and the changes you make to a selected layer affect only that layer. Make sure you have the correct layer selected before you begin formatting—although you can always use the Undo or History command to fix your mistakes!

Creating Object Layers

As mentioned, you can create up to 99 layers for any object in LiveMotion. Wow! In most cases, though, you will find that working with a small number of layers is enough to achieve the look you want. And, in fact, the more layers you have the larger the file becomes. There are a couple of different methods you can use to create object layers in LiveMotion, depending on your design needs. You can create a new layer by selecting the object in the composition and then clicking the New Layer button in the Object Layers palette, as shown in Figure C-10. The new layer appears directly behind the selected layer. The new layer has the same shape as the selected layer and is filled with black. The default name of the new layer (such as

"Layer 2") is based on its order in the layer stack. In the composition, a new object layer is unnoticeable because it appears directly behind the existing object. Using the New Layer button is the quickest and easiest way to create a new object layer, but it may not provide you with the type of layer you want. You may want to create an object layer that looks exactly like the selected layer with the same attributes, in which case you can make an exact copy of the selected layer using the Duplicate Layer button on the Object Layers palette.

Using the Object Layers Palette

Once you create a new object layer, it appears selected in the Object Layers palette. The Object Layers palette is used to create,

name, select, duplicate, restack, delete, show, and hide layers. As soon as you create a new object layer, it's a good idea to rename it so as not to confuse it with another layer. Renaming a new object layer gives that layer a unique identity and enables you to recognize it easily in the Object Layers palette. Naming layers with a description of what each layer does can be very helpful. For example, if you create an object layer that creates an embossed effect for another layer, you might name the layer "Emboss." You can easily hide or show a layer by clicking the Show/Hide button (eye icon) next to the layer you want to show or hide. Every visible layer displays a thumbnail preview of the layer's contents in the Object Layers palette. As you add object layers, each layer is arranged or **stacked** in a certain order in the

Object Layers palette, with the topmost layer in the palette representing the front layer in the composition. At some point, you may find it necessary to change the layer stacking order to achieve a different look. To move an object layer, you simply drag a layer up or down in the palette. If an object layer doesn't turn out the way you want it or if you are sure you have no further use for a layer, you can delete it using the Delete Layer button in the palette. Make absolutely sure you don't need the layer before you delete it. Remember that you can hide a layer, which you might want to do instead of actually deleting it.

QUICKTIP

If a selected layer is hidden from view, any changes you make to the layer still affect it.

FIGURE C-10
Object Layers palette

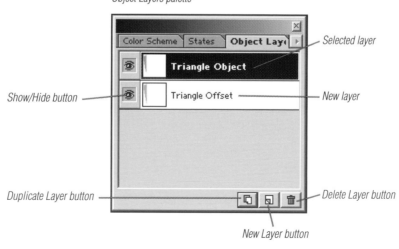

Show/Hide button

Duplicate Layer button

Selected layer

New layer

Delete Layer button

New Layer button

Create and name a new object layer

1. Click the red triangle object in site1, then, if necessary, click the Object Layers palette tab.

   Clicking the red triangle object will select the red triangle and the horizontal line across the top of the composition, thus the selection border of the object will be a large square.

2. Click the New Layer button in the Object Layers palette. 🔲

   A new layer named Layer 2 appears in the Object Layers palette—the triangle in the new layer thumbnail preview now has a black fill. In the composition, the new layer is positioned directly behind the top layer.

3. Double-click Layer 2 in the Object Layers palette.

4. In the Name dialog box, type **Triangle Offset**, then click OK.

5. Compare your Object Layers palette to Figure C-11.

You created and named a new object layer in the Object Layers palette.

FIGURE C-11
Object Layers palette

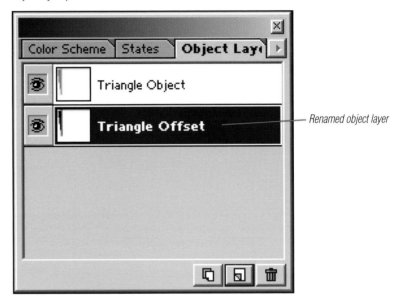

— *Renamed object layer*

1. Click the top layer, named Triangle Object.

2. Click the Duplicate Layer button in the Object Layers palette.

   An exact copy of the Triangle Object layer named Triangle Object copy appears in the Object Layers palette. Notice that the triangle object in the Triangle Object copy layer thumbnail preview has the exact same attributes as the triangle object in the Triangle Object layer thumbnail preview.

   > TIP You can also duplicate an object layer by clicking Layer on the menu bar, then clicking Duplicate Layer.

3. Compare your Object Layers palette with Figure C-12.

You selected an object layer, then created a duplicate layer.

FIGURE C-12
Object Layers palette

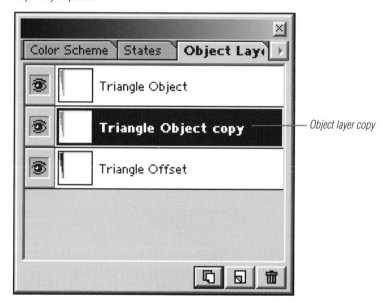

— Object layer copy

Hide and show object layers

1. Click the Show/Hide icon next to the thumbnail of the Triangle Object layer.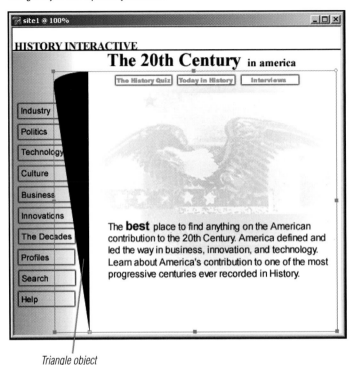

2. Click the Show/Hide icon next to the thumbnail of the Triangle Object copy layer.

   The top two layers of the object (red layers) are hidden and the bottom layer (black layer) is visible.

3. Compare your composition with Figure C-13 and your Object Layers palette with Figure C-14.

4. Click the Show/Hide button for the Triangle Object and Triangle Object copy layers to show the layers again.

You used the Show/Hide button on the Object Layers palette to hide and show two object layers.

FIGURE C-13
Triangle object with top two layers hidden

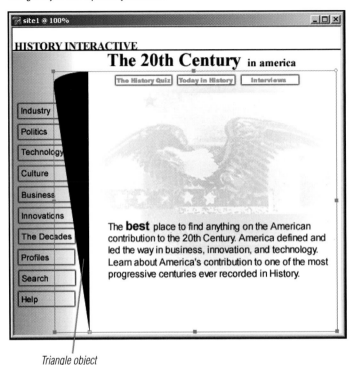

Triangle object

FIGURE C-14
Object Layers palette

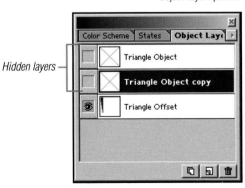

Hidden layers

FIGURE C-15
Object Layers palette

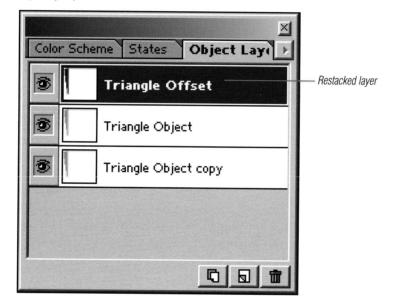

Restacked layer

Restack and delete an object layer

1. Click the Triangle Offset layer in the Object Layers palette.

2. Drag the layer to the top of the palette until it is directly over the Triangle Object layer.

   The Triangle Offset layer is now the top layer of the object in the Object Layers palette, as shown in Figure C-15. Notice that the color of the object in the composition is now the color of the Triangle Offset layer.

3. Drag the Triangle Offset layer back until it is directly over the Triangle Object copy layer.

   TIP You can also use the Arrange command on the Layer menu to rearrange the order of object layers.

4. Click the Triangle Object copy layer, then click the Delete Layer button at the bottom of the palette. 🗑

5. Save and close the file.

You changed the stacking order of an object's layers, then deleted a layer.

CHANGE LAYER OPACITY

What You'll Do

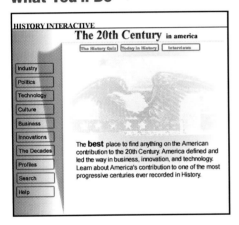

 In this lesson, you'll learn how to change the opacity of objects and layers using the Opacity palette.

Understanding Opacity

In LiveMotion you can adjust the opacity of objects, individual layers, or both. Opacity measures how transparent (clear) or opaque (dense) an object appears. When an object has a low opacity setting it is more transparent, and when an object has a high opacity setting it is more opaque. Each layer of an object can have its own opacity setting, or you can also change the opacity setting for an entire object. Opacity can be very useful, especially when designing multiple overlapping objects. To see an object that is behind another, simply adjust the opacity of the top object so it is more transparent. Adjusting the opacity of objects to see textures, images, or other styled objects can produce appealing Web elements. For example, if you create a colored layer with a textured layer underneath, you can decrease the opacity of the colored layer significantly to allow the textured layer to show through.

Copying and saving layer attributes

After you've worked hard to create a set of layer attributes just the way you want them, you can save the attributes as a style for future use, copy the attributes to another object, or both. To copy the layer attributes, select the object whose attributes you want to copy, select the appropriate layer, copy the layer using the Copy command, select the object and the layer to which you want to apply the copied attributes, then, using the Paste Special command, click Layer. The attributes from one object layer are applied to another object layer. If you want to save the layer attributes, you can save the attributes as a style using the Styles palette. You can then use the layer attributes any time by selecting an object layer, then clicking the style on the Styles palette.

Using the Opacity Palette

The Opacity palette, shown in Figure C-16, allows you to change the opacity of objects and object layers. If you move the Object Opacity slider or change the number in the Object Opacity text box, you change the opacity for the entire object. Moving the Object Layer Opacity slider or changing the number in the Object Layer Opacity text box modifies the opacity of a single selected layer.

Opacity can be applied evenly or as a gradient. To create an opacity gradient for a layer, you need first to select a gradient type from the Gradient Type list. You have four gradient types (other than No Gradient) to choose from: Linear, Burst, Double Burst, and Radial. See Figure C-17 for an example of how each gradient looks when applied to an object. Now, if you want to change how the

opacity gradient blends, all you do is drag either the Starting opacity stop or the Ending opacity stop along the Gradient selection bar. Blending occurs between the two opacity stops. You can also change the angle of the gradient by entering a number between 0 and 359 in the Angle text box or by dragging the Angle dial to a different position.

FIGURE C-16
Opacity palette

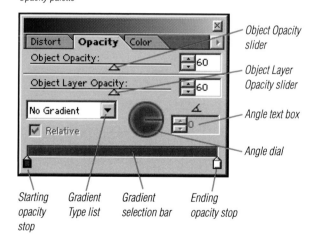

Object Opacity slider

Object Layer Opacity slider

Angle text box

Angle dial

Starting opacity stop

Gradient Type list

Gradient selection bar

Ending opacity stop

FIGURE C-17
Example of gradient types

No Gradient   Linear   Burst   DoubleBurst   Radial

Change object layer opacity

1. Open LMC-2.liv, then save it as **site2**.

2. Click the red triangle object, click the Opacity palette tab if necessary, then, if necessary, click the Triangle Object layer in the Object Layers palette.

3. Drag the Object Layer Opacity slider in the Opacity palette until the number 60 appears in the text box.

   TIP If necessary, you can make precise adjustments to the opacity by clicking the Object Layer Opacity up or down arrow.

4. Click the Triangle Offset layer in the Object Layers palette, then drag the Object Layer Opacity slider in the Opacity palette until 30 appears in the text box.

   By decreasing the opacity of both object layers, the Triangle object is more transparent.

5. Compare your composition to Figure C-18.

You changed the opacity of the red triangle's layers.

FIGURE C-18
Modified object layer opacity

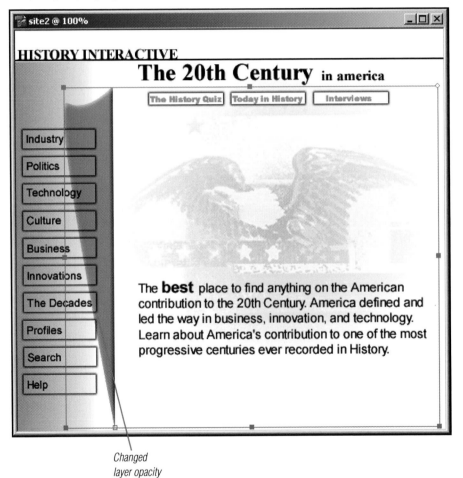

Changed layer opacity

FIGURE C-19
Changed object opacity and applied gradient

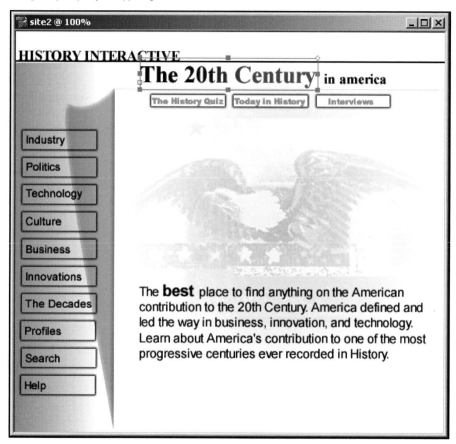

Change object opacity and apply a gradient

1. With the red triangle object still selected, drag the Object Opacity slider until 60 appears in the text box.

   The opacity of the whole object is changed.

2. Click the Drag Selection Tool on the toolbox, then select the The 20th Century text object.

3. Click the Gradient list arrow in the Opacity palette, click Linear, then compare your composition to Figure C-19.

   The blue color of the bottom layer of the text object gradually appears from left to right.

You changed the opacity of the entire red triangle object, then applied a layer gradient to a text object.

Modify a layer gradient

1. In the Opacity palette, drag the Angle dial until –90 appears in the Angle text box.

2. Drag the Ending opacity stop (right opacity stop) below the gradient bar to the left, then drag the Starting opacity stop (left opacity stop) to the right as shown in Figure C-20.

   The opacity stops define the starting and stopping points of the gradient opacity.

   (continued)

FIGURE C-20
Opacity palette

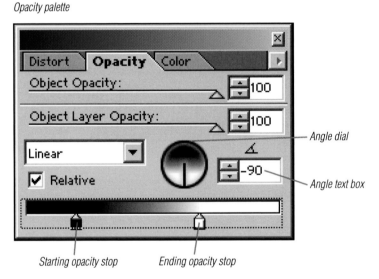

Angle dial

Angle text box

Starting opacity stop   Ending opacity stop

3. Click in a blank area of the composition, then compare your composition to Figure C-21.

4. Click the Selection Tool in the toolbox, then save your work.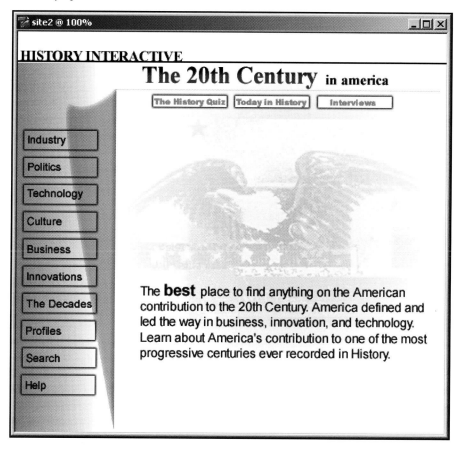

You changed the angle and opacity stops for the layer gradient of a text object.

FIGURE C-21
Modified layer gradient

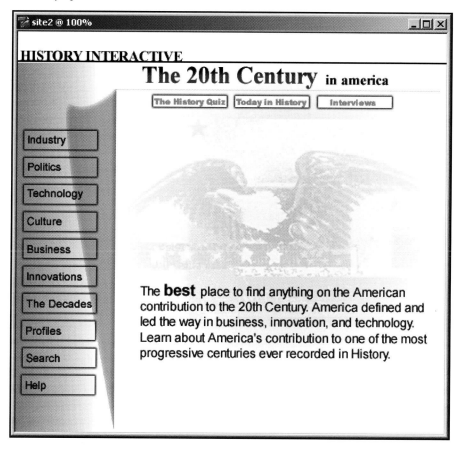

MODIFY OBJECT LAYERS

What You'll Do

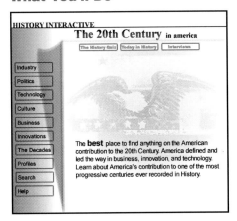

In this lesson, you will learn how to use the Layer palette to change layer properties.

Using the Layer Palette

So you've added a new layer to an object that appears directly behind the selected layer—now what? Well, the Layer palette (not to be confused with the Object Layers palette) offers you some options for customizing object layers. The Layer palette has five features, as shown in Figure C-22, to help you change the properties of a layer: Fill With, X Offset, Y Offset, Width, and Softness. The Fill With feature acts like a short term memory, remembering

the last type of fill you used to fill the layer. Let's say that, as you design a specific Web element, you decide to experiment with different types of fill, like an image or a texture. As you experiment with these different fills, LiveMotion remembers the last fill that you applied to the object layer. The Fill With feature has four options: Color, Image, Background, and Texture. The Fill With Color feature applies the current (or last) color, opacity, and gradient selected in the Color, Opacity,

FIGURE C-22
Layer palette

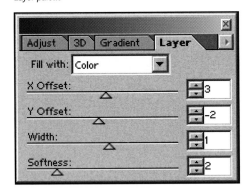

Working with Imported Images and Object Layers

and Gradient palettes. The Fill With Image feature applies the last image that the layer was filled with or, if the layer has not been filled with an image, then the last applied color is applied. The Fill With Background feature fills the layer with the color of whatever is behind the object, whether it is another layer or the composition background. The Fill With Texture feature fills the layer with the last applied texture. If no texture has been applied to the layer, the current color, opacity, and gradient are applied. Figure C-23 illustrates how the top layer of an object would look using each of the Fill With options.

FIGURE C-23
Object with image fill

Object with texture fill

Object with background fill

Object with color fill

The X Offset and Y Offset settings in the Layer palette allow you to offset one layer from another, as shown in Figure C-24. The X Offset moves the selected layer along the horizontal axis, and the Y Offset moves the selected layer along the vertical axis. You can adjust the offset of a layer in the Layer palette by moving the offset slider or by entering a value in a text box.

You can also adjust the offset of a layer using the Layer Offset Tool in the toolbox, but no matter which method you use, you can only offset a layer 50 pixels in any direction. The Width feature widens the selected layer horizontally and vertically from the center of the layer, which can give an outline effect to an object. And finally, the Softness feature of the Layer palette blurs the edges of the layer to create a glow around the object. You'll probably find the Width and Softness features very handy when designing elements for the Web. See Figure C-25 for an example of an object with a width and softness applied to its second layer.

FIGURE C-24
Example of an offset layer

— Offset layer

FIGURE C-25
Example of a layer displaying width and softness attributes

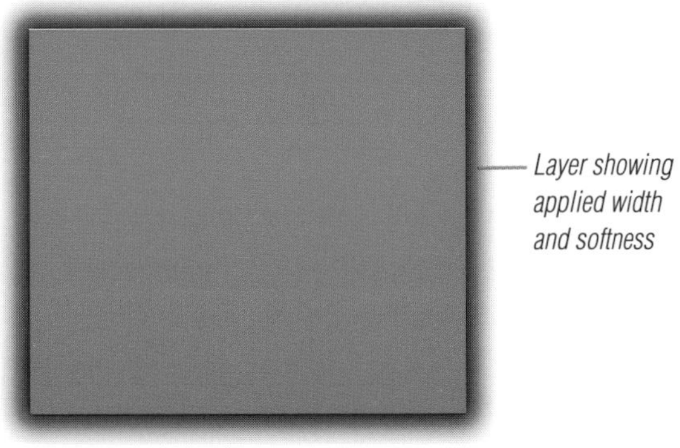

— Layer showing applied width and softness

FIGURE C-26
Offset object layer

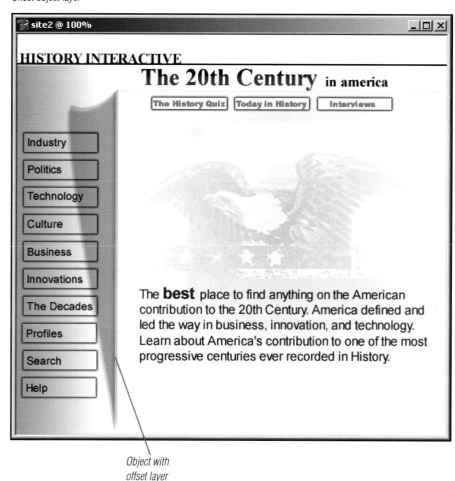

*Object with
offset layer*

1. Click the triangle object in the composition, then click the Triangle Offset layer in the Object Layers palette.

2. Click the Layer palette tab.

3. Click the X Offset up arrow until 3 appears in the text box, then click the Y Offset down arrow until –2 appears in the text box.

   The second layer moves up and to the right from the top layer.

4. Click in a blank area of the composition, then compare your composition to Figure C-26.

You selected an object layer and then offset it from another layer.

Widen and soften a layer

1. Click the red triangle object, then click the Triangle Offset layer in the Object Layers palette.

2. Click the Width up arrow on the Layer palette until 1 appears in the text box.

3. Click the Softness up arrow on the Layer palette until 2 appears in the text box.

   The second layer of the red triangle object now is slightly wider, with blurry or softer edges.

4. Click in a blank area of the composition, then compare your composition to Figure C-27.

You widened and softened the bottom layer of the triangle object.

FIGURE C-27
Triangle object with modified layer

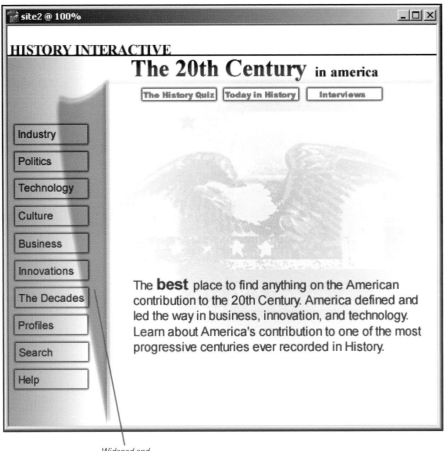

Widened and
softened layer

FIGURE C-28
Completed file

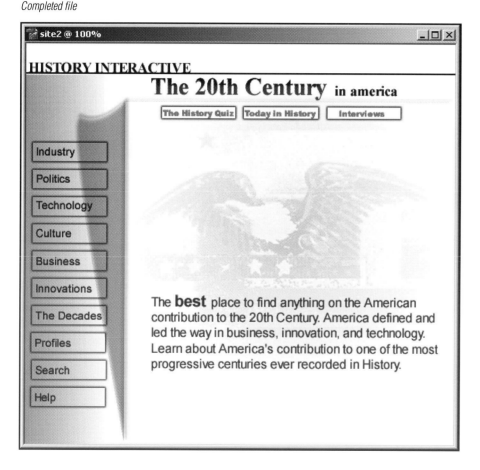

1. Click the red triangle object, then, if necessary, click the Triangle Offset layer in the Object Layers palette.

2. Click the Fill with list arrow on the Layer palette, then click Background.

   The fill of the Triangle Offset layer becomes transparent and the objects in the background are displayed.

3. Click the Fill with list arrow, then click Texture.

   The fill of the Triangle Offset layer changes to the last texture that was applied to the object—in this case the light green texture in the Texture palette.

   > TIP LiveMotion remembers the last texture that was applied to the layer even if the file has been saved, closed, and reopened.

4. Click the Fill with list arrow, then click Color.

5. Click in a blank area of the composition, then compare your composition to Figure C-28.

6. Save and close the file.

You changed the layer fill of the triangle object.

You work for a local Internet provider in a small mountain community outside of Denver, Colorado. Your company provides Internet service, Web site maintenance, and other Web related services such as Web page design to the community. One of the local resorts, The Peaks Resort, wants to upgrade their Web site design and you have been assigned the job. In this project you have already entered the basic text for the site; now all you need to do is enhance the page with an image and add some effects to some objects. Use Figure C-29 to help you finish the new home page for the site

1. Open the file LMC-4, then save it as **resort1**. (*Hint*: This file contains the Monotype Corsiva font in font sizes of 16 and 18. If your computer does not have this font, it may make a font substitution.)

2. Place the image file Lake.jpg into the composition from the drive and folder where your data files are stored for this section.

3. Use the Transform palette to adjust the image properties to the following settings: Width 493; Height 315; X coordinate 23; Y coordinate 28.

4. Select the image, apply the active matte to the image using the Properties palette, then apply a Radial gradient to the image using the Opacity palette.

5. Move the left gradient stop to the right until the image looks similar to Figure C-29. (*Hint*: Move the stop about an inch.)

6. Select the rounded rectangle object behind the text object Rocky News, select the layer Rocky News, then change the layer opacity to 75. Change the opacity of the Specials layer of the rounded rectangle behind the text object Specials to 75.

7. Create a new layer for the text object "Welcome to", then rename it **Welcome Background**.

8. Create a new layer for the text object "The Peaks Resort", then rename it **Web Title Background**.

9. Use the Layer palette to change the X Offset to −2 and the Y Offset to −2 for both new text object layers.

10. Use the Layer palette to change the softness of both new text object layers to 2.

11. Save the file, then compare your screen to Figure C-29.

FIGURE C-29
Completed Project 1

You are in the process of learning as much as you can about multimedia design and have a friend who owns a growing flower business. You offer your services to design a Web site to help grow your friend's business. Using the skills you have learned so far, finish the composition provided for you in this project.

1. Open the file LMC-5, then save it as **flowers**. (*Hint*: This file contains the Monotype Corsiva font in font sizes of 60 and 16, and the Microsoft Sans Serif font in a font size of 16. If your computer doesn't have these fonts, it may make font substitutions.)

2. Place the image file Photo1.jpg into the composition.

3. Use the Transform palette to adjust the image properties to the following settings: Width 109; Height 146; X coordinate 420; Y coordinate 24, and rotation –7.

4. Create a new layer for the Photo1 image object, then change the fill of the new layer to Background using the Layer palette.

5. Select Layer 1 of the Photo1 image object, then change the layer opacity to 75.

6. Use the Layer palette to change the softness of Layer 1 of the Photo1 image object to 5.

7. Create a new layer for the text object "Flowers by Linda", then rename it **Web Title Background**.

8. Use the Layer palette to change the X Offset to 2, the Y Offset to 2, and the softness to 1.

9. Select the rose image object, then change the object opacity to 85.

10. Select the rectangle object behind the paragraph text object, change the layer opacity to 70 using the Opacity palette, then change the fill of Layer 1 to Background using the Layer palette.

11. Select Layer 2 of the rectangle object, then change the width to 2, the softness to 2, and the fill to Texture using the Layer palette.

12 Save the file, then compare your screen to Figure C-30.

FIGURE C-30
Completed Project 2

SECTION D

WORKING WITH COLOR EFFECTS, AND ROLLOVERS

1. Adjust and apply color.

2. Add textures and gradients.

3. Apply 3D effects and distortion.

4. Work with styles and the library.

5. Create and edit a basic rollover.

6. Create a remote rollover.

WORKING WITH COLOR EFFECTS, AND ROLLOVERS

Giving Objects Personality

After you create or import objects for your Web page, you are ready to transform what might at first be a plain and ordinary composition into one that is vibrant and colorful. The best way to do this is with color and effects. Applying color to your composition definitely adds personality to your design and sets a certain mood or tone. For example, you can use warm colors such as red, orange, or yellow to express friendliness and compassion or you can use blue, black, or dark green to express a more sophisticated or professional tone. You can change the color of an object or a selected object layer using the Color palette. Once you have selected a color, you can change the color opacity, create a color gradient, or make other color adjustments. Applying effects such as textures, gradients, 3D effects, and distortion can add depth and dimension to object layers. Use the Texture palette, Gradient palette, 3D palette, and Distort palette to add effects to object layers. With so many color and effect options available to you in LiveMotion, it's easy to make a big impression with your Web design.

Learning about Rollovers

The best way to make a Web site compelling is to add interaction for the viewer. There are a number of ways to provide interaction, one of which is to create an object rollover in the composition. A **rollover** is a change that occurs to an object in response to a mouse action. For example, a rollover can be a text object that increases in size when you move the mouse over it. A rollover is actually a state that is applied to an object, which is triggered by the mouse to produce a specific result. A **state** is a collection of attribute changes that affect the way an object appears after being triggered by a mouse action or a script. Practically any object attribute that you can change, such as object color, opacity, or gradient, can be applied as a rollover state to an object. You can also create remote rollovers. A **remote rollover** is an event (such as clicking) that happens to one object that triggers one or more other objects to change states. For example, you can create a remote rollover that displays an image object when you move the mouse over a specific text object.

Tools You'll Use

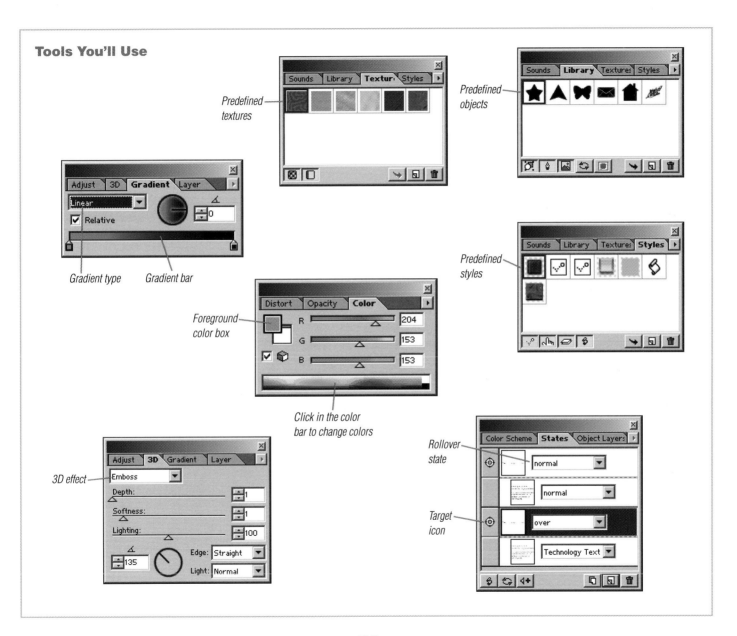

Predefined textures

Predefined objects

Gradient type · Gradient bar

Foreground color box

Predefined styles

Click in the color bar to change colors

3D effect

Rollover state

Target icon

ADJUST AND APPLY COLOR

What You'll Do

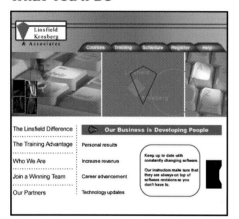

 In this lesson, you'll change the foreground color using the Color palette and apply colors to objects using the Eyedropper Tool and the Paint Bucket Tool.

Understanding Web Color

Before you learn how to apply or adjust colors in a composition, you need to learn a little about color and how it's used in Web design. Designing elements for the Web can present a unique challenge for any Web designer when it comes to the use of color. The basic issue is that color computer monitors and Web browsers do not display every color that is available for you to use in LiveMotion (or any other program for that matter), which limits your ability to control what color is actually displayed on a user's monitor. Color monitors and Web browser software only display RGB colors, which is any color created by the mixture of red, green, and blue. Another factor in the color dilemma is that color varies from computer to computer. The color seen on a computer is dependent upon the computer's hardware, such as its video card and monitor, and the computer's software, such as the operating system and the Web software being used.

So what can LiveMotion do to help with this issue? LiveMotion includes a Web-safe color feature that you can activate to limit the number of available colors to the 216 RGB colors most often used by Web browsers. Now, whether you use the Web-safe color feature depends largely on your audience. If your target audience has the color technology to display standard RGB colors, then you are better off not limiting yourself visually by only using Web-safe colors. However, if you are unsure of the color technology of your target audience, it is probably best to design your Web elements for as many people as possible, which means using Web-safe colors. One final note about colors is that you should always check your work on both the Mac and Windows platforms to be sure that the colors in your composition look good on both systems.

QUICKTIP

When you apply solid colors to objects in another program with the intention of importing them into LiveMotion, you should use Web-safe colors. Bitmap images from programs such as Photoshop that have gradual color changes, or dithering, generally look fine without Web-safe colors because the dithering is not as noticeable on the Web.

Changing Colors

The Color palette, shown in Figure D-1, displays the current foreground and background colors and values. The **foreground color**, shown in the Foreground color box, is the color that fills a selected object layer and newly created objects. The **background color**, shown in the Background color box, is the color that fills the composition background. The foreground and background colors remain the same until you specify a different color. To specify a different foreground or background color, select the Foreground color box or the Background color box, then do one of the following: (1) move one or more of the color sliders, (2) enter a value in one or more of the color value text boxes, (3) select a color from the Color bar, or (4) pick up a color from another object using the Eyedropper Tool from the toolbox. Be sure you verify which of the Foreground or Background color boxes is selected before you change a color, because it's easy to make a mistake and change one when you intend to change the other. You know a color box is selected when it is outlined in black.

You may have noticed that the toolbox has identical color boxes as those found in the Color palette. Both sets of color boxes function in the same manner, so it's up to you which ones you use (and it's fine to swap back and forth). When you want to use Web-safe colors, you can check the Set Web-safe colors check box in the Color palette. Clicking the Color palette menu in the upper right corner of the palette displays the Color palette menu, which lists six different color models that you can use to create different colors.

FIGURE D-1
Color palette

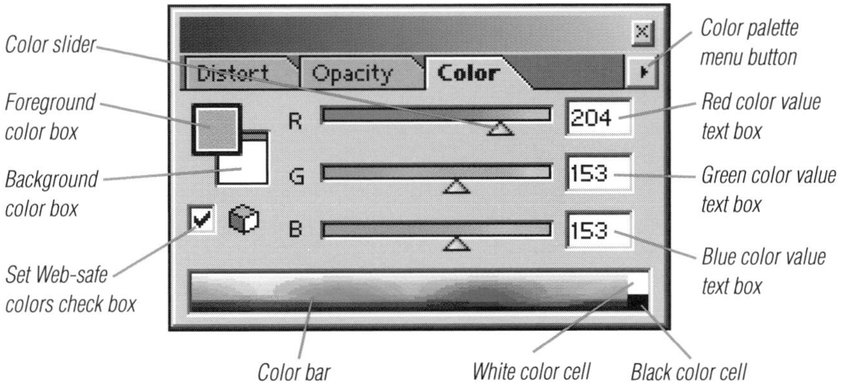

Color slider
Foreground color box
Background color box
Set Web-safe colors check box

Color palette menu button
Red color value text box
Green color value text box
Blue color value text box

Color bar   White color cell   Black color cell

Learning about Color Models

The six LiveMotion color models provide you with different ways to create colors based on certain aspects of color or a certain way of viewing color. For example, one color model may focus on the strength or intensity of pure color, while another color model may focus on a color's relative lightness or darkness. The color models include: Saturation View; Value View; Hue View; HSB View; RGB View; and CIE L View (the Web-safe color feature discussed previously is also a color model, though it is not listed on the Color palette menu). Saturation View, also referred to as chroma, identifies the purity or strength of a color. **Saturation** represents the amount of gray added to a specific color to change its hue to black. The Value View color model identifies how light or dark a color is. Hue View represents the literal color as it relates to other similar colors. **Hue** is a common way to identify a shade of color. Figure D-2 shows the Color palette with the Hue View displayed. HSB View stands for hue, saturation, and brightness. You have control over the hue (color), its saturation, and how bright it is using this color model. RGB View, which is the default view, assigns an intensity value for red, green, and blue. CIE L View represents only colors that are visible on a color monitor. Colors that are not visible on a color monitor are eliminated from the color model.

So which color model do you use? Well, it depends on your preference and your knowledge of how color models work. If you are really unsure about color models, then it's probably best to stick with the RGB color model, otherwise you might first try the Hue View color model when you are looking for different colors and then switch to the RGB color model to determine the specific color values. No matter which color model you choose, colors in LiveMotion still end up as RGB because everything you create is destined for the on-screen environment of the Web.

Applying Colors

When you are ready to apply a color to an object, an object layer, or the composition background, you can use the Color palette or the Paint Bucket Tool in the toolbox. To apply a color to an object using the Color palette, select or create the object you want, select the color model in the Color palette, then choose a new color. To apply a color to the composition background, use the same method as just described except select the Background color box first. When you have already selected a color and want to apply it to an object, simply select the Paint Bucket Tool from the toolbox and then click the object. The object is filled with the current foreground color.

FIGURE D-2
Color palette displaying Hue View

Working with Color, Effects, and Rollovers

FIGURE D-3

Color palette with the Hue View displayed

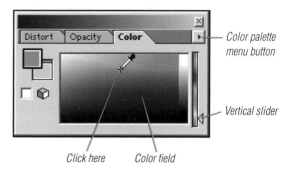

Color palette
menu button

Vertical slider

Click here   Color field

FIGURE D-4

Rectangle object showing new applied color

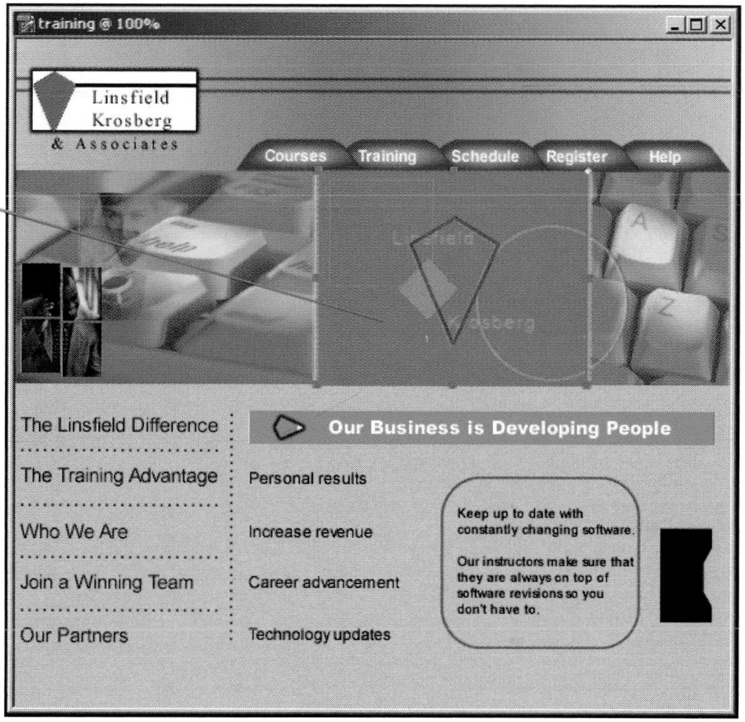

New color applied
to rectangle object

Apply a foreground color using the Color palette

1. Open LMD-1.liv, save it as **training**, click Window on the menu bar, then click Reset To Defaults.

2. Click the large black rectangle object to select it, then click the Foreground color box in the Color palette.

3. Click the Color palette menu button, click Hue View, then click in the color field as shown in Figure D-3.

   Notice that the color of the rectangle object changes to match the color you selected in the Hue View color field.

4. Slowly drag the vertical slider in the Color palette up to the top of the color bar, then back down to the blue portion of the color bar.

   Notice that the hue, or color, of the object in the composition constantly changes as you move the color slider along the color bar.

5. Click the Color palette menu button, click RGB View, double-click the Red color value text box, type **80**, double-click the Green color value text box, type **115**, double-click the Blue color value text box, type **195**, then press [Enter] (Win) or [return] (Mac).

6. Compare your composition to Figure D-4.

You selected a rectangle object, changed its color using the Hue View of the Color palette, then refined the color using the RGB View.

Sample a color using the Eyedropper

1. Select the Background color box in the toolbox, then click the Eyedropper Tool in the toolbox.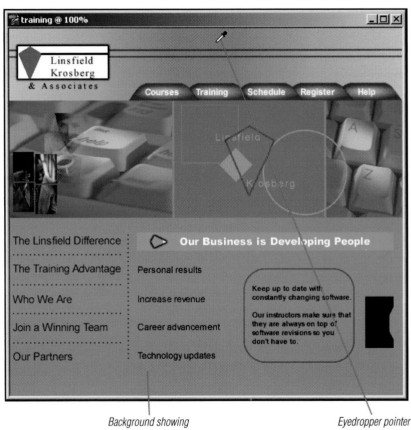

   TIP You can also select the Foreground color box to sample colors using the Eyedropper Tool.

2. Position the Eyedropper pointer in the dark blue color band at the top of the composition, then click.

   Because the Background color box is selected, the color of the area you clicked with the Eyedropper pointer is applied to the composition background, as shown in Figure D-5.

3. Position the Eyedropper pointer over one of the tabs (not the tab text) at the top of the composition, then click to change the background color again.

4. Position the Eyedropper pointer over the white rectangle, then click to change the background color to white.

5. Save your work.

You used the Eyedropper Tool to sample two colors other than white for the composition background.

FIGURE D-5
Composition with new background color

Background showing
newly sampled color

Eyedropper pointer

FIGURE D-6

Rectangle object with new color

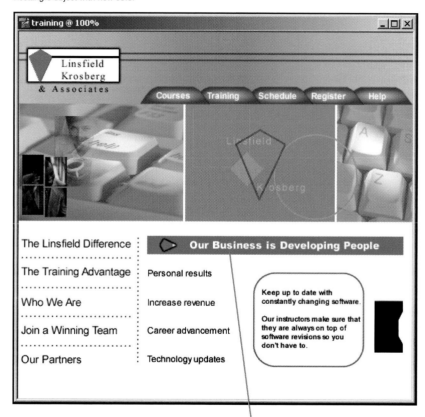

Rectangle object with
new applied color

1. Click the Foreground color box in the Color palette, then click the Paint Bucket Tool in the toolbox.

2. Position the Paint Bucket pointer over the long narrow blue/green rectangle object, then click.

   The rectangle object is filled with the current foreground color, which is the same color that you applied to the large rectangle object.

   TIP Objects don't have to be selected to use the Paint Bucket Tool to apply colors to them.

3. Click the Selection Tool in the toolbox, click in a blank area of the composition, then compare your composition to Figure D-6.

You applied the current foreground color to a rectangle object using the Paint Bucket Tool.

ADD TEXTURES AND GRADIENTS

What You'll Do

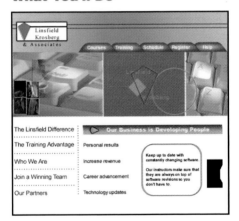

In this lesson, you'll apply a texture using the Textures palette and apply a gradient using the Gradient palette.

Understanding Textures

A **texture** is an image file that you can apply to an object layer or composition background. A texture can be either a bitmap or vector image, such as a photograph or other artwork, which can be modified in an image editing program like Photoshop by applying filters or effects to the image. For example, you might have a close-up photograph of a white tile roof, which you want to apply as a texture in an object you created in LiveMotion. The right texture can add a unique character to an object in a composition. The only limitation is that a LiveMotion texture can have only one layer, so any kind of grouped or layered image cannot be a texture. Depending on the size of the image you're

FIGURE D-7
Texture palette

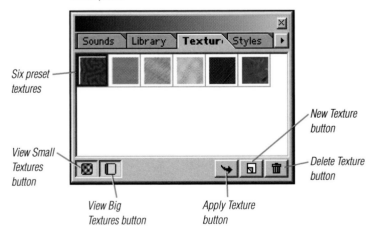

Six preset textures

View Small Textures button

View Big Textures button

Apply Texture button

New Texture button

Delete Texture button

using as a texture, it may be displayed in a tile pattern. A **tile** pattern is one that repeats over and over to fill a selected area.

Working with the Textures Palette

LiveMotion provides six preset textures in the Textures palette for you to use, as shown in Figure D-7. In addition, you can add your own textures to the palette as you create them. To help you manage your textures, there are five buttons along the bottom of the Textures palette. In the lower right corner of the palette is the Apply Texture button, which you use to apply a texture to an object or background; the New Texture button, which you use to add

a new texture to the Textures palette; and the Delete Texture button, which you use to delete a texture from the palette. In the lower left corner of the palette are two buttons, which narrow the available textures in the palette, depending on the size of the textures. The View Small Textures button displays textures that are less than 500 pixels in width or height and need to be tiled. The View Large Textures button displays textures that are more than 500 pixels in width or height and usually fill a background without tiling.

Applying Gradients

When you want to give an object layer some volume or depth, you can apply a

gradient. A **gradient**, which is similar to an opacity gradient that blends the opacity of one color, is the gradual blending of two colors. A gradient is applied to the active layer of the currently selected object. You can choose any two colors you want to blend, and you can modify the hue, saturation, or brightness of the colors used. You apply gradients using the Gradient palette shown in Figure D-8. To apply a gradient, select the object, click the Gradient Type list arrow in the Gradient palette, then select a gradient. You have four different gradient patterns from which to choose, as shown in Figure D-9: Linear, Burst, Double Burst, and Radial. You also have the ability to rotate the angle of the gradient by dragging the Angle

FIGURE D-8
Gradient palette

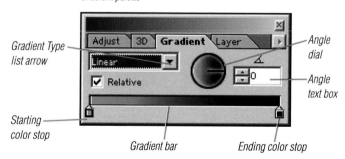

Gradient Type list arrow

Angle dial

Angle text box

Starting color stop

Gradient bar

Ending color stop

FIGURE D-9
Available gradient patterns

Original   Linear   Burst   Double Burst   Radial

dial, entering an angle in the Angle text box, or clicking the Angle up or down arrows. If you want the angle of the gradient to remain constant even if you rotate the object, you can uncheck the Relative check box in the Gradient palette, and then select the Shape Transforms option on the Transform submenu of the Object menu. As you can see by looking at Figure D-8, the Gradient palette has a Gradient bar with starting and ending color stops at the bottom of the palette. You can change the starting and ending gradient colors by clicking the appropriate color stop and then choosing a different color in the Color palette. And like the Gradient bar in the Opacity palette, you can move either color stop to adjust where the starting color begins blending into the ending color.

QUICKTIP
If you are concerned about the download speed of your composition, make sure that gradient objects are small and have a vertical gradient. Horizontal gradients download more slowly than vertical ones.

Using the Adjust Palette

When working with color, texture, and gradients in objects, you may need to alter the color slightly to achieve just the right look. For example, you may need to lighten an object to see some text better, or maybe you need to change the saturation of the object to see the object better without changing the color. The Adjust palette allows you to make adjustments to the brightness, contrast, saturation, tint, and posterization of an object's color. Brightness makes the object color lighter or darker. Changing the contrast of a color increases or decreases the difference between colors. Saturation adjusts the strength, or purity, of a color. Tint blends the current foreground color in the Color palette with the current fill for the selected layer. Posterize restricts the number of colors in an image layer. This option is commonly used to create effects in an image object, such as creating the appearance of a film negative.

FIGURE D-10

Textures palette with Name View displayed

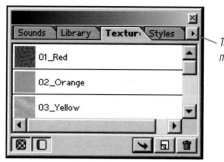

Textures palette
menu button

FIGURE D-11

Rectangle object showing applied texture

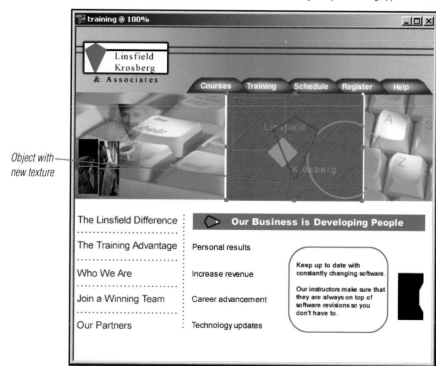

Object with
new texture

Apply a texture

1. Click the Selection Tool in the toolbox if necessary, then click the large blue rectangle object to select it.

2. Click the Object Layers palette tab if necessary, then click Texture layer.

3. Click the Textures palette tab, click the Textures palette menu button, then click Name View.

   The Textures palette now displays each texture by its name along with a small thumbnail picture of the texture, as shown in Figure D-10.

4. Click the down scroll arrow, click the 05_DarkGreen texture, then click the Apply Texture button.

5. Click Top layer in the Object Layers palette, then click the Opacity palette tab.

6. Drag the Object Layer Opacity slider until 75 appears in the text box, then drag the Object Opacity slider until 90 appears in the text box.

   Notice that the top layer of the object is now transparent enough to see the texture on the second layer. Changing the opacity of the texture on the second layer of the object helps soften the effect of the texture.

7. Compare your composition to Figure D-11.

   TIP   To apply a texture to a composition background, click the Background color box, then click the texture you want from the Textures palette.

You applied a texture to the bottom layer of an object, then changed the opacity of the object's top and bottom layers to display the texture more clearly.

Apply a gradient

1. Click the long narrow blue rectangle object to select it.

2. Click the Gradient palette tab if necessary, click the Gradient list arrow, then click Linear.

3. Drag the Gradient Angle dial until 90 appears in the text box, if necessary.

   A linear gradient is applied to the rectangle object with a 90 degree angle.

4. Drag the left color stop in the Gradient palette to the right about a half an inch, as shown in Figure D-12.

   (continued)

Gradient palette

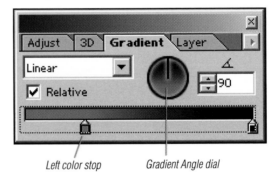

Left color stop   Gradient Angle dial

Working with Color, Effects, and Rollovers

FIGURE D-13

Composition showing modified blue rectangle

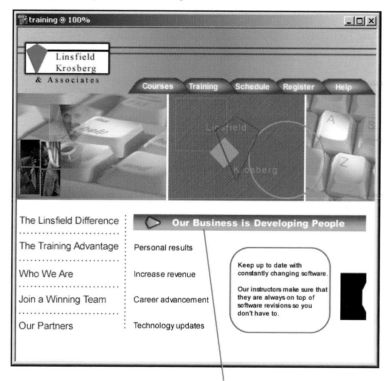

Modified rectangle object

5. Click the Adjust palette tab, then drag the Brightness slider to the right until 70 appears in the text box.

The rectangle object color is now brightened. Use the Brightness up or down arrow to adjust the brightness to 70 if necessary.

6. Click the Contrast down arrow until -20 appears in the text box, then click in a blank area of the composition.

The color of the rectangle object is adjusted so the text on top of the object is more easily readable.

7. Save your work, then compare your composition to Figure D-13.

You applied and modified a gradient to the narrow blue rectangle, then adjusted the color of the object.

APPLY 3D EFFECTS AND DISTORTION

What You'll Do

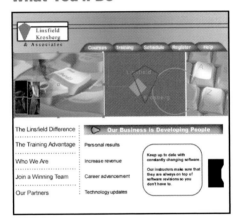

In this lesson, you will learn how to apply a 3D effect and a distortion to objects.

Creating and Modifying 3D Effects

When you really want an object, like a button, to stand out and be noticed, you can apply a 3D effect to it. To apply a three-dimensional effect to an object in LiveMotion, you need to open the 3D palette, as shown in Figure D-14. The 3D palette provides four different effects: cutout, emboss, bevel, and ripple. Each allows you to transform a flat two-dimensional object into a three-dimensional object that has depth and dimension. An example of each 3D effect is shown in Figure D-15. The cutout effect makes the object look like it is cut out from the background. The emboss effect adds a soft rounded edge around an object. The bevel effect adds an angled edge all the way around the object, and the ripple effect adds a series of waves from the center of the object to the outside. In LiveMotion, a 3D effect creates the illusion of three dimensions by adjusting the depth, softness, and lighting of the object. You can adjust each of these dimensions using the appropriate

FIGURE D-14
3D palette

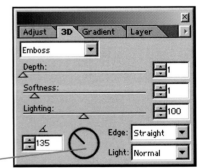

Angle dial

sliders on the 3D palette. Depth refers to the distance, measured in pixels, between the edge of the object layer and the most intense part of the effect in the layer. The higher the depth value, the greater the depth effect. Softness is used to measure the amount of blur or smoothing of the 3D effect. A high softness value increases the amount of blur and is useful in part for preventing jagged edges on the bevel effect. Lighting refers to the difference between the light and dark areas of the 3D effect. The higher the lighting value, the greater the contrast of the effect.

To create other interesting effects with light, you can change the angle direction of the light source by moving the Angle dial, entering a new angle in the Angle text box, or clicking the Angle up or down arrow. An angle of 0°, for example, lights the object from the right side, 90° lights the object from the top, 180° lights the object from the left, and 270° lights the object from the bottom. The Light feature on the 3D palette changes the type of light that is used to light an object, as shown in Figure D-16. The Normal setting, which is the default, applies neutral lighting, highlights, and shadows to an object. The Light Only

setting applies neutral lighting and high-lights to an object but no shadows. The Dark Only setting applies neutral lighting and shadows to an object but no highlights. To modify the 3D effect even more, you can change the edge type, which adds a certain style to the edge of the object. The Edge settings include Straight, Button, Plateau, and Ripple. An example of each type is shown in Figure D-17.

QUICKTIP

The Edge settings are unavailable when you use the Cutout effect.

FIGURE D-15
An example of each 3D effect

Original Cutout Emboss Bevel Ripple

FIGURE D-16
3D effect light settings

Normal Light Only Dark Only

FIGURE D-17
3D effect edge settings

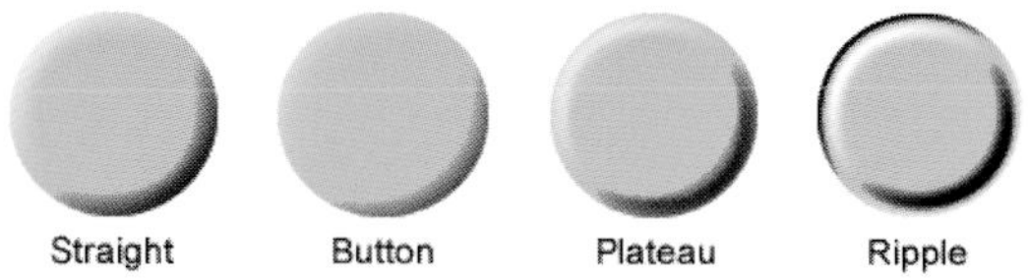

Straight Button Plateau Ripple

Applying Distortion Effects

Distortion effects are image-editing effects used on an image object, an object with a texture or gradient fill, or an object with multiple colors to distort the fill. Distortion effects have little to no effect on objects with solid colors. All distortion effects are found on the Distort palette and include the following effects: Displace, Lens, Twirl, Spherize, Quantize, and Radial Quantize. Figure D-18 illustrates each distortion effect in relation to the original object that has no distortion effect. The Displace effect shifts the fill of the object within the object's selection border (up and to the right by default). You can modify the distance in pixels and the angle of the shift to change the look of this effect further. The Lens effect magnifies or shrinks the object fill. The Twirl effect rotates the object fill more in the center than on the edges, like a tornado. The Twirl effect has two additional features, Turns and Band Size, which you can modify to customize the effect even more. Increasing the Turns option (either positive or negative) intensifies the distortion effect. The Band Size value splits the image into increasingly larger concentric bands. The Spherize effect wraps the fill around a sphere, like a fish-eye lens. Increasing the magnification value of this effect enlarges the fill and decreasing the magnification shrinks it. The Quantize effect breaks up the fill into mosaic-like tiles or blocks. The higher you set the size value, the larger the tile size. The last distortion effect, the Radial Quantize effect, fractures the fill into circular bands radiating from the center of the object. The higher you set the size value, the wider and more obvious the bands become and the more distorted the fill becomes. Ultimately, the result of a distortion effect depends on the type of object and fill you are using.

FIGURE D-18

An example of each distortion effect

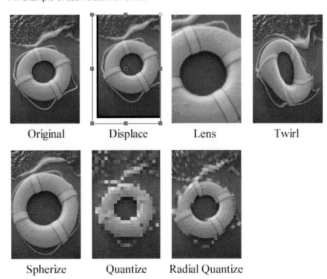

Original   Displace   Lens   Twirl

Spherize   Quantize   Radial Quantize

FIGURE D-19

Emboss effect applied to the rectangle object

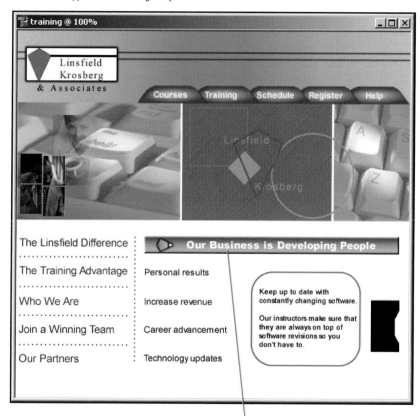

*Emboss effect
applied to object*

1. Click the narrow blue rectangle object, then click the 3D palette tab.

2. Click the 3D Effect list arrow, then click Emboss.

    An embossed effect is applied to the object, which makes it appear as if it is three-dimensional.

3. Click in a blank area of the composition, then compare your screen to Figure D-19.

You applied the Emboss 3D effect to an object.

Modify a 3D effect

1. Click the narrow blue rectangle object, then drag the Depth slider in the 3D palette to the right until 12 appears in the text box.

2. Drag the Softness slider to the right until 4 appears in the text box.

3. Drag the Angle dial to the left until 180 appears in the text box.

   Modifying the Emboss effect gives the object a distinct appearance.

4. Click in a blank area of the composition, then compare your screen to Figure D-20.

You changed the depth, softness, and lighting angle of the Emboss effect you applied to an object.

FIGURE D-20
Object showing embossed effect

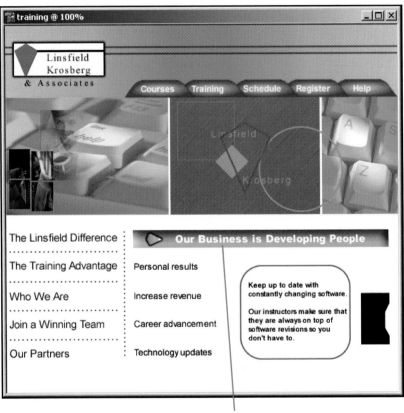

*Object with
modified effect*

FIGURE D-21

Distorted image object

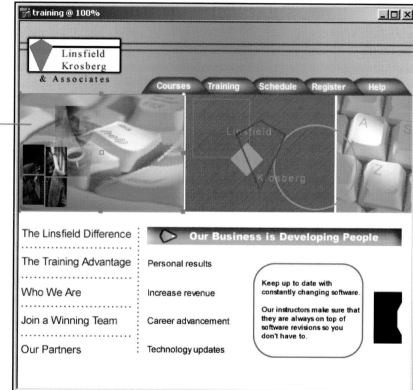

Image object with applied distortion effect

1. Click the large keyboard image object on the left side of the composition.

2. Click the Distort palette tab, click the Effect list arrow, then click Twirl.

   The Twirl distortion effect is applied to the image object.

3. Drag the Turns slider to the left until 10 appears in the text box.

4. Click the Band Size up arrow until 4 appears in the text box.

   The Turns option changes the amount of distortion that is applied to the image and the Band Size option changes how many bands appear in the distortion.

5. Click in a blank area of the composition, then compare your screen to Figure D-21.

6. Save your work.

You applied and modified a distortion effect on an image object.

WORK WITH STYLES AND THE LIBRARY

What You'll Do

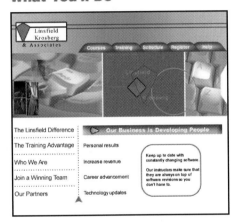

 In this lesson, you'll learn how to create a custom style, add it to the Styles palette, and then apply it to an object. You'll also learn how to use the Library palette and save an object to the Library palette to be used as an active matte.

Understanding Styles

The more you use LiveMotion to create customized objects using layers, color, gradients, distortions, and other effects, the more you'll want to save what you create for future use on other compositions. Saving and applying groups of attributes between objects and even between compositions is a fast and easy way to ensure consistency in your work. One way to save your work is to create a style. A **style** is a saved set of attributes that can include layer color, opacity, texture, 3D effects, distortion, and other palette settings. A style can contain multiple layers, animation directions, and rollovers as well. A style can't contain attributes such as the type of object (i.e., geometric, text, or image); the shape of an object (i.e., rectangle or polygon); or any settings from the Transform or Web palettes.

You can apply one of LiveMotion's six predefined styles to an object or create and apply one of your own styles. Once you apply a style to an object, the previous layers and layer attributes of the object are removed and the object takes on the layers and attributes of the style. You can apply styles, one at a time, to any of the three types of LiveMotion objects. LiveMotion's predefined styles offer a sample of the types of effects and behaviors you can create. Whether you create your own styles or use the predefined LiveMotion styles, make sure you use them consistently in your Web site.

Using the Styles Palette

The Styles palette, shown in Figure D-22, shows the set of predefined styles in the top row that are installed with LiveMotion and one custom style that has been added

Working with Color, Effects, and Rollovers

to the palette. To apply a style to an object, you first select the object in the composition, then select the style in the Styles palette and click the Apply Style button on the bottom of the palette. The Styles palette has seven buttons on the bottom of the palette that help you work with and manage the styles. The four buttons on the left side of the palette determine which styles are displayed in the palette and are selected by default. The View Styles with Animation button on the far left side of the palette displays styles that include animation. The next button, View Styles with Rollovers, displays styles with rollovers. The View Styles with Object Layers button displays styles that have multiple layers. The last button, View Styles with Scripts, shows all styles that include scripting. The three buttons on the right side of the palette allow you to apply a style to an object (Apply Style button), create a new style (New Style button), and delete a style from the palette (Delete Style button).

Using the Library Palette

The Library palette, like the Styles palette, is used to store information that you want to save for future use, as shown in Figure D-23. However, the Library palette stores actual objects or groups of objects as well as their attributes. The Library palette can store LiveMotion, vector, and

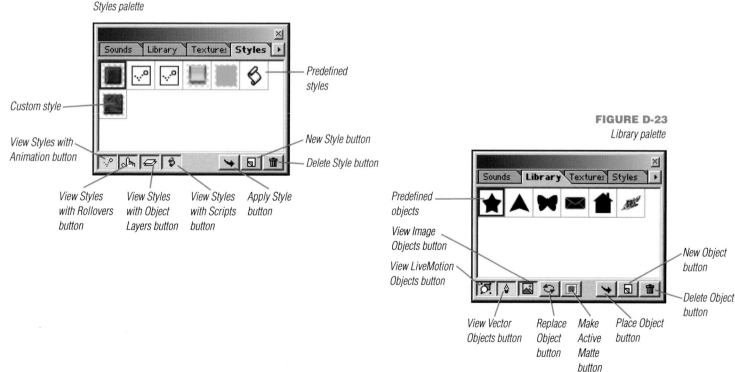

FIGURE D-22
Styles palette

Custom style

View Styles with Animation button

Predefined styles

New Style button

Delete Style button

View Styles with Rollovers button

View Styles with Object Layers button

View Styles with Scripts button

Apply Style button

FIGURE D-23
Library palette

Predefined objects

View Image Objects button

View LiveMotion Objects button

New Object button

Delete Object button

View Vector Objects button

Replace Object button

Make Active Matte button

Place Object button

image objects and all of their attributes, including animation and rollovers. The Library palette is a good place to store graphic elements such as logos, photographs, or navigation elements that you plan to use in multiple compositions. Similar to the Styles palette, the Library palette comes with six predefined objects that you can apply to your composition.

To apply an object from the Library palette to a composition, open the Library palette, select the object you want, then click the Place Object button. The Library palette has buttons along the bottom of the palette, which help you work with and manage objects in the palette. The three buttons on the right side of the palette allow you to place an object in a composition (Place Object button), create a new object in the palette (New Object button), and delete an object from the palette (Delete Object button). The first three buttons on the left side of the palette are object view buttons that display LiveMotion objects (View LiveMotion Objects button), vector objects such as EPS and PDF images (View Vector Objects button), and bitmap images (View Image Objects button). The next button on the palette is the Replace Object button which allows you to replace an object shape in the composition with a new object shape from the palette. One thing to keep in mind when you replace an object with a new shape is that the new object shape is forced to fit (stretched or squeezed) within the selected object's selection border. The next button, Make Active Matte, changes the active matte on the Properties palette to the selected shape in the Library palette. It's simple to add an object shape to the Library: just select the object in the composition, then drag it to the Library palette. You will be asked to name the new object shape and then it will appear in the palette. When you place a LiveMotion object from the Library palette into a composition, it can be edited like any other object.

FIGURE D-24

Object showing new custom style

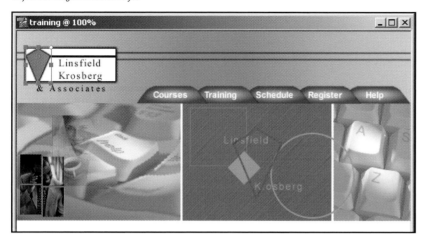

1. Click the small blue diamond shape in the white rectangle object in the top left corner of the composition.

2. Click the Object Layers palette tab if necessary, click Texture layer, then click the Textures palette tab if necessary.

3. Click the 04_LightGreen texture, then click the Apply Texture button. ↘

   The texture is applied to the Texture layer of the selected object.

4. Click Top layer in the Object Layers palette, then click the Opacity palette tab.

5. Drag the Object Layer Opacity slider to the left until 75 appears in the text box.

6. Click Outline layer in the Object Layers palette, click the Layer palette tab, click the Width up arrow once, then click the Softness up arrow once.

7. Compare your composition to Figure D-24.

8. Click the Styles palette tab, then drag the diamond object to the Styles palette.

   The Name dialog box appears, which allows you to name the new style.

9. Type **Logo Style** in the Name text box, then click OK.

   The new style appears in the Styles palette, as shown in Figure D-25.

You created a new custom style, then saved it to the Styles palette.

FIGURE D-25

New style in Styles palette

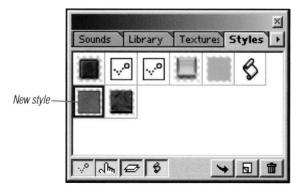

New style

Apply a custom style

1. Click the small light blue filled diamond in the center of the large rectangle object.

2. Click the new style (Logo Style) you just created if necessary, then click the Apply Style button. ↘

3. Click in a blank area of the composition, then compare your composition to Figure D-26.

   The small diamond object is filled with the new custom style.

4. Click the Logo Style style, click the Delete Style button, then click Yes (Win) or Delete (Mac) to accept the deletion of the style from the styles palette. 🗑

You applied a custom style to a small diamond object and then deleted the style from the Styles palette.

Diamond object with applied custom style

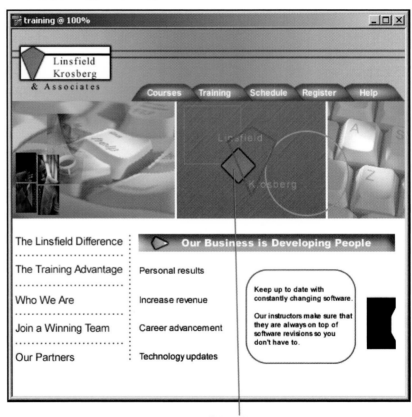

*Object with new
custom style*

FIGURE D-27

Composition showing new Library object

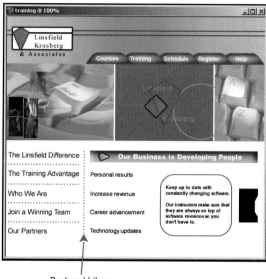

Replaced Library
object

1. Click the Library palette tab, then click the star object if necessary.

2. Click the Place Object button, then drag the new object to the bottom of the composition in a blank area. ➔

 The object from the Library appears in the composition filled with the current fill color.

3. Click the Arrowhead object (02_Arrow) in the Library palette, then click the Replace Object button. ⟳

4. Click the Transform palette tab, select the number in the Width text box, type **18**, select the number in the Height text box, then type **16**.

5. Drag the object to a new position in the composition as shown in Figure D-27, then click in a blank area of the composition

You added an object to the composition from the Library palette, replaced it with a different object from the palette, resized the new object, and then repositioned the new object.

Save an object to the Library palette

1. Drag the black box object in the lower right corner of the composition to the Library palette.

2. Type **Photo Matte 1** in the Name dialog box, then click OK.

   The object appears selected in the Library palette, as shown in Figure D-28.

3. Click the keyboard image object on the right side of the composition, then click the Properties palette tab.

4. Click the Make Active Matte button on the Library palette. 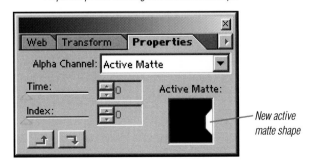 (inline button)

   The image object changes to reflect the active matte, which has now changed in the Properties palette, as shown in Figure D-29. This active matte is applied only to the currently selected image object and does not affect any other image object.

   (continued)

FIGURE D-28
Library palette showing newly added object

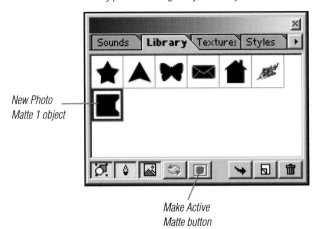

New Photo Matte 1 object

Make Active Matte button

FIGURE D-29
Properties palette showing new active matte shape

New active matte shape

5. Click the black box object in the composition, click Edit on the menu bar, then click Clear.

6. Compare your composition to Figure D-30.

7. Click the Photo Matte 1 object in the Library palette, click the Delete Object button, then click Yes (Win) or Delete (Mac) to accept the deletion of the object from the library palette. 🗑

8. Save your work.

You saved an object to the Library palette and then made the new object the active matte for an image object.

FIGURE D-30
Image object showing new active matte

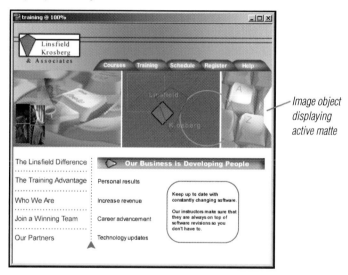

Image object
displaying
active matte

CREATE AND EDIT A BASIC ROLLOVER

What You'll Do

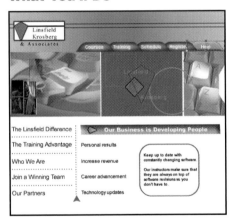

 In this lesson, you will learn to create and edit a basic rollover.

Creating Rollovers

So, why create rollovers? Rollovers can be important because they function as navigational tools that provide Web users with visual clues about where to click to get further information or to be linked to another Web page or Web site. A static Web page without any interaction can be uninteresting and unappealing.

To make an object into a rollover, you need to add a state to it using the States palette, shown in Figure D-31. As has been mentioned previously, a state is a collection of changes to an object that is triggered through mouse actions or scripts. A state can be a color change, an opacity change, or some other property change. You apply a rollover state by selecting the object in the composition and then clicking the New State button in the States palette. You then need to choose what type of state you want to use. LiveMotion has five state types to choose from including normal, over, down, out, and Custom. The normal state is the default state for every

Specifying the active area of a rollover

When you plan to export a composition with rollovers to a Macromedia Flash file, you may want to specify the active area for the rollover objects (that is, the area in the object that triggers the rollover in response to an action). If you have applied a rollover to a multilayered object, you can indicate which layer represents the area that triggers the rollover. For example, you might have applied a rollover to an object with an offset shadow layer. By default the entire object including the drop shadow becomes the active area, and you might want the shadow part not to be active. To specify which layer you want to be active, open the Object Layers palette, then double-click the desired layer. In the Name dialog box, add an asterisk to the beginning of the layer's name (for example, "*Object Front"), then click OK.

object you create or import into a composition. This is the state where the object is at rest and no action takes place. The over state is triggered when the mouse pointer is moved over the object. The down state is triggered when you click the object. The out state is triggered when the mouse pointer is moved off the object. The Custom state lets you create your own state. This state is used to create remote rollovers and other similar effects. After you have applied a rollover state type to an object, you can then change the object's appearance to create the rollover state. Using the States palette, you can also create a new state by duplicating an existing state using the Duplicate State button and then modifying it, and you can delete a rollover state by clicking the Delete State button.

Editing Rollovers

All of the changes you make to a rollover state's appearance are listed in the Changes list beneath the selected rollover state. You can expand, or view, this list by clicking the small arrow next to the word "Changes" and then modify any item in the list. Because the normal state defines the object, editing all of the states at once is easy because any change you apply to the normal state is also applied to the other states. However, if you make any modifications to the other states, they do not affect the normal state.

In the lower left corner of the States palette are three buttons that help you work with rollovers. The button on the far left is the Edit State Script button, which allows you

to open a Script Editor window for the selected state and modify the script code. You can also use this feature to create a new script to play when a state is activated. The next button is the Replace Image button, which allows you to replace a selected object with an image object. The last button on the left side of the palette is the Add/Remove Sound button, which allows you to add or remove a sound to a rollover state other than the normal state. The sound plays when you activate the rollover.

QUICKTIP

If you want to make a modification to a normal state without affecting the other states, temporarily change the normal state to another state, make your changes, and then change the state back to normal.

FIGURE D-31
States palette

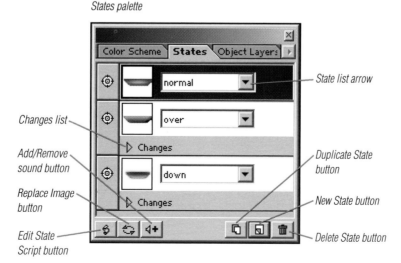

Changes list
Add/Remove sound button
Replace Image button
Edit State Script button

State list arrow
Duplicate State button
New State button
Delete State button

Create a rollover

1. Click the blue Help tab (not the text) in the composition.

2. Click the States palette tab, then click the New State button. 🔲

   By default, a new over rollover state appears in the States palette.

3. Click the Color palette tab, select the number in the Red color value text box, type **255** if necessary, select the number in the Green color value text box, type **130**, select the number in the Blue color value text box, type **140**, then press [Enter] (Win) or [return] (Mac).

4. Click the Opacity palette tab, drag the Object Layer Opacity slider all the way to the right until 100 appears in the text box, click the Opacity Gradient list arrow, then click No Gradient.

   You have now modified the color and gradient for the over rollover state, as shown in Figure D-32.

5. Click the Duplicate State button on the States palette.

   A new exact duplicate of the over state called the down state appears in the States palette, as shown in Figure D-33.

   (continued)

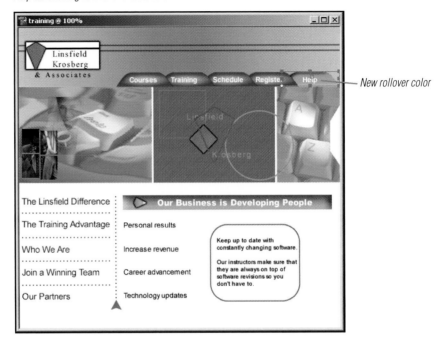

New rollover color

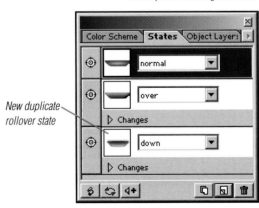

New duplicate
rollover state

Working with Color, Effects, and Rollovers

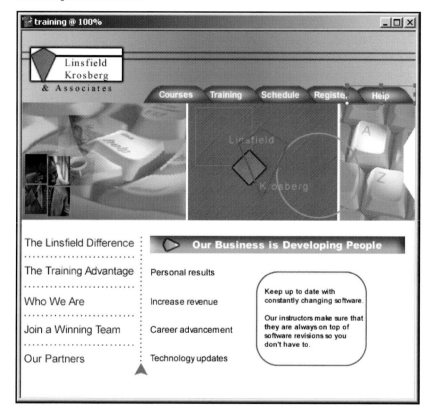

6. Click the 3D palette tab if necessary, then drag the Angle dial to the left until 270 appears in the text box.

7. Click the Object Layers palette tab, click Bottom layer, then click the Layer palette tab.

8. Click the Width up arrow once, click the Softness up arrow until 5 appears in the text box, click the States palette tab, then click the normal state.

9. Compare your composition to Figure D-34.

10. Click the Preview Mode button on the toolbox, move the pointer over the Help tab, click the Help tab, then click the Edit Mode button on the toolbox.

You created two rollover states for the Help tab in the composition.

Add a sound to a rollover

1. Click the down rollover state, then click the Sounds palette tab.

2. Click the 02_Event_Button_Push sound if necessary, as shown in Figure D-35, then click the Apply Sound button. ⬚

   Don't worry if you don't see anything happen after you apply the sound to the rollover, because the sound does not appear in the composition window. Notice that, as shown in Figure D-36, the Add/Remove sound button at the bottom of the States palette now has a minus symbol, indicating that a sound has been applied to the down rollover state.

3. Click the Preview Mode button on the toolbox, move the pointer over the Help tab, click the Help tab, then click the Edit Mode button on the toolbox. ⬚ ⬚

You added a sound from the Sounds palette to the down rollover state.

FIGURE D-35
Sounds palette

FIGURE D-36
States palette showing changed Add/Remove sound button

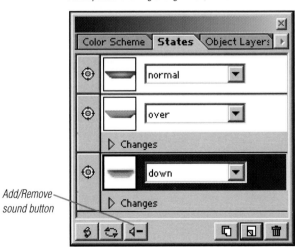

Add/Remove sound button

FIGURE D-37

Open Changes heading for the down rollover state

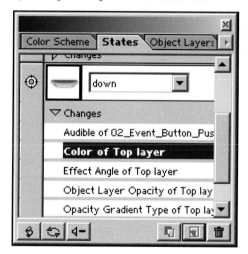

1. Click the triangle next to the Changes heading for the down rollover state, then click Color of Top layer in the list as shown in Figure D-37.

2. Click the Color palette tab if necessary, select the number in the Green text box, type **0**, then press [Enter] (Win) or [return] (Mac).

   The color for the down state changes to a darker pink.

3. Click the Up scroll arrow on the States palette, click the triangle next to the Changes heading for the down state to close the Changes list, then click the triangle next to the Changes heading for the over state.

4. Click Color of Top layer in the list, select the number in the Green text box in the Color palette, type **0**, then press [Enter] (Win) or [return] (Mac).

5. Click the triangle next to the Changes heading for the over state, click the normal state, then click in a blank area of the composition.

6. Click the Preview Mode button on the toolbox, move the pointer over the Help tab, click the Help tab, then click the Edit Mode button on the toolbox.

7. Save your work.

You darkened the color of two rollover states using the Changes heading option in the States palette, then previewed your work.

CREATE A REMOTE ROLLOVER

What You'll Do

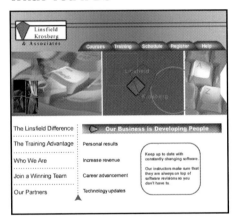

In this lesson, you will create a remote rollover.

Understanding Remote Rollovers

If you really want to add some excitement and helpful interactivity to your composition, you can add remote rollovers to it. A remote rollover is basically interactivity between different objects of your composition, where the action of one object causes another object to do something, as shown in Figure D-38. A typical example of a remote rollover is a button that, when clicked, triggers the display of a photograph or the playing of a movie. Another common example of a remote rollover is the clicking of a small photograph that causes the display of a larger version of the photograph.

Before we learn how to create remote rollovers, let's go over a few terms and concepts. For a remote rollover interaction to take place, you need to have an originating object, called a trigger object,

Creating linked images and image maps

Objects that you create in LiveMotion, including rollovers, can be linked to a Web page address and used to link a user to other Web pages. The linked image acts like a button that, when clicked, opens up another Web page or Web site. An image map is an image on a Web page that contains multiple links to other Web pages or Web sites. Areas of the image map, called **hotspots**, link you to various URLs. To create a linked image or an image map, select the object to which you want to assign a URL, open the Web palette, then enter the URL for the link. Once you have entered all of your URLs, select AutoLayout, GIF, JPEG, or PNG from the Export palette Format menu, then export the composition with the Make Page option selected. Note that if you are adding the page to a site in GoLive, you should internally link files from within GoLive in order to make site maintenance more efficient.

and a remote object, called a target object. A **trigger object**, as its name implies, triggers another object to do something, like appear on the screen or change colors. A trigger object usually has a rollover state attached to it that, when initiated by the user's mouse, causes the interaction with the target object. A **target object** (or objects) is the object that interacts with the trigger object. Target objects have custom states applied to them that are linked to the rollover states of the trigger object. A target

object needs to be prepared before you attempt to use it as a target object by creating a custom state for it and then modifying the custom state.

Creating Remote Rollovers

Remote rollovers are created the same way as regular rollovers, but with a few additional steps. First, you need to create or place both the trigger object and the target object in the composition. Next, you need to select the target object, apply a custom

state to it, and modify the custom state. Now, keep in mind that the state of the target object at this point is how it will look when the trigger object is triggered, but not until then. As a third step, you select the trigger object and apply a rollover state to it that will function as the trigger for the target object. To link the two objects together, you then drag a target icon from the desired state of the trigger object in the States palette to the target object.

FIGURE D-38
Example of a remote rollover

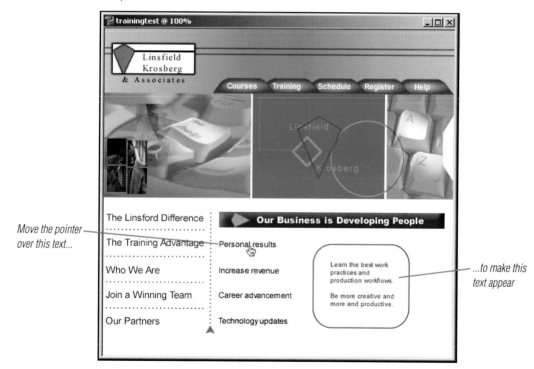

Move the pointer over this text...

...to make this text appear

Create a remote rollover target

1. Click the paragraph text object in the lower right corner of the composition.

   TIP Throughout these steps, make sure you are selecting the paragraph text object that starts with "Keep up to date." There are a number of text objects below this object, and it is important to select the correct one.

2. Click the Layer palette tab if necessary, click the Fill with list arrow, then click Background.

   The target object appears to disappear, but the object's selection box proves that it's still there. Changing the target object's normal state fill to background (white in this case) makes the text in the object invisible until the trigger object is activated.

3. Click the States palette tab, click the New State button, click the State list arrow on the new state, then click Custom State. 🗗

4. Type **Technology Text**, then click OK.

   A new custom state is added to the States palette, as shown in Figure D-39.

   (continued)

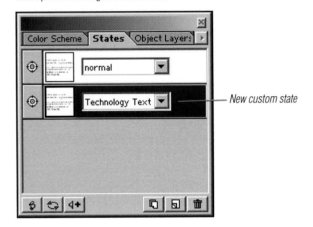

— *New custom state*

Working with Color, Effects, and Rollovers

FIGURE D-40

Composition showing target object in custom state

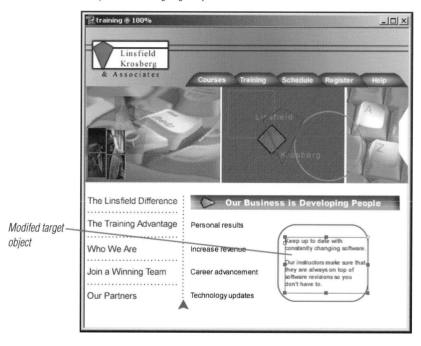

Modifed target object

5. With the Technology Text state selected, click the Fill with list arrow in the Layer palette, then click Color.

6. Click the Color palette tab if necessary, select the number in the Red color value text box, type **151**, select the number in the Green color value text box, type **53**, select the number in the Blue color value text box, type **53**, then press [Enter] (Win) or [return] (Mac).

7. Compare your composition to Figure D-40.

You selected the remote rollover target object, created a custom state for it, then modified the state's color.

Create a remote rollover trigger

1. Click the "Technology updates" text object, then click the New State button.

2. Drag the target icon for this new state (over) to the target object ("Keep up to date..." paragraph text object).

   A new rollover state (Technology Text) appears underneath the over state in the States palette, as shown in Figure D-41. The over state of the "Technology Updates" object will trigger the Technology Text state of the paragraph text object.

   > TIP Throughout these steps, make sure you drag the target icon so it is directly over the paragraph text and you see the correct text object's selection box. There are other remote rollover text objects below the Technology Text object, so be sure you target the correct object.

3. Click the Preview Mode button in the toolbox, move the pointer over the "Technology updates" text object, then click the Edit Mode button.

   The target object appears when you move the mouse over the trigger object ("Technology updates") and remains in view when you move the mouse off of the object.

   (continued)

FIGURE D-41
States palette showing new rollover state

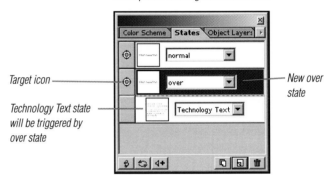

Target icon

Technology Text state
will be triggered by
over state

New over
state

FIGURE D-42

States palette showing modified rollover state

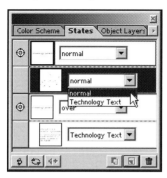

FIGURE D-43

Final composition

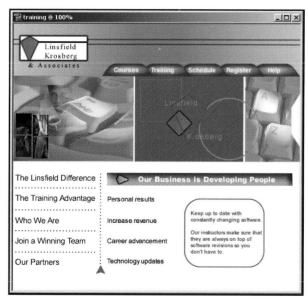

4. Click the normal state for the trigger object at the top of the States palette, then drag the target icon to the target object (paragraph text object).

5. Click the State list arrow of the new state, then click normal as shown in Figure D-42.

   The target object's normal state will now be triggered by the normal state of the trigger object. Thus the target object's text will be white and invisible when the trigger object is in its normal state, and it will be red and visible when the trigger object is in the over state.

6. Click the Preview Mode button, move the pointer over the "Technology updates" text object, then move the pointer over elements throughout the whole composition.

7. Click the Edit Mode button, click in a blank area of the composition, then compare your composition to Figure D-43.

8. Save your work.

You created a remote rollover trigger and then modified the rollover state.

Lesson 6   Create a Remote Rollover

You own a small Web site development company in Phoenix, Arizona called ProDesigns. Your company provides Web page design, maintenance, and Web hosting. A new senior living community, Oak Ridge, has contacted you about designing a Web site to advertise their retirement community. You have begun work on the Web site home page already and now you need to work with the background color, and the color of some objects, apply a style to an object, and create some rollovers. Use Figure D-44 to help you finish the new home page for the site.

1. Open the file LMD-3, then save it as **oaks1**. (*Hint*: This file contains the Monotype Corsiva font with font sizes of 16 and 48. If your computer does not have this font, it may make a font substitution.)

2. Click the Background color box in the Color palette, click the Textures palette tab, click the Textures palette menu button, then click Preview View.

3. Click the 04_LightGreen texture in the list, then apply the texture to the composition.

4. Click the Foreground color box in the Color palette, click the "Experience the difference" text object, then click the Color palette tab, if necessary.

5. On the Color palette menu, click Value View.

6. Drag the slider to the top of the color bar, then click RGB View on the Color palette menu.

7. Click the Paint Bucket Tool in the toolbox, then click the text "Oak Ridge."

8. Click the Selection Tool, select the "The Community" text object, then click the Paint Bucket Tool.

9. Click the white color cell in the Color palette, then click the other six text objects that appear around the central image.

10. Click the Selection Tool, then select at the same time the ellipse behind the text "Local News" and the ellipse object behind the text "Specials."

11. Click the Styles palette tab, click the Styles palette menu, then click Name View.

12. Click the 01_EmbossGradTexture style if necessary, then click the Apply Style button.

13. Change the object opacity of each ellipse object to 70 and the object layer opacity of each ellipse to 50.

14. Click the text "Getting Here," click the States palette tab if necessary, then click the New State button.

15. Click the Font list arrow in the Properties palette, click Garamond, click the Font Size list arrow, then click 48. (*Hint*: If you do not have the Garamond font, choose a different font.)

16. Click the black color cell in the Color palette, then click the normal state in the States palette.

17. Click the Preview Mode button in the toolbox, then move the mouse over all the elements in the composition.

18. Save the file, then compare your screen to Figure D-44.

FIGURE D-44
Completed Project 1

You work for Corporate World, a company that specializes in developing corporate identities, logos, and product branding. One of your jobs is to maintain the company Web site and update the site with new features, information, and design. You are currently working on a new version of the Web site design in LiveMotion. Using the skills you have learned so far, finish the composition provided for you in this project.

1. Open the file LMD-4, then save it as **cpworld1**.

2. Click the blue rectangle object, then click the Gradient palette tab.

3. Change the gradient to Burst, then move the left color stop about a half an inch.

4. Click the 3D palette tab, then apply the bevel effect to the object.

5. Click the Edge list arrow, then click Button.

6. Change the Depth to 12.

7. Drag the Angle dial to the left until 90 appears in the text box.

8. Click the image object, then click the Distort palette tab.

9. Use the Spherize effect to distort the object.

10. Click the Magnification up arrow until 105 appears in the text box.

11. Click the Library palette tab, click the Library palette menu button, then click Name View.

12. Click the New Object button in the palette, locate the Fisheye object file in the drive and folder where your data files are stored, click Open, then click OK to accept the name "Fisheye."

13. Click the down scroll arrow in the Library palette, click Fisheye, then click the Place Object button.

14. In the Transform palette, change the X text box value to 175, then change the Y text box value to 357, change the Width value to 67, change the height value to 42.

15. Click the small circle object to the left of the text object "Contact Us," then add a new, custom state to the circle object called **Contact Circle**.

16. Click the Color palette tab (make sure RGB View is displayed), then drag the Red slider all the way to the left.

17. Add a new state to the Contact Us text object, then drag the target icon to the circle object.

18. Click the normal state, drag the target icon to the cyan circle, click the State list arrow of the state directly under normal (should be a new Contact Circle state), then click normal.

19. Click the Preview Mode button in the toolbox, move the pointer over all of the text objects, then click the Edit Mode button in the toolbox.

20. Click in a blank area of the composition, save the file, then compare your screen to Figure D-45.

FIGURE D-45
Completed Project 2

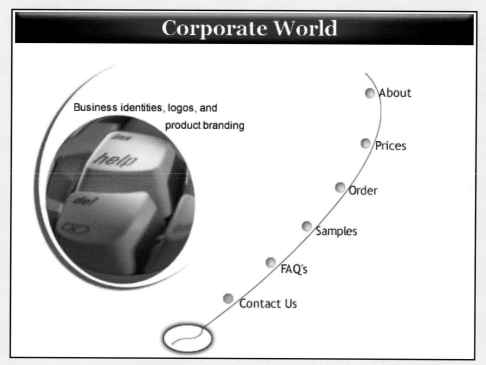

SECTION E

CREATING ANIMATIONS AND EXPORTING A COMPOSITION

1. Use the Timeline window.

2. Work with keyframes.

3. Create motion.

4. Animate object attributes.

5. Animate text and use sounds.

6. Export a composition.

CREATING ANIMATIONS AND EXPORTING A COMPOSITION

Understanding the Basics of Animation

What do you think of when you hear the word animation? You might think of cartoons that you watch on television, or maybe you think of high-tech computer animation that you see in a movie at a theater. Well, today many Web sites include animation that is designed to entertain you, advertise a product or service, or draw your attention to something specific on the Web page. No matter the content, all animation is developed using some sort of animation design tool like LiveMotion. In LiveMotion, you can animate an object's movement across the screen or animate an object's properties, such as its color, opacity, or size.

Producing an Animation

In LiveMotion, an animation is developed using the objects that you create or place in a composition. You can animate an entire object or just a layer of an object, depending on what animation effect you are trying to achieve. So, where exactly do you develop animation in LiveMotion? You develop animation in LiveMotion using the Timeline window. The **Timeline window**

displays all of the objects in a composition and their associated animation events. The Timeline window enables you to control the duration of an animation. The entire composition has a **duration bar** that represents how long the composition is animated. Individual objects within the composition also have duration bars that identify how long they are animated. By default the durations of newly created objects match the duration of the composition. To create an animation, you'll first need to decide how long and when you want to animate the object using its duration bar. Next, you'll set a **keyframe**, which marks the point in time that the animation of the object begins. The properties of the object remain constant until you set another keyframe in the Timeline window and modify the object properties. LiveMotion automatically creates a series of steps between the keyframes so that the object properties blend smoothly from one to the other. This blending between keyframes is called **tweening**. In a nutshell, that is how digital animation is developed—now get ready to try it for yourself!

Tools You'll Use

Play/Pause button   Current-time marker

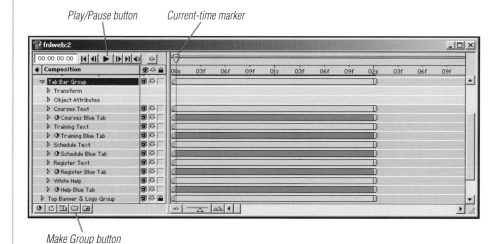

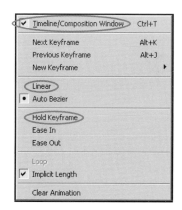

Make Group button

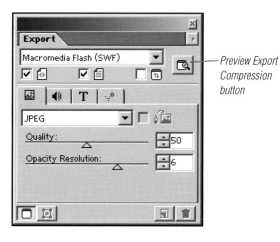

Preview Export
Compression
button

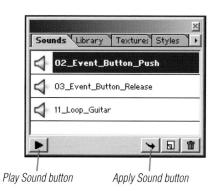

Play Sound button   Apply Sound button

USE THE TIMELINE WINDOW

What You'll Do

 In this lesson, you'll view the Timeline window and identify the features of the window.

Understanding the Timeline Window

The Timeline window, shown in Figure E-1, is the staging area for all animation in LiveMotion. You know by now that the Composition window is used to create and modify the individual elements of a composition. Well, the Timeline window is used to move and modify the elements of the Composition window over time. In other words, the Timeline window allows you to display the composition at different points of time. These points of time are called **animation frames**, or just **frames**. The frame rate for each composition, for example 12 frames per second, is set in the Composition Settings dialog box when you initially create a composition; you can modify the frame rate later by opening the Composition Settings dialog box using the Composition Settings command on the Edit menu.

A key component of the Timeline window is the object hierarchy list, which appears in the left side of the window. When you add an object to the Composition window, it is added to the object hierarchy list in the Timeline window for the composition and automatically given a descriptive name. The name of the object changes automatically if you modify the object in any way (such as altering its color or shape); you can also edit the object name manually. Below each object row in the hierarchy list are object property rows that you can use to animate an object by changing its properties over time. To view (expand) or hide (collapse) the property rows for each object, click the small triangle next to object's name.

QUICKTIP

If you rename an object in the object hierarchy list, LiveMotion no longer automatically changes the object's name when you modify its color or shape.

There are three types of object properties that you can animate using LiveMotion's palettes: transform properties (rotation, position, and scale), object properties (shape and active matte), and layer properties (color, 3D effects, and distortions). An object property row contains the keyframes that identify when the properties of that object change. For example, if you animate an object to move across the Composition window, the Position object property row for that object would display the keyframes that indicate when the object moves.

In the upper left corner of the Timeline window, the current-time display (in hours, minutes, seconds, and frames) identifies the location of the current-time marker on the right side of the Timeline window. The current-time marker at the top of the timeline is used to identify the current frame in

the Composition window; for example, if the current-time marker is moved to the 2 second mark in a 4 second animation you will see the animation as it looks at that point in time in the Composition window. Drag the current-time marker or click on the timeline to move the marker in the timeline. Dragging the current-time marker forward or backward along the timeline is called **scrubbing**. The faster you drag the current-time marker, the faster the animation plays.

QUICKTIP

To hear sound while scrubbing, press [Ctrl] (Win) or [Command] (Mac), then drag the current-time marker.

The playback and sound buttons appear just to the right of the current-time display. The playback buttons allow you to play or pause the animation, go forward or backward one frame at a time, or go to the beginning or the end of the animation. The sound button simply turns sounds on and off in the animation.

FIGURE E-1
Timeline window

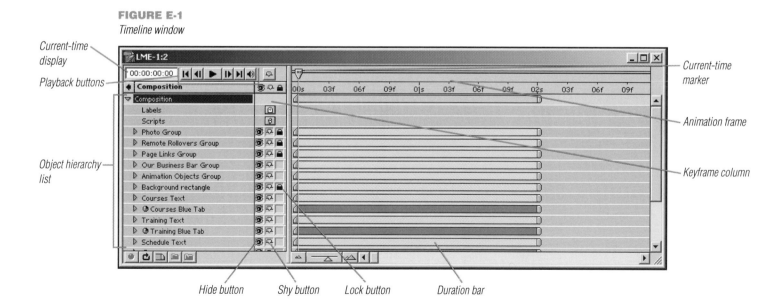

Current-time display
Playback buttons
Object hierarchy list
Current-time marker
Animation frame
Keyframe column

Hide button Shy button Lock button Duration bar

Below the object hierarchy list are five buttons that help you manage animations that you create. The Make Movie Clip button changes the object into a movie clip. A movie clip is a time-independent or **nested animation** that plays independently from the composition animation. This is useful when you want an animation to play only when triggered by the user or when you want it to remain playing after the composition animation has finished. For example, you might want a certain part of an animation, such as a product name, to continue playing after the main animation stops. An icon appears next to the object name in the object hierarchy list when you create a movie clip. The Loop button makes the object repeat its animation. The Explicit/Implicit button allows you to switch between two types of duration time for objects: explicit and implicit. An object with explicit time duration appears for the amount of time in its duration bar and is not affected by any other object's duration. An object with an implicit time duration is linked to the length of the composition, to

the end handles of other objects, or to the position of its own keyframes. The Make Group button groups two or more objects in the object hierarchy list into a group, which is helpful when you want to animate a complex composition with numerous objects. The Make Movie Clip Group button groups one or more objects and turns them into a movie clip, similar to the Make Movie Clip button except with a group of objects.

The timeline, which takes up the majority of the Timeline window, shows the lifetime of the animation from start to finish. Each object's duration bar and keyframes are identified in the timeline. A duration bar has a start point and an end point, each of which can be moved in the timeline to adjust when the object is animated. At the bottom of the timeline are zoom controls that allow you to magnify or shrink the timeline view. Zooming into the timeline displays a shorter duration in the window, making it easier to work with keyframes that are close together. Zooming out of the timeline shows you more of the timeline

and gives you an overview of the whole animation. You can either click one of the Zoom buttons or drag the Zoom Slider to zoom in or out of the timeline window.

Managing Objects

Just to the right of the object hierarchy list is the keyframe column, which has three buttons for each object: the Hide button, the Shy button, and the Lock button. The Hide button hides the selected object in the Composition window, while still displaying it in the Timeline window. This is useful when objects overlap in the composition. The Shy button hides a selected object in the Timeline window, while displaying the object in the Composition window. You would use this feature when you want to show only those objects you want to modify in the Composition window. The Lock button makes an object unselectable and uneditable in the Composition window and in the Timeline window. Use this feature when you want to protect objects from accidentally being changed.

Composition window and Timeline window

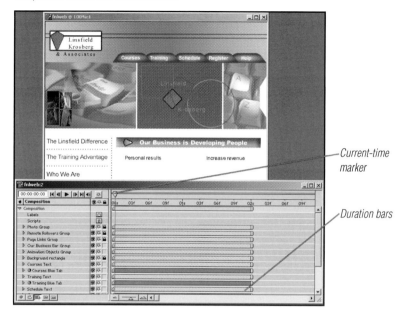

—*Current-time marker*

—*Duration bars*

FIGURE E-3

Timeline window showing renamed objects

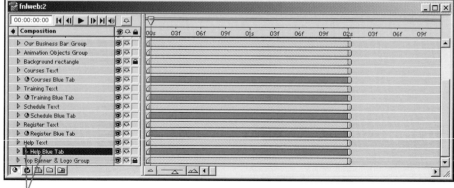

Renamed objects

Lesson 1   Use the Timeline Window

Open the Timeline window and rename objects

1. Open LME-1.liv, save it as **fnlweb**, click Window on the menu bar, then click Reset To Defaults.

2. Click Timeline on the menu bar, then click Timeline/Composition Window.

   The Timeline window appears below the Composition window, as shown in Figure E-2. Notice that the current-time marker is set at 0 and that all of the object duration bars in the timeline are set at 2 seconds, indicating that at least one object has been animated already. Also notice that most of the objects in the object hierarchy list have been grouped together to help organize the objects.

   TIP   If you are using a Mac, the title in the Timeline window title bar will differ from that shown in Figure E-2.

3. Click the down scroll arrow in the Timeline window, then click the White Help object in the object hierarchy list.

4. Click Object on the menu bar, click Edit Name, type **Help Text**, then click OK.

   The name of the object changes in the object hierarchy list.

5. Click the White Geometric object in the object hierarchy list, click Object on the menu bar, click Edit Name, type **Help Blue Tab**, then click OK.

6. Save your work, then compare your Timeline window to Figure E-3.

You opened the Timeline window, then changed the names of two objects in the object hierarchy list.

Group objects and view object properties

1. Click the Courses Text object in the object hierarchy list, press [Ctrl] (Win) or [Shift] (Mac), then click the next nine objects below in the list, so that a total of ten objects are selected.

2. Click the Make Group button in the Timeline window. ▭

   All of the selected objects are grouped together into one object heading. The objects can be displayed by clicking the triangle next to the object heading.

3. Click Object on the menu bar, click Edit Name, type **Tab Bar Group**, then click OK.

4. Click the small triangle next to the Tab Bar Group object.

   The first two properties listed, Transform and Object Attributes, are the available properties for the object group as a whole, not for each individual object. As you can see in Figure E-4, each individual object in the group is listed below the two group properties. The properties of the individual objects can be displayed and changed by expanding their object properties.

5. Click the small triangle next to the Courses Text object, then click the small triangle next to Transform.

   The available properties that you can change for this text object appear in the object hierarchy list, as shown in Figure E-5.

   (continued)

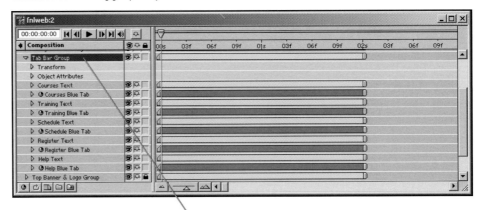

New object group

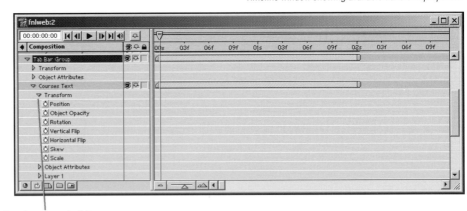

Transform property list

FIGURE E-6

Timeline window showing played animation

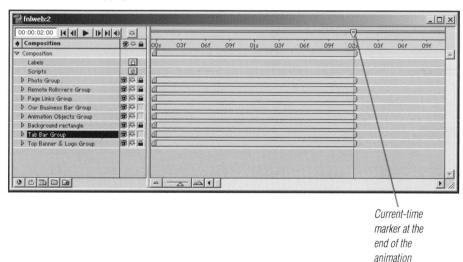

Current-time
marker at the
end of the
animation

6. Click the small triangle next to Transform, click the triangle next to Courses Text, then click the triangle next to Tab Bar Group to collapse all of the lists.

You grouped objects together and named the group. You then expanded and collapsed the property list for the Tab Bar Group object.

Play and rewind an animation

1. Click the Play/Pause button in the Timeline window, then watch the Composition window and the Timeline window. ▶

   The diamond object, which was previously animated, plays. Notice that the current-time marker is now at the end of the animation as shown in Figure E-6.

   TIP Move the Timeline window as necessary if it obstructs your view of the Composition window.

2. Click the Go to the first frame button to reset the current-time marker to the beginning of the animation. ◀

3. Save your work.

You played an animation and then reset it to the first frame.

WORK WITH KEYFRAMES

What You'll Do

 In this lesson, you'll place and move keyframes in the timeline.

Learning Keyframe Basics

To animate an object it usually takes at least two keyframes: one to begin the change of the object and the second to end the change of the object. At each keyframe specific properties of the object, such as object color, position, or opacity, change to produce the animation (the object changing over time, or from keyframe to keyframe). The keyframe also identifies the value of the property being changed, such as the color value, as well as the type of change (smooth or abrupt) between the keyframes. By default, LiveMotion adjusts the property value of an object at each regular animation frame in the timeline to create a smooth transition from one keyframe to another.

Working with Keyframes

You can create a keyframe for any object property at any time in the timeline. You can change one or more object properties at different times in the timeline by creating keyframes with different values for each of the properties. For example, you can move an object from one side of the composition to the other and change its

Reversing keyframes

Sometimes the property changes you have developed for an object would look better if they occurred in reverse order. For example, let's say that you animated an object to change its color from red to green and then move across the screen from right to left. By reversing the object's position keyframes you would cause the object to move across the screen in the opposite direction, from left to right, but the colors would still change from red to green. To reverse an object's individual keyframes you can drag the keyframes past each other. If you want to reverse an object's keyframes using its duration bar, press [Alt] (Win) or [Option] (Mac) and then drag one end of the duration bar past the other.

color and shape while the object is moving. Each object property in the object hierarchy list has a Stopwatch button next to it that you click to begin the process of animating that particular object property. Clicking the Stopwatch button for the object property places a starting keyframe in the timeline, which indicates when the animation begins for that object property. See Figure E-7. Once the stopwatch has been activated, a new keyframe is added to the timeline any-time you change the current time and prop-erty value for that object. After you set the starting keyframe for an object, move the current-time marker to a different position in the timeline and then change the value of the property to establish another keyframe. When you set different object property states at different keyframes, you are animating!

What's great about working with keyframes is that they can be managed much like other objects in LiveMotion. For instance, you can copy and paste keyframes to other locations in the timeline, duplicate keyframes within a property, move keyframes to different posi-tions in the timeline, or delete keyframes from the timeline.

QUICKTIP

If you adjust the duration bar of an object, its keyframes proportionally adjust automatically to match the new duration time.

Changing Keyframe Interpolation

In LiveMotion you have the ability to choose how an object transitions or blends between keyframes. See Table E-1 for a description of the different keyframes in LiveMotion. Keyframe **interpolation** deter-mines how an object changes between keyframes. Each keyframe has an interpola-tion method applied to it when it is created. For example, you can apply an interpolation setting that causes an object to accelerate from the first keyframe to the second keyframe and then quickly bounce and speed away after passing the third keyframe. When necessary, you can apply multiple interpolation methods to a keyframe for most object properties. There are five inter-polation methods to choose from: Linear, Auto Bezier, Hold Keyframe, Ease In, and Ease Out. The Linear interpolation method changes the object property value evenly

FIGURE E-7
New keyframe in timeline

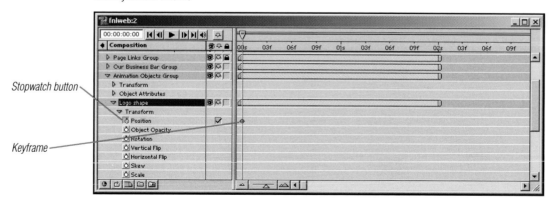

Stopwatch button

Keyframe

between keyframes. You would use this interpolation method when you want to create angled turns or sharp transitions, such as a ball bouncing off the floor. There is also the Auto Bezier interpolation method, the default method, which adjusts property values slowly to create a smooth or curved transition. This method is useful when you want to create a smooth animation movement, such as an object following a curved path. The Hold Keyframe method creates an abrupt change from one keyframe to another—in other words, there is no interpolation. An object using this interpolation method holds its property value until it reaches the next keyframe. This is useful when you want to create a dramatic animation, such as a burst or explosion. The Ease In interpolation method slows the rate at which the object property blends from one keyframe to the next. You would use this interpolation method when you want to illustrate an object slowing down, such as a car at a stop sign. The last interpolation

method, Ease Out, produces a slow property transition rate immediately following a keyframe and then gradually increases the transition rate to the next keyframe. This method could be used to show a car speeding up after having stopped at a stop sign. Now, not every object property has all five interpolation methods available for you to use. Some object properties, such as the Text property for a text object, are limited to one interpolation method: the Hold Keyframe interpolation method. Keep this in mind as you develop your animation.

Playing Animations

As you develop an animation you'll find that you will need to make constant adjustments to the object properties. Playing the animation repeatedly during its development is the best way to test the animation. Of the different ways to play an animation in LiveMotion, the playback buttons in the Timeline window are the easiest to use. The playback buttons are especially useful when

you are developing an animation because they provide a quick and easy way to preview your work. Starting at the current-time marker position the playback buttons allow you to play or pause the animation, move the animation forward or backward one frame at a time, or move to the first or last frame in the animation. Once you believe an animation is complete, you can test it in LiveMotion's Preview mode or a Web browser. Playing an animation in Preview mode gives you the best indication of how an animation will play in a Web browser because Preview mode executes any scripts or rollovers that might be present. When you are completely finished with your animation, you should test it in both Microsoft Internet Explorer and Netscape Navigator on both the Windows and Mac platforms. You should find that the features in LiveMotion make animating an object fairly simple, and with just a little experimentation you will be surprised at what you can create. This is where the real fun begins!

TABLE E-1: Keyframe Symbols	
symbol	**symbol description**
◈	Starting keyframe
◈	Ending keyframe
◁	Hold keyframe
▷	Ease In
◁	Ease Out
⚍	Both Ease In and Ease Out

Creating Animations and Exporting a Composition

Create a new keyframe

1. Click the triangle next to the Animation Objects Group object, click Ellipse, click the triangle next to Ellipse, then click the triangle next to Layer 1.

   The ellipse is selected in the composition and the Layer 1 properties available for the object are displayed in the Timeline window.

2. Click the Stopwatch next to Color in the object hierarchy list.

   A starting keyframe is placed in the timeline, as shown in Figure E-8.

3. Drag the current-time marker to the 2 second mark (02s) in the timeline, then click the empty check box in the keyframe column for the Color property row to place a new keyframe.

4. Click the Color palette tab if necessary, then click the white color cell at the far right of the color bar.

   Now when the animation plays, the color of the ellipse will steadily change between its starting blue color and white.

   (continued)

FIGURE E-8

Timeline window showing new keyframe

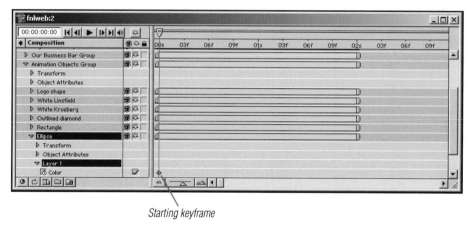

Starting keyframe

5. Click the right window scroll arrow once in the Timeline window, click the 03s mark in the timeline, then in the Color palette change the Red color value box to **120**, the Green color value box to **174**, and the Blue color value box to **206**.

Notice that the duration bars for all of the objects move to the 3 second mark. Now when you run the animation, the ellipse will change from blue to white and then back to blue again.

6. Click the Go to the first frame button, click the Play/Pause button, then watch the animation. ◄◄ ►

7. Drag the right edge of the Timeline window to increase the width of the window, click the Timeline window left scroll arrow and down scroll arrow if necessary, then compare your composition to Figure E-9.

You created two new keyframes for the ellipse object that change its color from blue to white and then back to blue, then played the animation.

FIGURE E-9
Timeline window

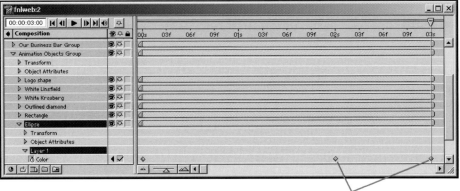

Additional keyframes

FIGURE E-10

Keyframe with changed interpolation

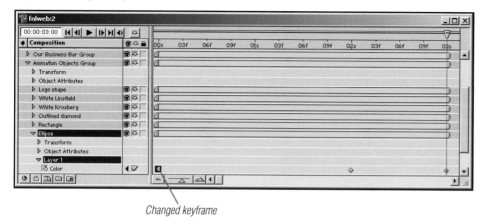

Changed keyframe

FIGURE E-11

Timeline window showing moved keyframe

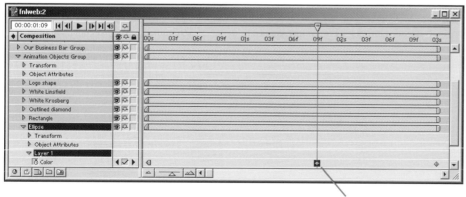

Dragged keyframe

Change keyframe interpolation

1. Click the starting keyframe (far left) for the ellipse object.

2. Click Timeline on the menu bar, then click Hold Keyframe.

   Notice that the keyframe in the timeline changes shape, as shown in Figure E-10, indicating that the interpolation method has changed.

3. Click the Play/Pause button, then watch the animation. ▶

   Notice that the ellipse color doesn't change color until the current-time marker reaches the second keyframe and then the color abruptly changes to white. Between the second and third keyframes, the color gradually changes back to blue.

You changed the interpolation method between two keyframes.

Move a keyframe

1. Drag the current-time marker to 02s in the timeline, then click the Go to the previous frame button three times until the current-time marker is over the 09f mark in the timeline. ◀|

2. Drag the second (middle) keyframe to the current-time marker.

   The keyframe moves in the timeline.

3. Save your work, then compare your screen to Figure E-11.

You moved the current-time marker and then moved a keyframe to the current-time marker.

CREATE MOTION

What You'll Do

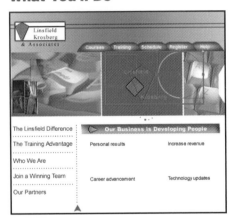

In this lesson, you will animate an object's position.

Putting Objects in Motion

When you change the position of an object in the timeline, LiveMotion creates a **motion path**, which is a visual representation of the path that the object follows during the animation. Figure E-12 shows an example of a motion path created in LiveMotion. The dots in the motion path represent the object's position at each frame of the animation. The squares in the motion path represent the object's position at keyframes. Since the frame rate of an animation is consistent through the whole animation, the greater the distance is between the dots and squares in a motion path, the faster the object moves along the motion path.

Editing Motion Paths

Once you create a motion path, you may want to change the path or edit the path by adding additional keyframes to it. A motion path can't be edited directly in the Composition window; however, you can edit it using one of three methods in the Timeline window. One way to edit a motion

Animating objects off the screen

You can set object properties of an object so that it travels off the screen during an animation. An object can be set to begin or end off the screen or simply travel off the screen during the animation. You accomplish this by changing the position of the object so that it exceeds the dimension of the composition. Simply enter X or Y values in the Transform palette that are larger than the composition, or just drag the object off the composition at a Position keyframe. It can be helpful to see beyond the borders of the Composition window when you are animating an object off the screen. In order to see beyond the borders of the Composition window, use the Zoom Out command on the View menu to decrease the size of the Composition window.

Creating Animations and Exporting a Composition

path is to change the position of the object at an existing Position keyframe. To change the motion path of an object at a Position keyframe, drag the current-time marker to the keyframe you want to change, then drag the object to a new location in the Composition window. You can also edit a motion path of an object by adding a new Position keyframe. Drag the current-time marker to the point in the timeline where you want the object to be in another place and then drag the object to a new location in the Composition window. Finally, you can edit a motion path by applying one of the interpolation methods, which changes the way the object moves in or out of keyframes. To apply an interpolation method to a keyframe, select one (or more) of the Position keyframes and then choose one of the interpolation methods from the Timeline menu. When you are done editing, the motion path reflects the changes.

QUICKTIP

You can right-click (Win) or press [control] and click (Mac) a Position keyframe in the Timeline window to display the five interpolation methods.

FIGURE E-12
Object motion path

Motion path

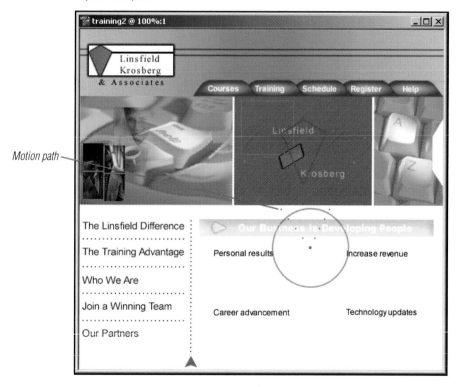

Add motion to an object

1. Click the triangle next to Layer 1 in the object hierarchy list, then click the triangle next to Transform.

2. Drag the current-time marker back to the beginning of the animation, then click the Stopwatch next to Position.

   This sets the starting point for the motion path of the ellipse.

3. Drag the current-time marker to the first occurrence of 09f (before 01s) in the timeline, then drag the ellipse in the Composition window below the textured blue rectangle as shown in Figure E-13.

   Notice the motion path (dotted line) that is created when you move the position of the ellipse object.

4. Click the Timeline window title bar, drag the current-time marker to the 06f mark after 01s in the timeline, then drag the ellipse object to the top left corner of the blue rectangle as shown in Figure E-14.

5. Click the Timeline window title bar, drag the current-time marker to the 06f mark after 02s in the timeline, then drag the ellipse object to the top right corner of the blue rectangle as shown in Figure E-15.

6. Save your work.

You animated the motion of the ellipse object to move to three spots in the composition.

FIGURE E-13
Ellipse moved to first point on motion path

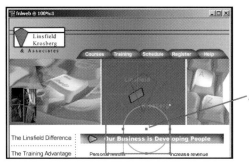

—Moved ellipse object

FIGURE E-14
Ellipse moved to second point on motion path

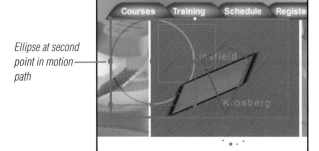

Ellipse at second point in motion—path

FIGURE E-15
Ellipse moved to third point on motion path

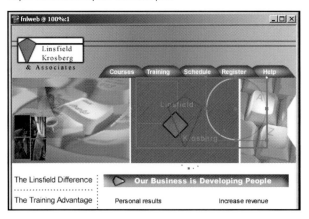

FIGURE E-16
Edited motion path

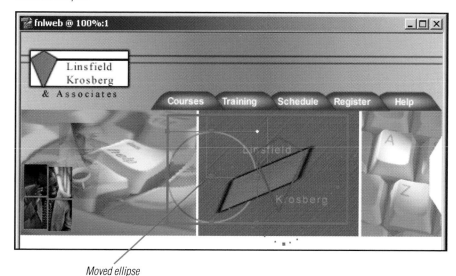

Moved ellipse

1. Click the Timeline window title bar, then drag the current-time marker to the previous keyframe in the timeline.

   Notice that the ellipse object moves backward in the animation.

2. Drag the ellipse to the middle left side of the blue rectangle as shown in Figure E-16.

3. Click the Timeline window title bar, click the current keyframe, click Timeline on the menu bar, then click Linear.

4. Drag the current-time marker to the previous keyframe in the timeline, then click the keyframe.

5. Click Timeline on the menu bar, then click Linear.

   The Linear interpolation method will create a sharp angled turn at each of these keyframes.

6. Click to collapse all of the Ellipse object's triangles.

7. Click the Go to the first frame button, click the Play/Pause button, then watch the animation in the Composition window.

8. Click the Go to the first frame button.

You edited the motion path for the ellipse object and changed the interpolation method for two keyframes.

ANIMATE OBJECT ATTRIBUTES

What You'll Do

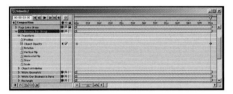

 In this lesson, you'll animate the properties of individual and grouped objects.

Animating Object Properties

In the Timeline window, LiveMotion splits up the attributes that you can animate into three categories: Transform, Object Attributes, and Layer. Each object in the object hierarchy list has a small arrow beside it, which you click to expand and thus reveal the attribute categories for that object. The Transform attributes include the following properties: Position, Object Opacity, Rotation, Vertical Flip, Horizontal Flip, Skew, and Scale, as shown in Figure E-17. Each of these individual properties modifies specific attributes of the object and is applied to the whole object. The Object Attributes include specific additional properties for the selected object type, such as font for a text object or shape for a geometric object. The properties in this category change depending on which object is selected in the composition. The Layer category lets you modify the properties of individual object layers. Properties that you can modify in this category include color, 3D effects, distortion effects, and gradients, to list just a few. The properties in this category vary depending on what modifications you have made to the object. For example, if you have added a texture or changed the tint of an object, those attributes would be available under the Layer attribute category. To animate the attributes of an object or an object layer, open the Timeline window, reveal the object property you wish to change, then move the current-time marker to where you want the property change to begin. Now, you are ready to change the individual property of the object by selecting the Stopwatch button and then changing the object's property using the appropriate LiveMotion palette.

QUICKTIP

When changing the color or hue of an object, you might consider changing one of the color's attributes instead of changing the whole color. Animating the color in this way produces a smooth color transition.

Animating Grouped Objects

When you have grouped objects, LiveMotion animates them in much the same way as it does individual objects. However, there are a few differences that you should be aware of before you decide to group objects together. When you group objects together, the available object properties that you would use to animate the grouped object are restricted to what can logically be applied to the group of objects as a whole. So, for example, you could change a grouped object's position, rotation, and opacity. It is possible to animate individual objects, group them together, and then animate the grouped object. If you group individual animated objects, the individual animations will run along with the grouped animation. For example, you could individually animate the properties of two geometric objects, group the objects together, and then animate the grouped object to move across the screen. Once you group objects together, they are no longer listed individually in the object hierarchy list, but are listed as subheadings beneath a grouped object heading. Grouping objects in the Timeline window, if you don't plan to animate the grouped object, is a great way to organize the Timeline window, especially when you have a complex composition.

FIGURE E-17
Timeline window displaying available object properties

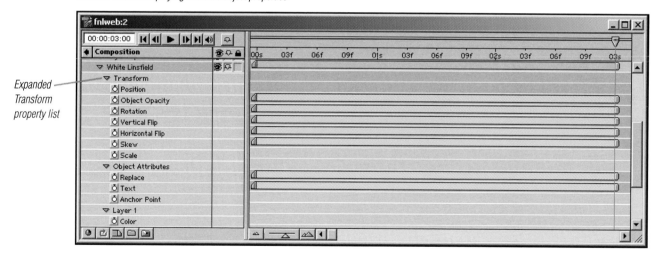

Expanded
Transform
property list

Animate Object Properties

1. Under the Animation Objects Group in the object hierarchy list, click Rectangle, click the triangle next to Rectangle, then click the triangle next to Object Attributes.

2. Drag the start point of the Rectangle object duration bar to the first 06f mark (before 01s) on the timeline, then click the Implicit/Explicit button in the Timeline window to deselect it.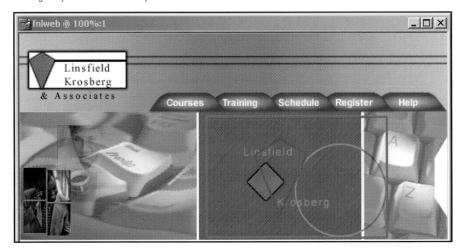

   Moving the start point of the object's duration bar adjusts when the object starts in the animation. With the current-time marker at the beginning of the animation, notice that (as shown in Figure E-18) the rectangle object no longer appears in the composition because the start point for the object is now later in the timeline.

3. Drag the current-time marker to the 06f mark in the timeline, then click the Stopwatch next to the Outline Width property.

   Now the rectangle animation will begin 6 frames after the start of the animation.

   (continued)

FIGURE E-18

Rectangle object not shown in composition

Creating Animations and Exporting a Composition

4. Drag the current-time marker to the 03f
mark after 01s in the timeline, then click the
Properties palette tab if necessary.

5. Drag the Width slider until 35 appears in the
text box.

6. Drag the current-time marker to the 06f
mark after 02s in the timeline, then drag the
Width slider in the Properties palette until 2
appears in the text box.

The width of the rectangle will now change
and then return to its original state as the
animation plays. Notice in Figure E-19 that
LiveMotion placed keyframes in the timeline
when you simply adjusted the width of the
rectangle at different points in the timeline.

7. Click the Go to the first frame button, click
the Play/Pause button, then watch the animation in the Composition window.

You animated the Outline Width attribute of the
rectangle object and then played the animation.

FIGURE E-19
Timeline window showing new keyframes

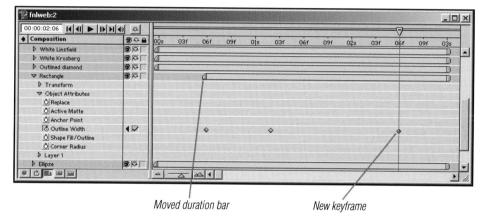

Moved duration bar   New keyframe

Animate Grouped Object Properties

1. Collapse the triangles for the rectangle object in the object hierarchy list, then click the triangle next to Our Business Bar Group.

2. Click the triangle next to Transform, click the Go to the first frame button, then click the Stopwatch next to Object Opacity, as shown in Figure E-20. ◄|

3. Click the Opacity palette tab, then drag the Object Opacity slider to the left until 0 appears in the text box.

   The object appears to disappear in the composition, which is how it will appear when the animation begins.

   (continued)

Timeline window showing the Object Opacity Stopwatch selected

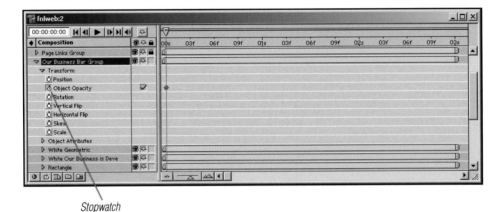

Stopwatch

Creating Animations and Exporting a Composition

FIGURE E-21

Timeline window showing new keyframes for grouped object

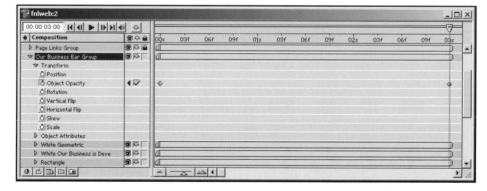

4. Drag the current-time marker to 03s on the timeline, then drag the Object Opacity slider in the Opacity palette to the right until 100 appears in the text box.

5. Click the Play/Pause button, watch the animation in the Composition window, then compare your Timeline window with Figure E-21. ▶

6. Collapse the triangles for Our Business Bar Group, click the Go to the first frame button, then save your work. ◄

You animated the opacity of a grouped object and then played the animation.

ANIMATE TEXT AND USE SOUNDS

What You'll Do

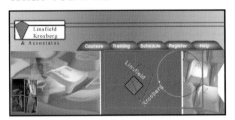

 In this lesson, you will animate text and use sound in an animation.

Animating Text

Using LiveMotion, you can create exciting animations with geometric and image objects, but you can also create striking animation effects with text objects. Because LiveMotion treats different types of objects in the same way, animating a text object is functionally no different than animating any other object. The primary difference between animating a text object and animating another type of object is the properties that are available for you to change. When animating a text object, a Text property option appears in the Object Attributes category on the object hierarchy list as shown in Figure E-22, which allows you to change any of the text properties on the

Properties palette. So, you can change such text attributes as font size, font type, leading, tracking, and alignment. Having the ability to change these properties along with other text object properties, such as color, opacity, position, and gradient, provides you with an array of options from which to choose to create dynamic text animation. Keep in mind as you plan your text animation that some Text property changes are limited to the Hold Keyframe interpolation method. This interpolation type, as you remember, does not produce property transition stages between keyframes, so each property transition happens abruptly at its corresponding keyframe.

Looping sounds

After you apply a sound to a composition, you can modify the sound object so that it loops repeatedly. To loop a sound you can either drag the end handle of the sound duration bar to the point where you want the sound to repeat or you can make the sound a movie clip and then click the Loop button at the bottom of the Timeline window.

Animating with Sound

As you develop your animation, you might consider adding sound to it. Maybe there is a specific sound related to your company, product, or service that is appropriate to use on the Web page. Sounds can be used in a variety of ways to draw a user's attention to a specific area of the Web page or just to enhance a user's experience at the Web page. The ability to use sound on a Web page is great and can add a new dimension to the content; however, be careful what kind of sounds you use and how many sounds you use. Sounds can be fun and entertaining, but they can also be annoying for the user, especially sounds the user has no control over.

There are two types of sounds used on the Internet today: event sound and streaming sound. **Event sound** is sound that needs to be downloaded completely before it can play. You generally use this type of sound when you are playing a short or small sound file or a sound file that continually repeats itself, such as background music on a particular Web page. **Streaming sound**, on the other hand, is a sound that can play while it is being downloaded. This type of sound is useful when you have a very long sound or large sound file. You would also use streaming sound when you need to synchronize a sound with a specific frame in an animation. As you work with sound there are some considerations that you need to keep in mind. One is the size of the sound

file you decide to use. Large file sizes can severely decrease the performance of your Web site, so it's a good idea to limit sound files to 16-bit sound. (16-bit sound will generally give you the best sound quality for the smallest file size.) Also, if you are planning to export the sound in a Macromedia Flash (SWF) file, the Flash player plays the sound independently from other elements unless you use streaming sound. LiveMotion supports the following sound file formats: .aif; .av; QuickTime; and .wav.

QUICKTIP

One major difference between a looped event sound and a looped streaming sound is that the overall file size of the looped streaming sound increases with each sound loop.

FIGURE E-22
Timeline window showing Text property

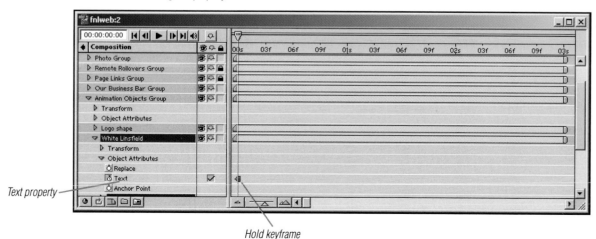

Text property

Hold keyframe

Applying Sounds to an Animation

So how exactly do you work with sounds in LiveMotion? Well, sounds in LiveMotion, except for those triggered by rollovers or manipulated by scripts, exist in the timeline as shown in Figure E-23. When you add a sound to a composition, it appears as a separate object in the timeline. Depending on what your needs are you can add sounds to a composition timeline or to a movie clip timeline. Sounds can be added using the Place command on the File menu, the Sounds palette, or by dragging the sound to a timeline. As with any other object that

you animate in LiveMotion, before you apply a sound to a timeline, you need first to move the current-time marker to the time at which you want the sound to play. Once you have moved the current-time marker, you can add the sound to the timeline and then modify the sound's properties if necessary.

Working with Sound Properties

Every sound that you add to a composition has two object properties that can be modified or animated. When you click the triangle next to a sound to expand its properties list, you'll find these two properties under

Object Attributes: pan and volume, as shown in Figure E-24. When the sound object is selected either of these property values can be changed using the Properties palette. The pan sound property simply shifts the audio signal between the left and right channels (or speakers) and the volume property controls how loud or soft the sound plays. You can set these properties so they are constant or you can animate them to change as the sound plays. Like animating other object properties, you place keyframes in the timeline and then change the sound property value at each keyframe as necessary to achieve the effect

FIGURE E-23
Timeline window showing added sound

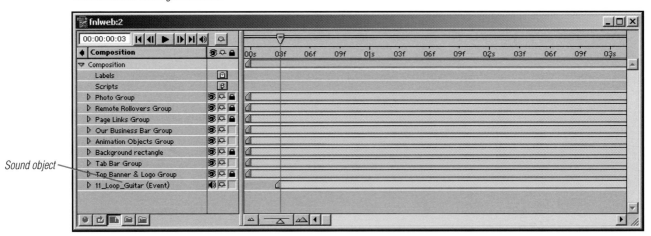

you want. Now, depending on what you want the sound to do in the animation, you might need to change the sound type in the Properties palette. If you click the Sound Type list arrow in the palette, you'll reveal three sound types: Event Sound, Solo Event Sound, or Streaming Sound.

You have already learned about the two basic sound types Event Sound and Streaming Sound; however, LiveMotion includes an additional sound type option, the Solo Event Sound, which is used in specific instances. The Solo Event Sound, which is actually an Event Sound, stops the

playing of additional instances of the sound once the sound has been played completely. In other words, this sound type prevents a sound from being played multiple times even if a button is continually clicked, for example.

FIGURE E-24

Timeline window showing Text property

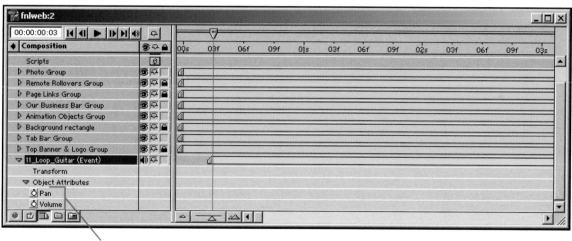

Sound properties

Animate text

1. Click White Linsfield in the Animation Objects Group in the object hierarchy list, click the triangle next to White Linsfield, then click the triangle next to Transform.

2. Click the Stopwatch next to Object Opacity, drag the current-time marker to 01s, click the Opacity palette tab if necessary, then drag the Object Opacity slider to 75.

   The opacity of the text object will change from 40 to 75 during this part of the animation.

3. Drag the current-time marker to the 06f mark after 01s, click the Stopwatch next to Rotation, then drag the current-time marker to 03s.

4. Click the empty check box in the keyframe column for the Rotation property, click the Transform palette tab, select the number in the Rotation text box, type **320**, then press [Enter] (Win) or [return] (Mac).

5. Click the empty check box in the keyframe column for the Object Opacity property, then drag the Object Opacity slider to the right until 100 appears in the text box.

   You have now changed the opacity of the text object from 40 to 100 and you have rotated the text object 320 degrees, as shown in Figure E-25.

6. Press [Shift], click all of the keyframes you just added to the White Linsfield object, click Edit on the menu bar, then click Copy.

(continued)

FIGURE E-25
Timeline window showing keyframes for text object

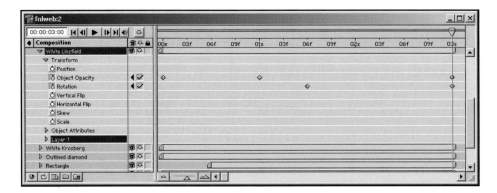

FIGURE E-26

Composition window showing the end of the animation

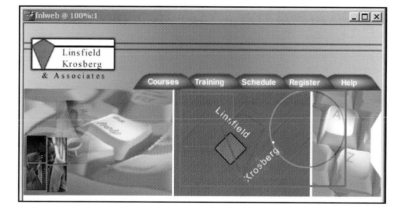

7. Click White Krosberg in the object hierarchy list, click the triangle next to White Krosberg, click the triangle next to Transform, click the Go to the first frame button, click Edit on the menu bar, then click Paste. ◄|

   All of the keyframes you created for the White Linsfield object are now applied to the White Krosberg object and appear in the timeline at the same frames.

8. Drag the current-time marker to 03s, select the number in the Rotation text box in the Transform palette, type **-315**, then press [Enter] (Win) or [return] (Mac).

9. Save your work, click the Play/Pause button, then compare your composition to Figure E-26. ▶

You animated one text object by changing its opacity and rotation, cut and pasted the object's animation attributes to another text object, then changed the rotation property of the second text object.

Add a sound to an animation

1. Collapse all of the triangles in the object hierarchy list, except the Composition triangle.

2. Click the Sounds palette tab, click the 11_Loop_Guitar sound in the list, then click the Play Sound button to preview the sound. ▶

3. Click Composition in the object hierarchy list, drag the current-time marker to 03f (before 01s) in the timeline, then click the Apply Sound button in the Sound palette.

   The sound object appears at the bottom of the object hierarchy list, as shown in Figure E-27.

4. Click the Go to the first frame button, click the Play/Pause button, then watch and listen to the animation. |◀ ▶

   Notice that the overall animation length and all of the objects' duration bars are now at just below five seconds due to the length of the sound.

5. Click the Go to the first frame button, then save your work. |◀

You added a sound to the animation, and then played the animation.

FIGURE E-27
Timeline window showing new sound object

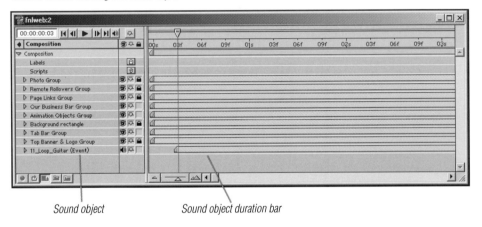

Sound object   *Sound object duration bar*

FIGURE E-28

Timeline window showing volume keyframe

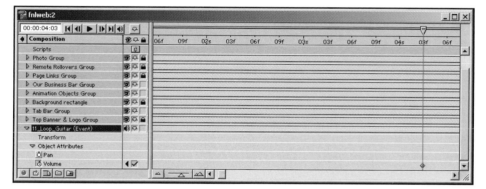

1. Click the sound object, 11_Loop_Guitar (Event), in the object hierarchy list, then drag the current-time marker to 03f (before 01s) in the timeline.

2. Click the triangle next to 11_Loop_Guitar (Event), then click the triangle next to Object Attributes.

3. Click the Stopwatch next to Volume, drag the current-time marker to 03f past 04s in the timeline, then click the empty check box in the keyframe column as shown in Figure E-28.

4. Click the Properties palette tab, then drag the Volume slider to the left until 0 appears in the text box.

   The sound will now start at full volume at the beginning of the animation and then fade to no sound near the end of the animation.

5. Click the Go to the first frame button, click the Play/Pause button, then watch and listen to the animation. ▐◀ ▶

6. Click the Go to the first frame button, collapse the sound object triangles in the object hierarchy list, then save your work. ▐◀

7. Click Timeline on the menu bar, then click Timeline/Composition Window.

You modified the volume of the sound to play at full volume at the beginning of the animation and then fade out completely by the end of the animation.

EXPORT A COMPOSITION

What You'll Do

 In this lesson, you'll optimize and export a LiveMotion composition.

Exporting Basics

Once you have completed all of the work on your composition, you are ready to export it to a Web page design program like Adobe GoLive for further Web page development. **Exporting** is the process of saving a composition in a different file format to be used by another program. This final step of optimizing and exporting your LiveMotion composition is critical to creating a high-quality Web page that loads quickly and runs smoothly. **Optimization** is the process of reducing a composition's file size while maintaining visual quality. You optimize a composition by modifying the settings in the Export palette shown in Figure E-29. The Export palette allows you to choose a specific export method, or file type, and any number of specialized settings. In LiveMotion you have different exporting options from which to choose, including Macromedia Flash (SWF) and QuickTime.

Understanding File Types

Since Web browsers can't read native LiveMotion files, you need to convert the composition into a file that Web browsers can read. This process exports the native LiveMotion composition file (.liv) into one of ten file formats: Macromedia Flash (SWF); AutoLayout; Live Tab; GIF; Animated GIF; QuickTime Video; JPEG; Photoshop; PNG-Indexed; and PNG-Truecolor. The format you choose depends on the characteristics and purpose of the composition, so let's spend a little time getting to know the different file types. The Macromedia Flash (SWF) file format is used to export animated compositions. In order to see this animation in a browser, a user needs the Flash plug-in player, which can be downloaded from the Macromedia Web site. The SWF file format saves the information in your composition as vector images, so it is a good choice if your animation has elements with solid colors and defined edges. There are a couple of things to consider when you export to an SWF file—such as that objects with more than one layer cannot be exported as vector objects and LiveMotion must reference a bitmap file to recognize these objects, which increases the file size. All non-vector objects are converted to JPEG, GIF, or PNG and embedded in the SWF file. The AutoLayout file format actually slices the composition into pieces and makes a separate image file for each object or group of objects. Any background color or texture that is applied to the composition is preserved in the individual object files. Overlapping or grouped objects are exported as a single object and rollover objects become their own slice. The Live Tab format saves the composition as a Live Tab, which is basically a predefined animation that you can then load into another composition. The GIF format is a good format to use when your composition is composed of text, line art, logos, or illustrations that have solid colors and sharp details. GIF limits the number of colors that are used in the file by supporting 8-bit indexed color for a display of up to 256 colors. Thus, image objects that are created using more than 256 colors will probably appear degraded on the Web. The Animated GIF format uses the same export criteria as GIF; however, instead of exporting the current frame in the composition like a GIF, it exports the animation frames as an animated sequence. The QuickTime Video format is the standard Apple multimedia file format. You can use this format for movies, animation, sound, and text on the Web. The JPEG format is designed for use with bitmap image objects. JPEG uses 24-bit color and preserves the color in photographs.

FIGURE E-29
Export palette

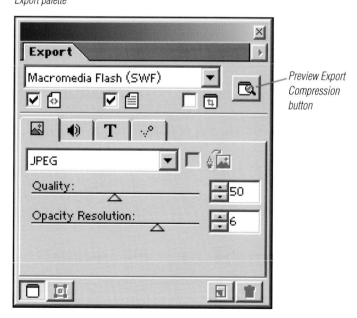

Preview Export Compression button

The JPEG format does not support animation. The Photoshop file format exports a flattened image of the composition to the Adobe Photoshop format. This format is useful when you want to open the file in Photoshop, Adobe ImageReady, or Adobe Illustrator. The PNG-Indexed file format supports 8-bit indexed color. This format is good for exporting compositions with areas of solid color and text. LiveMotion uses the composition's alpha channel or active matte information to create a file with one level of transparency. This format does not support animation. The PNG-Truecolor format supports 24-bit color and preserves the wide range of tone and color in photographs. Like PNG-Indexed, PNG-Truecolor exports files with one level of transparency. PNG-Truecolor exports small bitmaps very well.

Previewing and Exporting a Composition

Before you export your composition, you should preview the effects of the current export settings on the composition. With the Preview Export Compression button selected in the Export palette, the composition file size and the size of any selected object appear in the bottom left of the Status bar (Win) or the Composition window (Mac). To see the size of your composition using other export options, simply change the option and LiveMotion updates the file size data automatically.

Once you have verified all of your export settings, you are ready to preview the composition. You should always preview your composition in both computer platform environments (Win and Mac) before you export it. You can use the Preview mode in LiveMotion, or you can select the Preview In command on the File menu and preview the composition in a Web browser. Previewing a composition in a Web browser using the Preview In command is the best way to see how it will appear in that browser. After you set the export settings in the Export palette and preview the composition, you are ready to export it. You can export parts of a composition or an entire composition, depending on your needs. Depending on which export format you choose, LiveMotion creates one or more files when you export a composition. For example, when you export a composition as a SWF file, LiveMotion creates an HTML file, which allows a Web browser to view your composition; an HTML export report file (identified by a capital R at the end of the file name), which provides details on the composition, including estimated download times, number of keyframes, and file size; and a Shockwave Flash object file, which holds the animation information for the composition.

FIGURE E-30

Export palette

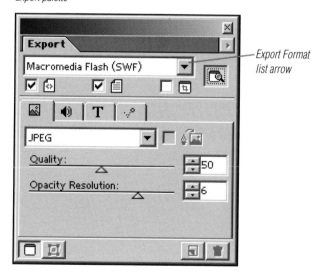

Export Format
list arrow

1. Click File on the menu bar, then click Export Settings.

2. Click the Preview Export Compression button. 🔍

   LiveMotion displays the file size of the composition in the lower left corner of the Status bar (Win) or the Composition window (Mac), which is the approximate size of the composition file with the current export settings.

3. Click the Export Format list arrow, then click AutoLayout.

   Notice the change in the file size display at the bottom of the screen with the current export format. LiveMotion will display an approximate file size each time you select a different export file setting in the Export palette.

4. Click the Export Format list arrow, then click Macromedia Flash (SWF). Compare your Export palette to Figure E-30.

You previewed the composition file size using two different export file types.

Preview a composition in a Web browser

1. Click File on the menu bar, point to Preview In, then click Internet Explorer.

   LiveMotion generates a Macromedia Flash preview file and opens it up in Internet Explorer, as shown in Figure E-31. The animation plays immediately when the browser window opens.

   TIP If the Internet Explorer browser does not appear in the Preview In submenu, use another browser.

2. Move the mouse over all of the rollovers.

3. Click the browser window close button when you are finished previewing the composition.

4. Click Window on the menu bar, click Export to close the Export palette, then save your work.

You previewed the composition in a Web browser.

FIGURE E-31

Composition in Internet Explorer Web browser

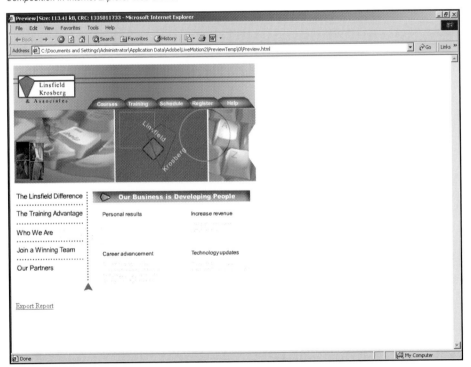

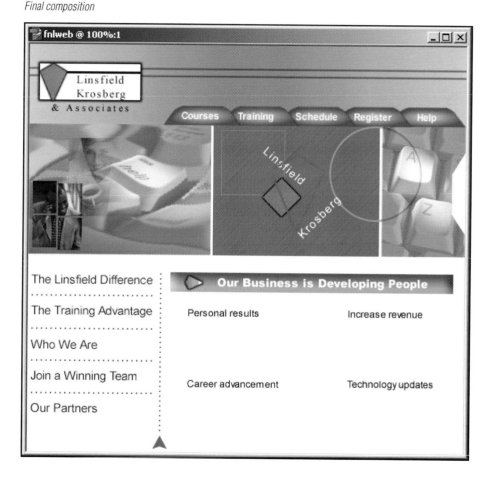

Export and view a composition

1. Click File on the menu bar, then click Export.

2. In the drive and folder where you are storing your work for this section, select the name in the File Name text box, type **fnlweb1**, then click Save.

   LiveMotion exports your composition as a Macromedia Flash file and saves it in the drive and folder you indicated.

3. Open Internet Explorer (or your Web browser), click File on the menu bar, then click Open (Win) or Open File (Mac).

4. Browse to fnlweb1 in your data files, click fnlweb1, click Open, then click OK.

   Your composition opens in your Web browser and the animation in the composition immediately plays.

5. Click the Close button in the browser window, click the Timeline window title bar if necessary, click the Play/Pause button in the Timeline window, then click the Composition window title bar. ▶

6. Save your work, then compare your composition to Figure E-32.

7. Close your composition file.

You exported your composition file, and then viewed the exported Flash file in a Web browser.

You work for an Internet multimedia company, World Media, that is bringing major motion pictures from all of the major studios in Hollywood to the Internet. Part of your job as this project unfolds is to produce a simple Web animation that a test group will use to interact with the new online movie product. You have put together a very simple Web page and now you need to animate some of the elements.

1. Open the file LME-3, then save it as **movie1**.
2. Open the Timeline window if necessary, click the White object in the object hierarchy list, then rename it **Title Group**.
3. Select all of the White Ellipse objects in the object hierarchy list, group the objects, then rename the group **Ellipse Object Group**.
4. Animate the Moving Ball object in the object hierarchy list so that it moves to the edge of the movie reel object and then down the line between the ellipses and the text objects, stopping finally just below the line. Make the total animation 3 seconds long.
5. Animate the individual text objects in Text Link Group so that each text object changes color from black to white and to a new font size of 18 when the Moving Ball object passes by it in the animation. (*Hint*: you'll need to change the interpolation of a Color keyframe to prevent the color change until the Moving Ball object passes the text object.)

6. Animate the individual white ellipse objects in Ellipse Object Group so that the lighting angle on the 3D palette changes to -45 when the Moving Ball object passes by it in the animation. (*Hint*: change the Effect Angle property under Layer 1 for each ellipse object and use a Hold keyframe so the effect happens when the Moving Ball object reaches the ellipse and not before.)

FIGURE E-33
Completed Project 1

7. Export the composition as a Macromedia Flash (SWF) file, save the file as **moviewb**, then watch the animation in your browser.
8. Save the file, then compare your screen to Figure E-33.

You work for Corporate World, a company that specializes in developing corporate identities, logos, and product branding. One of your jobs is to maintain the company Web site and update the site with new features, information, and design. You have been working on a Web page design and now you are ready to add some animation to the page and export it to be used on the Web. Using the skills you have learned so far, add animation to the composition, then export it.

1. Open the file LME-4, then save it as **worldfnl**.
2. Click the Ellipse object in the object hierarchy list, then change its name to **Fisheye Ellipse**.
3. Select all of the White Ellipse objects in the object hierarchy list, group them together, then rename the group White Ellipse Group.
4. Animate the Fisheye Ellipse object so that it travels down the arc line in 3 seconds, stopping at the bottom with the ellipse over the last part of the line. (*Hint*: you'll need to create quite a few keyframes along the arc in order for the ellipse to follow the arc.)
5. Animate the Business Text 1 and Business Text 2 objects so that they change color during the animation. Change the Business Text 1 object to from black to red and then black again. Change the Business Text 2 object from black to dark green to black again.
6. Play the animation.

7. Export the composition as a Macromedia Flash (SWF) file, save the file as **worldwb**, then watch the animation in Internet Explorer (or other Web browser).

FIGURE E-34
Completed Project 2

8. Save the file, then compare your screen to Figure E-34.

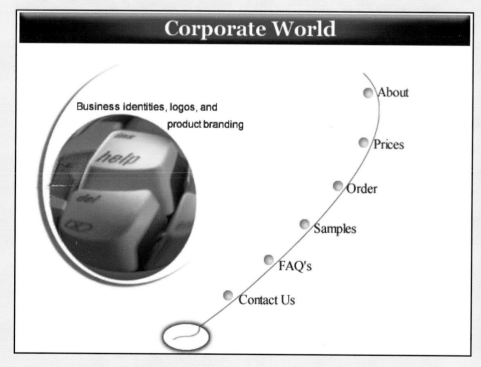

SECTION A

INTEGRATING PHOTOSHOP LIVEMOTION, AND GOLIVE

1. Understand Adobe program integration.

2. Add a Photoshop file to a GoLive page.

3. Animate Photoshop layers in LiveMotion.

4. Add a LiveMotion file to a GoLive page.

5. Create and modify a Web Photo Gallery.

SECTION A
INTEGRATING PHOTOSHOP, LIVEMOTION, AND GOLIVE

Taking Advantage of the Adobe Web Collection

The Adobe Web Collection is a powerful collection of software programs that provides everything you need to express your imagination on the Web: Photoshop offers a wide range of sophisticated tools for image editing; LiveMotion simplifies image animation with a straight-forward interface; and GoLive manages Web site content dependably and easily. As you have probably realized by now, once you've learned how to use any one of these programs, learning other Adobe programs is easier. The similar interfaces enable you to focus on learning program features, rather than focusing on where to find things on the interface.

Using Adobe Web Collection Programs Together

Once you have developed skills in each of these three programs, integrating those skills by using the programs together becomes a great way to create and publish robust sites on the Web. You can create and modify photo images and text in Photoshop, then use ImageReady to add elements for Web functionality, such as button styles and rollover effects, and to embed optimization settings within the file. You can add these files directly to a Web page using GoLive, and GoLive will automatically create the compressed files for the Web page and include any subsequent changes you make to the Photoshop files. You can create an entire Web site of images using Photoshop templates, and modify the templates in GoLive. You can place a layered Photoshop file in LiveMotion, then animate each layer as an object in a composition. Placing a LiveMotion file in a GoLive page generates a Flash file that will be automatically updated upon subsequent modifications. Because you can add a Photoshop or LiveMotion file to a GoLive Web page in its original format, using the three programs together helps you manage the multitude of files involved in creating a Web site. You maintain the source images, and GoLive converts them for the Web.

Tools You'll Use

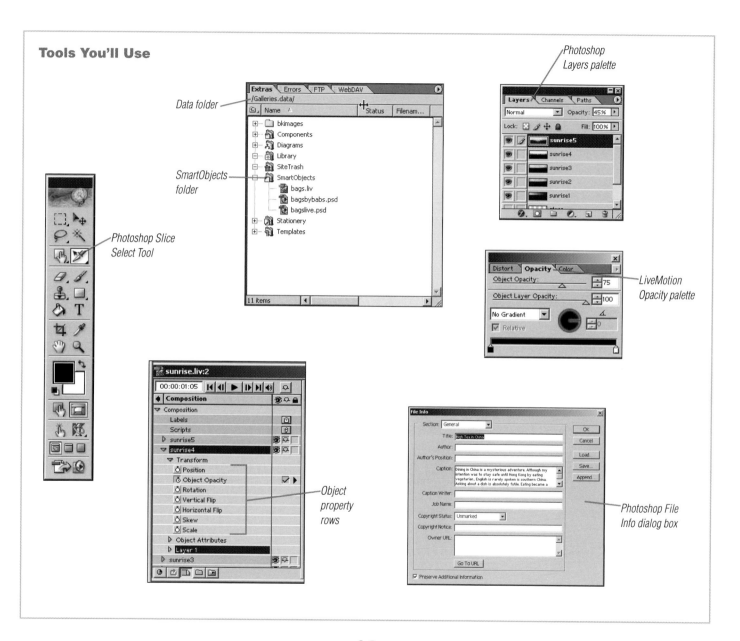

Data folder

SmartObjects folder

Photoshop Slice Select Tool

Photoshop Layers palette

LiveMotion Opacity palette

Object property rows

Photoshop File Info dialog box

UNDERSTAND ADOBE PROGRAM INTEGRATION

What You'll Do

In this lesson, you'll compare features of the Adobe Web Collection programs.

Integrating Photoshop, LiveMotion, and GoLive

Adobe Photoshop, LiveMotion, and GoLive, when used together, enable you to create images and image behaviors and assemble them into a Web page layout easily. Although each program is designed for a different purpose, the programs do have some overlapping features, as described in Table A-1. Not everyone will use all three programs together. If you have access to all three programs, you may find that you prefer creating certain design elements in one program over another based on the differences in program features or methods. If appropriate, the recommended program to use for a particular feature is indicated by a checkmark in Table A-1. However, because each Web site design element is different (as are the designers creating them), your preferences will develop with experience.

If you are using more than one program, embedding information in a source file,

the original file, simplifies file maintenance, because Adobe programs preserve information contained in a file imported from another Adobe program. Generally, if you are using an image in all three Adobe programs, your development of the image will progress from left to right in Table A-1. For instance, you might create a file in Photoshop, modify it in LiveMotion, then add it to a page in GoLive. Or, you might create a file in Photoshop, add it to a page in GoLive, then modify it's text in GoLive using variables. When possible, embedding information in a file using the features in the program used earliest in the process will simplify file maintenance. For example, by defining the optimization settings for a file in ImageReady, or loop properties in LiveMotion, you can use the file in multiple GoLive pages without having to define the settings each time you add the file to a page or update the original file.

TABLE A-1: Feature comparison

Feature	Photoshop/ImageReady	LiveMotion	GoLive
Create vector images	Text (vector images rasterized on save)	✓Geometric, text, and image objects	Convert text to image using presets only
Photo editing	✓Filters (14 categories), crop, transform, opacity, layer styles, color correction, masking, clipping, paths, channels	Opacity, color adjustments, and filters	Crop and opacity (tracing images)
Create animations	Yes (ImageReady)	✓Yes (including Scripts, Movie clips)	Macros, actions, and limited edit only: SWF (quality, loop, scale); QuickTime (full editing, apply controls); RealPlayer (apply controls)
Sound	Annotations	✓WAV, AIFF, AVI, MPEG, MP3 (embed only, no editing)	No
Create slices	✓Layer slices, user guide slices, draw a custom slice	No	Imported from Photoshop or ImageReady as images
Create links	Slice URL (absolute)	Object URL (absolute)	✓Image/Text URL (absolute); Image/Text Point and Shoot (relative with maintenance)
Image maps	Yes (ImageReady)	Yes	Yes
Rollovers	Yes (ImageReady)	Yes	Yes
Rollover Alt text (Win only)	Slice Message text	Object Alt text	Inspector Alt Text
Remote rollovers	Layer visibility applied to rollover state (ImageReady)	Remote rollover; animated rollover, scripting	Show/Hide Action; import Photoshop layers as floating boxes
GoLive Smart Object format	GIF or JPG	SWF	N/A
GoLive Smart Object variables	Text, optimization, matte	Matte; replacement tags: link, target, font, font size, tracking and leading, color, style, texture	Photoshop: crop, opacity (tracing image); LiveMotion: text (convert text to banner)
Web optimization	Per slice: Optimization palette (ImageReady)	Per object (or group of touching/overlapping objects); per file (Export settings)	Per slice or file (Save for Web dialog box)
Web output formats	GIF, JPG, animated GIF, QuickTime, html (Web Photo Gallery), PNG	GIF, JPG, animated GIF, QuickTime, html, SWF, PNG	GIF, JPG, Animated GIF, Quicktime, html, SWF, PNG, SVG, Realmedia, ACTION, ASA, ASP, CFM, CHTML, CSML, DWT, HTT, HTX, IHTML, JSP, LASSO, LBI, PHP, SSI, XHTML

ADD A PHOTOSHOP FILE
TO A GOLIVE PAGE

What You'll Do

In this lesson, you'll add a Photoshop file to a GoLive page as a Smart Object.

Adding a Sliced File to a GoLive Page

A Photoshop image can be sliced into rectangular areas that can each be individually optimized and linked for use on the Web. A sliced Photoshop image is added to a GoLive page as a Smart Object. GoLive saves each slice of the Smart Object as a separate Web-ready image and arranges these images in an invisible table to resemble the original single image. Each slice can be selected and linked within GoLive, or the original image can be opened in Photoshop from the GoLive site window for modifications.

The topmost text layer in a Photoshop Smart Object is variable. This text can be modified within GoLive, and the color, font, and other text formatting originally applied in Photoshop will be maintained. This is especially useful for using a single image to create multiple buttons.

Optimizing Slices for the Web

ImageReady allows you to embed Web optimization settings in slices. For example, if you are using a combination of photographs and graphic elements, you can specify a different file format (JPEG or GIF) for each slice. This enables you to optimize your images for the best quality display and download speeds on the Web. It is useful to embed optimization settings, because doing so means that optimization doesn't need to be reset each time an image is added to a GoLive Web page or updated. When you add a Photoshop file to a GoLive page, the Save for Web dialog box opens regardless of embedded optimization settings; in this dialog box, you can specify, or change, the settings for each slice.

Organizing Smart Objects with GoLive

It is important to keep the Smart Object source files you use in a Web site in an easily accessible place. Photoshop files that you add to a GoLive site must be stored in the site's project folder. By storing Photoshop files in this folder, you maintain the relationship between the Photoshop file and its Web-ready target files. More specifically, it is also useful to store the files in the site's data folder (within the project folder); doing so helps you manage and find these files easily for updates. In addition, using the GoLive site window, you can open the original files in Photoshop from the data folder for modifications.

When you are working with sliced Photoshop Smart Objects, the contents of your site expand when you add the files to your GoLive site. Adding a sliced Photoshop file to a page in GoLive adds a folder to your site window, which uses the file's name followed by ".data_." This folder contains an HTML page, a document used by the Save for Web process for assembling slices, and an image folder that contains the Web-ready image files created by GoLive for each slice. Photoshop files that have rollovers applied to slices in ImageReady create a multitude of images, name the images effectively, and store them all in the ".data_" image folder in the site window.

QUICKTIP

The naming conventions for rollover images in Photoshop Smart Objects are different than those used in GoLive; thus the Inspector does not display rollover states for Smart Objects. Any modifications that need to be made to rollovers created in ImageReady must be made in ImageReady.

Linking Slices
It is possible to embed URLs for links and other link information in a Photoshop slice

Photoshop images as GoLive rollovers

You can create rollovers in ImageReady, LiveMotion, or GoLive. If you create rollovers in GoLive, you can simplify the process using Photoshop Smart Object variable text. For instance, suppose that you needed to create three identical buttons, each with a different button label, and each with three rollover states. First, in Photoshop, create one image for each button state, using the filename suffixes _base, _over, and _down to indicate the state. Next, add a button label to the top layer of each image, using the longest label (to be sure it fits). Then, save the three images in the SmartObjects folder in the data folder for your GoLive site.

In GoLive, add each button state image to a GoLive Component. As you add these .psd files, GoLive will create a target file for each. Save these target files to a new folder within your GoLive site folder, possibly one called "rollovers." Add all three button state images to the Component again, changing the variable text of the button label and target filename for each button when saving each target file to the same rollover folder. Repeat this process until you have created all of the buttons that you need in the Component. Lastly, delete all of the buttons except the _base images from the Component. (You can do this because you added the _over and _down state images to the Component only to create the target files in the folder. These target files will automatically be applied to the states implied in their suffixes by GoLive.) Finally, add the Component to the appropriate pages.

by double-clicking on the slice in Photoshop, then using the Slice Options dialog box (as shown in Figure A-1) to enter an absolute address for a link. External links embedded using Photoshop will be maintained if the file is added to a Web page. However, if you are using a Photoshop Smart Object in GoLive, it is strongly recommended that you create

internal links from the object using GoLive. The paths between links in a site are critical for that site's functioning and efficient maintenance, and maintaining absolute paths for internal links can become complex over the life of the site. The site window in GoLive simplifies the task of creating and maintaining links to pages within a site.

To add internal links to a sliced image, create the sliced image in Photoshop, save the file to the SmartObjects folder in your GoLive site, add the Smart Object to a page, then link the slices to other pages in the site within GoLive.

FIGURE A-1
Photoshop slice options dialog box

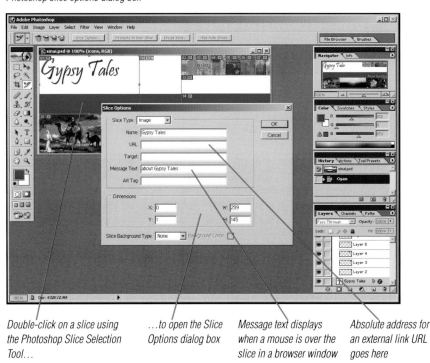

Double-click on a slice using the Photoshop Slice Selection Tool…

…to open the Slice Options dialog box

Message text displays when a mouse is over the slice in a browser window

Absolute address for an external link URL goes here

FIGURE A-2
Sliced image in ImageReady

Slice Select tool

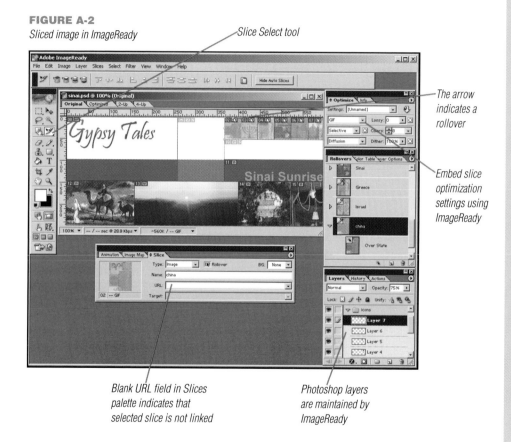

The arrow indicates a rollover

Embed slice optimization settings using ImageReady

Blank URL field in Slices palette indicates that selected slice is not linked

Photoshop layers are maintained by ImageReady

Modify a sliced Photoshop file in ImageReady

1. Open GoLive, create a new, single user, blank site named **GypsyTales,** then save the site to the drive and folder where you are storing your work for this section.

2. Using your file management tool, navigate to the drive and folder where your data files are stored, copy the contents of the SiteIntA-1 folder into the GypsyTales.data folder (in the "GypsyTales folder" folder), then click Yes (Win) or Replace (Mac) to replace the SmartObjects folder.

   The SmartObjects folder from the SiteIntA-1 folder will replace the empty SmartObjects folder created with the GypsyTales site.

3. Open ImageReady, then open sinai.psd from the GypsyTales.data/SmartObjects folder.

4. Click the Slice Select Tool to show the numbered slices in the file as shown in Figure A-2, then click on slice 02 in the upper-right area of the image.

   > TIP If the Slice Select Tool does not appear in your toolbar, click and hold the mouse button down on the Slice Tool until a short menu appears next to the tool, then click the Slice Select Tool on the menu.

5. In the Optimize palette, set the file format to JPEG and the Quality to 50.

   The opacity of the rollover states for this image is automatically updated.

6. Save and close the file.

You viewed a sliced file in ImageReady.

Add an ImageReady Smart Object to a GoLive page

1. In GoLive, add a new page to the GypsyTales site, then save the page as **sinai.html** in the GypsyTales site folder.

2. Arrange your workspace so you can see both the site window and the sinai.html window.

3. In the site window, click the double-arrow in the bottom right corner to view site Extras, then expand the SmartObjects folder and refresh the window.

4. Drag the sinai.psd file to sinai.html, then click OK in the Variables Settings dialog box to accept no variable changes.

5. In the Save For Web dialog box, click on slice 02 using the Slice Select Tool.

   Note that the optimization settings are preserved from ImageReady, as shown in Figure A-3.

   TIP If you don't see the slices, click the Toggle Slices Visibility button.

6. Click Save.

7. Click Save again to accept the name sinai.data and the GypsyTales site folder location for sinai.data.

   Sinai.data is a folder that will contain your Save for Web settings and a target Web-ready image for each slice in the source image.

You added a Photoshop file to a page in GoLive, maintaining the optimization settings preset in ImageReady.

FIGURE A-3
Save for Web dialog box

Slice Select Tool

Toggle Slices Visibility button

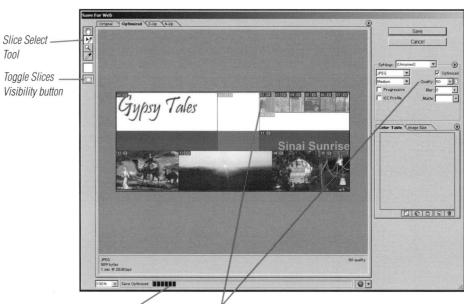

Saving each slice as an optimized image may take a few minutes

Slice optimization settings in ImageReady are maintained; they don't need to be set each time in the Save for Web dialog box

FIGURE A-4

Photoshop Smart Object in GoLive

Rollover states set in ImageReady   Message text set in Photoshop is
are maintained in GoLive   maintained (Win only)

1. Click the Preview tab, then move the mouse pointer over each slice in the upper right corner, noting the change in the image and the text displayed next to the pointer, as shown in Figure A-4.

   The message text that appears when the mouse is over the slice, and the rollover attributes of the slices, were set in Photoshop and ImageReady and maintained when the file was added to a GoLive page.

   > TIP If you are using a Mac, click the Show in Browser button to view the page in a browser; on a Mac the rollovers will not be visible in Layout Preview. Note that Mac browsers do not display message text. Close your browser when you are finished viewing the page.

2. Save the page and minimize GoLive.

You viewed a Photoshop Smart Object's rollover properties in a GoLive page.

ANIMATE PHOTOSHOP LAYERS IN LIVEMOTION

What You'll Do

 In this lesson, you will place a layered Photoshop file into a LiveMotion composition, convert the layers to objects, and animate the objects.

Preparing Photoshop Layers for an Animation

Using Photoshop layers to create the objects in a LiveMotion animation can streamline the development of your animations. You may find that layers in several of your existing Photoshop files actually provide a natural series of objects for an animation. When creating new files for animation in Photoshop, you can use the Duplicate Layers command and create slight variances in layers, resulting in an animation-ready file. To animate a series of photographs, you can use opacity settings to align them (as shown in Figure A-5) for a video-like effect.

Converting Layers into Objects in LiveMotion

Once you have created Photoshop layers for an animation, you can put the file into a LiveMotion composition using the Place command. This adds the file to the composition as a single object. Using the Convert Into command on the Object menu, you can convert the layers of the Photoshop file into a sequence or convert each layer into an object, thus enabling you to use the resulting sequence or objects as an animation. Converting layers to objects gives you flexibility in applying durations and effects to each object, while converting layers to a sequence is quick and simple but doesn't allow you to modify the sequenced layers.

FIGURE A-5

Animation layers in Photoshop

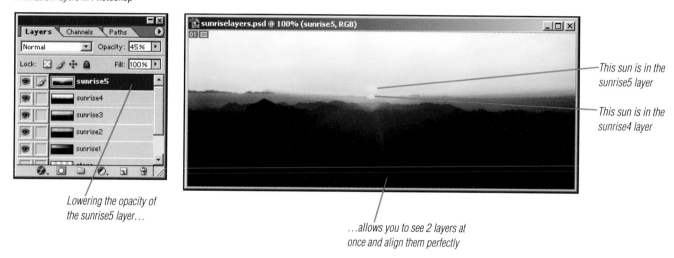

This sun is in the
sunrise5 layer

This sun is in the
sunrise4 layer

Lowering the opacity of
the sunrise5 layer…

…allows you to see 2 layers at
once and align them perfectly

Preview a layered file in Photoshop

1. In Photoshop, open sunrise.psd from the GypsyTales.data/SmartObjects folder.

   When the file opens, only the black background layer is visible.

2. In the Layers palette, click the Indicates layer visibility icon next to the stars layer to view the layer. 👁

3. Click the Indicates layer visibility icon next to each hidden layer, moving from bottom to top, to view each layer of the image.

   | TIP   If the Layers palette is not open, click Window on the menu bar, then click Layers.

4. Click Image on the menu bar, click Image Size, then note that the size of the image is 600 pixels by 235 pixels, as shown in Figure A-6.

   The size of the Photoshop image will be used as the size for the LiveMotion composition created next.

5. Click Cancel, then close and save the file.

You viewed a layered file in Photoshop, then made each layer in the file visible.

FIGURE A-6
Photoshop Image Size dialog box

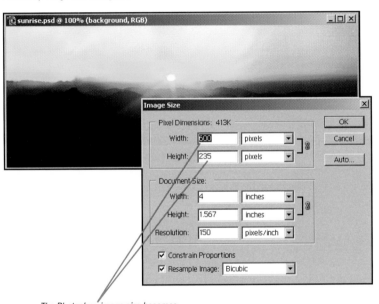

The Photoshop image size becomes the LiveMotion composition size

FIGURE A-7

Photoshop layers converted into LiveMotion objects

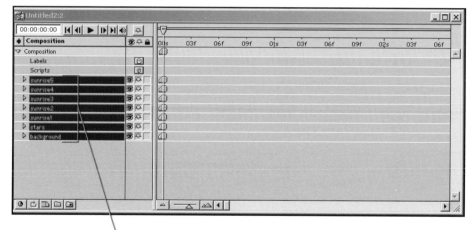

*Photoshop image layers are converted into
modifiable LiveMotion animation objects*

1. Open LiveMotion, click File on the menu bar,
   then click New Composition.

2. In the Composition Settings dialog box,
   specify a width of **600** pixels and height of
   235 pixels, then click OK, accepting the
   frame rate of 12 per second.

3. Click File on the menu bar, click Place, navigate
   to the sunrise.psd file in the SmartObjects
   folder in the GypsyTales.data folder, then click
   Open (Win) or Choose (Mac).

4. Click Timeline on the menu bar, then click
   Timeline/Composition Window to open the
   Timeline window.

   Note that the sunrise file is a single object in
   the timeline and a single layer in the Object
   Layer palette.

5. Click Object on the menu bar, point to
   Convert Into, click Objects, then compare
   your window to Figure A-7.

   Each layer in the file becomes an object that
   can be manipulated in a LiveMotion animation.

6. Save the file as **sunrise.liv** in the GypsyTales
   SmartObjects folder.

*You placed a Photoshop file in a LiveMotion com-
position, then converted the layers in the file into
LiveMotion objects.*

Animate Photoshop layers in LiveMotion

1. Click the Zoom Out button at the bottom of the Timeline window until you can see the 09s time marker, then drag the Composition duration bar's end point to the 09s time marker. ⌧

2. Move the start point of the sunrise5 object's duration bar to 04s, then move the current-time marker to 04s.

3. Click the triangle to the left of the sunrise5 object, click the triangle to the left of Transform under the sunrise5 object, then click the Stopwatch next to Object Opacity to set an opacity keyframe at the 04s time marker.

4. In the Opacity palette, set the Object Opacity to 30%.

5. Set the current time to 05s06f, click the check box to the right of Object Opacity in the Transform list to set another opacity keyframe, then in the Opacity palette set the Object Opacity to 100%.

6. Click the triangle to the left of sunrise5 to collapse it, click sunrise4 to select the object, then click the triangle to the left of sunrise4 to expand its object property rows.

7. Repeat Steps 3-6 above and set the duration for each layer, using the settings for each layer listed in Table A-2, making sure that you have selected the layer that you intend to affect. Compare your Timeline window to Figure A-8. Then save the file.

You animated in LiveMotion the layers of a file that was created in Photoshop.

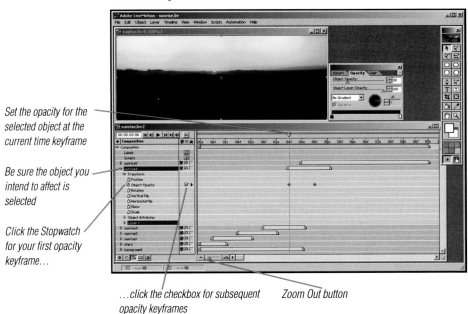

Set the opacity for the selected object at the current time keyframe

Be sure the object you intend to affect is selected

Click the Stopwatch for your first opacity keyframe…

…click the checkbox for subsequent opacity keyframes   Zoom Out button

TABLE A-2: Animation Settings

| Object | Duration | | Opacity Settings | | | |
	Start	End	keyframe 1	Setting	keyframe 2	setting
Sunrise4	03s06f	05s	03s06f	30%	04s06f	100%
Sunrise3	02s06f	04s	02s06f	30%	03s06f	100%
Sunrise2	01s06f	03s	01s06f	30%	02s06f	100%
Sunrise1	00s06f	02s	00s06f	30%	01s06f	100%
Stars	00s	01s	00s	100%	00s06f	0%
background	00s	04s	00s	100%		

1. Click the Go to the first frame button in the animation window, then click the Play/Pause button. ◄◄ ▶

2. Click the Composition object in the Timeline window, then click the Loop movie clip button at the bottom of the window, as shown in Figure A-9. ⟳

   This animation will be positioned at the bottom of a Web page. Looping the animation ensures that the reader will see it when he or she reaches it. The lack of movement in the animation in its last few seconds keeps the animation from looping too fast—which can be distracting.

3. Click the Preview Mode button in the toolbox to view the looped animation. 🖐

4. When you have viewed the animation, click the Edit Mode button in the toolbox. ▶

You set the animation to loop, then viewed the animation in Preview Mode.

FIGURE A-9
Final Timeline window

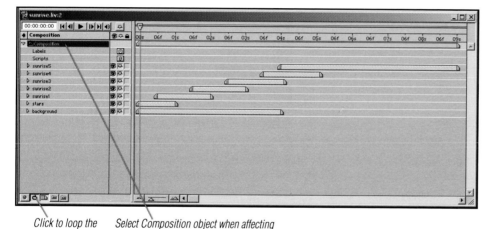

Click to loop the composition

Select Composition object when affecting the entire composition

ADD A LIVEMOTION FILE TO A GOLIVE PAGE

What You'll Do

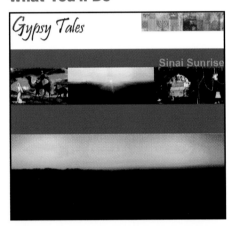

In this lesson, you will place a LiveMotion composition into a GoLive page as a Smart Object.

Using LiveMotion Smart Objects in GoLive

Adding a LiveMotion file to a GoLive page as a Smart Object automatically converts the LiveMotion file to a Macromedia Flash file (SWF). The advantage of using a LiveMotion Smart Object (as with all Smart Objects) is that modifications to the source LiveMotion file will be updated automatically in a GoLive page the next time the page is opened. This is helpful because you only need to maintain the source file—not both the source and the exported Web-ready files.

Objects in LiveMotion files can have variables (such as text properties, color, style, and texture) that you can modify when you add the file to a GoLive page, enabling you to create several Web-ready files from the same source file. To make the settings of an object in LiveMotion variable when added to GoLive, the object must be

assigned a value in the Replace field of the LiveMotion Web palette. When the file is added to a GoLive page and one or more of its objects has a Replace value, the Variable Settings dialog box opens to enable you to modify the variables for the object. These objects can also be linked to internal pages from within the Variable Settings dialog box, and the link address will be relative (the preferred path for an internal link); however, since these links are not maintained when a linked file is moved in GoLive, it is recommended that you link animated Smart Objects from within GoLive rather than by changing variable settings.

QUICKTIP

Although you can assign a Replace value to any object, only vector objects can be modified within the Variable Settings dialog box.

FIGURE A-10
Web palette

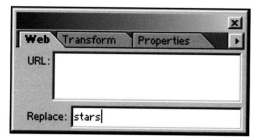

1. Open sunrise.liv if necessary.

2. Click Window on the menu bar, then click Web to open the Web palette.

3. Click the stars object in the Composition window to modify the object.

   | TIP   Move the current time marker to a point within the stars object's duration to make sure you are selecting the stars object in the Composition window.

4. Type **stars** in the Replace field in the Web palette, as shown in Figure A-10.

   This designates the stars object as having variable properties when the LiveMotion file is added to GoLive.

5. Close and save the file.

You set a LiveMotion object as a variable in GoLive.

Prepare a GoLive page for an animation

1. Open GypsyTales.site in GoLive, then open sinai.html if necessary.

2. In the Layout Editor, add a layout grid under the existing images, stretching it to the width of the images, then set its background color to **#660099** in the Layout Grid Inspector.

3. Add a text box to the layout grid, leaving one grid line to the left and above the text box, then drag the bottom right corner resize handle of the text box to the last gridline on the right side and down two gridlines.

   This text box adds space to the page between the images at the top of the page and the LiveMotion Smart Object that will be added.

4. Change the page title to **Sinai Sunrise**, then click the Page icon.

5. In the Inspector, set the Text color to white (**#FFFFFF**) and set the Margin Width and Height to **0**. Compare your window to Figure A-11.

You added a layout grid and a layout text box to a Web page, and changed the page title and text colors in preparation for the addition of an animation to the page.

FIGURE A-11
Layout text box in layout grid

Putting the animation in the layout grid (versus below) better controls the spacing between the story and the animation

FIGURE A-12

Sunrise.swf file in sinai.html

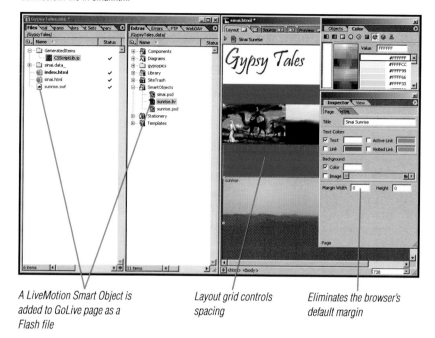

A LiveMotion Smart Object is
added to GoLive page as a
Flash file

Layout grid controls
spacing

Eliminates the browser's
default margin

FIGURE A-13

Sinai.html

1. Arrange your workspace for adding a Smart Object to the bottom of the page, then click the Refresh View button to refresh the contents of the right side of the site window.

2. Drag sunrise.liv to the left edge of the sinai.html layout grid, below the text box.

3. In the Variable Settings dialog box, click the stars object, click the check box next to Set Style, click the Set Style list arrow, click 14_Gel, then click OK.

   You applied a LiveMotion style to the stars that includes highlight, refraction, gel, and shadow properties.

4. Click the Set to Background button to match the matte color to the background, click OK, then save the file to the GypsyTales site folder, accepting the name sunrise.swf.

   The matte color is used for blending transparent pixels. Although this file doesn't have transparent pixels, the background color would normally be selected as the matte color if it did.

5. Align sunrise.liv to the left side of the layout grid, then resize the layout grid to the width of sunrise.liv if necessary.

6. Compare your screen to Figure A-12, then save sinai.html.

7. Preview the file in a browser, compare your screen to Figure A-13, then close the file.

You added a LiveMotion Smart Object to the page.

CREATE AND MODIFY A WEB PHOTO GALLERY

What You'll Do

 In this lesson, you'll add File Info to a Photoshop image, create a Web Photo Gallery from a folder of images, then edit the Gallery using GoLive.

Understanding Web Photo Galleries

If you have spent time creating a gallery page or looking for art on the Web, you will be pleased with the elegance of Web Photo Gallery pages that Photoshop can create automatically for you. This feature of Photoshop enables you to create an elegant Web site speedily for viewing a collection of images; you can then modify that site in GoLive. Creating a Gallery will compress, save for the Web, and create a Web-enabled thumbnail for each image in a designated collection of images. The Gallery consists of one page of thumbnail images and individual pages for each full size image. Each thumbnail in the Web Gallery links to the page with the full size version of the same image. Depending on the gallery template used, full size image pages may include buttons that link to the next full size image page.

Using Photoshop File Info in a Gallery

File information such as title, author information, caption, and copyright status can be embedded in a Photoshop file using the File Info command in the File menu and the File Info dialog box. File information adds some level of security to your electronic images and provides data for automated processes. File Info is embedded, saved, and loaded in an XMP format. This format is recognized by XML technologies for automating electronic processes with images, such as searching for an image using some image browsers. The fields in File Info correspond to the standards for identifying files set by American and international press associations.

The text values entered in the File Info for an image can also be used as text on the pages within a Web Photo Gallery. You can select whether to display the values next to an image, or on the image itself, such as information in the Copyright field of the File Info. Because the File Info is embedded in the image, if you want to replace an image and maintain the same File Info for the new image, you must re-enter the File Info unless you first save the File Info from the file being replaced. To save File Info, click the Save button from within the File Info dialog box, shown in Figure A-14. You can use the Load or Append button in the File Info dialog box to embed the File Info in the new file once it replaces the previous file.

Using Photoshop Web Photo Gallery Templates

Photoshop provides 11 different templates for Web Photo Gallery pages. There are basically two types of templates. Three of the templates use entirely separate windows for the thumbnails page and the large images pages: Simple (as shown in Figure A-15), Table, and Table-Blue. In these templates, clicking a thumbnail opens a new page in the browser containing the large image. Each of the large image pages include buttons for flipping through large images without returning to the thumbnails page, along with an "up" arrow that links to the thumbnails page. The other eight templates use HTML

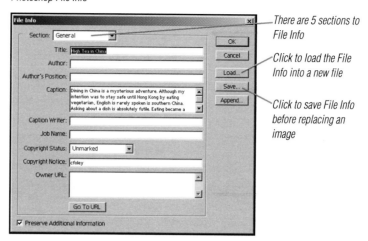

There are 5 sections to File Info

Click to load the File Info into a new file

Click to save File Info before replacing an image

Creating a Photoshop Web Photo Gallery template

If you are working on your own computer (and not a shared computer or in a lab), you can create new templates by modifying copies of the templates Photoshop provides. If you modify the Web pages Photoshop creates, you will have to make these same modifications each time you create, or recreate, a gallery. By copying and then modifying the copy of a gallery template, you need only make such modifications once.

Modifying a template is a bit more complicated than modifying the resulting files, but with a little focus, it can be done. To make modifications, make a copy of a similar template folder, modifying its name—this way you won't lose any templates that already exist. Template folders can be found in the Presets/Web Contact Sheets folder (Win) or Presets/WebContactSheets folder (Mac) in the Adobe Photoshop program files. Each template folder consists of an images folder, and five files, of which three can be modified: FrameSet is used in templates with frames; IndexPage results in the page of thumbnails; and SubPage results in the full image file. Text in the template files that is surrounded by "%" (for example: %Caption%) represents the value of a field in the image's file information. You can add any field from File Info to a template using these variables. You can replace the images in the template by replacing the files in the images folder with files of the same name and size. Play with patience!

frames to display the thumbnails page and a large image page in the same window (as shown in Figure A-15), allowing you to keep thumbnails in view while viewing the larger images. The frame templates arrange thumbnails either horizontally or vertically.

As you go through the process of creating the Web Photo Gallery in Photoshop, you can customize its appearance using the options in the Web Photo Gallery dialog box, including the size of the images, the file information displayed with an image, and colors in the Gallery, then further customize the resulting Web pages using GoLive. These features will save you hours in creating a Web Gallery that looks just the way you want it to.

QUICKTIP

You can customize the colors of any Gallery using the Custom Colors option in the Web Photo Gallery dialog box. However, Photoshop retains this setting—even if you select a different template. The Custom Colors option includes one text color and one background color, while many of the templates include two of each. To return to the default settings, you must restart your computer.

FIGURE A-15
Two sample Photo Web Gallery templates

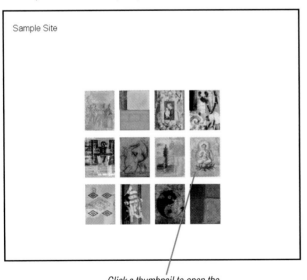

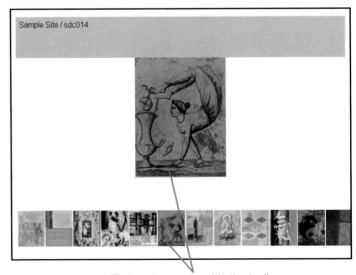

Click a thumbnail to open the larger image in a new page

The larger image page and the thumbnails are displayed in the same window; clicking a thumbnail replaces the larger image

FIGURE A-16

File Info dialog box

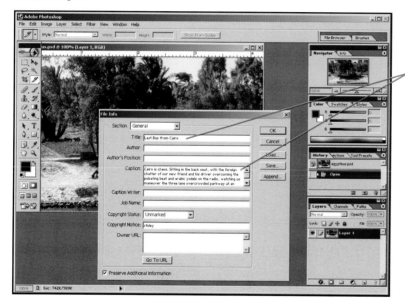

These values will be displayed with the image in the Gallery

View Photoshop images and modify File Info

1. Open Photoshop if necessary, click the File Browser tab, navigate to the gypsypics folder in the GypsyTales.data folder, then click the folder.

2. Double-click chinatea.psd to open it in Photoshop, click File on the menu bar, then click File Info.

   Note that the Title and Caption fields have text values in them. These File Info fields can thus be displayed with images in the Photo Web Gallery.

3. Change the value of the Title field to **High Tea in China**.

4. Click OK to close the File Info dialog box, then close and save the file.

5. Click the File Browser tab, double-click egyptbus.psd to open it in Photoshop, then view the File Info for the file.

6. Change the value of the Title field to **Last Bus from Cairo**, as shown in Figure A-16.

7. Click OK to close the dialog box, then close and save the file.

You viewed and changed the File Info for two Photoshop files that will be included in your Web Photo Gallery.

Create a Photoshop Web Photo Gallery

1. Click File on the menu bar, point to Automate, then click Web Photo Gallery.

   The Web Photo Gallery dialog box opens.

2. Click the Styles list arrow, click Vertical Frame, click the Extension list arrow, then click .html.

3. Click the Browse (Win) or Choose (Mac) button, navigate to the GypsyTales.data folder, click gypsypics, then click OK (Win) or Choose (Mac).

   This designates gypsypics as the folder of images from which the Web Photo Gallery will be created.

4. Click the Destination button, navigate to the GypsyTales site folder, then click OK (Win) or Choose (Mac) to designate the folder as the location of the Web Photo Gallery file when it is created.

5. Click the Options list arrow, then click Banner if necessary to edit the fields displayed in the site banner.

6. Type **GypsyTales** in the Site Name field, then clear the Date field so it is not displayed.

   TIP The next time you use the Web Photo Gallery, the options values will be preserved from your previous use, except the Date field. The Date field is repopulated with the current date each time you open the Web Photo Gallery dialog box.

7. Click the Options list arrow, click Large Images, click the Resize Images list arrow, click Small, click the Caption and Title check boxes to check them if necessary, then click any other checked check boxes to uncheck them, as shown in Figure A-17.

   (continued)

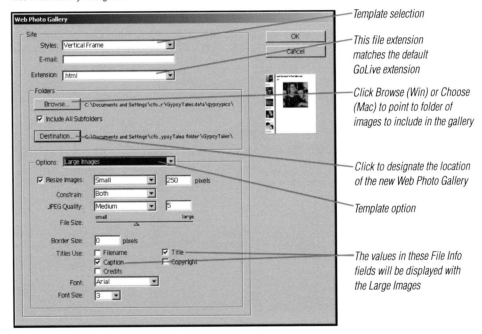

Template selection

This file extension matches the default GoLive extension

Click Browse (Win) or Choose (Mac) to point to folder of images to include in the gallery

Click to designate the location of the new Web Photo Gallery

Template option

The values in these File Info fields will be displayed with the Large Images

8. Click the Options list arrow, click Thumbnails, uncheck all Titles Use check boxes except for the Title check box, make sure the Title check box is checked, then set the Font Size to 1

9. Click the Options list arrow, click Custom Colors. Click the Banner color box, click the Only Web Colors check box to select it, in the Color Picker # field type **FFFFFF**, as shown in Figure A-18, then click OK.

10. Click OK in the Web Photo Gallery dialog box.

Photoshop creates a Web Photo Gallery using the Vertical Frame template and the images in the gypsypics folder (and their File Info), saves the resulting files in the GypsyTales site folder, then displays the Gallery in a browser.

11. In the browser window, click each of the thumbnails to display the larger image and its File Info, then close the browser window.

You have created a Photoshop Web Photo Gallery using the images in the gypsypics folder.

FIGURE A-18
Color Picker

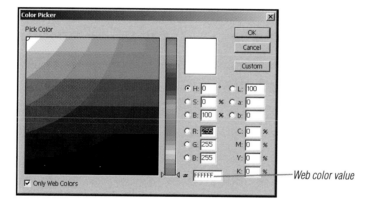

—Web color value

Modify the Gallery in GoLive

1. Open GypsyTales.site in GoLive, then click the Refresh button in the toolbar. 🔄

   TIP If both sides of the site window are open, it may be necessary to click the left side prior to clicking Refresh.

   Photoshop has added to the site the images, pages, and thumbnails folders for the Web Photo Gallery, along with the files ThumbnailFrame.html and UserSelections.txt, as shown in Figure A-19. In addition, it has replaced the index.html file.

2. Open index.html.

   The Layout Editor displays a message that the page requires a browser capable of displaying frames; they are not viewable in the Layout Editor.

3. Click the Frame Editor tab to view the frames in this page, then open the Inspector, if necessary. 🔲

   The Frame Editor displays the position and names of the two pages displayed within the frames, along with the names of the frames, as shown in Figure A-20.

4. Click the left frame, change the Width to 15 Percent in the Inspector, click the Scrolling list arrow, then click No.

   (continued)

FIGURE A-19
Web Photo Gallery added to GoLive site

The pages folder stores pages and images for the large images

Index.html has been replaced with the Photo Gallery frames page

This file is displayed in the left frame of index.html

This file keeps track of your gallery options

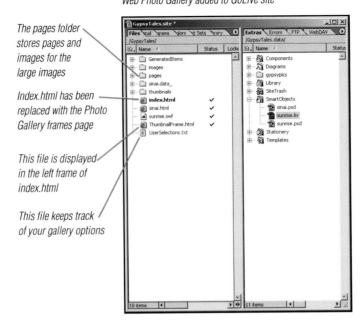

FIGURE A-20
Frames in index.html

Frame Editor tab

Frame names

The pages to be displayed in the frame

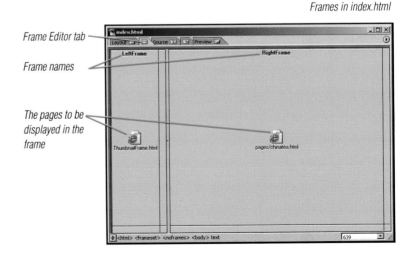

FIGURE A-21

Modifications to index.html frames

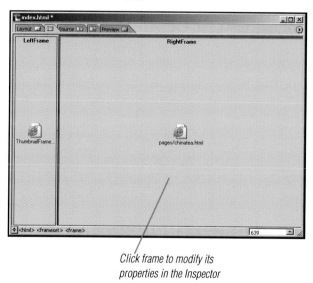

Click frame to modify its
properties in the Inspector

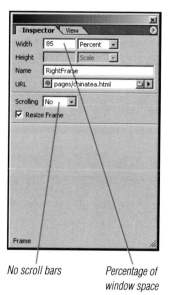

No scroll bars   Percentage of
window space

5. Click the right frame, change the Width to
85 Percent in the Inspector, click the Scrolling
list arrow in the Inspector, then click No.
Compare your screen to Figure A-21.

6. Close and save the file.

7. Open ThumbnailFrame.html, click the Page
icon, then in the Page Inspector set the
background color for the page to **#660099**
and the text color to **#FFFFFF**.

8. Close and save the file.

*You modified the frames in one Web page and the
background and text colors in another page in the
Photoshop Web Gallery.*

Link a Web Gallery image to a page

1. Using the site window, open the pages folder, then open sunrise.html.

   This is the page displayed in RightFrame when the sunrise thumbnail is clicked in the Gallery.

2. Arrange your workspace for creating an internal link, making sure the Inspector is open.

3. Click the sunrise image, click the Link tab in the Image Inspector, then use the Point and Shoot button to link the image to sinai.html in the site window.

4. In the Inspector, click the Target list arrow, then click _top, as shown in Figure A-22.

   This target sets the link so that when the sunrise image is clicked, sinai.html will replace all frames in the Gallery window.

5. Close and save the file, then save the site.

6. Click index.html in the site window to select it, click the Show in Browser button on the toolbar, then view the site in a browser of your choice. Compare the site to Figure A-23.

You linked a gallery image to a GoLive page.

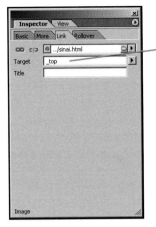

— *Target field set to_top will replace both frames with the sinai.html page*

FIGURE A-23
Modified Web Photo Gallery

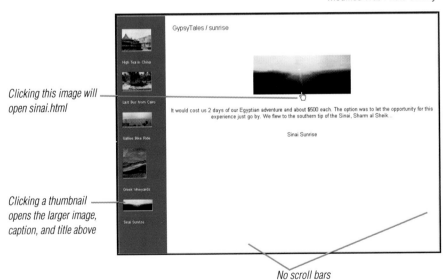

Clicking this image will open sinai.html

Clicking a thumbnail opens the larger image, caption, and title above

No scroll bars

FIGURE A-24

Upload files to the server

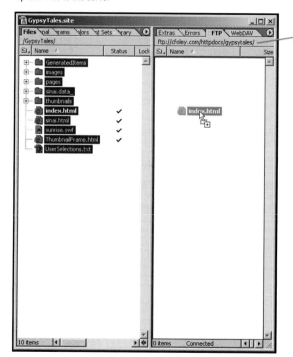

Your FTP server
location will differ

1. Click the Site Settings button, click FTP & WebDAV Server on the left side of the dialog box, click the FTP Server list arrow, click the name of the FTP server to which you will upload your site, then click OK.

2. Click the FTP Server connect/disconnect button on the toolbar.

3. Click the New Folder button on the toolbar to create a new folder on the FTP server in the right side of the site window, name it **gypsytales**, then double-click the folder to open it.

4. Drag to select all of the folders and files in the left side of the site window, then drag the selected folders and files to the FTP window on the right, as shown in Figure A-24.

   An initial upload of a large number of files is easier to do by dragging rather than by using the Incremental Upload button, because there is no check for existing files on the server or warning if a file doesn't exist.

5. Click the FTP Server connect/disconnect button on the toolbar, then close GoLive.

6. In your browser, enter the URL for the site you uploaded and test the site.

You uploaded and viewed the Web Photo Gallery and its links.

China Mist Gourmet Tea Company's loyal business using you as a Web designer is very much appreciated. To thank them for their business and make their site even more engaging, you have decided (with their approval) to add a fun animation to one of their pages. You have a Photoshop file that you would like to animate and add to the China Mist Web site.

1. Copy the lmnpull.psd file from the SiteIntA-4 folder in the drive and folder where your data files are stored to the SmartObjects folder in the China Mist site, then open the file in Photoshop.

2. Using some or all of the layers, make modifications to the file to create layers that can be animated.

3. Using LiveMotion, animate the objects in the Photoshop file, then save the animation to the China Mist SmartObjects folder as **lemon.liv**.

4. Using GoLive, add the LiveMotion file to recipes.html in the China Mist site (replacing the existing lemon). (*Hint*: Be sure your animation is slow enough so that it will be seen and won't be distracting if looping.) Compare your screen to Figure A-25.

FIGURE A-25
Completed Project 1

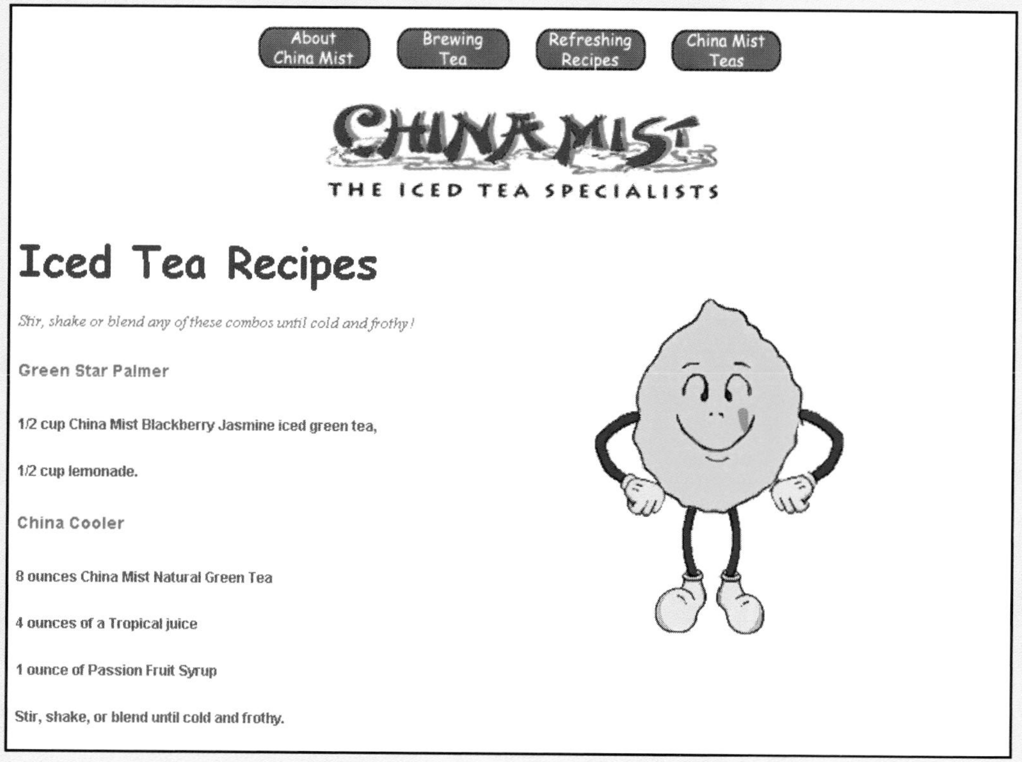

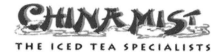

About China Mist
Brewing Tea
Refreshing Recipes
China Mist Teas
CHINA MIST
THE ICED TEA SPECIALISTS
Iced Tea Recipes
Stir, shake or blend any of these combos until cold and frothy!
Green Star Palmer
1/2 cup China Mist Blackberry Jasmine iced green tea,
1/2 cup lemonade.
China Cooler
8 ounces China Mist Natural Green Tea
4 ounces of a Tropical juice
1 ounce of Passion Fruit Syrup
Stir, shake, or blend until cold and frothy.

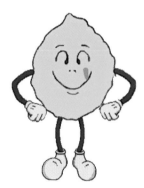

China Mist likes the use of animation on its site. To add to the activity on the Teas page in their Web site, they ask you to make the image of China Mist's owners, John and Dan, on the page appear to have a conversation about teas.

1. Copy the johnanddan.psd file from the SiteIntA-5 folder in the drive and folder where your data files are stored to the SmartObjects folder in the China Mist site.

2. Open johnanddan.psd in Photoshop and view the layers. Modify the layers to prepare them for an animation in which John and Dan are having a conversation in their beach chairs.

3. Add the johnanddan.psd file to a LiveMotion composition, then convert the layers and modify the composition to complete the animation, as shown in Figure A-26.

4. Save the LiveMotion file as **johnanddan.liv** to the China Mist SmartObjects folder.

5. Add johnanddan.liv to teas.html replacing the existing john and dan.jpg image, test the animation in a browser, then save and close teas.html.

FIGURE A-26
Completed Project 2

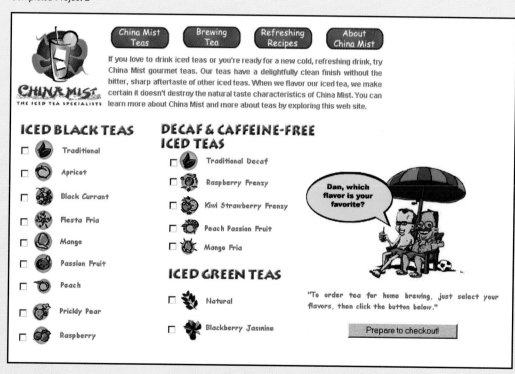

Read the following information carefully!!

Copy and organize your Data Files.

- Use the Data Files List to organize your files to a zip drive, network folder, hard drive, or other storage device.

- Create a subfolder for each section in the location where you are storing your files, and name it according to the section title (e.g., GoLive Section A).

- For each section you work with, copy the files listed in the **Data Folder Supplied** column into that section's folder.

- Store the files you modify or create in each section in the section folder.

Find and keep track of your Data Files and completed files.

Photoshop and LiveMotion

- Use the **Data File Supplied** column to make sure you have the files you need before starting the section or exercise indicated in the **Section** column.

- Use the **You Save File As** column to find out the filename you use when saving your changes to a provided Data File.

- Use the **You Create File** column to find out the filename you use when saving your new file for the exercise.

GoLive and Integration

- Use the **Data Folder Supplied** column to make sure you have the files you need before starting the section or exercise indicated in the **Section** column.

- Use the **You Use Site File** column to find the name of the site provided for use in the current section.

- Use the **You Create Site** column to find the name you use for the new site created in the current section.

Files used in this book

Photoshop

Section	Data File Supplied	You Save File As	You Create File	Used in
A	PS A-1.psd Butterfly.tif	Vacation.psd		Lessons 2–7
	PS A-2.psd	Zenith Design Logo.psd	Review.psd	Skills Review
	PS A-3.psd	Kitchen World.psd		Project 2
B	PS B-1.psd Gourds.psd	New England Fall.psd New England Fall copy.psd		Lesson 1–4
	PS B-3.psd Cell Phone.psd	Fraud Magnet.psd		Project 1
	PS B-4.psd Gorilla.psd	Zoo Billboard.psd		Project 2
C	PS C-1.psd Sheepdog.tif Butterfly.tif Photographer.tif	Family Portrait.psd		Lesson 1–4
	PS C-3.psd Plug.tif Satellite.tif Headphones.tif	FBI.psd		Project 1
	PS C-4.psd	Marathon Contest.psd		Project 2
D	PS D-1.psd PS D-2.psd	Chili Shop.psd Chili Shop Colorized.psd		Lessons 1–6 Lessons 5–6
	PS D-5.psd	Restoration.psd		Project 1
	PS D-6.psd	Preschool.psd		Project 2
E	PS E-1.psd	Fresh Ideas.psd		Lessons 1–6
	PS E-3.psd	Beautiful Blooms Ad.psd		Project 1
	PS E-4.psd	Spilled Milk.psd		Project 2
Bonus A	PS Bonus A-1.psd	Bloom Island.psd		Lessons 1–5
	Day Lily.psd	Day-Lily.gif		Lesson 2
	PS Bonus A-2.psd	Rose Morph.psd		Lessons 6–7
			Xtream Charity.psd	Project 1
			Countdown.psd Countdown Browser.psd	Project 2

LiveMotion

Section	Data File Supplied	You Save File As	You Create File	Used in
A			basic_button.liv	Lessons 1–6
			client1_buttons.liv	Project 2
B	LMB-1.liv Logo Wave.liv	navbar_1.liv		Lessons 1–2 Lesson 1
	LMB-2.liv	navbar_2.liv		Lesson 3
	LMB-3.liv	navbar_3.liv		Lessons 4–6
			theater.liv	Project 1
	LMB-6.liv	webbar.liv		Project 2
C	LMC-1.liv Buildings.jpg Patriotic.jpg	site1.liv		Lessons 1–3 Lesson 1 Lesson 1
	LMC-2.liv	site2.liv		Lessons 4–6
	LMC-4 Lake.jpg	resort1.liv		Project 1
	LMC-5.liv Photo1.jpg	flowers.liv		Project 2
D	LMD-1.liv	training.liv		Lessons 1–6
	LMD-3.liv	oaks1.liv		Project 1
	LMD-4.liv Fisheye.liv	cpworld1.liv		Project 2
E	LME-1.liv	fnlweb.liv		Lessons 1–6
			fnlweb1.html fnlweb1.swf fnlweb1R.html	Lesson 6
	LME-3.liv	movie1.liv		Project 1
			moviewb.html moviewb.swf moviewbR.html	
	LME-4.liv	worldfnl.liv		Project 2
			worldwb.html worldwb.swf worldwbR.html	

GoLive

Section	Data Folder Supplied	Student Uses Site File	You Create Site	Used in
A	SiteA-1	Eucalyptus.site		Lessons 1–6
	SiteA-2	UncleLouie.site		Project 1
	SiteA-3	GrowUp.site		Project 2
B	SiteB-1		IslandFever!.site	Lessons 1–5
	SiteB-3		China Mist.site	Project 1 Project 2
C	SiteC-1	IslandFever!.site		Lessons 1–6
	SiteC-3	China Mist.site (created in Section B)		Project 1
	SiteC-4	China Mist.site (created in Section B)		Project 2
D	SiteD-1	GrowUp.site		Lessons 1–4
	SiteD-3	China Mist.site (continued from Section C)		Project 1
	SiteD-4	China Mist.site (continued from Section C)		Project 2
E	SiteE-1 (if no Internet connection)		growup.site	Lessons 1–4
		China Mist.site (continued from Section D)		Project 1
		China Mist.site (continued from Section D)		Project 2

Integration

Section	Data Folder Supplied	Student Uses Site File	You Create Site	Used in
A	SiteIntA-1		GypsyTales.site	Lessons 2–5
	SiteIntA-4	China Mist.site (continued from GoLive Section E)		Project 1
	SiteIntA-5	China Mist.site (continued from GoLive Section E)		Project 2

Absolute address

A page reference that includes the page's entire path; in a Web page an absolute address is a URL.

Actions

Scripts, small programs, included in GoLive that can be used to make a page element or elements respond to a specified event.

Active matte

The matte currently applied to an image object.

Additive colors

Colors that are used for lighting, video, and computer monitors; color is created by light passing through red, green, and blue phosphors. When combined, the colors create white. When the values of R, G, and B are zero, the result is black; when the values are all 255, white results.

Alias

A linked duplicate of the original object. Changes made to either object are reflected in the other.

Align

Position objects relative to the horizontal or vertical axes or to specific points on the axis.

Alpha channel

A grayscale image that is added to the color channels that make up an image. Use an alpha channel to create and store a matte whose shape is defined by the image object to mask or hide a portion of the image.

Altitude

Bevel and Emboss setting that affects the amount of visible dimension.

Anchor point

A fixed point identified by a hollow circle in the middle (by default) of an object that determines how an object is transformed. All transformation actions, such as rotating and skewing, occur in relation to the object's anchor point.

Angle

Setting that determines where a drop shadow falls relative to the text.

Animation

The movement of one or more objects on the screen or the changing of an object attribute, such as color or opacity, over time.

Animation frames

Points of time on an animation timeline. An animation is measured in frames per second.

Anti-aliasing

The addition of pixels around the edges of an object, such as text in a text object. Reduces the jaggedness that appears around the object.

Applying an element tag

Assigning the properties of a predefined, named object type using an element name.

Attributes

An object's properties for which values can be specified.

Auto-slice

A slice created by ImageReady. An auto-slice has a dotted line border.

Background color

The color that fills the composition background. The default background color is white.

Base color

The original color of the image.

Baseline

An invisible line on which type rests.

Baseline shift

The distance type appears from its original position.

Bitmap

A geometric arrangement of different color dots on a rectangular grid.

Bitmap mode

Uses black or white color values to represent image pixels: a good choice for images with subtle color gradations, such as photographs or painted images.

Bitmap type

Type that is composed of pixels and may develop jagged edges when enlarged.

Blend color

The color that is applied to the base color when a blending mode is applied to a layer.

Blending mode
Affects the layer's underlying pixels, or base color. Used to darken or lighten colors, depending on the colors in use.

Bookmark
A URL address saved from within a browser using the Favorite (Explorer) or Bookmark (Netscape) menu.

Brightness
The measurement of relative lightness or darkness of a color (measured as a percentage from 0% [black], to 100% [white]).

Bug
In the GoLive site window, a bug icon indicates unresolved references in a page.

Button
A graphical interface that helps visitors navigate and interact with a Web site easily.

Cascading style sheets
A collection of attributes that are applied to elements in a Web page or multiple Web pages. An external cascading style sheet has the file extension .css, an internal style sheet is within the <head> element of a page. An internal style sheet takes precedence over the attributes specified in an external style sheet referenced by the same page; hence, the style sheets are "cascading".

Character palette
Helps you control type properties. The Character palette is located on the tool options bar.

Check box
An element within a form for selecting one or more values.

Class style
A property or set of text properties that can be added to any element using a class attribute.

Clipboard
Temporary storage area provided by your operating system.

Closed path
A path that consists of segments that form a closed shape, like a circle.

CMYK image
Has at least four channels (one each for cyan, magenta, yellow, and black).

Color Mode
Amount of color data that can be stored in a given file format, and determines the color model used to display and print a document.

Color Model
Determines how pigments combine to produce resulting colors, and is determined by the color mode.

Color palette
A window that contains color libraries for modifying object properties.

Color Picker
Feature that lets you choose a color from a color spectrum.

Color Range command
Used to select a particular color contained in an existing image.

Color separation
Result of converting an RGB image into a CMYK image.

Combined objects
Two or more objects that are joined together to create a new object. Using one of the combine commands you can create a specific effect where the objects overlap or don't overlap.

Component
A GoLive Smart Object that can be reused within any number of pages within a GoLive site.

Compositing
Combining images from sources such as other Photoshop documents, royalty-free images, pictures taken from digital cameras, and scanned artwork.

Composition
The basic LiveMotion document (with the file extension of ".liv") that you create when you open a new file.

Compressed
State of an image file that is prepared for display on the Web. Compression methods remove all information from a file that is not required for its display on the Web and can dramatically decrease its file size.

Contrast
Increases or decreases the difference between colors.

Control point
Each end of a path segment, identified by a square or circle. The shape of a path is changed by modifying a control point.

Corner point
A type of control point that can connect both straight and curved path segments.

Crisp
Anti-aliasing setting that gives type more definition and makes it appear sharper.

Crop
Exclude part of an image without losing resolution quality.

Current-time marker
Used to identify the current frame of an animation in the Timeline window.

Data folder
A folder within a GoLive site's project folder for storing files that are used in creating a Web page, but not required on the Web server. The contents of the data folder appear in the Extras tab of the site window.

Deselect
Command that causes the marquee to disappear from an area.

Direction line
Appears when you select a smooth point of a path segment. The angle and length of a direction line determines the shape and size of the curved segment.

Direction point
A small black circle at the end of a direction line that is used to adjust the size and shape of a curved path segment.

Distance
Determines how far a shadow falls from the text. This setting is used by the Drop Shadow and Bevel and Emboss style.

Distort filters
Used to create three-dimensional or other reshaping effects. Some of the types of distortions you can produce include Glass, Pinch, Ripple, Shear, Spherize, Twirl, Wave, and Zigzag.

Distortion
A type of special effect usually used on an image object or an object with a texture, gradient fill, or an object with multiple colors.

Distribute
Spread the space between objects out evenly along the horizontal or vertical axis.

Division element
A named HTML element that can be used as an object to apply style properties or actions to a range of child elements within a page.

Duplicate
Makes an exact copy of a selected object. The duplicated object is a separate and distinct object.

Duration bar
Represents in the Timeline window how long an object or the composition is animated.

Endpoints
Control points at each end of an open path.

Event sound
A type of sound used on the Internet that needs to be completely downloaded before it can play.

Export
The process of saving a composition in a different file format to be used by another program, such as a Web page design program.

External links
Hyperlinks that reference a URL on a remote Web server.

Extract command
Used to isolate a foreground object from its background.

Fastening point
An anchor within the marquee. When the marquee pointer reaches the initial fastening point, a small circle appears on the pointer, indicating that you have reached the starting point.

Feather
Method used to control the softness of the selection's edges, by blurring the area between the selection and the surrounding pixels.

File Transfer Protocol (FTP)
A method for moving files over the Internet, unopened.

Filters
Alters the look of an image and gives it a special, customized appearance by applying special effects, such as distortions, changes in lighting, and blurring.

Flattening
Merges all visible layers into one layer, named the Background layer, and deletes all hidden layers, greatly reducing document size.

Floating box
A GoLive object with layer properties that can be used within an action. A floating box can contain any other GoLive object.

Font
Characters with a similar appearance.

Font family
Represents a complete set of characters, letters, and symbols for a particular typeface. Font families are generally divided into three categories: serif, sans serif, and symbol.

Foreground color
Used to paint, fill, and stroke selections. The default foreground color is black.

Form
An HTML element that provides fields for collecting data provided by the user.

Frame delay
Length of time that each animation frame appears.

Frame rate
The rate an animation plays in frames per second.

Geometric object
An object that you create using one of LiveMotion's drawing tools, such as the Ellipse or Rectangle tools.

Gloss Contour
Bevel and Emboss setting that determines the pattern with which light is reflected.

GoLive site
A Web site's file within GoLive, along with a site folder, a data folder and a settings folder—which are used to effectively manage the site using GoLive.

Gradient fill
A type of fill in which colors appear to blend into one another. A gradient's appearance is determined by its beginning and ending points.

Gradient
The blending of two colors in a pattern to form an effect.

Grid
A series of non-printing connected boxes used to help you position objects precisely in the Composition window.

Grouped object
Two or more objects joined together to form one object.

Guides
Horizontal and vertical non-printing blue lines that you create to help you align objects.

Handles
Small blue boxes that appear on the selection border of a selected object that are used to change the size, skew, or rotation of an image.

Highlight Mode
Bevel and Emboss setting that determines how pigments are combined.

History palette
Contains a record of each action performed during a Photoshop session. Up to twenty levels of Undo are available through the History palette.

Hotspot
Area within an object that is assigned to a URL.

Hspace
Horizontal space added to the boundaries of an image in a Web page.

Hue
The color reflected from/transmitted through an object and expressed as a degree (between 0° and 360°). Each hue is identified by a color name (such as red or green).

Hyperlink
An element, property, or action applied to text or an object in an electronic file that causes a new page to display when the text or object is clicked.

Hypertext
Text that has been assigned an element, property, or action that causes a new page to display when clicked.

Hypertext Markup Language (HTML)
Text that includes special codes understood by a browser to describe a Web page's appearance, deliver text content, display images, and provide links to other Web pages on the Internet.

Image editing program
Lets you manipulate graphic images that can be reproduced by professional printers using full-color processes.

Image Inspector
A GoLive window that displays the properties of an image, including file and rollover image addresses, placement properties, image map properties, and link properties.

Image map
An image on a Web page that contains multiple links to other Web pages or Web sites.

Image object
An imported image, such as a bitmap image from an image editing program like Photoshop.

Incremental upload
A GoLive method for uploading files to a server using FTP that uploads only the files that have been modified, which is determined by comparing a file's modification date in the site window to the file's modification date on the FTP destination server.

In-line property
An object property specified by a tag surrounding an object.

Input elements
Elements within a form element for collecting user data, including text fields, check boxes and radio buttons.

Inspector
A GoLive window that displays the selected object's properties. Changing a value in the Inspector modifies the object's properties.

Internet Service Provider (ISP)
A business that provides user connections to the Internet.

Interpolation
Determines how an object changes between keyframes.

Kerning
Controls the amount of space between two letters or characters.

Keyframe
Marks a point in the timeline when the animation of an object changes.

Landscape orientation
A document with the long edge of the paper at the top and bottom.

Layer
A section within an image on which objects can be stored. The advantage: individual effects can be isolated and manipulated without affecting the rest of the image. The disadvantage: layers can increase the size of your file.

Layer set
An organizing tool you use to group layers on the Layers palette.

Layer thumbnail
Contains a miniature picture of the layer's content, and appears to the left of the layer name in the Layers palette.

Layers palette
Displays all the layers within an active document. You can use the Layers palette to create, delete, merge, copy, or reposition layers.

Layout Editor
A GoLive environment for visually modifying the appearance, content and links in a Web page.

Layout Preview
A GoLive rendition of a Web page in a browser, which is based on Explorer 5.

Leading
The vertical amount of space between lines of type.

Logo
A distinct image that you can create by combining symbols, shapes, colors, and text.

Luminosity
The remaining light and dark values that result when a color image is converted to grayscale.

Marquee
The dotted bounding box created when you drag your mouse to select an object.

Matte
The background or shape that defines the visible area of an image.

Menu bar
Contains menus from which you can choose commands.

Monotype spacing
Spacing in which each character occupies the same amount of space.

Morph
Blending multiple images in the animation process. Short for metamorphosis.

Motion path
The visual representation of the path an object follows when its position is moved during an animation. A motion path is identified in the composition window by green dots (that identify frames) and green squares (that identify keyframes).

Navigation link
Text or object in an electronic file that causes a new page to display when clicked.

Navigation view
GoLive's hierarchal rendition of the pages and links within a site.

Nested animation
A movie clip that plays independently from the composition animation.

Nested object
An object that is contained within another object, such as a small object on top of a large object.

None
Anti-aliasing setting that applies no anti-aliasing, resulting in jagged edges.

Object
A single element in a composition or page that has distinct attributes and characteristics that can be formatted.

Object palette
A window of icons representing objects that can be added to a Web page.

Opacity
Determines the percentage of transparency an object has in relation to its background. An object with 100% opacity will obstruct objects beneath it, while an object with 1% opacity will appear nearly transparent.

Opacity gradient
Gradually blends the object or the object color with the background object or color.

Open path
A path that consists of segments that don't close the shape, like an arc.

Optimization
The process of reducing a composition's or image's file size while maintaining visual quality.

Orientation
Direction an image appears on the page: portrait or landscape.

Other filters
Allows you create your own filters, modify masks, or make quick color adjustments

Outline type
Type that is mathematically defined and can be scaled to any size without its edges losing their smooth appearance.

Out-of-gamut indicator
Indicates that the current color falls beyond the accurate print or display range.

Page Inspector
A window that displays the properties of a page, including title, text colors, background images, background colors and margins.

Palette well
An area where you can assemble palettes for quick access.

Palettes
Floating windows containing groups of object properties that are used to modify objects. Palettes contain name tabs that can be separated and moved to another group.

Paragraph text
A word, string of characters, sentence, or paragraph created by dragging a bounding box in the Composition window and typing using the Type Tool.

Path
A freeform object made up of one or more straight or curved segments created using the Pen Tool.

Pixel
Each dot in a bitmapped image that represents a color or shade.

Point text
A word, string of characters, or sentence created by clicking in the Composition window and typing using the Type Tool.

Points
Unit of measure for font sizes. Traditionally, 1 inch is equivalent to 72.27 points. The default Photoshop type size is 12 points.

Portrait orientation
A document with the short edge of the paper at the top and bottom.

Posterize
Restricts the number of colors in an image object layer that is visible. Often used to create a film negative effect.

PostScript
A programming language, created by Adobe, that optimizes printed text and graphics.

Preferences
Used to control the software environment using your specifications.

Proportional spacing
Each character may take up a different amount of space, depending on its width.

Radio button
An element within a form for selecting one value from a group of values, as defined in the form.

Raster program
A bitmap program, such as Adobe Photoshop, that develops objects using individual pixels.

Rasterize
Converts a type layer to an image layer.

Rasterized shape
A shape that is converted into a bitmapped object. It cannot be moved or copied, and uses a much smaller file size.

Remote rollover
An event, such as clicking, that you perform on one object to trigger another object to change states.

Render filters
Transform three-dimensional shapes and simulated light reflections in an image.

Resolution
Number of pixels per inch.

Resulting color
The outcome of the blend color applied to the base color.

Rollover
An interactive behavior that causes an object to change on the screen when you click or move the mouse over the object.

Rulers
Rulers appear along the left and top of the Composition window and can help you precisely measure and position an object.

Sans serif fonts
Fonts that do not have tails or strokes at the end of some characters, and are commonly used in headlines.

Saturation
The strength or purity of the color, representing the amount of gray in proportion to hue (measured as a percentage from 0% [gray], to 100% [fully saturated]). (Also known as *chroma*)

ScreenTip
Identifies the name of the tool in the toolbox and its corresponding shortcut key.

Scrubbing
Dragging the current time marker back and forth along the timeline to make an animation play.

Selection
An area in an image that is surrounded by a selection marquee.

Selection border
A dotted border that appears around an object when the object is selected.

Serif fonts
Fonts that have a tail, or stroke, at the end of some characters. These tails make it easier for the eye to recognize words; therefore, serif fonts are generally used in text passages.

Settings folder
A folder within a GoLive site's project folder for storing information and preferences associated with a site, including workspaces, FTP server address, and upload instruction settings.

Shading
Bevel and Emboss setting that determines the lighting effects.

Shadow Mode
Bevel and Emboss setting that determines how pigments are combined.

Sharp
Anti-aliasing setting that displays type with the best possible resolution.

Sharpen More filter
Increases the contrast of adjacent pixels, and can focus blurry images.

Shortcut keys
Combinations of keys that can be used to work faster and more efficiently.

Site file
The source file of a GoLive site.

Site folder
A folder that contains the Web pages and the pages' referenced files within a GoLive site, sometimes referred to as the root folder. The contents of this folder are uploaded to the Web when the site is published.

Site wizard
A series of GoLive screens for creating the initial settings of a new site. The site wizard can be opened by choosing New Site from the File menu.

Smart Object
Objects that are not Web-ready that can be easily added to and modified in a GoLive Web page. The translation and management required for the Web are handled by GoLive.

Smart Object variable
Content or settings in an image file that can be modified when added to a GoLive page as a Smart Object.

Smooth
Anti-aliasing setting that gives type more rounded edges.

Smooth point
A type of control point that connects two curved segments of a path.

Snap (layout grid)
A property of the layout grid that pulls an object close to a gridline.

Sound object
An audio file that you use in a composition from the Sounds palette or that you import from your hard drive, the Web or a CD.

Source Code Editor
A GoLive environment for modifying the HTML code of a Web page.

Span element
An HTML element that can be used to apply style properties to a range of content within an element.

Spread
Determines the width of the drop
shadow text.

Stack
The order that each new object is created or
imported in a composition. The first object
created or imported is on the bottom of
the stack and the last object created or
imported is on top of the stack. The stacking order of objects can be changed.

State
A collection of attributes that affect that
way an object appears after being triggered
by a mouse action or a script (a rollover).

Status bar
This area is located at the bottom of the
program window (Win) or the bottom of
the document window (Mac) and displays
information such as the file size of the
active window and a description of
the active tool.

Streaming sound
A type of sound used on the Internet that
can begin playing before it is completely
downloaded.

Stroking the edges
The process of making a selection or layer
stand out by surrounding it with a border.

Strong
Anti-aliasing setting that makes type appear
heavier, much like the bold attribute.

Structure
Bevel and Emboss setting that determines
the size and physical properties of the object.

Style
A saved set of attributes that can include
object layer color, opacity, texture, 3D
effects, and distortion effects. A style can
have multiple layers, animation directions,
and rollovers.

Submit button
An element in a form for invoking an action
that writes the form's input values to a
specified location.

Subtractive colors
The result of cyan, magenta, and yellow
absorbing all color and producing black.

Swatches palette
Contains available colors that can be
selected for use as a foreground or background color. You can also add your own
colors to the Swatches palette.

Symbol fonts
Used to display unique characters (such as
$, ÷, or ™).

Table
An arrangement of cells into a series of
rows and columns. In HTML, a table
element consists of table row elements,
<tr>, and their embedded, child, table data
elements, <td>.

Tagging an element
Assigning the properties of a pre-defined,
named object type using an element name.

Target (link)
The browser window specified for displaying a linked page.

Target file
The file resulting from the translation of a
Smart Object for uploading to the Web. In
the case of an image Smart Object, the target file is the compressed image file.

Target object
The object that interacts with the trigger
object in a remote rollover.

Text object
A word, a sentence, or a paragraph created
using the Type Tool or the Text Field Tool.

Texture
A texture is a bitmap or vector image file
that has been customized using filters and
other effects. A texture can be applied to an
object or the composition background.

Texture filters
Give the appearance of depth or substance.

Tile
A pattern that repeats over and over to fill a
selected area.

Timeline window
Displays all objects in a composition and
their associated animation events.

Tint
Blends the current foreground color in the Color palette with the current fill for the selected object layer.

Tool options bar
Displays the settings for the currently active tool. The tool options bar is located directly under the menu bar, but can be moved anywhere in the work area for easier access.

Toolbox
A window that contains 18 tools for frequently used commands that you can use to create, select, and edit LiveMotion objects.

Toolbox
Contains tools for frequently used commands. On the face of a tool is a graphic representation of its function. Place the pointer over each button to display a ScreenTip, which tells you the name or function of that button.

Tracking
The insertion of a uniform amount of space between characters.

Trigger object
The object that causes, or triggers, another object to change its state in a remote rollover.

Tweening
The process of selecting multiple frames, then inserting transitional frames between them. This effect makes frames appear to blend into one another and gives an animation a more fluid appearance.

Type spacing
Adjustments you can make to the space between characters and between lines of type.

User-slice
A slice created by the user in ImageReady. A user-slice has a solid line border.

Vector program
A program, such as LiveMotion, that develops objects using mathematical coordinates instead of pixels.

View palette
Contains a list of browsers that can be selected for rendering a simulation of a page in a browser, within Layout Preview.

Vignette
A feature in which a picture or portrait whose border fades into the surrounding color at its edges.

Vignette effect
Feature that uses feathering to fade a marquee shape.

Vspace
Vertical space added to the boundaries of an image in a Web page.

Web colors
216 colors that appear consistently in all Web browsers on all platforms. Web colors are represented by RGB hexidecimal value pairs, preceded by a pound (#) sign. (Examples: Red = #FF0000, Green = #00FF00, Blue = #0000FF)

Web server
A computer that is configured for serving Web pages across the Internet.

Web-safe colors
Limits the available colors in the LiveMotion Color palette to just the 216 RGB colors most often used by Web browsers.

INDEX